6/09

Dime Novel Desperadoes

The Notorious Maxwell Brothers

John E. Hallwas

University of Illinois Press
Urbana and Chicago

© 2008 by the Board of Trustees
of the University of Illinois
All rights reserved
Manufactured in the United States of America
C 5 4 3 2 1
∞ This book is printed on acid-free paper.

Library of Congress Cataloging-in-Publication Data
Hallwas, John E.
Dime novel desperadoes : the notorious
Maxwell brothers / John E. Hallwas.
p.   cm.
Includes bibliographical references and index.
ISBN 978-0-252-03352-0 (cloth : alk. paper)
1. Maxwell family.
2. Outlaws—Illinois—Biography.
3. Outlaws—Wisconsin—Biography.
4. Brothers—Illinois—Biography.
5. Brothers—Wisconsin—Biography.
6. Illinois—Biography.
7. Wisconsin—Biography.
8. Illinois—History—19th century.
9. Wisconsin—History—19th century.
I. Title.
F546.M39H35   2008
977.3'0410922—dc22 [B]   2008002174

Dime Novel Desperadoes

is dedicated to the following archivists, genealogists, and local historians who responded to many inquiries during a period of several years, generously shared their knowledge and their accumulated records, and helped to bring this long-forgotten story to the modern public:

Walter Brieshke, Illinois Department of Corrections (retired)

Catherine Dodson, Davee Library, University of Wisconsin–River Falls

Gary L. Jacobsen, Maxwell family genealogist, Colorado

Marion C. Johnson, Fulton County (Illinois) Historical Society

Terry Mesch, Pepin County (Wisconsin) Historical Society

Stanley N. Miller, Cumberland County (Pennsylvania) Historical Society

Kathy Nichols, Archives, Malpass Library, Western Illinois University

Brent T. Peterson, Washington County (Minnesota) Historical Society

Catherine Renschler, Adams County (Nebraska) Historical Society

Kevin Thorie, Library Learning Center, University of Wisconsin–Stout

Donna (Maxwell) Tivener, genealogical researcher, Ohio

Stephanie J. Zeman, Davee Library, University of Wisconsin–River Falls

It is very easy to blame a wrongdoer; it is very difficult to understand him.

—attributed to novelist Fyodor Dostoyevsky

≈⋇≈

By the time we reach an age at which we can critically reflect on who we are, we are already somebody we did not choose to be.

—Douglas V. Porpora, *Landscapes of the Soul*

≈⋇≈

None of us enjoys the thought that what we do depends on processes we do not know; we prefer to attribute our choices to *volition, will,* or *self-control.* . . . Perhaps it would be more honest to say, "My decision [or act] was determined by internal forces I do not understand."

—Marvin Minsky, *The Society of Mind*

≈⋇≈

For men who have lived . . . on a diet of contempt and disdain, the temptation to gain instant respect [with a gun] can be worth far more than the cost of going to prison, or even of dying.

—James Gilligan, *Violence: Reflections on a National Epidemic*

Criminals are made by environment and circumstance.
. . . The worst thing you can do to a criminal is to put
him in a class by himself, to treat him as if he were a
creature set apart. He is just an average man who has
gone wrong. . . .

 —bandit Henry Starr, in George D. Hendricks,
  The Bad Man of the West

"The facts are, Lon, we seem born to be unfortunate,"
[said Ed]. "We have been wronged, and when we
retaliate . . . the world turns against us. We are branded
as outlaws and hunted as if we were wolves."

 "We seem likely to never get justice here," said Lon.

 —the Maxwell brothers, in a dime novel,
  December 31, 1881

Contents

Illustrations follow pages 108 and 218.

Preface

No outlaws who achieved nationwide notoriety have been so thoroughly forgotten as the Maxwell brothers. Except for occasional retrospective newspaper items and one poorly researched article in *Real West* magazine, they have not received any historical attention. Even supposedly thorough reference books, such as Bill O'Neal's *Pimlico Encyclopedia of Western Gunfighters* and Jay Robert Nash's *Encyclopedia of Western Lawmen and Outlaws,* fail to mention them, while including hundreds of less noted figures.

Surely one reason is geographical: The Maxwell brothers committed most of their crimes, including the one that made them notorious, east of the Mississippi River, in Illinois and Wisconsin. Had they killed lawmen from two counties in a gunfight at Deadwood or Tombstone, or had they been the focus of a huge multistate manhunt in the far West, they would still be well-known desperadoes. This suggests an ongoing problem with scholarship on American outlaws: Historians have usually limited their focus to the region west of the Mississippi River, simply because so much outlawry took place there. O'Neal, for example, refers to no gunfighters who developed their reputations east of the big river, while Nash's list of 1,100 outlaws mentions only the Reno brothers and a few other figures from that area.

Also, the outlaw career of the Maxwells was brief, essentially confined to the summer of 1875 and the summer and fall of 1881. During most of the intervening years, Ed, the instigator of their lawbreaking, was in prison, and Lon, after a much shorter term behind bars, was struggling to go straight.

The recovered story of the Maxwells is important not just because it adds two figures to the short list of American outlaws who achieved national attention in their own time, but also because it provides insight into the character of violent men and sheds light on a notably violent era in American history.

The notorious Maxwells received so much newspaper coverage, which included several interviews of Ed and letters by both brothers, that their psychological makeup can be readily reconstructed. They provide a compelling case study of rootless, alienated men whose inner problems fostered ongoing conflict with society—and made them dangerous. By the same token, we can understand Ed and Lon well enough to regard them as complex figures who had positive qualities too and felt disrespected by others and oppressed by powerful forces. Neither monsters of evil nor innocent victims, they were very much like the rest of us, which makes for sympathetic comprehension of their struggle and emotional engagement in the story of their unfolding destiny.

The Maxwell saga also reminds us that identities are deeply related to cultural values and social conditions. Individuals become who they are partly because of where they live, who they know, and what they experience or struggle with. For that reason, *Dime Novel Desperadoes* reflects in some detail the rural and small-town world of the Maxwell brothers—a world of destabilizing westward movement, frustrating failure, extreme poverty, frontier rowdyism, conflict over Civil War issues, prejudice against landless workers, escalating crime, ineffective courts, and harsh, often counterproductive penitentiaries. It is not surprising that the Maxwell story symbolizes the anxieties of an era. Indeed, it reflects perennial forces that prompt disorder in American culture.

Moreover, this is a book about the social response to outlaws. Because newspaper coverage of the Maxwells' short outlaw career was extensive and American readers were deeply engaged with their story—so much so that the infamous brothers inspired many folkloric reports and a dozen dime novels—the Maxwell saga illuminates the psychological relationship between notorious lawbreakers and the general public. It becomes clear, in fact, that the figure of the "outlaw" or "desperado" was a mythic construction, an expression of the public's need to variously demonize and admire opponents of the social order. Indeed, the Maxwell brothers eventually contributed to the rise of the outlaw hero in American fiction precisely because of the public's fascination with, and ambivalence toward, such committed lawbreakers.

This heavily contextualized biographical narrative is, then, about the perennial problems of knowing and evaluating—the difficulty of knowing the truth about people and events featured in the news and the challenge of evaluating the character of others. For that reason, it quotes from and comments on a variety of newspaper reports. As *Dime Novel Desperadoes* reveals, accounts about the Maxwell brothers were often inaccurate, and assessments of their character and motivations were frequently shallow. Of course, with regard to lawbreakers, folklore and misjudgment are almost unavoidable because people want violent stories to make sense, believe almost everything they hear or read, and often see in criminals what they admire and want to promote or fear and try to restrain in themselves.

As all of this suggests, *Dime Novel Desperadoes* is necessarily a kind of anti-western. The most deeply American of all literary forms—which the dime novel prefigured—the western is devoted to a mythic conflict between good and evil, in which a gun-toting hero, without much complexity or self-comprehension, feels driven to assert himself, display his manhood, and seek revenge or protect some group by eradicating the "bad guys." Strangely enough, those enemies of society often share the hero's own desires to remain apart from society, resist authority, reach for a gun, and evoke admiration. They are just more apt to break the law and harm the innocent than he is.

Psychologically probing westerns are rare because complex characters challenge the mythic limitations of the genre. Fictional gunfighters, whether good or evil, typically have no childhood experience that readers can ponder and few, if any, meaningful relationships. Nor do they grow. The heroic ones simply crystallize courage and the sense of honor while the "bad guys" crystallize dishonorable, self-serving brutality. Hence, westerns are inherently devoted to portraying lawbreakers, and lawmen or other "justice" seekers, in melodramatic terms.

Dime Novel Desperadoes does the opposite, chronicling the background and career of two actual outlaws who lived in a fascinating era of social change and chronic violence; in the process, it reflects some of the cultural and literary roots of the western novel and film. Ed and Lon Maxwell are neither condemned as inherently evil nor celebrated as dark heroes. Our mythic view of outlaws notwithstanding, they are portrayed as essentially decent, if seriously troubled, young men who go astray under the influence of powerful cultural and psychological forces.

As superb naturalistic novels like Theodore Dreiser's *An American Tragedy* and Richard Wright's *Native Son* reveal so convincingly, we can never understand violent men if we do not recover, in some measure, their past experience and consider things from their perspective. The Maxwells were clearly alienated, neurotic, and potentially dangerous, but their view of life—as a harsh, unfair struggle for poor outsiders like themselves—was not mistaken. Driven by deeply American desires, they were also creatures of fate, trapped by cultural concepts and psychological problems as well as socioeconomic circumstances. By pursuing better social conditions, broader awareness of cultural myth, and greater sensitivity to others, rather than by celebrating aggressive, gun-toting heroes, we will eventually address America's unfortunate preeminence in violent crime.

Dime Novel Desperadoes

Prologue

A Desperado
in McDonough County

The people of McDonough County long remembered how it began, the story of the Maxwell brothers, how it first became part of their common experience—only to escape the limits of their knowing and grow bigger than any of them ever dreamed that it might, becoming a noted part of the American struggle for law and order, and the quest for justice, in a strange and violent time.

It was in 1874, during a mild winter—what the old-timers sometimes called "an open winter" because the ground failed to stay frozen very long. By mid-February, melting snow and rain had turned the thawing dirt roads into troughs of mud. The merchants at the county seat, busily working in their narrow and dimly lit shops, knew that trading would be slow in Macomb that Saturday. And it was. Impassable roads, like hard economic times, were troubles that people back then simply learned to cope with—part of an array of uncontrollable forces that shaped their lives and tested their character.

At times like that, Macomb still seemed isolated, despite the regular coming and going of the trains, announced by shrill whistles and blasts of steam at the red-painted depot just one block north of the square. The dray drivers were pulling their "mud-boats"—smooth-bottom carts without wheels—that glided over the slippery surface of the streets behind teams of plodding horses. Invented by a local man in 1867, the "mud-boats" were a common sight in wet weather, moving goods to and from the depot in an enterprising prairie town that thought of itself as an up-and-coming community, like so many other places in Illinois, and the entire Mississippi Valley, in that first generation after the Civil War.

The symbol of Macomb's rising sense of "prosperity, progress, and enterprise" was the magnificent new three-story opera house, known as Chandler's Hall. Built in 1873 by banker and investor C. V. Chandler, who had been raised in a modest frame house on the very spot where the hall then stood, it reflected his vision for the town as well as his socioeconomic status as "McDonough County's most prominent citizen." Located just off the northwest corner of the square, the building was dubbed "The Most Beautiful and Well-Arranged Hall in the West" by the town-boosting editor of the *Macomb Journal.* On show nights the polished, ornamented doors led into a lobby with frescoed walls and a high ceiling, lit with a hundred oil lamps in magnificent chandeliers. Farther on, the elegantly decorated "opera hall" (auditorium) held seats for as many as eight hundred people, who might see a play, a musical, an orator, a singer, a vaudeville act, or some other entertainment brought in from almost anywhere in the country.

The most popular play of that era at Chandler's Hall was *Buffalo Bill,* performed soon after the opera house opened. Promoted as "a drama presenting many wild scenes of frontier life in the far West," it celebrated the buckskin-clad title character, the daring sharpshooter of dime novel fame, who was fast becoming the most renowned symbol of western manliness. Courageous in the face of Indians and outlaws, Buffalo Bill was portrayed as a defender of American culture and a hero of self-assertion, who was always ready for violent action and refused to knuckle down to anyone. With either a rifle or a revolver, he was a deadly opponent. The audience was thrilled.

The most noted speaker at the new hall in the 1870s was Schuyler Colfax, who was vice president under U. S. Grant. According to the newspaper, he "held his hearers spellbound" with a ninety-minute lecture on Abraham Lincoln, whom he had known well during the turbulent Civil War years, when Colfax had served as Speaker of the House. He portrayed the martyred leader as an inspiring figure, whose "struggles with poverty and adverse circumstances" had shaped his character for the great challenges that he faced as president. Lincoln was the nation's ultimate success story, the triumphant validation of American beliefs in equality, individualism, and opportunity.

It was also in Chandler's Hall during the 1870s that Henry Ward Beecher, billed as "the greatest living pulpit orator," gave his well-known lecture on "The Reign of the Common People," asserting that Americans do indeed have the freedom "to rise up from the lower stations of life"—but also reminding his listeners that "the great undermass of society . . . less fortunate in every respect than those who are advanced, are now seeking to go up, but no road has been found along which they can travel far, as yet."

On lecture occasions the hall was a kind of temple, where the people of nineteenth-century Macomb celebrated their beliefs and, sometimes, reexamined their lives. But on that Saturday evening in the winter of 1874, there would be nothing so meaningful—just a minstrel show, where performers with burned-cork-blackened faces, imitating low-class "darkies," would make the all-white audience roar with laughter.

The only other thing for the townspeople to look forward to that day was the appearance of a weekly newspaper, the *Macomb Eagle*. Published upstairs in a new brick building on the north side of the courthouse square— in quarters dubbed "The Eagle's Nest"—it was a staunchly Democratic sheet that often traded political insults and personal attacks with the Republican *Macomb Journal*. The most widely circulated newspaper in the county, with a flair for reporting local events, the *Eagle* frequently had the edge on news from nearby small towns like Blandinsville, Bushnell, Colchester, Industry, and Tennessee.

The February 21 issue was uncommonly interesting. On the local news page, along with the usual announcements, "personals," and ads, there was a lead article that many people surely read more than once and then talked about for the next month or so. It reported, with some excitement, that McDonough County had a budding outlaw:

A DESPERADO.

Burglary and Horse Stealing.
Ed Maxwell "on His Muscle."

A young man named Edward Maxwell, aged about twenty-five years, whose father resides in the vicinity of Tennessee, in this county, is fast developing into a desperado of no mean proportions. A complete history of this young man, written out, would render insignificant the thrilling legends and incidents in the life of "Jack the Giant Killer." And the hair-breadth escapes and exciting adventures of Gil Blas lose all their charming novelty when Edward Maxwell enters the arena to display the instincts of his nature. True, Edward has never yet killed anybody, so far as we know, but he has shown a disposition to be dangerous, and the killing process would come as natural to him as it is for water to trickle over the plumage on a gosling's back. . . .

That was Ed Maxwell's introduction to the public, leading into an account of his arrest for burglarizing a store in nearby Blandinsville, his escape on horseback with a drawn revolver, and his subsequent capture in the next county. He had been jailed in Macomb for several days by the time that story appeared—long enough, perhaps, for the editor to hear a few rumors about the young hired hand, who was awaiting trial.

As the newspaper report suggests, there was something about Ed Maxwell—his boldness, perhaps, his readiness to flash a gun and defy the authorities—that set him apart from most other lawbreakers. He was "A DESPERADO"—a man given to violence, a daring outlaw—and as such, he was a threat to the social order in McDonough County. By assigning him that identity, the editor was labeling the young man as an outsider, an inherently "dangerous" figure whose "instincts" were not at all like those of the essentially virtuous, socially restrained general public.

But there was an almost heroic quality about him, too, as the editor's literary comparisons suggest. A very popular folk story, *Jack the Giant Killer* was focused on "a famous Cornwall boy, who, gifted with great bravery, went all over the lands of England, Ireland, and Wales, exterminating awful giants," as another Macomb newspaper put it. Jack was a kind of nineteenth-century superhero. And Gil Blas was the roguish hero of a popular picaresque novel, written in French but translated into most other European languages. As a young man, Gil has an exciting series of adventures, including some exploits with a band of robbers, which the *Eagle* editor was perhaps recalling.

No other criminal in the county's history, before or since, was ever introduced to the public in such hyperbolic terms. It was almost as if the editor, reflecting what local folks had told him, could not resist celebrating the bold, defiant, courageous actions that he was also condemning. He was, in fact, not just convicting Ed Maxwell of burglary and horse theft without a trial, he was mythologizing the young man, declaring him a lawbreaker with a special destiny, a desperado who was born to kill—and to fascinate the public with his unrestrained self-assertion. As it turned out, the presentation of Ed Maxwell as an outlaw-hero, long before his deeds justified it, helped to shape his emerging identity, and perhaps guarantee that the killings would finally come.

It was, after all, the 1870s, when the public mind was stirred time and again by stories of outlaws—exciting tales that often depicted gun-toting desperadoes in heroic terms. The social and economic disturbance of the Civil War had spawned a postwar crime wave like nothing else Americans had ever experienced. In the West, it was an era of defiant lawbreakers.

Right after the war, the Reno gang, formed by four outlaw brothers and their friends, had robbed trains, banks, and county treasury offices in Indiana, Kentucky, Missouri, and Iowa. Pinkerton detectives finally brought in seven of them—including Frank, Simeon, and William Reno—but Indiana lynch mobs hanged them all, three on one occasion and four on another, during 1868, before any of the desperadoes could be tried.

More notably, the James-Younger gang had been robbing banks since 1866—and had recently held up trains and stagecoaches in Iowa and Missouri. Jesse and Frank James, along with Cole, Jim, and Bob Younger, were still on the loose in 1874, despite the efforts of lawmen and vigilantes in several states.

Horse thieves did not receive such widespread publicity, but there were several large gangs in operation. For example, Frank Sidney's "Western Bandit Volunteers," organized during the war, eventually operated from Kansas to Minnesota in the later 1860s and 1870s. Kentucky, Nebraska, and other states also had huge gangs in that era.

At the same time, in Texas, New Mexico, Kansas, and other places, gunfighters like Clay Allison, John Wesley Hardin, and Ben Thompson had gained wide notoriety. Soon Sam Bass and Billy the Kid would emerge as nationally famous outlaws, the latter eventually becoming, in the public mind, the quintessential American gunfighter.

As frontier conditions slowly faded east of the Mississippi River, and the Civil War brought hardship, animosity, and violence to many localities, central Illinois also produced an array of less-noted outlaws. In the 1850s Joe Brice became the leader of a gang that stole horses and held up stores in Fulton and McDonough counties. During the mid-1860s he killed a man in Iowa and was captured, convicted, and sentenced to hang, but he escaped from jail and fled to the West. At the same time, Harrison Johnson (alias "Kansas Red"), who hailed from that state but had lived for some years in Oquawka, led a gang of horse thieves and robbers. He eventually moved to McDonough County, near the village of Blandinsville, but operated in several states. Shortly after the war he was lynched for horse stealing by vigilantes near Wyandotte, Kansas. In 1869 the Berry gang of Tazewell County, also known for horse stealing and robbery, killed Deputy Sheriff Henry Pratt, who was leading a posse, and soon afterward local citizens lynched the leader of those outlaws, William Berry, at the Tazewell County Jail.

As these examples suggest, the often-fascinated public was also frustrated by the apparently ineffectual justice system in many localities, and lynchings were not uncommon. Just across the big river, in Missouri, Jesse James claimed that he would never surrender because, as he put it in an 1870 letter, "I would be mobbed and hanged without a trial."

Ed Maxwell did not have to worry—yet. In that soggy winter of 1874, he was simply headed for a short stay at the Illinois State Penitentiary at Joliet. But he would later team up with his brother Lon, and together they would become nationally famous outlaws, much-feared desperadoes hunted in half a dozen states and discussed extensively in the newspapers, before a lynch mob would finally get him too.

For many years, folks in McDonough County and other places, especially western Wisconsin, would remember the Maxwells and would shape their legend. Stories even circulated about their childhood in Arkansas during the Civil War, their crimes in a dozen other Illinois counties, their robberies with the James gang, and their epic escape down the Mississippi River—none of which was true. But their real exploits were daring enough to fascinate the public, and when the end of their career finally came, it was national news—and it triggered a vast discussion of violence and American justice.

Later, at the turn of the century, long after the Maxwell brothers were gone and the crime wave of the post–Civil War decades was just an unpleasant part of the midwestern past, folks in McDonough County still recalled their daring exploits—and their remarkable skill with guns. Ed, in particular, was a legendary figure, viewed as a treacherous desperado who feared nothing, struck without warning, and "was more like a panther than a human being," as one prominent citizen put it.

In 1903, the editor of the *Macomb Journal,* in a stirring account called "THE MAXWELL BOYS: Two Noted Desperadoes Who Commenced Their Wild Career in This County," summarized their fame, apparently for the benefit of younger readers and newer residents who could not recall that violent era: "So daring were their deeds that they gained a national reputation, and were the subject of stories in the dime novel trash. They were [later] known, in Wisconsin, as the Williams brothers, and under that name they were the heroes in the novels."

He was referring to dime novels like *The Williams Brothers, or a Thousand-Mile Chase* and *The Williams Brothers and the Detectives,* which circulated nationally in the 1880s and 1890s, introducing thousands of readers to the exploits of those desperadoes, who were once more well-known across America than any other outlaws except the James and Younger brothers, and possibly Billy the Kid.

More than twenty years later, in 1924, a local historian named Quincy Hainline, who had known the Maxwells in the 1870s, recalled their exploits for yet another generation. His two-part newspaper series, "The County's Worst Desperadoes," reminded readers that their career had started with a local "reign of terror," and by the time it had ended elsewhere, they had achieved "national notoriety."

Now no one in Illinois, or in Wisconsin, can remember when the legend of the Maxwell brothers still excited the public mind, when horse stealing, outlaw gangs, sheriff's posses, jailbreaks, and lynch mobs had not yet faded from the Mississippi Valley—back when it too was still called "the West."

1

The Maxwell Family Moves West

We know little about the background of the Maxwell brothers, but some things, unknown to the public in their time, are now perfectly clear. Of first importance is the fact that they were born to a poor tenant farmer who moved west in the mid-1800s, chasing the fabled American Promise across several states, but repeatedly failed to rise—at least until the closing years of his life. And because they participated in that long, hard, frustrating process, the Maxwell brothers did not belong very deeply to any community or local cultural tradition, and they often felt that their very identities were at risk. Although they eventually regarded themselves as radically free, they were, in fact, profoundly constrained—driven by inner forces they did not fully comprehend, forces rooted in the desperate struggle of their parents.

The Maxwell family was Scotch-Irish. During the mid-1700s, the earliest American Maxwells left Scotland or northern Ireland and settled in southeastern Pennsylvania. The colony's chief proprietor, Thomas Penn, directed them and many other Scotch-Irish immigrants to a beautiful wooded area just west of the Susquehanna River. In 1750 that stretch of land became part of a massive new county called Cumberland, which encompassed the entire southwest quarter of the state. As Pennsylvania pioneers continued to arrive, the county's population grew from 5,000 in 1750 to 24,000 by the Revolutionary War—while its borders shrank through a series of legislative changes. By 1790 the county's width had been reduced to roughly forty miles, and its length was just slightly bigger.

Running through that area, from southwest to northeast, was the heavily timbered Cumberland Valley, which led across the Susquehanna into the Lebanon and Lehigh valleys, on the east, and at the western end curved down through Franklin County into Maryland and Virginia, where it was known as the Shenandoah. In Pennsylvania, to the north and south of the valley, there were hills and mountains, largely unsuitable for agriculture, where deposits of iron, copper, and lead were mined, but in the center of the great valley were rolling plains where the soil was rich and fertile, ideal for growing grains and hay. For the land-hungry pioneers, it was a good place to establish farms.

The great-grandfather of the Maxwell brothers was born in 1755, probably in America, although that is uncertain, and he was twenty-one when the Revolutionary War broke out. William Maxwell served in the Cumberland County militia, First Battalion, commanded by James Dunlap, and his name shows up on several company rolls produced between 1779 and 1782. Stories of his long service in the war were part of family lore for many years. A man of action and courage, he was surely respected and admired by the Maxwells who came along after him.

During the war, William married a woman named Sarah, and in the years that followed they established a farm along the Walnut Bottom Road, three miles east of Shippensburg and sixteen miles southwest of Carlisle. The Maxwells eventually had five sons and four daughters. Because land was cheap but hired labor was expensive, a large family was clearly a long-term asset: Sons cleared fields, plowed and planted, put up mowed hay, hauled grain (wheat was the key crop), and did other heavy work, while daughters planted gardens, kept chickens, churned butter, spun cloth, made candles, and did other household chores. Although many farms were eighty to one hundred acres in size, William's was larger. By the time he died in 1808, he had amassed 248 acres in Southampton Township.

The Maxwell clan in Pennsylvania's Cumberland Valley was clearly off to a good start in a promising place. It is not surprising that most of William's sons remained there. Among them was the outlaws' grandfather, also named William, who was born in 1784 and spent most of his life in Southampton Township, living along the same well-traveled dirt road, probably on or near the land once owned by his father.

Young William eventually married a woman named Rebecca, and they journeyed to "the Queen City of the West," Cincinnati, where their first child, James D., was born on May 9, 1821. The infant died at Louisville in late July, so they had apparently moved during the summer. For unknown reasons, they soon returned to Pennsylvania, and they were living in nearby Franklin County when their daughters Harriet and Sarah were born, on June 28, 1828, and May 1, 1830. Rebecca may have had relatives there.

In 1817 a man named George Lee purchased a two-story log house just south of the Walnut Bottom Road, in Southampton Township, and operated a tavern there until his death in 1824. His widow ran it for six more years and then sold it to William Maxwell, who had just moved from Franklin County back to Cumberland. By that time, the locality was known as "Lee's Cross Roads," and perhaps a dozen families lived there.

William Maxwell was forty-six years old in 1830, and his wife Rebecca was thirty-three. Two years later, on April 6, 1832, they had their fourth child, David D. Maxwell, whose sons, more than forty years later, became the noted outlaws. David's younger sister, Margaret, was also born in that log building, on January 31, 1834.

In about 1840 William built a brick tavern near the old log one, and he apparently operated that until his death. The 1850 Southampton Township tax roll lists him as the owner of seventy acres, consisting of a "Farm and Tavernstad," with a gross value of $1,750. For the 1850 federal census he listed his occupation as "Innkeeper," and his household then included wife Rebecca, son David, and daughter Margaret, as well as a certain Harriet Anderson, age seventeen—who may have been a relative—and a man named Levi Strohm, age thirty, who was a butcher. Early in that year, William and Rebecca had sold seven adjoining acres to Strohm, who was surely living with them while building, or planning to build, a residence.

William was sixty-six in 1850, and one year later he died. An inventory of his possessions, for an 1852 estate sale, includes agricultural implements as well as sixteen hogs, showing that he was indeed a farmer as well as an innkeeper. The entire sale netted just $385.75 for William's wife, son, and daughters. Along with his small acreage, the sale shows that the second William Maxwell was not as successful as his father.

Increasing population and sharply rising land prices in southern Pennsylvania—especially after the Cumberland Valley Railroad arrived in 1838—were making it difficult for descendants of the pioneers to thrive. According to tax records, a typical cleared, cultivated acre in Cumberland County was valued at thirty to forty-five dollars in 1850, and that figure rose sharply in the following decade. As elders passed away and farms were sold, there was commonly not enough inheritance for any one descendant to establish a similar farm, especially since there was no longer any cheap, uncultivated land. To make matters worse, wheat yields tended to slowly decline, from twenty or thirty bushels per acre on newer land, to just twelve or fifteen bushels on older land.

Many younger men became tenant farmers or hired hands. The same 1850 tax roll that lists William's "Farm and Tavernstad," for example, also lists one hundred acres of "Prime Land" owned by the heirs of his older brother George, who had died in 1847. George and his wife Mary had raised eleven children, so it is not surprising that two of their sons, William and John, are already listed as "tenants" on the roll. The once-prosperous Maxwell clan was producing landless tenant farmers and agricultural laborers.

David D. Maxwell was also one of them. In the 1850 federal census, the eighteen-year-old youth listed his occupation as "Farmer," and he had probably been doing most of the work on his father's small farm because William was sixty-six in 1850 and was probably already ill with whatever he died from a year later. But the estate sale of 1852 left David without a farm residence, and he was not old enough to even bid on the livestock and equipment. He was forced to work as a hired hand.

Growing up as an innkeeper's son along a well-traveled road that was part of the network of routes stretching from Philadelphia west to Harrisburg, on the Susquehanna, and beyond, David must have met a number of west-going pioneers, who dreamed of a better life in Ohio and other places. Like everyone else, David knew that land was cheap there, and perhaps a few years of work as a hired hand or tenant would provide enough money for him to start his own farm. One thing was sure: Land was too expensive in Cumberland County—and that was aside from the $500 that it would take for livestock, seed, tools, and other supplies.

Little is known about the outlaws' mother. Born in 1833, Susan B. Ott was nineteen when she married David Maxwell on August 26, 1852, at the Lutheran church in Carlisle, the county seat. She was a small, slim, brown-eyed woman, whose long brown hair was parted down the middle and surely pinned up in a bun. The daughter of Henry and Margaret Ott, about whom nothing is known, she was related to the Jacob Ott family that lived near Lee's Cross Roads—a factor that probably brought her into contact with David. By her early teens, Susan was an orphan, being raised by the John Beatty family on a farm in nearby Newton Township. Perhaps one thing that attracted David and Susan to each other was that each had been, in a sense, dispossessed or marginalized by the loss of parents (or one parent, in David's case). They both knew what it meant to become more socially insecure.

In the winter of 1853, David, Susan, and several other members of the Maxwell family moved to Ohio. Included among them was David's sister Sarah, who had married William Clark (another resident of Lee's Cross Roads), and with that couple was Sarah and David's widowed mother, Rebecca. David's older cousin and namesake, David R. Maxwell (Uncle George Maxwell's son), who lived nearby, also traveled with the group. Eight years older, David R. had already been working as a tenant farmer and had acquired horses and farm equipment, but he was still unmarried. Like the other Maxwells, David and Susan must have been excited about the prospect of settling in the fabled West, and they were surely hopeful of one day having their own farm.

The 500-mile-long journey, by covered wagon, across southern Pennsylvania and most of Ohio took the Maxwells several weeks. The first hundred and fifty miles or so were the hardest, as they encountered the mountains west of the Cumberland Valley. Then came the Ohio River Valley and the rolling hills that lay beyond it. For twenty-one-year-old David and his wife, it was a grand adventure as well as a test of endurance.

And for all of the Maxwell group, it was the start of a new, destabilized spiritual orientation. The decision to move west meant the exchanging of home and tradition—a century of Maxwell family life in the Cumberland Valley—for the challenges of journeying, establishing a farm, and breaking in socially at a new place. It meant the abandonment of stability, order, community, trust, and recognition, for separation and seeking, for self-reliance and struggle, for instability and alienation, and for the promise of transformation coupled with the anxiety of rootlessness.

Their destination was northwestern Ohio, where some land could still be acquired from the federal government for $1.25 per acre—and settlers had four years to finish paying for it. Because of such cheap and fertile land, easy access via the Ohio River and Lake Erie, and a long canal that connected those two bodies of water, the state's population had doubled and redoubled in the 1830s and 1840s. By 1850, Ohio was the third most populous state in America, and when the Maxwells arrived a few years later, the settlement period was almost over.

The Maxwell clan was headed for Wyandot County, about fifty miles north of Columbus. Located at the eastern edge of the geographic area called the Central Plains, the county had a gently rolling to flat landscape, one-third of it prairie, which was much easier to traverse than the hilly, heavily wooded Allegheny Plateau through which the two Davids, Susan, William and Sarah Clark, and Rebecca Maxwell had journeyed, probably as a group.

The settlement of Wyandot County had been delayed because of Indians. The Wyandots, Ottawas, Delawares, Senecas, and Shawnees once held a vast reserve in common, in northwestern Ohio, but in the Treaty of 1817 they agreed to occupy smaller reservations, located in or near what later became Wyandot County. The former Indian territory surrounding the reservations was then opened up for settlement. Many farms were established, and a few log cabin villages appeared.

Some additional Indian land was acquired in the 1830s, but still, a twelve-mile-square Wyandot Reservation occupied the heart of what later became the new county. As white settlement continued, there was no effort to respect the needs and interests of the remaining native Americans. The tribe was continually pressured to leave, and the members finally agreed to do so in 1842—setting out for the strange, empty prairies of Kansas in the following year. The departure of the Wyandots—perhaps 750 men, women, and children who sadly abandoned their ancestral home—marked the end of a cultural era, for they were the last native Americans to occupy lands in Ohio.

The village they left behind was already named Upper Sandusky, so that is what white settlers called the place when Wyandot County was formed in 1845 and the new seat of justice was established. Land sales were held that year—long after most government land in Ohio had been sold and settled. A courthouse and county jail were erected in the later 1840s, as shops, taverns, and hotels sprang up, and a stagecoach line connected the village to a host of other small communities. By 1850, Upper Sandusky had 786 people, all of them focused on the American Promise for themselves and surely none of them concerned about the fate of the people they had displaced.

When the Maxwells arrived, in the spring of 1853, David R. immediately bought eighty acres of land along the Sandusky River, just two miles northeast of the county seat. For him and his younger cousin, the balance of the year was spent doing the arduous work of clearing the land, planting and harvesting crops, and building a log farmhouse.

Three years after he arrived, David R. Maxwell married, and he eventually fathered eight children. Also, in the 1860s and 1870s he bought other small parcels of land. He eventually became "one of the best known citizens of the county, whose friends were numerous," according to his 1894 obituary.

David D. Maxwell's destiny would be very different. He never bought land in Ohio, so he must have worked as a tenant farmer or hired hand—probably on his cousin's land. Since farm labor was in short supply, he surely worked for other nearby settlers as well. But accumulating enough money to buy land was very difficult.

David's sister Sarah, her husband William Clark, and the matriarch Rebecca Maxwell also do not appear in the Wyandot County land records, so they apparently had the same problem. They stayed in Ohio for several years, but later records find them in Indiana and Illinois, where land was cheaper.

During that difficult first year in Ohio, Susan was pregnant, and on August 15, 1853, the Maxwells' first child was born. Named William, like his grandfather and great-grandfather, he was always called Ed, a shortened version of his middle name, Edmuston. That unusual name was surely derived from family tradition, too. Ed never used it—and eventually replaced it with Edward.

At the time Ed Maxwell was born, railroads were spreading throughout Ohio. The miles of track jumped from 299 at the start of the decade to 2,974 by 1860—and that changed things dramatically. The frontier vanished, as hitherto isolated farms were connected with distant markets, and the Buckeye State became a national leader in wheat, corn, sheep, and hog production. As newspapers boasted all over the state, people could also travel to cities like Pittsburgh and Chicago in a matter of hours.

In Upper Sandusky, the Ohio and Indiana Railroad had just arrived, and the residents of Wyandot County were aglow with the thought that they were living in the Land of Promise, the golden West, the new America, where everyone's dreams would soon be realized. The editor of the town's first newspaper, the *Democratic Pioneer,* expressed the hope and excitement of that moment in a November 17, 1853, article:

GOING BY STEAM.

When we think that but a few years ago this was the home of the redman, and now we see the steam cars rolling through our town, it astonishes even our own eyes. The progress of the western people and country is not to be equaled in any other region of our union. Look at the railroads and other

improvements that are now going on in all the western portions of our new world.

Here, but a short time ago, the wilderness covered our
whole country. In fact, not a cultivated field was to be seen.
And now we have beautiful, well-cultivated farms, and little
towns, well built up. . . .

Who can beat our rapid strides of progress? Soon we will
be ahead of the old, settled land of "steady habits" . . . and
ere long the western country will be the Garden of Eden of
the new continent.

The energetic Pioneer of the West will soon find himself
in the midst of the world, and [of] business.

It would be hard to find a more forceful vision of the West as an agrarian Promised Land, a realm of economic hope and social transformation,
where vigorous effort will soon make marginal places important and struggling pioneers successful. As the same editor said early in 1854, "we are
bound to rise," and Upper Sandusky will soon become "one of the noted
places [in Ohio]."

That optimistic mind-set was undoubtedly shared by the Maxwells, who
had just settled in Wyandot County.

But even in a period of astounding progress, David D. Maxwell did not
thrive. The coming of the railroad to Upper Sandusky also brought rapidly
rising land prices, as farmers expanded from a subsistence operation to
a market function, so many poorer people—including tenant farmers and
hired hands—came no closer to purchasing their own land. And things got
worse when the Panic of 1857 brought widespread joblessness in the cities,
which lasted for several years, and depressed wage levels on the farms.
As poor people became frustrated, there was rising animosity—toward
farm owners, business leaders, politicians, immigrants, and others who
had an impact on economic conditions.

That probably contributed to the rise of rowdyism in many areas of
the country during the late 1850s. In the western states, however, exces-
sive self-concern (because family and church influence had diminished),
anxiety about being respected, and lack of commitment to the new, still-
developing social order may have been just as important. By 1857 the
editor of the *Wyandot Pioneer* was bringing the issue of frequent "street
brawls" to public attention, decrying "the lawless spirit that is now rife

in our midst." He called for "morality and public order," as well as better law enforcement, matters that increasingly stirred the public mind in the early Midwest.

For David and Susan, the economically troubled later 1850s also brought two more children: Alice, born on April 6, 1856, and David, born on June 17, 1858. Like Ed, the latter was always called by his middle name, Alonzo—or Lon. With three children to feed and care for, and none big enough to be of any help with farm chores, the Maxwell family must have faced hard times.

In the later 1850s, the prospect for advancement in Ohio did not equal that of Illinois or Iowa, and everyone knew it. Many frustrated settlers were moving on. By 1859 the state had, in fact, been losing more population than it had been gaining for several years, and it was clear to David and Susan Maxwell that because of rising land prices and the depression they would not soon become land owners and, hence, would not rise in Wyandot County. Like so many others, they too decided to move farther west.

Illinois had been widely celebrated as a land of opportunity for settlers, especially since the 1830s, when pioneers had begun arriving in large numbers and hundreds of towns had been established. A popular folk song about the Prairie State, called "Elanoy," depicted it as an American Eden and, in the two-line refrain, appealed to the struggling pioneers in precisely the right terms: "Then move your family westward; good health you will enjoy,/ And rise to wealth and honor in the State of Elanoy."

"Illinois Fever" persisted through the 1850s, when Ohio's population was declining, and as late as 1861 an article on "The Prairie State" in *The Atlantic Monthly* proclaimed that "a man of very small means can become independent on the [Illinois] prairies," a place where "land is cheap and plenty, but labor is scarce and dear." That was exactly what a farm worker like David Maxwell wanted to hear—and he probably had heard it from more than one source.

David's much-older cousin, Sarah Maxwell, had moved to Woodford County in central Illinois with her husband, William Woodburn, during the early 1850s, so she may have written to him about the prospects for settlers in the fabled Prairie State. Her older brother William had also moved to that county and had settled near the village of Washburn, so he was another possible source of information and encouragement.

Whatever and whoever prompted them to go, when the fall of 1859 arrived and the crops were harvested, the Maxwells were again on the road, traveling across Indiana to central Illinois. Alice and Lon were mere toddlers, but Ed was six—perhaps old enough to share the frustration of his hardworking parents, who were not economically better off than they had been six years earlier, when they had left Pennsylvania.

2

≈)✦(≈

The Maxwells
in Troubled
Fulton County

In the winter of 1859–60, the Maxwells settled in Fulton County, just west of the Illinois River. The decade that was just starting would bring challenges and hardships that neither David nor Susan could have anticipated, and the family's struggle, as well as the troubled social environment, would have an impact on their sons, especially Ed.

The 1860 federal census, taken in June, records the presence of "David D. Maxwell," a farmer, age twenty-eight, who owned no real estate and, thus, was a tenant. He claimed only $200 in personal property. At that time Ed was six, Alice was four, and Lon was two. The Maxwells lived in northern Waterford Township, just three and a half miles south of the county seat, Lewistown, which had been founded in 1822 and had the closest post office.

Waterford was a fractional township, sharing the normal thirty-six sections of land with Isabel Township, located to the west and south across the Spoon River. It was also the least populated and developed township in the county, with fewer than 500 residents, and less than 100 horses and mules, during the 1860s. Waterford had just seventy farmers in 1860, and only half of them owned any land. Many of the 500 residents were hired hands, tenant farmers, and subsistence, log-cabin settlers who lived by hunting, fishing, gardening, and raising a few hogs. It was a place

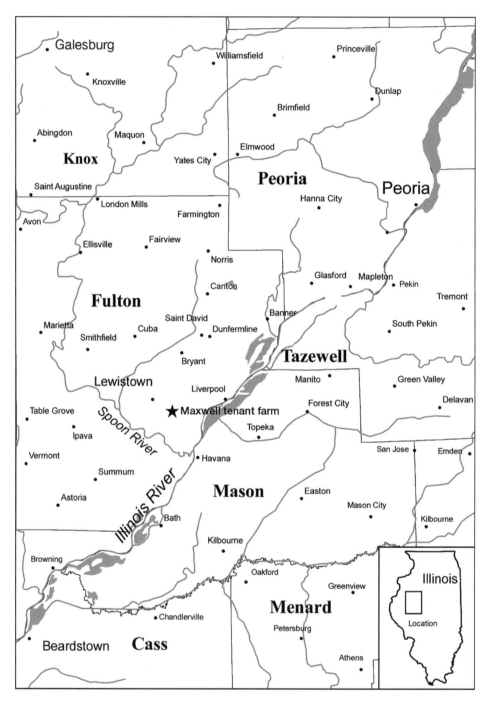

Fulton County and the Illinois River Valley, showing the approximate location of the Maxwell tenant farm during most of the 1860s. The outlaws were pursued through this region in both 1875 and 1881.

of significant poverty. A mile or two west and south of their home was the placid, winding Spoon River, and along its banks were the hamlets of Duncan Mills and Waterford, each of which had a mill. The hilly landscape was extensively wooded, and Ed, if not Lon as well, must have learned to hunt raccoons, squirrels, quail, and deer there.

The movement westward of David and Susan Maxwell had followed a well-established pattern. Just as Pennsylvanians like them had been the largest immigrant group in early Ohio, former residents of Ohio were, by the 1850s, the third largest immigrant group in Illinois, and they tended to settle in a dozen central Illinois counties, with Fulton County drawing the largest number. In Waterford Township, most of the substantial farmers were from Ohio, so David probably had an invitation to work there as a tenant farmer before he came to Illinois. The name just before his in the 1860 census is Hiram Johnson, a substantial farmer who owned one-third of Section 3, so David may have rented land from him.

In 1860 Fulton County had more than 33,000 people, and all the best land had been settled. Railroad connections had recently been established with Peoria, on the Illinois River, and other communities, so farms were becoming market oriented. Once again, David Maxwell had come to an area where land prices were starting to rise and the dream of farm ownership, for landless tenants, was fading. Moreover, the depression of the late 1850s was still having an impact throughout the Mississippi Valley, including central Illinois, where money was extremely tight and business was slow, according to the *Canton Register.*

By 1860 Lewistown had about 1,000 people, and its leading business enterprises were pork packing, wagon making, and woolen manufacturing. It also had a sawmill, a gristmill, two hotels, and more than a dozen stores. A few buildings were brick; the rest were frame—and all were long and narrow, with board sidewalks and hitching rails in front of them. A small, white, Greek Revival–style courthouse sat in the center of town. Lewistown was a typical farm center village and county seat of the pre–Civil War era. Because it still had no railroad connection (the first tracks crossed the county farther north), the editor of the *Fulton Democrat* admitted, "We have not yet fully caught the impulse of enterprise and prosperity. We have not gone ahead as fast as some of our neighbors."

Farm life in that era, before horse-drawn implements became common, was a continuous round of hard work, done with a sense of urgency as the warmer weather came and passed. A vivid recollection by James W. Madison, who was raised near Fulton County, reflects the world of manual labor that was typical on most early Illinois farms, including David Maxwell's:

> We got up at 4 A.M. and saw the sun rise, and by that time we were in the field. Twenty acres of corn was a big amount for . . . us to manage. We had to [plow] up the ground with an old bar-shear, or afterwards with a diamond plow . . . and then scratch it over with a brush or an old wooden tooth harrow. Then we crossed off the land with a go-devil or a little diamond [plow], one furrow at a time, both ways, and the fellow who could run a straight row was in demand. Then the corn was dropped in, three grains in a cross.
>
> I dropped [seed] for a neighbor three whole days once, and he gave me 25 cents, and I thought I was well paid, too. Good farm hands only got about $10 a month up until the time of the Civil War.
>
> When the corn was dropped, then a man with a hoe went along and covered it, one hill at a time. When he had it covered, he set his foot on it.

Later, the corn was picked, shucked, and shelled by hand. Other grain, especially wheat, was also planted on almost every farm, and that was later cut, with a scythe or cradle, and then raked, tied into bundles, and threshed.

As Madison's comments suggest, there was often work for boys to do—and both Ed and Lon began their involvement in farm work as youngsters in Fulton County. By the age of seven, in 1860, Ed would have been bringing in firewood, shelling corn for the chickens, hauling water from the pump, and doing other light chores. Within a year or so, he would have been working in the field, dropping seed and raking wheat, and soon afterward he would have learned to pitch hay, split wood, and drive a plow or harrow.

Field work was often arduous, and most boys hated it. In the classic account of childhood farm life of that era, *A Son of the Middle Border* (1914), Hamlin Garland recalled that at age ten, "to reach the plow handles I was obliged to lift my hands almost to my shoulders," and in that struggling position he trudged "eight or nine miles in the forenoon and as many more in the afternoon," enduring the heat, mud, dust, and flies, until "all sense of being a man evaporated," and he was just a physically abused little boy who could "scarcely limp home to supper." An intelligent, sensitive youth, like Ed apparently was, Garland admitted that "my heart sometimes felt bitter and rebellious" during such grueling forced labor. He eventually rebelled by leaving rural America and telling the awful truth about his boyhood experience there. As an outlaw who later plundered farmhouses, Ed may have rebelled in a different way.

Women's work was not much easier, and Susan must have labored to the limit of her strength on many a day. Aside from preparing and preserving food and caring for the children, she tended the garden, raised chickens and collected eggs, milked the family cow, helped with the butchering, sewed clothes, washed clothes by hand and mended them, made soap and candles, kept the fireplace, and cleaned the hopelessly dirty cabin or frame shack—which was surely infested with flies, gnats, fleas, spiders, and mice.

Maxwell family relationships probably adhered closely to nineteenth-century standards. A hard-driving, sin-conscious churchgoer who later headed a frontier Sunday school, David was almost certainly an authoritarian father who enforced discipline and demanded hard work and self-restraint from his children. As Hamlin Garland said of his similarly religious prairie-farming grandfather, "he was just, but he was not tender." Ed and Lon were coached to be little men—and were probably slapped or otherwise abused when they failed to meet rigid expectations.

For the sons of a struggling tenant farmer who was driven by desperate hope and constant privation, childhood was not a distinctive and precious stage of life, but an extended period of servitude, focused on learning to work. Ed's childhood must have been especially unfortunate, for adult chores were commonly thrust upon the oldest son before he was capable of doing them well enough to avoid verbal or physical abuse.

Ed's predicament was complicated by something that affected him profoundly throughout his life: He was small for his age and of slight build. Things that a bigger, huskier boy might do well—digging potatoes, swinging a scythe, handling a plow horse—were very challenging for him. Like another "undersized" boy of that era named Henry Antrim (later known as Billy the Kid), Ed became obsessively concerned about measuring up—about being regarded as a man.

By the same token, Ed Maxwell eventually became remarkably strong for his size, as the lawmen who struggled with him later discovered.

Most of Ed's formal education came in Fulton County, at a country schoolhouse. In the early 1860s he almost certainly attended Waterford School, a small frame building with two tall windows on each side and a plain door on one of the gable ends. Built in 1839, it sat on a hill along a dirt road that led south along the Spoon River to Havana. Inside, it was a bare, drab, uninsulated room, heated only by a potbellied stove.

Later documents reveal that Ed could read and write well—and he even briefly tried his hand at teaching—so he probably enjoyed his schooling, but it must have been interrupted by the seasonal demands of farm labor.

A year or so after the Maxwells moved to Fulton County, the Civil War erupted. As the father of three small children whose move to the West had separated him from kinfolk in Ohio and Pennsylvania, David must have felt initially that his family could not survive if he was in the Union Army. Indeed, Susan was pregnant again when the war broke out, and a fourth child, Flora, was born on Christmas Day, 1861.

But many other Fulton County men joined up as the wave of patriotism swept through central Illinois. By May the first company of local soldiers, the Fulton Blues, had departed from Lewistown for camp in nearby Peoria. Other military units would follow, especially later in 1861 and 1862.

Sometime after the war began, the Maxwells moved again. According to the Illinois state census, taken early in 1865, David and his family were then living in Lewistown Township, about two miles southeast of the county seat—and three miles north of their former location in Waterford Township. He was again working as a tenant farmer, almost certainly on land owned by Jonathan Bordner, Moses Bordner, or Charles C. Clark, substantial farmers who had come from Pennsylvania in the 1830s and 1840s. The census reveals that Clark's livestock was valued at $1,000—a hefty sum—and his stored grain was worth another $700. The Bordners were even more well-to-do, and they dominated that rural neighborhood. By contrast, David Maxwell, whose name appears right after Clark's in the census, simply had livestock worth $50—probably a horse, a cow, and a few hogs.

While living near Lewistown, the Maxwells attended "Christine" Church, a nondenominational neighborhood church, which had been erected by the Bordner brothers and named in honor of their mother. It was surely within sight of the Maxwell tenant farm. Like virtually all nineteenth-century Protestant churches, it was committed to a sin-focused, repent-and-pray-for-help kind of Christianity, often touted as the key to God-given prosperity, as well as salvation. Ed, and later Alice and Lon, must have sat through many a tedious service there.

Some in the Bordner neighborhood were also associated with the influential Presbyterian Church in Lewistown. Charles Clark, for example, was a "ruling elder" there for forty years, and was "a devout Christian," according to his 1887 obituary. He was from the same area of Southampton Township, in Cumberland County, that David Maxwell hailed from; in fact, David's sister Sarah had married into the Clark family. That surely explains why David and Susan became aware of tenant farming opportunities in the Bordner neighborhood, and the family connection also made it likely that Clark's piety would influence, or reinforce, the religious orientation of the Maxwells.

To most ardent Protestants, like the Clarks, the Bordners, and the Maxwells, all people were "inclined to evil," but church members like themselves experienced "regeneration by the Holy Ghost," so the world was divided into them and us, the lost and the saved, with no middle ground. Moral choices were supposedly clear and absolute rather than conditioned or contextual. If nineteenth-century churchgoers were often long on righteousness and moral fervor, they were sometimes short on the sympathetic understanding of others.

In a county deeply divided by social class and plagued by rowdyism, most of the Protestant congregations also crusaded against a variety of sins and vices, from adultery and drunkenness to gambling and card playing. In that way, they strove to develop an accepted moral framework that would limit bad behavior. Like so many others, David and Susan were opposed to drinking and saloons. Their sons never drank—or smoked or chewed tobacco, for that matter.

If church experience contributed anything else to the psychological makeup of Ed and Lon Maxwell, it was probably "an individualistic mind-set [that] did not look to authority for guidance but to internalized standards," which was common to mainline Protestantism, and a "tight suppression" of emotional life as a means of shaping their social experience. For alienated youngsters like Ed and Lon, that apparently meant doing as you pleased when alone but always acting restrained and respectful in social situations.

While living southeast of Lewistown, the Maxwell children also must have attended the Bordner School, which was located very close by, in Section 25. The small white building stood on land owned by Moses Bordner, who had several school-age children. A widely respected farmer, with some 800 acres, and eventually an influential Lewistown bank president, he was also a deeply religious man.

More than a year after the war began, David finally decided to join the Union Army. He enlisted at Lewistown on August 11, 1862, becoming a private in the 103rd Illinois Infantry, composed almost entirely of Fulton County men. Within a month the new regiment had almost 900 recruits, and on September 12 they departed by train for Peoria. According to the *Fulton Democrat,* published at Lewistown, the men lined up at the depot, a band played, and after the railroad cars were filled, "the crowd offered their salutes of hurrahs, waving handkerchiefs and hats, and the gallant soldiers, suppressing their sobs for the moment, made answer with wild shouts that sent a thrill of satisfaction through those left behind. . . ."

Before leaving, David had his photograph taken—an image that he wanted to leave with Susan and the children. It shows a handsome, determined-looking young man, with blue eyes and an Amish-type beard, dressed in a military jacket that sported a row of brass buttons.

During November and December the regiment was in Jackson, Tennessee, and Bolivar, Mississippi. On November 9, the inexperienced soldiers fought rebels near Coldwater, killing fifteen and capturing seventy; and two weeks later they met another enemy force along the Tallahatchie River and drove those Confederates from their position. Much of 1863 and 1864 was spent in noncombat operations, but during that time, David was frequently sick. A brief letter "From the 103d Reg't" to the Lewistown newspaper, dated January 25, 1863, reported "considerable sickness in this regiment," which "can only muster four hundred"—or less than half the soldiers. David was "excused from duty," probably because he had measles, which ravaged the camp at that time. A month later he was treated for "parotitus," which was an inflammation of the parotid gland, located in the cheeks, and was associated with mumps.

David's worst illness came in late July and August 1863. According to the official history of the 103rd Illinois Infantry, the men suffered from intense heat and lack of water while laying siege to Jackson, Tennessee: "During the siege and the march we suffered greatly from want of water. There being no wells and the cisterns soon giving out, we were forced to use the water collected in pools, in nearly all of which General Johnson had caused to be killed an ox or a mule. . . ." David was soon very sick with "Int. [Intestinal] Fever," which was also called typhoid fever. Caused by the ingestion of contaminated food or water, its symptoms included intestinal bleeding. According to a later account by Susan, David was so ill that he "came home in the month of August or September 1863, and staid [*sic*] at home between five and six weeks with sickness, as near as I can remember, and was treated by Doctor Robert McDowell of Lewistown. . . ."

Also, in the spring and early summer of 1864, the 103rd Infantry fought in the Atlanta Campaign as part of the Fifteenth Army Corps under Major

General John A. Logan, remaining under fire for some one hundred days and losing several dozen men, including Colonel Willard Dickerman. David was wounded in the engagement at Resaca, Georgia, near Dalton, but not severely enough to end his military service. Eventually promoted to corporal, he remained with the regiment until he was mustered out at Louisville, Kentucky, on June 21, 1865.

While David was away, the Maxwell family suffered grinding poverty. He had received a $27 bounty for enlisting, but afterward, there was little money to send home. Of course, there was no way for Ed, who was just nine years old when his father left, to effectively support a family with three smaller children, although he may have worked as a chore boy or a helper in the field for a nearby farmer.

It is easy to see how a sensitive, undersized boy placed in that circumstance might feel chronically inadequate and harbor self-contempt—be ashamed that he was never the man his mother needed. That was probably at the root of Ed's lifelong neurotic drive to convey an image of manliness, and like so many American males with that problem, he projected his own negative self-assessment onto others, tending to see "hostility and contempt everywhere," as psychologists who later studied such people have pointed out.

At an early age Ed undoubtedly hunted alone, developing grim self-reliance as well as skill with a gun—skill that may have assuaged his sense of inadequacy. In future years, when hiding from the law, he would often pass himself off as a hunter, an identity that he surely felt comfortable with. It is also very possible that Ed's practice of petty theft from neighboring farms, evident during his teens in McDonough County, began sometime during the war years as he struggled to help his mother put food on the table.

Was Ed also emotionally neglected as Susan was preoccupied with two small children and an infant, not to mention the challenge of making ends meet in devastating hard times? Probably—and "[a] man who has had inadequate mothering and fathering often has difficulty envisioning himself as a worthwhile individual" and "attempts to make up for his feeling of worthlessness by constantly 'proving' his importance," according to noted psychiatrist Alfred Messer. For those with opportunity, that can result in high achievement; for Ed, it apparently prompted another kind of "proving," which increasingly emerged as he got older.

For Lon, who was almost three when the war started and almost seven when it ended, those years were the beginning of his deep bond with Ed, whom he admired as the brother who could do so much that he could not.

In a sense, Lon would spend most of his life trying to measure up, to be a worthy comrade. He was also surely taught to "mind" his older brother, who must have had charge of Alice, Lon, and Flora when Susan had to be away. So, before he was ten, Ed became an authority figure, a substitute parent—someone whose impact on Lon would be enormous.

By September of 1863, the editor of the *Fulton Democrat,* William T. Davidson, was leading a campaign to help support the destitute families of local soldiers. One of his articles, "Shame on Lewistown," depicted the desperate wife of a soldier in the 103rd Infantry, begging a local merchant for help to provide for her family—and being refused. If that wasn't Susan, it was surely someone in precisely the same situation. Despite his general opposition to the war, Davidson was a man of social conscience and became alarmed at the poverty and suffering of many military families, especially when the breadwinner was a poorly paid private, like David Maxwell. As he reported at the end of that year, "We learn that there are thirty-four families of private soldiers in the town alone, besides many others in the township outside of the town. Many of those families are in need of the commonest necessities of life. . . ." It was a call for compassion and community in the face of shattering hardship and emotional stress caused by the war.

The ladies of Lewistown raised some money that Christmas season with a "Festival and Fair," but that only helped temporarily. By the following fall, a permanent Relief Society was operating in Lewistown to supply at least some food for the destitute families, but the only effective solution came in April 1865, when the war finally ended.

Unfortunately for the Maxwells, the end of the war did not end their poverty. David had developed heart problems, perhaps as a result of his severe illnesses. According to a document later written by Susan, "At the time he was discharged he was using patent medicine, and for several years afterward he was never able to do much work." Of course, that placed a continuing burden on Ed, who was not yet twelve years old when Lee surrendered at Appomattox.

It is tempting to speculate that David's return, physically damaged but no doubt anxious to reassert his position as head of the household, may have led to dominance disputes with his adolescent son, who was so used to acting on his own—and perhaps thought of himself as the potential replacement for David in his mother's affections. (The circumstances for producing an Oedipus complex were certainly present.) If so, that father-son conflict could only have resulted in bitter tension and the enforced subjugation of Ed—for whom damaged self-esteem and resentment of authority became life-shaping psychological problems.

To make matters worse, the people of Fulton County were deeply divided over the war. Before it began, during the 1860 presidential race, county residents had cast slightly more votes for Stephen Douglas than for Abraham Lincoln. In Lewistown Township, for example, the count was 254 for Douglas and 250 for Lincoln. That political split continued as many Democrats became opposed to the conflict, and the Lewistown area became "a hot-bed of rebellion," as one nearby newspaper put it. Of course, local Republicans vigorously supported Lincoln and the war—and viewed the anti-war Democrats as traitors, or "Copperheads." Distrust, anger, and hostility were starting to rise in Fulton County at the very time when the Maxwell family arrived.

During the summer of 1861, "zealous Republicans" threatened to mob "certain secessionists" and destroy the *Fulton Democrat* office. Editor Davidson responded by promising violent retaliation if any of those plans were carried out. As the Civil War dragged on, bringing more suffering and death than anyone had anticipated, and as the draft—very unpopular with Democrats—was eventually being enforced, local animosity grew between pro-war and anti-war factions. Family was set against family.

During the summer of 1863 there was armed resistance to the arrest of local deserters and to the draft. In Isabel Township, adjacent to Waterford, three soldiers who went to arrest a deserter struck the man's wife with a gun, and that "Brutal Outrage," as the *Fulton Democrat* put it, led to the formation of a posse with a warrant for their arrest and an upsurge of anger among anti-war Democrats. On August 13, the Illinois provost marshal sent in sixty-one Union cavalrymen, from the military camp at Quincy, to round up the many other deserters. Raids on some homes led to gunfire and the wounding of a few men, but at the end of it all, nine prisoners were brought in, then shipped off by railroad to stand trial. That, in turn, prompted a huge demonstration by "six or seven hundred armed citizens . . . in the environs of Lewistown," according to a report by the Fulton County provost marshal. Fear that angry local residents would attack the soldiers led to the arrival of fifty more cavalry and an eighty-man infantry unit as well, to guarantee order. In a lead story, the *Fulton Democrat* termed the whole military operation a "REIGN OF TERROR." All of that occurred just a few miles south of the Maxwell home.

Angry rhetoric persisted, and in the fall of that year some three thousand Copperheads rallied at Lewistown to condemn the war and the violations of civil rights that were occurring. A local lawyer, S. Corning Judd, was in fact the state commander of a society of Southern sympathizers called "The Order of the American Knights," which soon changed its name to

"The Sons of Liberty." No wonder there was ongoing political friction and partisan resentment in Fulton County.

Occasional fights also continued to erupt, and in the following spring, on May 9, 1864, returned soldiers and Lincoln supporters clashed with opponents of the war in the streets of Lewistown. As the editor of the newspaper described it, "our streets were the scene of such tumult and disorder as was never witnessed in this town before," and for several hours, under the influence of liquor, "a mob with murder and destruction in their hearts" seemed to control the town. There was, in short, a radical loss of community in Lewistown, and in all of southern Fulton County, during the Civil War years.

Some individual acts of violence against officials were also related to the war. On August 9, 1864, for example, Assistant Provost Marshal Charles Phelps was ambushed near the village of Otto. Wounded in his left side, he survived, but his horse was killed. In late October of that year, Fulton County Enrolling Officer and Assistant Provost Marshal John Criss was fired upon in Liverpool Township while "he was out notifying drafted men." He received two wounds but also survived. Neither of the assailants was ever identified.

By the close of 1864, the newspapers in both Canton and Lewistown were calling for a reassertion of law and order in Fulton County.

For Ed Maxwell, the struggling, insecure son of a tenant farmer who had been caught up in the issues of the conflict and had departed for the battlefield, the home front in Fulton County was an emotionally harsh, semi-lawless social environment, where deprivation, ideological conflict, and intolerable stress generated resentment and brutality. Men, and boys, had to be prepared for confrontation.

Other local acts of violence were also clearly related to animosity over the war. Late in 1863, for example, a man named Jackson Bolen killed a certain James Mahary of Vermont (village) because the latter had charged him with being a Missouri jayhawker, or Union Army pillager. Bolen supposedly went to Mahary "for satisfaction" and ended up stabbing the man to death. Bolen was indicted and tried in 1863 but was acquitted, the jury accepting his improbable assertion that the deed was committed in self-defense.

The killing of Mahary vividly illustrates that "the code of the West," demanding confrontation and revenge for injury and insult, operated in mid-nineteenth-century Illinois, especially in frontierish areas like Fulton County, as it did in states and territories west of the Mississippi River.

That code not only prompted Bolen's violent confrontation with Mahary but also influenced his acquittal, for juries were composed of men who were just as obsessed with masculine honor as he was. The willingness to commit violence was, in fact, regarded as a demonstration of manliness.

As the Ringo Kid (John Wayne) would later put it in John Ford's classic western film *Stagecoach,* "There are some things a man just can't walk away from." But beneath that obsession with honor was insecurity—as men strove for acceptance and stature in a new and turbulent social environment where masculine identity was always at issue.

In the same way, other Fulton County court cases show local reluctance to convict a man of violence if he could make any claim whatever to self-defense. In June 1863, for example, the Lewistown newspaper recorded the following circuit court decision: "The people vs. Samuel Goodman, for gouging Shadrack Lewis' eyes out. Acquitted." Goodman had simply claimed that Lewis had caused the fight, and of course, a man had a right to defend himself.

It is not surprising that an 1881 researcher who examined the local circuit court records asserted, "Of the fifty-two murders committed [in the county] . . . there has not been a single conviction." That was not quite accurate, but the justice system clearly failed most of the time. The underlying reason: Most men in Fulton County feared and resented authority—and also felt that dependence on a lawman undermined the assertion of one's manhood. It was a sign of weakness. Consequently, they were unable to employ the justice system to force compliance with a common moral standard regarding assault and murder. They settled things themselves—and gave their approval when others did the same.

As the war dragged on, there was also a general increase in lawbreaking. Rowdyism became a major problem. Early in 1863 the editor of the *Fulton Democrat* asserted, "The morals of Lewistown, as illustrated by the daily brawls upon our streets, are almost at the lowest possible ebb. We are virtually without law and order. . . . Never was another town so completely at the mercy of lawbreakers and ruffians." He also complained of boys "from twelve to eighteen, [who] smoke cigars, play cards, drink whisky, and swear in a style that would astonish a Texas lawyer." Some of the older ones even wore revolvers or bowie knives, like the tough, assertive men they admired. Lewistown, where the Maxwells shopped and attended events, was becoming a place where bravado and self-assertion were part of everyday male behavior. All of that may well have influenced young Ed, who later carried both a gun and a bowie knife.

Even after the war, that kind of disorder remained a deep concern. In fact, just a few months after the conflict ended, the editor of the *Fulton Democrat* asserted, "No town in our knowledge is cursed with a more malignant and depraved set of desperadoes than Lewistown. . . . Jack Ross and Joe Brice [local outlaws] are gentlemen, when compared with some of the devils that perambulate our streets daily, with an impudence that would shame an imp of darkness." Some of those men were returned soldiers, who got drunk, fought in the streets, and committed acts of theft and vandalism, but such social disorder and street violence at the county seat continued through the 1880s.

Like so many other places in the West, Fulton County also saw a rise in robbery and horse stealing during and after the war. In the late 1860s and 1870s, dozens of such criminals—including repeat offenders like Dan Ryan, Jacob Spidell, and Henry Trent—were caught, jailed, tried, and sentenced to the state penitentiary at Joliet, but it was also easy for lawbreakers to vanish into the heavily timbered, thinly settled country along the Illinois River, and to escape by raft or boat down the river itself.

Horse stealing was especially alarming. An 1865 letter to the *Chicago Tribune,* by a resident of nearby Woodford County, asserted that horse theft was "rampant in central Illinois," and it pointed to the rise of "organized bands" of horse thieves, which apparently "had little fear of punishment."

In June 1865, the editor of the *Fulton Democrat* stated that "horse stealing is being done to an alarming extent in this county," and again, early in 1866, he reported that the county was full of horse thieves, and recommended that local people resort to lynching: "There will be no security from horse thieves until people commence taking them from the clutches of attorneys and hanging them up as fast as found." A year later, the editor of the *Fulton County Ledger,* at Canton, made a similar comment: "Stealing horses has become so common that it almost seems that the best way to treat a horse thief is to try him by Judge Lynch's court." Vigilantes in some counties did that: Both St. Clair and Jersey counties had five such lynchings in 1866, but Fulton County apparently had none.

Horse thieves aroused the ire of residents in Illinois and other western states like no other robbers, simply because people were so dependent on horses for work, travel, and emergency situations. And like America's soon-to-be-mythic cowboys, many homesteaders deeply prized their horses. So, prosecution for assault of some kind, and even murder, often resulted in acquittal or a light sentence, especially in turbulent Fulton County, but horse theft was more dependably and severely punished. A circuit court report from the 1863 *Fulton Democrat* shows this clearly:

> *The People vs. John Metzer*—Assault with intent to kill Patrick Lynch. 30 days in the county jail.
> *The People vs. J. B. Johnson*—Larceny of a horse. Three years in the penitentiary.

In fact, Illinois law prescribed a three- to twenty-year prison sentence for horse stealing.

Assaults and murders were not uncommon, but few of those crimes ever led to a conviction, especially if the victim was an outsider. For example, a few months after the Civil War ended, a hired hand named Daniel Lash, who worked for a well-to-do farmer near Marbletown, ten miles southeast of Lewistown, got into an argument with a nearby saloonkeeper named Thomas Richardson. The latter assaulted him, beating him repeatedly with a hatchet. As he was dying, the brutalized farmhand staggered out of Richardson's saloon and told nearby people, "He has killed me!" Then he collapsed. Although Lash had been unarmed, the local grand jury refused to even indict the well-liked local businessman, who simply asserted that the impoverished drifter had used "threatening language" to him—and that was sufficient excuse for the killing. Richardson had demonstrated, by his action, the local public's willingness to defend the established social order, which he represented, against lower-class outsiders, who could be trouble, so the townspeople ignored his violence. Inequality had both encouraged the brutal act and kept the justice system from dealing with it.

Several years later, at another saloon near Lewistown, a tenant-farming Swede who had just come to the West, "a very quiet, inoffensive man," was clubbed to death by three local men who had taunted him. Although the bullies were indicted for murder, sympathetic local juries acquitted two of the men, and the third, a certain Lem Purdy, was tried in nearby Mason County, where the prosecution got a better result, but he received only a five-year sentence for manslaughter. Incredibly, one local account of the killing, which appeared in 1879, commented that "All [three] of these parties were accounted good, respectable citizens." Indeed, they must have been, to get away with murder.

As those disgraceful episodes show, in Fulton County the justice system was often perverted to shield well-known local figures from suffering serious consequences for their violent acts. And surely many beatings and threats were never even prosecuted. The Maxwells were probably aware of that double standard, which militated against impoverished outsiders—people like themselves.

Of course, the ineffective county court tended to foster private vengeance, which sometimes took the form of lynching. For example, in the summer of 1870 the *Chicago Tribune* carried an article titled "Murder and Lynching in Fulton County," which tersely reported, "During a drunken quarrel at Otto, in Fulton County, on Sunday, a man named Craig shot another man, named Brown, twice, killing him instantly. The murderer fled, but was found by Brown's friends at Ipava, and hung to a tree. . . ." This act of mob violence was never recorded in a local history, so it eventually passed from memory, cleansing the county of yet another aspect of its violent heritage.

After the war, shooting incidents were on the rise, in Fulton County and elsewhere, partly because ex-soldiers had become accustomed to self-assertion, and some still carried handguns. Late in 1866, for example, a Christmas dance at Lewistown led to a fight in which two men drew their revolvers and one was shot dead. Both men were former Union soldiers. Six months later, a robber and horse thief named John Yarnell, who had served in the Seventeenth Illinois Infantry, killed a marshal during a confrontation at Lewistown. Sheriff David Waggoner, himself an ex-soldier, then managed to arrest the killer, who was tried in nearby McDonough County on a change of venue, convicted, and sentenced to the penitentiary at Joliet.

By then, Waggoner already had a fine reputation as a lawman. A tall, handsome man, with striking blue eyes and a short beard, he was good with horses and guns. After serving as a deputy for four years, he was first elected county sheriff in 1850, when he was only twenty-seven. In later life he often told stories about enforcing the law in those early days, when Illinois was still a frontier state.

The most noted lawman in the county's history, Waggoner was sheriff or deputy sheriff for most of the 1850s, the later 1860s, the 1870s, and the early 1880s before finally retiring. During the Civil War he was a major in the Eleventh Illinois Cavalry, serving under Colonel Robert G. Ingersoll, and in December 1862, while fighting a battle against overwhelming odds in Tennessee, he was captured by the Confederates. Later paroled, he was allowed to return home. By then, his exciting story had appeared in a New York newspaper, and he was regarded as a war hero.

Perhaps his greatest exploit was bringing in the notorious Fulton County horse thief and robber Joe Brice, who had been accused of killing a man in Iowa. Waggoner was serving as a deputy in 1865 when he tracked Brice to Okaman, Minnesota, where the latter was living under an alias. He then notified the local authorities and assisted them with the capture. He brought the outlaw back to Fulton County, where Brice was held for extradition to Iowa—and where Waggoner was celebrated as an intrepid lawman.

When Waggoner again ran for sheriff in 1866, the *Fulton Democrat* remarked that his reputation was "more than statewide" and asserted his preeminence as a lawman: "He has received, and justly merits, the title of 'the model sheriff of Illinois.'" Despite the fact that Democrats were not often chosen to fill county offices after the war, he was elected.

David Maxwell probably knew Sheriff Waggoner, who was popular throughout the county and was a hero both as a Civil War veteran and a lawman. Moreover, like the Maxwells, he had been raised in southern Pennsylvania and, like David, he had a background in farming and had married just before immigrating to the West.

Later in his career, Waggoner would be on the trail of the Maxwell brothers.

The postwar rise in crime, in Illinois and elsewhere, was partly fueled by an increase in poverty and frustration. While popular images still portrayed the West as a Land of Promise, economic realities made the rise to success difficult, and social class divisions were advancing everywhere in the upper Mississippi Valley. Tenant farmers like David Maxwell were simply not on the same social level as doctors, lawyers, bankers, businessmen, and established farmers. An 1868 newspaper poem called "Song of the Emigrant," by a poet in nearby McDonough County, conveys the popular myth of the West as an egalitarian paradise:

> Away, away, away,
> Where souls, like wild game, are free,
> Where the human heart is true and gay,
>   And brothers together agree.
> There equals *are equal*—then hasten away;
> My country the Great West shall be.

And it was precisely that hope, of being truly equal, rather than second class, that prompted David and Susan to move—not once, but three times as the 1860s closed and the next decade began. In 1881 Ed Maxwell himself chronicled his family's moves, in a newspaper interview: "He told the reporter that he had been born in Wyandot County, Ohio, and lived there till he was 6 years old; moved to Fulton County, Illinois, and settled near Lewistown; lived there until 16; thence moved to Woodford County, one year; then west, to Iowa, and then back to McDonough County, Illinois. . . ." While this account is roughly true, it is slightly inaccurate—perhaps the reporter's fault. Ed must have been only fourteen or fifteen when the Maxwells moved from Fulton County, probably late in 1868, after the harvest. By then, the impoverished tenant family had a fifth child, George, born on September 15, 1866.

The move to Woodford County, across the Illinois River from Peoria, was surely prompted by the hope that relatives there could provide work and perhaps help them become established. Those relatives included David's much-older cousin, Sarah, and her sixty-six-year-old husband, William Woodburn. Like David and Susan, the Woodburns had settled in Ohio before moving to Illinois, but by the late 1860s their land was worth some eight to ten thousand dollars. David may have worked for them as a hired hand on their prairie farm in Section 24 of Linn Township, through the harvest season. The Woodburn farm was located several miles southeast of Washburn, a village of 300 people, and several miles southwest of Minonk, which had a population of about 1,100. The landscape of Linn Township was rolling prairie that stretched away to occasional groves of timber, and most of it had been "improved" into farms that were already worth about twenty dollars per acre. Like the Woodburns, many of the early settlers there had come from Pennsylvania.

In Clayton Township, just east of William and Sarah Woodburn's place, was the farm of William Maxwell, another much-older cousin of David's, who had also homesteaded in Ohio before moving to Illinois. William was then sixty-two years old and had a substantial farm, so David may have worked for him as well.

While the Maxwells struggled in Woodford County, yet another child, John, was born, on March 30, 1869. He was the sixth child in a family perennially faced with hard times.

A commentary on the Maxwell brothers, written after they had become infamous, mentions that Ed was "detected in petty thieving" while in Woodford County, but no details were provided. He was sixteen then, in 1869, and was surely permitted to hunt alone and travel to Washburn on his own, so he had the opportunity for theft—while his status as the son of impoverished outsiders may have made the more prosperous local folks seem like fair game.

Interestingly, the only surviving signatures by Ed are inside the front and back covers of a book that he once owned, in Woodford and McDonough counties. Entitled *The Prodigal Son; or the Sinner's Departure and the Sinner's Return,* by the Reverend E. P. Rogers, it is a religious tract based on the famous parable about a rebellious son and a forgiving father—or, as the book says, "a kind father" and "a restless, wayward, impatient son" who experiences "ruin and wretchedness" but repents and returns home. Was the book presented to Ed by his religious father, or both parents, in an effort to prompt reflection on his bad behavior and encourage repentance? Probably—but in any case, it is a tract that recommends self-surrender rather than self-assertion, and promotes guilt, self-doubt, and a sense of inner deficiency. If that book was typical of the religious-based instruction of his father, no wonder Ed developed low self-esteem and created an alternative identity as a desperado that everyone had to respect.

Such a book reminds us, too, that "the law, which exercises authority over the citizen, represents [an extension of] the parent, who exercises authority over the child," as one scholar has put it, so for some people, at least, "the law thus serves as a repository of powerful feelings from early childhood—complex feelings of love and hatred . . . submission and defiance." For Ed Maxwell, defiance of the law and resistance to lawmen may well have been an extension of his troubled relationship with his father.

Inside the book's front cover is Ed's signature: "William E. Maxwell, Woodford Co., Illinois." Another signature, inside the back cover, is accompanied by "McComb [Macomb], Ill," so he kept the book during the 1870s while the family was living in McDonough County—where he eventually got into bigger trouble.

When no prospects for economic stability materialized, the Maxwells set out, late in 1869, for Taylor County, Iowa, sixty miles east of the Missouri River. That county had been established in 1847, but its seat of government, Bedford, was not laid out until 1853. Taylor County was, then, a new area, without any sizable towns, when the Maxwells spent some weeks or months there late in 1869 and early the next year. Strangely, Taylor County was the place where Fulton County outlaw Joe Brice had murdered a man in 1865, and where he was afterwards convicted and sentenced to hang— but escaped, stole a horse, and vanished into the West. It is unlikely that the Maxwells knew Brice, but they must have heard stories about him— tales of his bold robberies and his jailbreaks—both in Fulton County and again in Iowa.

Although the precise reason why David and Susan Maxwell journeyed to Taylor County is unknown—they may have simply heard good reports about that area—they surely expected to find land to rent and obviously failed to do so. The deeply frustrated couple, with six children to care for, then headed back to Illinois, where they would try again to establish a foothold.

So, when Ed was in his mid-teens, the Maxwell family was reduced to drifting from place to place, and their hope for social transformation was surely beginning to wear thin. For the undersized youth, who wanted so much to be well-regarded, there were bitter memories of poverty, insecurity, failure, and disrespect—his father struggling, worrying, giving up in place after place; his mother slaving, making do, and coping with young children and babies in one bare, cold shack after another.

Ed must have shared his parents' desperation as they headed their tightly packed wagon back to western Illinois. And he surely absorbed their sense of alienation as well. They had a stable social background, however, allowing them to put their recent plight into perspective—to regard their frustrating tenant-farming life as a series of temporary failures, part of the long, necessary struggle for prosperity. But for an insecure, friendless adolescent like Ed, it was the only kind of life he had ever known. It was the way things were.

3

The Maxwells in McDonough County

The Maxwells did not travel all the way back to where they had lived during the troubled 1860s but, instead, moved into a tenant house in McDonough County, which was just to the west of Fulton. Their rented farm was on the northern edge of Tennessee Township, in Section 4, just a mile or so above the heavily wooded banks of the Lamoine River and a half mile west of the road leading from the hamlet of Tennessee across the huge North Prairie to the village of Blandinsville.

Like so many counties in western Illinois, McDonough had been organized in the 1820s. At that time, most of the region's villages—such as Peoria, Quincy, Beardstown, and Fort Edwards (Warsaw)—were scattered along the Illinois and Mississippi rivers, which lay more than thirty miles away, to the east and west. The steamboat era soon arrived, and because McDonough County was not on a major river, it developed slowly. The county seat, Macomb, was not laid out until 1831—five years after the county had been formed—and twenty years later, the town still had only 700 people.

The coming of the Northern Cross (later Chicago, Burlington, and Quincy) Railroad in the mid-1850s spurred development, generating new farm-center villages like Prairie City, Bushnell, Bardolph, and Tennessee, as well as the coal-mining community of Colchester. In Macomb the first

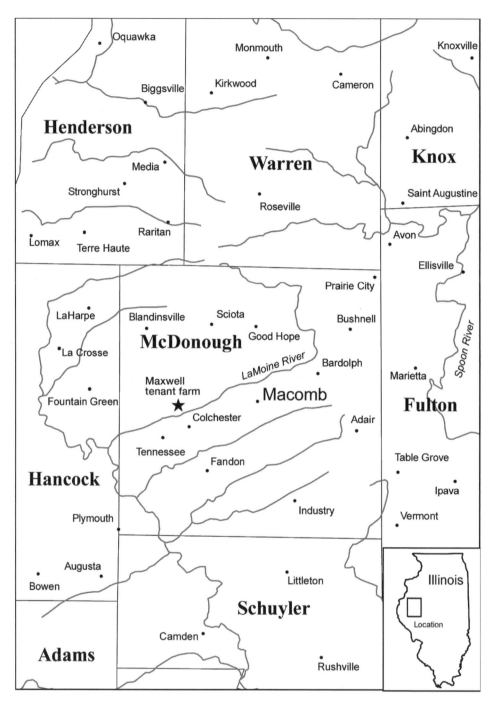

McDonough County and surrounding areas, showing the approximate location of the 1870 Maxwell tenant farm and several communities related to the outlaw career of Ed and Lon.

depot was erected a few blocks west of the square, and strange new signs went up that warned, "Look out for the cars when the bell rings or the whistle sounds." A new, more progressive era had dawned, and the county's population soon doubled. But the coming of the Civil War slowed the pace of progress once again.

As in Fulton County, local people were badly divided over issues related to the war. Some wanted strict enforcement of the Fugitive Slave Law while others opposed slavery and approved of the Underground Railroad, which had operated in McDonough County since the 1840s. Some viewed Lincoln—who had visited Macomb twice in 1858—as a destroyer of the Union and a threat to constitutionally guaranteed rights, while others viewed him as the preserver of the Union and a champion of freedom. Some opposed the draft and rejected the war itself, as "a foolish, vain, wicked, and impossible attempt to break down the sacred barriers of the Constitution and abolish slavery," while many others served in the Union Army—or supported the effort of their husbands and brothers, and prayed for their safe return.

With almost 2,700 men from McDonough County serving in the conflict, and hundreds of them not returning, there was widespread hardship and suffering.

The close of the war brought steady population growth, new business initiatives, and a renewed impulse toward local development. In 1871 the *Atlas Map of McDonough County* appeared, underwritten by the more prosperous businessmen and landowners. In lithographs, maps, and historical-biographical sections it celebrated the county as a localized version of the American Promise—an agrarian empire, newly wrested from the wilderness and characterized by lovely, productive farms, progressive villages, and a splendid, substantial county seat. From the look of things in that grand, oversized book—itself a symbol of social status—no one had failed and no one was poor. The achievers had created a great localization of American culture, and prosperity was available for all.

Published at a time of rising expectations, the *Atlas* testified to a prevailing philosophy of life—the Gospel of Success. It seemed to demonstrate that economic independence was the natural order of things, open to all "through diligent effort and pursuit of the main chance"—especially if you possessed certain virtues. You simply shaped your character, which prompted the right choices and, in turn, shaped your life. That was also the message preached at home, school, and church—and it was often reflected in local newspapers as well. In 1875, for example, the *Macomb*

Journal printed a column that reinforced the Gospel's message, and it also revealed that ordinary activities were often loaded with moral meaning:

PROVERBS OF TRUTH

Diligence commands success. . . .

An oak tree is not felled with one blow. [Persistence will prevail.]

Always put your saddle on the right horse. [Make good choices.]

Never split wood against the grain. [Follow the natural order of things.]

Borrowed clothes never fit. [Don't try to be other than who you are.]

Better go to bed supperless than get up in debt. [Do whatever you must to avoid economic dependence.]

Fortune knocks at least once at every man's gate. [Your opportunity to prosper will eventually come.]

Like a light, a good name keeps its lustre in the dark. [A virtuous reputation never fades, and will persist in adversity.]

Give a rogue enough rope, and he will hang himself. [People of bad character will inevitably destroy themselves.]

In post–Civil War America the call on every side was for an orderly, self-disciplined life, which would supposedly bring sure rewards—opportunity, prosperity, respectability.

But too often, it brought only frustration. And as the *Atlas Map of McDonough County* so clearly implied, respectability—or adherence to an established moral order—was always judged by outward appearances, by socioeconomic standing. Shaping one's character to achieve success was admirable, but appraising someone's character by his success, or failure, was unjust—and oppressive to those on the bottom, who often felt socially discarded and even morally condemned. It was unjust because many components of any person's character are not a matter of choice but are determined by genetic inheritance, cultural forces, and psychological factors stemming from personal experience. More than people like to admit, their lives are impacted by fate and circumstance.

Seldom critiqued, the Gospel of Success also fostered an intensely competitive, self-focused mind-set, which bred tension, distrust, judgmentalism, and resentment. It tended to limit sympathetic identification with others—people who failed where you succeeded or succeeded where you failed—laying the groundwork for animosity.

The coming of the Maxwells to McDonough County, where the outlaw career of Ed and Lon began, was apparently accidental. They had probably intended to return to Fulton County, where they had lived for eight years and surely had friends. But they were questing for a new situation, another tenant farm, and then fate intervened—in the person of Ebenezer Hicks. A November 24, 1881, article in the *Macomb Journal,* titled "How They Began," reconstructs the scene of their arrival:

> In the winter of 1869–70, a "mover" with a wife and children—two sons, lads, and a daughter—drove up to the residence of E. Hicks, of Hire Township, this county, and asked permission to stay overnight. It was granted. The man had, a year previous, emigrated from Woodford County, this state, to Iowa, but not liking the country, was on his way back. It was stormy weather at the time, and the following day they asked to occupy a vacant tenement house on Mr. Hicks' farm until the roads became fit for traveling. He gave them permission, and the family remained a few days, and finding their quarters comfortable, and an opportunity to work, they made arrangements to stay until spring. In the spring he rented land for a year, and after a year, he stayed another, and still another.

At first, this seems plausible enough, but David and Susan Maxwell had six children then, not three, and their move to Iowa had come only a few months earlier, not "a year previous." Nor was the move back from Iowa simply a matter of "not liking the country" in that state, which had a prairie-and-timber landscape like Illinois. The memory of those local folks who had informed the newspaper reporter was clearly inaccurate. They probably knew very little about the Maxwells.

More to the point: The very idea that seeking refuge from a storm had accidentally brought them to the door of Ebenezer Hicks, the richest farmer in McDonough County, who was known far and wide for renting land to tenant families, is ridiculous. The Maxwells surely came to his door because, while moving through that part of western Illinois, they had heard about Ebenezer Hicks.

Born in Ross County, Ohio, in 1816, Hicks had come to McDonough County in 1842. He had started out by purchasing the southwest corner of Section 33, in Hire Township, ten miles west of the county seat, and by hard work and shrewd dealing, he eventually owned more than four thousand acres in McDonough County—and some in Hancock County as well. By 1870 he had a kind of mythic stature, as the ultimate pioneer farmer, symbolizing the incredible potential for success that local folks associated with their county and with agricultural life in the West.

The 1885 *History of McDonough County, Illinois* celebrates the achievement of Ebenezer Hicks—and suggests something about his character:

> When he purchased his place, there was but 16 acres broken and a small shanty built. He improved the farm and subsequently built a good house and other buildings. Mr. Hicks has been a man who always attended strictly to business, driving all before him. He has a very strong constitution. . . . In a short time he commenced buying more land, as he was able to pay for it . . . and he now owns about 4,000 acres, scattered around in various townships, especially in Hire, Tennessee, Colchester, and Scotland. The most of this is rented; only about 1,000 acres is retained for the management of his sons. Mr. Hicks oversees the whole thing, thereby causing himself much hard labor. . . . Stock-raising is the especial feature, and large herds of cattle roam over his dominions.

As this suggests, Ebenezer Hicks was a hard-nosed businessman. In fact, he had a reputation for ferreting out distressed farmers and purchasing their lands at bargain prices—sometimes by paying the back taxes that were owed. And he never took a personal interest in the tenant families who occupied his land. They paid on time, or they got out. Local folks respected "old man Hicks," as they did anyone who achieved notable success and seemed invulnerable to failure, but no one liked him. A much-discussed self-made man, he demonstrated that the Gospel of Success had little to do with social commitment.

As he aged, Ebenezer Hicks became the physical symbol of his forceful, grasping, dominating reputation. He was a strong, burly hulk of a man, with piercing eyes, a prominent nose, and a powerful jaw—not to mention graying, unruly hair that he never bothered to comb. He looked like a man who did not trust people, but inspected them for signs of weakness.

Chronically afraid that someone would get back at him, Hicks descended into paranoia. In 1885 his family succeeded in having him committed to the state insane asylum at Jacksonville, where he died one year later. But when the Maxwell family arrived at the start of 1870, he was a legendary cattle rancher and farmland manager, focused on enlarging his empire.

The Maxwells were on the southern edge of the vast prairie-and-timber holdings of Ebenezer Hicks, and, at times, they must have felt an almost feudal insignificance. Nowhere else in the county was the social and economic gulf between owner and tenant so dramatic.

The 1881 article on the coming of the Maxwells depicts David as a shiftless sort of person, a drifter without plan or purpose: "Maxwell (the father) was a quiet, well meaning man with not much education, itinerant in his habits, a sort of 'come-day, go-day, God-send-Sunday' man, as is plainly evidenced in his stopping over for a night at a place, and then for a few days, and then until spring, and then lengthening it into years." This comment reveals more about the public attitude toward tenant farmers, and itinerant farm laborers, than it does about David Maxwell. Because they were landless, and were often temporary residents, tenants were on the bottom of the social scale—not really part of the cultural enterprise in McDonough County, or Woodford County, or any other fairly progressive agricultural area where they happened to be. Their lives were commonly beneath public notice, or at least any genuine concern.

A brief item in the November 1868 *Macomb Eagle* reflects the anonymity of such "movers," as tenants were often called: "On Wednesday last, a mover's team became frightened at a locomotive, and ran away, spilling himself, the family, and their 'plunder' into the ditch near the railroad, and smashing the wagon up considerably. Nobody hurt."

Because tenant contracts extended for one year only, and might not be renewed, uncertainty haunted the lives of tenant families. In the 1870s roughly one-third of the tenants moved every year, typically leaving in November—like the "movers" mentioned above—after the fall crop was in and the owner was paid, or else in March, when the worst of the winter was over. Life was a relentless quest for security and prosperity—a cycle of extreme struggle, periodic exploitation, and inevitable dissatisfaction, if not despair.

The coming of horse-drawn and steam-powered farm machinery—reapers, threshers, cultivators, corn planters, and the like—in the post–Civil War era was of little benefit to tenant farmers, who could not afford those new implements and would not have been able to transport them to the next rented place anyway. So, those marginal farmers slowly became less productive—as well as less needed by farm owners who had those machines.

Because they were not rooted in local culture, like landowners—or home owners in a village—tenant families such as the Maxwells usually did not relate as closely to social institutions, like churches and schools, nor did they participate much in local politics. Spiritually, they were often outsiders—tolerated but not embraced by the more prosperous citizens of the county where they lived. And as the years passed, their struggle was not remembered—or recorded in the county histories that always celebrated the successful.

One of the long-forgotten McDonough County murder cases of the 1870s dramatized this social class division. On November 21, 1874, a certain Luther Courtwright, born into a respected, landowning farm family, shot and killed a hired hand named Moore—whose exact identity was so inconsequential that the Macomb newspaper never even printed his first name. The trouble started when Moore, described by some as "uncouth," was made "the butt of many jokes," which supposedly originated with Courtwright. In short, Moore was a victim of blatant disrespect. That led to an encounter on a country road, where Moore supposedly threatened the young farmer—according to Courtwright's later testimony—and the latter clubbed him to the ground. A few days afterward, the two men encountered each other again, in the darkness outside a neighbor's farmhouse, and supposedly Moore fired a shot at Courtwright, who then fired back, twice, and killed the hired hand. A coroner's jury, composed of landowners, soon exonerated Courtwright, who pleaded self-defense, despite the fact that no shot by Moore was seen or heard by anyone (except the defendant) and no revolver belonging to Moore was ever found at the crime scene. The *Macomb Journal,* anxious to persuade readers that somehow justice had been done, ended its report with the following comment: "The general character of the two men: Moore, as stated, was a very bad man, while on the other hand, Courtwright, who was raised in this county, has born the character of a quiet, inoffensive, orderly citizen. Moore, we believe, has no relations in McDonough."

It would be hard to find a case of violence, and subsequent injustice in the courtroom, more obviously influenced by the victim's lack of social status. If Courtwright was a "quiet, inoffensive" citizen, why did he repeatedly make Moore the butt of jokes, or club him down in the roadway instead of just riding off, or carry the gun that finally killed the unarmed and impoverished hired hand? The Moore murder case symbolized the increasing social divide between owners and workers, the insiders and the outsiders, and demonstrated that in the public mind, relative poverty and criminal propensity were fused. A landless worker was readily regarded as a "bad man" if a landowner who disliked him simply made that assertion.

The 1870 McDonough County census, recorded in July, found David and Susan Maxwell living in Tennessee Township, with their six children: William E. (Ed), age 16; Alice M., age 14; David A. (Lon), age 11; Flora, age 8; George W., age 3; and John, age 1. By then, Ed had a listed occupation: "works on a farm." Because David had lingering health problems related to his Civil War experience, Ed's work must have been arduous and indispensable.

Lon and his sisters attended the Hicks School, a sparsely furnished frame building along a dirt road on the open prairie, a mile or so north of the Maxwell tenant farm. Reading, writing, and recitation from memory were central to the country school experience, along with basic math and a little history and geography.

Almost nothing is known about the lives of David and Susan Maxwell in McDonough County, but they did have their seventh and eighth children there. James D. Maxwell—always called "Jimmie"—was born on the farm they rented from Ebenezer Hicks, on December 15, 1871. Charles Gilbert Maxwell—always called "Gabe"—was born on another nearby tenant farm, on March 11, 1874.

During those years, David and Susan did their weekly "trading" at Colchester, a poor mining community located just a few miles south of their farm, beyond the rugged bluffs of Crooked Creek. Founded in 1855, when the railroad had come through, allowing the miners to ship their coal, it was a struggling village of less than a thousand people in the early 1870s. Known for its several saloons, and consequent Saturday night drunkenness and rowdyism, the coal-dust-covered town was nevertheless a useful place for farm families to do "trading"—exchange eggs, chickens, cream, and butter for goods—because the villagers did not produce any agricultural products.

Very little is known about the early activities of Ed and Lon, but the 1881 newspaper account of their beginning portrays them as young comrades who were naturally inclined to lawbreaking, despite their apparent intelligence:

> They were quick and sharp, and a peculiar fact, when connected with their subsequent career, is that a Bible prize offered in the neighborhood Sunday School to the pupil that would commit the most Bible verses [to memory] in the course of a year, was captured by Lon, whose recitals footed up over 3,000 verses. . . . Be this as it may . . . it was not long before they developed a difference from their associates. While other boys were full of the fun of

harmless adventures and pranks, the Maxwells were always eager to turn those adventures into destruction of property and petty thieving.

An example: going coon-hunting one night, nothing would satisfy them but to steal a number of chickens, which they took to a schoolhouse to roast and eat. To add to their meal of poultry, they went to the premises of a man living near, and not only robbed his bee-stands of all the honey they could carry away, but also upset the hives, and destroyed the bees. . . . The facts came to light as to who were the depredators, and there was talk of arresting them. Immediately, they took to the woods with rascally instinct and 'laid out' until the matter blew over or was fixed up.

The memorizing of Bible verses by Lon is another indication of the Protestant religious vision that was part of the Maxwell brothers' upbringing. Ed must have been required or pressured to do that too—a demand that could have triggered resentment. There was a nearby church, and without a doubt, Sundays were dedicated to a long morning service, with sermonizing on sin, guilt, and salvation, followed by Sunday school in the afternoon.

It is unlikely that, in 1870, when Ed was perhaps sixteen or seventeen and Lon was only eleven or twelve, they hid in the woods for a period of days to avoid capture for petty theft. While Ed was a young farm worker, Lon was still a schoolboy. But they did have some lawbreaking exploits together. Another account, from the 1889 *Colchester Independent*, provides the recollections of a local school superintendent:

Prof. George Fentem, of this city, who remembers them as schoolboys, says they were models of behavior and brightness. Contrary to the rule, their earlier career did not evidence their after career. But when nearer grown they became wild. Their first depredations were of the nature of practical jokes. The first was the erection of a fence one night across the road near Allen Murray's. Next they stole beehives from Thomas Caldwell and Jesse Martin. Then they took the taps off Matt Foltz's wagon one night, and on another occasion stole a wheel from William Foster's buggy, which Bill never did find. They took intense delight in such escapades.

It is interesting to note that Ed, who was already sixteen when his family arrived, spent some time as a "schoolboy" in McDonough County. That was surely because his education had been interrupted by the Maxwell family's frequent moving—and by the Civil War, when he was forced to shoulder some adult responsibilities while David was in the army. Falling behind other boys his age was a blow to Ed's fragile self-esteem. And if he felt compelled by his parents to complete a country school education while in his later teens—perhaps by attending in the winter term, when there was little farm work—he may have resented their assault on his emerging manhood.

Murray, Caldwell, Martin, and Foltz were neighbors, living in the southeast corner of Hire Township, in the early 1870s, which reveals that the David Maxwell family had moved there, either to occupy other land owned by Ebenezer Hicks or to rent from someone else. That corner of Hire Township was three miles from where the Maxwells had lived when the 1870 census was taken.

Another account of Ed and Lon's "petty thieving," by farmer and local historian Quincy Hainline, asserts that "the family attended church and Sunday school at Argyle," a heavily wooded rural area two miles north of Colchester. But according to Hainline, despite their religious training, the boys "robbed melon patches, apple and peach orchards, chicken roosts, and beehives." Those minor thefts, of food items, are precisely the kind of foraging activity that Ed might have felt pressed to do, and become accustomed to doing, when the family was in desperate need during David's long absence in the Union Army.

Petty theft from neighbors also suggests the alienation of Ed Maxwell, who apparently never bonded very deeply with others and had no sense of belonging to a rural community, largely because of his parents' frequent moving from place to place. Such psychic separation commonly fosters insecurity and resentment—and often diminishes the influence of the moral order. Also, Ed's thefts must have put him increasingly at odds with his demanding father, whose values were being rejected and who was surely embarrassed by his wayward son.

It is probable that Ed drifted into trouble now and again without any assistance from Lon, who was much younger, but local memory of their pranks and petty thefts reveals that they did some things together, despite the age difference. Perhaps Ed needed an admiring, younger audience to whom he could display his manly assertiveness. In any case, he was clearly the instigator of their lawbreaking, whenever it began, and Lon was being coached to defy authority and to share his brother's sense of alienation.

Just as helpful to understanding Ed was his early failure as a rural schoolteacher. According to the *Macomb Journal* account, "he could make pretty good flourishes with a pen, and so, set himself up as a 'writing master,' opening a number of [writing] schools one winter. We believe, however, that no good came of them. . . . Evidently he was out of his element when attempting something useful. His bent was destruction."

The reporter clearly knew little about Ed's venture into teaching during his late teens, and was anxious to portray that as an obvious failure because of his criminal character. A more evenhanded account was provided by Quincy Hainline: "Ed was a fine penman and taught writing schools. He came to our school, but failed to get the required number of pupils, but he taught in some of the adjoining districts." That effort also shows Ed's interest in getting ahead by doing useful work in the wintertime, when farm labor was not in demand. And for a slim young man, not quite five feet, four inches tall, who was self-conscious about his smallness, teaching was a means of commanding the respect that he sought throughout his life.

But collecting pay from the parents of one's pupils, at the end of a term, for teaching a subscription class (probably on Saturdays or in the evening) was notoriously difficult, so that alone may have doomed whatever writing schools he may have launched. Perhaps that is what the *Journal* editor meant when he said that "no good came of them." The experience probably further damaged Ed's fragile self-esteem. And one wonders if his early failure to make a success of teaching prompted feelings of animosity toward the rural culture that had not responded to his initiative. Ed may have felt rejected. In any case, he would eventually raid the social order in that part of the county.

By 1871, when he was eighteen, Ed began to work as a hired hand on one or more farms located a few miles southwest of Sciota, a hamlet of 250 people, and three or four miles southeast of Blandinsville, a village of well over a thousand people. Both were in the northern part of McDonough County. Exactly who he worked for is unknown, but later records show that he became acquainted with farmers like John Isom and J. E. Carlisle, who lived in northern Hire Township, perhaps six or seven miles from David Maxwell's tenant farm. Of course, living apart from the family only increased Ed's sense of alienation.

By 1873 he was working on a sizable stock farm located a few miles northeast of Blandinsville. His employer was a middle-aged man named John Terrill, who apparently rented land and used several hired laborers to help him work it. The land rent, plus the labor cost, made it unlikely that Terrill would succeed, and in fact, his operation lasted only a few years.

Little is known about John Terrill, who may have been a very decent man, but the typical farmer who employed hired hands expected constant, often exhausting toil—plowing, planting, harvesting, cutting wood, feeding livestock, and the like—during fourteen-hour days, beginning at four o'clock in the morning, in exchange for just $15 per month, plus room and board. Such low pay had become a political issue, demonstrating to some activists that wealthy owners did not care "whether the farm laborer lives or starves," as the *Macomb Journal* editor put it. It was a bleak, unpromising life for the smallish teenager who had always been a good student and yearned to be highly regarded. But by herding cattle on a sizable stock farm—as a kind of Illinois cowboy—Ed became a very good horseman.

For the young hired hand, whose twentieth birthday came in that summer of 1873, the most interesting time of the week was surely Saturday night, when nearby farmers drove their wagons into Blandinsville to get supplies and socialize. (Sciota was a little closer, but it had only a few small shops.) A village with two dozen wooden business buildings and board sidewalks lining the dusty street, Blandinsville also had livestock pens near the railroad depot, just like a Kansas cattle town. After the Toledo, Peoria, and Warsaw Railroad had come through in 1867, the population had almost tripled, so by the early 1870s the town had about 1,600 people. On Saturday nights, it had at least a few hundred more. For Ed, it was a chance to see other people—at the barbershop, the pool hall, the livery stable, and the clothing and grocery stores—and perhaps hang out with other young men.

Blandinsville also had several saloons, but Ed did not drink. His religious parents had seen to that. However, in that town where so many young people caroused, his temperance may even have furthered his alienation.

Blandinsville also had some association with a gang of horse thieves and robbers. During the Civil War, the sleepy village of several hundred people had been frequented by horse thief Harrison ("Kansas Red") Johnson. His gang had been located twenty-five miles north, near the Mississippi River town of Oquawka, but Johnson knew people in Blandinsville, and during the war he bought a farm for his family (his widowed mother and sisters) a few miles outside of town—where he apparently kept stolen horses from time to time. In the spring of 1866 he was captured while plying his trade back in Kansas and was lynched, along with two members of his gang. Several weeks later, another of his comrades, a man named Blaker, was murdered by two unknown men at the Johnson farm.

Blandinsville had, in fact, developed a reputation for violence during the 1860s and early 1870s. In November 1864, McDonough County Provost Marshal William Randolph—a former county sheriff and a "radical Republican"—was killed in a gunfight there while trying to arrest draft resister John Bond. A kind of local hero in that strongly anti-war village, Bond fled from Illinois with his brothers, Miles and James, who were also involved in the gunfight. Outraged pro-war citizens of the county offered a big reward for their capture. Finally arrested in Kentucky during 1868, Miles Bond—who had apparently fired the fatal shots—was tried in nearby Schuyler County on a change of venue, and was eventually acquitted by a jury sympathetic to the anti-war cause, in a case that revived Civil War animosities. Two years later, his brothers were captured in Missouri and were also tried and acquitted. For McDonough County residents, that was the most disturbing murder case of the century. As with the war itself, some people never got over it.

Several other murders took place in Blandinsville during the late 1860s and 1870, prompting the *Macomb Journal* editor to assert, in January 1871, "There are bold, bad men there, and the very atmosphere seems impregnated with awful murder and death." After a near-fatal, crowd-witnessed knife fight a few months later, he commented on the causes of that town's violence in a piece called "MORE LAWLESSNESS IN BLANDINSVILLE":

> Blandinsville needs a lesson in law and order. More cases of bloodshed occur in the six miles square comprising that township than in the rest of the county. This is said by some to be unfortunate—that there are as good citizens there as elsewhere—and in being thus visited by these unforeseen murders and bloody affrays, [Blandinsville] is *unlucky.*
>
> While we cheerfully submit that there are a class of men there who will compare favorably with any other community, we further say that . . . it is overruled by those who, fearing neither God nor the law, find their keenest enjoyment in crime. Hence, they [the violent men] make the public opinion in that place, and that opinion is in favor of the murderer and against the victim. As examples, when the Bonds murdered Randolph, every aid was extended to them to escape, and not a single effort to arrest them was put forth. When the Huston boys killed [John] Fitzgerald, if they were not lauded they were generally excused, while not a word was said in favor of the dead man. . . .
>
> Whenever Blandinsville ceases to do these things, when the murderer is execrated instead of praised, when the arm of justice

is raised to preserve law and order, when the law-abiding instead
of the law-breaking men rule the place, then, and not till then, will
that cease to be an *unlucky* community.

The editor's commentary sheds light on the relationship between violence and the public mind. In an era that praised self-assertion, resistance
to authority was often admired. That was the essence of the Bond brothers' defense in the Randolph murder trials that resulted in their acquittal.
Also, the unpopularity of the victim often legitimated the killer's act. As
a draft enforcer—and a wealthy, powerful, outspoken pillar of the estab-
lishment at the county seat—Randolph was hated in Blandinsville. Many
poor, struggling local people also disliked the wealthy, domineering farmer
John Fitzgerald. And then there was the complex matter of manhood, of
maintaining respect and avoiding shame in a culture that celebrated toughness—which obviously contributed to the bloody and public knife fight.

The periodic eruption of violence and disorder was characteristic of
Blandinsville, as it was to a greater extent in towns like Dodge City and
Deadwood farther west. It is impossible to know how much that rampant
lawlessness, and the values that made it possible, influenced young Ed
Maxwell, but those values, evident in Lewistown as well as Blandinsville,
later contributed to his outlaw career.

Ed's outlook was also decisively shaped by the poverty, insecurity, and
disrespect of tenant farming—and, worse yet, of working as a hired hand.
Like his father, who had pursued the American Dream without success, Ed
had a deep longing to be more than he was, and by the time his teenage
years were coming to an end, he was frustrated, if not humiliated, by his
position at the bottom of the social scale. As he rose before dawn on John
Terrill's farm to work long days for little money, with no hope of buying his
own land, he surely knew the cruelty of a culture that promised success
to the sharp, the bold, the diligent, but failed to give people like himself,
and his father, a decent chance to make it. The same American belief that
asserted, "those with merit will rise," also implied that those who failed to
rise had no merit. Apparently pointless toil was surely eroding his sense
of self-worth. As twentieth-century author Harry Crews once said about
his similar childhood circumstance, he was ashamed, humiliated, that
he was a tenant farmer's son—and "had fear and loathing for what I was
and who I was." For Ed, too, the underlying issue was always the struggle
to maintain a positive identity in a culture that felt the perennial poor
deserved their place at the bottom.

Then came the Panic of 1873, which brought a fearful, lingering depression—"a vale of tears that grew wider and deeper, until by 1876 it seemed like the valley of death itself," as one historian later described the economic downturn. Although it was worse in the cities, where joblessness, hunger, and lawbreaking reached unprecedented proportions, rural life became a grim struggle too. Agricultural prices dropped by two-thirds; wages and property values also declined. As men lost their land, the number of tenant farmers increased, and thousands of others gave up and headed for the western frontier. Despite what the Gospel of Success asserted, the harsh fortunes of many people seemed to bear little relationship to their merits and efforts, calling into question the ordinary virtues of diligence, patience, honesty, and unselfishness.

Small wonder that petty theft was soon on the rise, as the *Macomb Eagle* reported early in 1874: "Macomb has more than her full quota of thieves. Every day or two we hear of petty thieving in various parts of the city."

Distress and dislocation caused by the depression soon compounded the problem. In Illinois and other states, jobless men from the cities swarmed into the countryside and its villages, looking for work, and they sometimes resorted to petty theft as a means of survival. The usually optimistic *Macomb Journal* editor was soon forced to report the pressing economic and social problem, but like so many nineteenth-century businessmen, he had little sympathy for the unemployed—viewing them as men who simply lacked personal responsibility. They were "Tramping Loafers," unattached outsiders, and in a society that celebrated landowners as the moral backbone of the nation, drifters were automatically suspect. Like Indians on the frontier, they were useful scapegoats who could be accused of any crimes that local people needed to blame others for. And they were also denigrated as the source of socioeconomic conflict.

In contrast, among those poor workers the depression brought widespread resentment—against owners, railroads, banks, and politicians—which surged over the country like an epidemic. Poverty and hardship, bravely endured by those on the bottom when there was hope for the future, now seemed intolerable to many distressed Americans.

A new organization of farmers, the Patrons of Husbandry—always called the Grange—encouraged the farmer to see himself as a victim of ruthless forces. By 1875 there were more than two dozen chapters in McDonough County—some with names like "Liberty" and "Equality," showing that rural activism was infused with deeply held American beliefs. The Blandinsville area had no less than five chapters of the Grange, including those two. And in Macomb, agricultural supporters launched a new weekly newspaper, *The Illinois Granger,* which carried increasingly strident editorials.

Looking back over the years of depression at the end of the decade, the angry editor of the *Macomb Independent* (which was also outspokenly supportive of farmers and laboring men) pointed out that since 1873, the value of real estate and personal property in the county had declined by 50 percent, and he blamed "the money mongers" who had victimized their fellow citizens.

Like many who were on the bottom in the mid-1870s, Ed surely saw himself as the victim of uncaring social forces. Farm owners and town leaders—people he envied and resented—had the power to affect his life, but he had little control over his own circumstances. Men in authority, those who controlled the world he struggled in, were not on his side and could not be trusted. Especially to a young man who had moved so many times, they were always strangers who didn't really know him or appreciate him, and he realized that they could damage his life, so they had to be defended against. As events soon demonstrated, Ed must have felt that he had to be wary, assertive, and ready to stand his ground against those who continually undervalued and disregarded him. Harsh circumstances, as inescapable as prison walls, were shaping the experience of an already troubled young man whose dream of respectability and freedom would soon become a nightmare of disrespect and confinement.

Ed's first serious crime, beyond petty theft in the countryside, was the exploit in February 1874 that resulted in his being labeled "a desperado" by the editor of the *Macomb Eagle.* That hyperbolic article also gave the particulars of the crime and the story of Ed's escape:

> On the night of the 10th inst., the store of Charley Dines, at Blandinsville, was broken into and two full suits of clothing abstracted. It was known that Ed Maxwell had been in the neighborhood—working on the farm of John Terrill, four miles northwest of Sciota, and as he was known to be capable of that kind of business, suspicion naturally pointed to him. . . .
>
> On Thursday, the 12th inst., Charley and Lorenzo Dines got on their horses and rode over to Terrill's, to see if Maxwell was there. They found several hired men on the farm, and among the number was the aforesaid Maxwell. . . . Lorenzo then mounted his horse and rode off to the nearest justice, to obtain a [search]

warrant. [James Andrews, another hired hand, was asked to watch Maxwell.]

Charley Dines' horse was in the stable feeding, and Charley was in the house . . . [while] Maxwell was out in the yard prancing about like a caged bear, and Andrews, unarmed, was keeping him company, to prevent his escape. . . . Maxwell asked Andrews, "What's those Blandinsville fellows doing out here today?" Andrews finally replied that he understood "they come out to levy on the old man's corn"—meaning Mr. Terrill's. Maxwell replied, "I know a d—d sight better. They're after me, and I'm going to light out of this d—d quick."

With that, Maxwell bolted into the stable, and seeing a saddle on Dines' horse, proceeded very coolly to put on the bridle, Andrews all the time urging him not to go. Maxwell led the horse out of the stable, got on, and then ordered Andrews to let the bars down [on the corral], so he could get out. Andrews refused to do it, but Maxwell presented a revolver and said he would "blow him through if he wasn't damned quick about it!" The bars went down on the double-quick, and Maxwell disappeared, on the wings of the wind—and Charley's horse.

In his hasty flight, Maxwell left his carpet sack, which, on examination, was found to contain the two suits of clothing stolen from Dines' store in Blandinsville. . . .

While the article claims that Ed had a reputation for theft, which immediately caused suspicion to fall on him, that seems unlikely. A hired hand with such a reputation would probably not have a job on John Terrill's farm—or any farm. A 1917 *Macomb Journal* article, "Reminiscences of the Maxwell Boys," provides a better explanation, "Ed, the day before the robbery, had gone into the store and tried on a suit and other clothing, selecting an outfit that fitted him, and had it laid away for him, saying that he would call for it and get it. That night the store was robbed, and that outfit was taken. Suspicion at once fell on Maxwell. He was not well known, and it was some time before he could be identified by name, as the clerk in the store did not know him." This also explains how a burglar, working in the dark, would be able to locate clothes that he wanted, which fit him. He knew where they would be. If Ed did not give the clerk his name, or his right name, he might have expected to get away with it.

Perhaps more important for understanding Ed Maxwell is the very fact that he did steal new clothes—whether two suits or just one—which clearly symbolized his desire to transcend his status, to be regarded as a man of some quality, rather than a destitute, insignificant hired hand. And as a man who resented others with money and power, Ed could not have picked a better victim: Charles Dines was the leading businessman in Blandinsville, owner of the largest store in town and also a livestock and grain dealer. He was also the former mayor and would soon be elected county clerk. He belonged to all the fraternal lodges in town. Successful, admired, popular—and part of the power structure in McDonough County—Dines was the polar opposite of Ed Maxwell.

It was not the theft itself, however, but Ed's dramatic escape on horseback that fascinated the public in McDonough County. Stealing the horse of the very man he had already robbed—an incidental crime, done on the spur of the moment, to avoid arrest—suddenly elevated Ed to the stature of a bold outlaw. An 1881 *Macomb Journal* article gives a more complete account:

> The wily thief mounted Dines' horse and fled. The officers pursued, and word getting out of the double theft [the clothing and the horse], neighbors joined, and in an hour a score of horsemen were galloping after the fugitive, who made for the timber on Crooked Creek, at breakneck speed. The stream at that time was high and filled with ice. The pursuers gained the bridges on either side of the thief and expected to catch Maxwell in "a pocket," feeling confident that he would not dare attempt to cross the swollen stream, but they could not find him. . . . It then transpired that the reckless fellow *did* ford the icy creek, and while the officers and citizens were scouring the woods, he was resting and lunching quietly in Macomb, gathering strength for his night ride. . . .

For Ed, the satisfaction of outwitting his pursuers must have been immense—a validation of his inner conviction that, despite his small physical stature and current poverty, he was a man to be reckoned with. Like a dime novel hero, he could outwit and outride the forces arrayed against him. For the unhappy twenty-year-old farmhand who had known only deprivation and disrespect, it was a thrilling escape—into another identity.

Ed soon abandoned the stolen horse and took a train to the next county, where he was arrested. Brought before a justice of the peace in Blandinsville and then "bound over in the sum of $1,000," he was jailed in Macomb by Saturday, February 14.

The "desperado" article in the *Macomb Eagle* ends with a remarkable paragraph, based on a report of Ed's comments in the McDonough County

Jail, which clearly suggests that his recent experience, of daring and danger, had brought some of his deep, repressed feelings to the surface: "He is evidently a dangerous customer, as he makes his boast that he 'would rather be a first-class thief than a prince among men.' The penitentiary, he says, has no terrors for him, as he is 'up to snuff' anyhow."

The comment that he was "a dangerous customer," like the labeling of him as "a desperado" in the same article, shows the readiness of more well-established local citizens, like the newspaper editor, to identify and proclaim "who is in and who is out, who is deviant and who is mainstream," as one scholar has put it, so that the socially prominent can be protected from "the poor, the deviant, the unpopular."

And as his brief comments at the jail show, Ed was exhibiting, or trying on, his new identity as an outlaw, a desperado. Always equating manhood with self-assertion and toughness, he had worried that if he did not impress people in that way, he would be seen as a weakling, a loser, a candidate for further disparagement. That was surely why he carried, as one article said, "a large Bowie knife and a loaded revolver," intimidating weapons for a mere hired hand—weapons that symbolized his almost pathetic desire to be regarded as tough. They were all-too-obvious signs of inferiority compensation, which was rooted in both Ed's psychological background (his smallness, his inability to replace David during the war, and his probable conflicts with him afterward) and his social circumstance (the impoverished son of a tenant farmer, the perennial outsider, the inconsequential hired hand). It was precisely his anxiety about being viewed as unmanly, as undeserving of respect, as not "up to snuff," that had prompted him, under stress, to steal a horse, ride like the devil, and elude his pursuers. Now they had given him a label that made his smoldering defiance seem real, his new self achievable: "desperado."

In later years Ed would be driven by the need to create other situations in which his manhood could be validated and the public would continue to realize that he was formidable and fearless, "a dangerous customer." In a sense, his entire outlaw career would be a desperate effort to compensate for his sense of unworthiness.

In the twentieth century, young men gripped by the same fear of not attaining their desired masculine identity would show up from time to time in western films. Among the more memorable examples of such anxiety-ridden figures hoping to prove themselves with a gun are Hunt Bromley (Skip Homeier) in *The Gunfighter,* Chico (Horst Buchholz) in *The Magnificent Seven,* and "The Schofield Kid" (Jaimz Woolvett) in *Unforgiven.* Like Ed, they admired and wanted to imitate assertive, violent men.

With his comment about preferring to be "a first-class thief" rather than "a prince among men," Ed was also asserting his spiritual and moral autonomy, as a desperado, and his rejection of the social system, which demanded conformity and public approval. Even a prince had obligations to the community—a position "among men"—but the young burglar and horse thief now saw himself as a permanent outsider. He was no longer struggling to rise.

And the notoriety he had suddenly achieved was itself a powerful psychological force, dispelling his awful sense of anonymity, as a man beneath the notice or concern of others. For Ed, social impact as a budding desperado was an acceptable substitute for more positive kinds of regard. After all, he now commanded respect for his manly daring, as the heroic comparisons to "Jack the Giant Killer" and "Gil Blas," which opened the *Eagle* article, revealed, and there was also a certain fascination with what he might do as his outlaw career unfolded, for "he had shown a disposition to be dangerous."

With the 1874 robbery and escape, Ed Maxwell had left the hired hand's realm of toil, monotony, shame, and restriction for a new world of defiant self-assertion, thrilling excitement, and public recognition. But his bold run from the authorities—a lone horseman on a desperate ride, a train passenger heading nowhere—also dramatized his alienation, which would increase with every phase of his outlaw career and would ultimately reach a sensational climax in the state of Wisconsin.

4

≈⟩✦⟨≈

Law and Order, and Prison Life

Ed Maxwell spent a few weeks in the McDonough County Jail, waiting for the circuit court to convene. One can only imagine his father's response to seeing his wayward son behind bars—and labeled as a dangerous "desperado."

In late March 1874, Ed pled guilty to burglary, but his sentencing was delayed, pending court action on the charge of larceny (horse stealing). Apparently, there was considerable discussion of that act. After all, Ed did not keep or sell the horse; he just used it to escape. Fortunately, he had the finest lawyer in the county, Damon G. Tunnicliff, a distinguished-looking man with a close-cropped gray beard who would later serve on the Illinois Supreme Court. And Tunnicliff must have been effective: When it was all over, Ed was sentenced to just "one year in the penitentiary"—for the burglary.

Not everyone liked that decision. A week later, the Blandinsville correspondent for the *Macomb Eagle* reported the response there: "Charley Dines and a host of others have made up their minds not to hunt up and catch any more burglars. One year in the penitentiary don't pay for the wear and tear of conscience in catching such fellows as Ed Maxwell." Instead of "wear and tear of conscience," a modern commentator would have said "stress," but the point is clear: Dines and others in that trouble-prone town felt the sentence was too lenient. Most people of that era wanted severe punishment for theft crimes, to instill fear in those socially marginal men, like Ed Maxwell, that the law was designed to control.

When he left town in handcuffs on the morning train with Sheriff Samuel Frost, bound for Joliet, Ed was surely apprehensive about what lay ahead. The penitentiary was a place of legendary toughness. But he was determined to show them all—any people who might view him with disrespect— that he was "up to snuff."

Undoubtedly, McDonough County residents were glad to be rid of him— and hoped that he would stay gone. But the Blandinsville robbery was just the beginning. He would come back, to create an unforgettable episode of lawbreaking and public alarm in a county that was struggling to control crime.

At the time Ed Maxwell was sent to prison, Macomb looked like a thriving prairie town, despite the recent Panic of 1873 and the encroaching depression. The courthouse square was lined with stores, most of them in two-story, red-brick buildings, although the east side still had some small, wooden, false-front shops that dated from the pioneer decades, the 1830s and 1840s. There were no less than a dozen grocery stores and ten dry goods stores on or near the square, not to mention other clothing stores, shoe stores, millinery shops, hardware stores, drug stores, dressmaking and tailor shops, bookstores, harness shops, hotels, banks, bakeries, and barbershops. Upstairs rooms were occupied by doctors, dentists, photographers, and lawyers—and a few were devoted to newspaper offices and meeting halls. Just off the square were six blacksmiths, four wagon makers, four implement dealers, three livery stables, three furniture stores, two lumberyards, and two machine shops. Grain elevators and livestock pens near the depot, just north of the square, attested to the town's importance as an agricultural shipping point.

The editor of the *Macomb Eagle* had recently bragged that "Macomb is outstripping in progress and prosperity all the towns between Chicago and Quincy." Some other communities, such as Ottawa and Galesburg, might have challenged that assertion, but the town was doing very well. By 1875 Macomb had 3,368 people, representing a population jump of more than 20 percent in five years.

The more well-established McDonough County residents had a profound sense of participation in a great struggle and achievement, creating a local version of the American good society in what had been, less than a half century before, a wilderness, inhabited by those two frightening symbols of disorder and hostility, Indians and wolves. While Macomb was being established as the seat of government, local pioneers brutalized, threatened, and displaced a dozen Indians who were staying at a seasonal hunting camp that the whites called Wigwam Hollow, northwest of the village. The whites were never endangered; they just had anxiety. They soon eradicated the wolves too—with countywide hunts that involved hundreds of men—during the 1840s.

But strangely enough, in the winter of 1874, the very season when the Maxwell saga began, wolves were again seen in the county, alarming some of the farmers and reminding folks that the uncivilized frontier was not so thoroughly vanquished after all. When a band of local men pursued "a large gray timber wolf" northeast of Macomb, they wounded it with a gunshot, chased it for miles, and then allowed their dogs to attack it for a solid hour, as a kind of grim amusement, until it was finally killed. No one pondered the pent-up cultural anxieties reflected in that brutality. The hunters were celebrated, and two days later the wolf's pelt was displayed for all to see at the new courthouse—the very building that symbolized the moral order that local folks felt they had established.

That was McDonough County's third courthouse. The first was a mere log building, used for only a few years. Then a permanent one was erected, in the center of the square—in the exact center of the county—in 1834. A two-story brick building set among the log cabins and small frame shops, it was an imposing icon of democracy and justice in pioneer days, when county officials came there to plan roads and bridges, license mills and saloons, record town plats and land sales, and prosecute lawbreakers— mostly thieves, rustlers, and brawlers. Lincoln spoke there, by the west entrance, in 1858, urging his listeners to look more deeply at the issue of slavery.

It is not surprising that the most significant structure of the entire century, the third McDonough County courthouse, was built on precisely the same spot during the postwar period of growth and optimism. Contracts were let in 1868, and the elaborate cornerstone ceremony was held on August 14, 1869. It began with a procession around the square, continued with speeches, and concluded with the placing of time capsule items in a cornerstone and the raising of an American flag. On that day, local residents—at least, those with a firm sense of belonging—reflected on the progress their county had made in just four decades, recognized the old settlers as cultural heroes, and celebrated their own participation in a common story. They felt focused, included, and significant.

When it was finally completed in 1872, the magnificent red-brick court-house—trimmed with gray stone, lighted by a hundred windows, adorned by columned porticos on all sides, and crowned by a stately clock tower on the western façade—was not only a sacred center where the work of a supposedly just society went on; it was also a symbol of the county's struggle for civilization and an expression of communal confidence in the unfolding future. It stood for what local folks believed in and felt they belonged to—a meaningful, encompassing moral order in which their lives were securely grounded.

But in the minds of most people, there was a lingering threat to local culture in McDonough County, and it wasn't the returning wolves. It was lawlessness. As the many recent murders in Blandinsville suggested, everything was not as stable and civilized as the presence of the imposing courthouse seemed to imply.

Moreover, theft was widespread. As the *Macomb Eagle* reported in the summer of 1868, "The county seems to be infested with thieves, and it behooves our citizens, both in town and country, to guard against their depredations." The assumption was that itinerant thieves were raiding in the countryside, but by 1872, it was clear that McDonough County had a gang of "Resident Thieves," as the *Macomb Journal* put it, and several were arrested by the end of that year.

In that same era saloons were licensed, and Macomb had no less than eight of them, on and near the square. Especially on Saturdays, they drew self-assertive, often frustrated men from throughout the county into the center of things, the town that maintained the social order, where some got drunk, fought in the streets, and resisted local authorities. In 1869 the *Macomb Journal* editor lamented that "during the past week, our city has been overrun with rowdyism, drunkenness, and brawls. . . ." Not only Blandinsville, but other outlying villages, such as Bushnell and Colchester, had similar problems.

Poverty and low social status were the preconditions for drunken belligerence, which was often a kind of self-assertion by men who felt disrespected. Because the local marshal in any community symbolized the social system that seemed to marginalize, or oppress, those at the bottom, the anger that was aroused during bouts of drinking, as repressed feelings surged to the surface, was often turned on him.

Karr McClintock, a former wagon maker, was the longest-serving Macomb marshal (1874–78; 1880–82) and was probably the most effective city law officer of the century. During his first year in office, the year of

Ed Maxwell's robbery in nearby Blandinsville, the Macomb Police Department was organized under his supervision. In the summer of 1875 he was severely beaten when four men assaulted him, one using brass knuckles, and that was not his only fight with lawbreakers. In April 1876, for example, he won a long and bloody fight with a man named Charles Bonham, who had pulled a gun and tried to kill him. After that, he was a hero in the community—although Bonham promised to kill him when he got out of the penitentiary, and apparently tried.

Posse members were always endangered too. In 1870 a young farmer named Joseph Johnson, living in nearby Henderson County, just north of Blandinsville, shot and killed a tenant who lived on his father's land—another case where the low social class of the victim may have emboldened his assailant—and when a posse came to make the arrest, other family members killed one of those volunteer officials and wounded another. Five members of that violent family were eventually arrested, but no one was ever convicted of anything. Johnson asserted that he had been threatened when he killed the tenant, and the other family members claimed that they had been afraid of mob violence when the posse arrived and were just trying to protect themselves. So, everything came down to a claim of self-defense.

Disgusted with the result of that case, which had been tried in McDonough County on a change of venue, the *Macomb Journal* editor remarked that "juries are not always made up of sensible, honest men," and commented on the difficulty of achieving murder convictions: "If a man steals a horse, a pocket-book, or any other article of value, justice—swift, winged justice—is sure to overtake him; but if he *only kills a man,* there are thousands who are ready to sympathize with him, and it is no trouble to find a jury which will set him at liberty—and bid him go kill another man."

As the population of Illinois steadily increased and the depression of the 1870s deepened, a record number of lawbreakers were being sent to the penitentiary at Joliet, most of them for theft-type crimes. By 1874 it had almost 1,400 inmates and was the biggest prison operation in the United States. It would soon grow even larger. Ed Maxwell was sentenced to serve time in a nationally prominent penal institution.

Constructed in the late 1850s and opened in 1860, the prison was located on a vast plain just north of Joliet and a few hundred yards east of the Des Plaines River. Running near the huge complex on the river side were the tracks of the Chicago, Alton, and St. Louis Railroad, which brought in criminals from throughout the state. Sheriffs and deputies from 102 counties made regular trips to the huge facility.

The state penitentiary was, in a sense, the dark side of the justice system in Illinois—the grim shadow of the shining courthouse in every county. One article in *The Illinois Granger,* titled "Hell and Joliet," reported that it was a harsh institution, but generally, few people cared about how it operated or what happened to the hundreds of men—and the few dozen women—who were sent there.

The penitentiary had dark gray limestone walls, twenty to forty feet high and five feet thick at the base, enclosing a fifteen-acre compound filled mostly with drab stone factory buildings. Prior to 1886, Illinois prison authorities sold convict labor to companies who bid for the privilege of manufacturing products with a kind of legalized slavery. Some of the early wardens were, in fact, simply contractors. In the 1870s, convicts at Joliet worked mostly as stonecutters, cigar makers, barrel and chair makers, machinists, wagon and implement makers, harness makers, and shoe makers. The inmates thereby learned a trade, and the income from the sale of their labor supported the penitentiary, which was intended to be a self-sustaining institution.

It was a cold, winter-like April day—part of "a backward spring" that kept everything brown and barren-looking—when Ed Maxwell stepped off the train just north of Joliet with handcuffs on his wrists and chains on his legs. Sheriff Samuel Frost walked him over to the south side of the prison, which housed the entrance. From that view, it looked like a grim, forbidding castle built of rock-faced stone blocks that had stood for centuries. Eight hundred feet wide, it was by far the largest structure Ed had ever seen—or would ever see. At the corners were sixty-foot towers manned by blue-coated guards with Winchester rifles. In the middle of the massive, castellated gothic façade was the four-story, turreted administration and inmate-processing building, which was flanked on either side by high walls with tall, narrow, barred windows that stretched away toward the guard towers. Architecturally, it was an image of impersonal authority and collective hostility, meant to inspire fear and submission.

In the center of that dark, threatening south wall were huge iron double doors that swung open to engulf the shackled prisoners. About one-third of them came from nearby Chicago, which was experiencing fabulous growth, and increasing crime, as it recovered from the great fire of 1871.

Ed left no record of his coming to the famous penal institution, but another prisoner of his era did. In an anonymous book called *An Ex-Convict's Story: Life in Joliet Penitentiary,* the author depicts in some detail the booking ritual that transformed convicted criminals into prison inmates, and in the process he evokes the common emotional response:

> The creaking of the big iron doors as they swung open . . . sent a cold shudder throughout my frame. . . . It meant ostracism from home, family and friends. It meant confinement within circumscribed quarters, prison food, hard beds, hard work, and loss of society. It meant that we were to become merely a piece of human mechanism, simply to do as we were bidden. . . . Our life was to be one routine. Our individuality was to be lost. While we remained within these four walls, we were simply to be chattels.
>
> The door closed with a clang, and we stood in the office of the prison. We were at once turned over to the receiving officer, who forthwith took off our irons. Our commitment papers were handed to him. We were then registered and given a number, by which we were to be known so long as we were confined within those walls. We were then turned over to another officer, who ordered us to fall into line, and marched us to the bath-room, where we were made to strip and bathe. The bath-room contains 60 large iron tubs. There was plenty of water, soap, and towels. After bathing, we were taken to the barber-shop, shaved, and our hair cut short. Then we were critically examined for any marks, scars, or deformities, all of which were noted down opposite our names and numbers in a book kept for that purpose. We were then dressed in an old suit of prison clothes, taken to the office, and questioned as to age, religion, education, whether married or single, family, business, habits, whether temperate or intemperate, whether ever arrested before, &c. . . .
>
> From the examination and measurement room we were taken to the clothing department, and there fitted out with our full prison outfit. This consisted of two pairs of socks, one pair of drawers, one shirt, one pair of shoes, a pair of pants, a jacket, cap, and handkerchief. . . .
>
> We were a peculiar looking lot—all smooth-shaven, all with short hair, and dressed exactly alike, in stripes. We hardly recognized ourselves, let alone one another, so great was the transformation.

However necessary, the booking process was a rite of shame and humiliation, forced submission to authority, and devaluation of the self—which could only foster resentment.

Prison records show that Ed was processed on April 2, 1874. His height was five feet, three and a half inches; his hair was brown and his eyes were dark brown. He was twenty years old and, like most of the convicts, he could read and write. He professed no religion—and so, had apparently rebelled against the strict Christian faith of his parents. To put it another way, Ed's defiance of authority, in order to carve out a meaningful destiny, had metaphysical implications. He also listed his occupation as "farmer" and asserted that he was "temperate" (a nondrinker). He became prisoner number 8126.

After being processed, Ed spent one night in "solitary"—the final phase of the prison's acculturation ritual. Another inmate of his era recalled the emotional impact of that first-night experience, which must have been typical: "In the stillness of the night, when nothing could be heard but the solemn tramping of the guards, then I felt my utter loneliness and desolation. Visions of days gone by came and went with wonderful rapidity—so fast, in fact, that my brain began to whirl and I feared I would go mad. . . . I had forfeited everything dear to man on earth, the love of family, the respect of friends; I was an outcast from society. . . ."

After a similar nightmarish realization of his profound alienation, Ed was taken to his cell on the following morning. In each cell block there were four or five tiers of cells, stacked atop each other in long rows, and they were fourteen feet back from the stone walls with their barred windows.

Although Joliet was a modern penitentiary for its time, conditions were spartan. Each cell was a tiny, tomblike, stone enclosure, only four feet wide, seven feet long, and seven feet high, with a door of heavy iron bars that was double-locked when the inmate was supposed to be there. Isolation was then total and movement was very limited. As every convict soon realized, occupying a cell was a dreary, mind-numbing ordeal. A three-legged stool and an iron bedstead—with a husk mattress, a straw-filled pillow, and two woolen blankets—were the only furniture. Each cell also had a water crock with a tin cup, a wash basin, and in one of the corners, a "slop bucket" that had to be emptied into the prison sewer every morning.

By 1900 even prison officials were protesting that the cells at Joliet were "so contracted, so repellant, and so utterly unfit for [habitation] that their very existence is a disgrace to the state." But Ed Maxwell arrived in 1874.

After breakfast the inmates assembled in long, silent lines and marched, in lockstep—with one hand on the shoulder of the convict in front—to their shops. In their black and gray striped uniforms, moving their legs in unison, they looked like gigantic caterpillars crawling among the rows of blank, grayish buildings—an appropriate image, perhaps, of their awful dehumanization. Once in the shops, they huddled over rough wooden benches, with eyes directed steadily at their work, from 7:00 A.M. until 6:00 P.M., with only a short lunch period. And when the shop day ended, they walked silently out, and marched in lockstep to get their supper and return to their cells. The routine did not vary except on Sundays, when the shops did not operate and the convicts were required to attend chapel services.

That strictly regimented, semi-isolated, industrial-work-oriented approach to incarceration was the "Auburn System," modeled on a noted prison in New York.

No one was excused from work on account of age or illness if he could stand up. In the very month when Ed Maxwell was arrested, an inmate named William Greenup, who had been sent up from Macomb for horse stealing, "dropped dead [at the prison] . . . while marching in line to commence the day's work." He was seventy-five years old.

The deprivation, hard work, strict rules, and monotonous routine were designed to effect the moral reclamation of the inmates through daily suffering that would prompt repentance—but the impact of it all was often quite the opposite. As one astute Joliet newspaper editor remarked, the rigid, dehumanizing routine "engenders a secret hostility on the part of the convicts . . . [only] held in check by fear of punishment or loss of 'good time,' [so] they nurse their wrath"—which of course boils over now and again, as "a convict loses control of his passion and . . . violently assaults his keeper."

A "keeper" was a guard charged with the daily moving, watching, and controlling of an assigned portion of the inmates—a man deeply and inexorably affected by their suppressed hostility to him, and who typically became, as one commentator said, "silent, crabbed, and unapproachable," an increasingly rigid and threatening figure himself. So, the keepers and the convicts were locked in a constantly degenerating cycle of distrust, anger, and emotional violence that could, and did, from time to time become physical.

Ed was assigned to the boot and shoe factory, which occupied two stone buildings located in the northwest corner of the prison compound. Because Joliet was a noted prison, visitors were regularly shown around, on tours, and one 1876 visitor described the shop where Ed had worked only a year earlier:

> M. Soley and Co. are working 470 of the convicts in the boot and shoe business. . . . It is a great curiosity to go through this shop and

observe all the workings of a boot or shoe, from the first cutting until the final finish. Everything goes on like clockwork—and not a slow time-keeper either. . . . Everything was business, energy, and order. . . . On some [convicts] we thought we could detect mental suffering, and some worked with a desperate energy, as if to drown thought.

It was work without the slightest social interaction or emotional respite. The inmates strove to perform their assigned tasks perfunctorily, like components of a vast machine, and the psychological impact of that was what this visitor observed. One convict who suffered through that arduous, repressive work routine, at the time Ed was there, later commented that he could only cope with "such revolting, degrading self-effacement" by assuming "the semblance of stupidity."

Every man who worked those long, pointless days in the shops and quarries knew that he had simply become a thing, enslaved to a brutal, authoritarian system—a system that was, in his mind, a harsh reflection of the impersonal, uncaring, control-oriented culture that he had encountered on the outside, and had rebelled against. The penitentiary seldom changed a convict's mind about the world that he had known, while it fostered anger, self-absorption, and despair.

After work, in the evenings, the stench in the poorly ventilated cellblocks was appalling. The convicts were required to bathe once a week, in the "bath-room" lined with tubs, but still, they seldom changed their black and gray zebra-suits, or underwear, and by late in the evening, the slop-buckets also stunk, in every part of the cellblock. Worse, the dozens of gaslights that burned until 9:00 P.M. gave off an acrid odor, and convicts also lit candles in their cells, which compounded the problem. As an 1876 prison report mentions, "the air in the cell houses towards the latter part of the night . . . becomes foul to a degree scarcely endurable." Many inmates died of respiratory disease.

The crowded confinement and stultifying labor were bad enough, but the prison regulations were also spiritually deadening. The hardest to endure was the rule of silence: "All conversation between convicts, and familiarity between convicts and guards, is strictly prohibited. . . ." By the time Ed arrived, the prison was overcrowded, so some metal bunk beds had been installed, and half of the convicts had a cell mate—in a space designed for just one man. In such cases, conversation between cell mates, in an undertone, was permitted in the evenings. Otherwise, the sheer lack of talk—at meals, at work, in lines, in the "bath-room," at Sunday services—was a torment to the men, and was violated whenever they could get away with it. Other interaction was also forbidden: "The convict must always approach an officer in a respectful manner, always touching his cap or forehead, and must not gaze, motion, or laugh at any person whatever." While in their shops, the convicts were not even permitted to look up momentarily from their work, no matter what else was going on around them.

As this suggests, the prison enforced spiritual isolation, and inmates learned to function without a normal emotional life—without being cordial to people, without showing an interest in what happened to others, and without expressing their feelings. As one ex-con from Joliet put it, "we had to annihilate the mind and the soul."

Most penologists thought that such dehumanizing regimentation and emotional restriction were just what convicts needed to discipline their weak wills and train them to control their passions, but novelist Charles Dickens knew better, and called that kind of punishment—which he had witnessed at a prison in Pennsylvania—what it was: "slow and daily tampering with the mysteries of the brain," brutality that "extorts few cries that human ears can hear" but eventually renders men "dead to everything but torturing anxieties and horrible despair."

It is not surprising that many inmates at Illinois State Penitentiary became more psychologically troubled—withdrawn and defensive, focused on survival, insensitive to others, resentful of authority, primed to be violent—while serving their time. Any lingering sense of connection with the social order was stamped out—and replaced by a fierce autonomy.

The penitentiary was, in fact, a finishing school for criminals, devoted to producing men who were thoroughly alienated and completely self-absorbed—if not overtly hostile. Each tormented inmate became the hero of his own psychic drama, battling against dehumanizing forces to avoid complete destruction. Most of them incurred psychological damage; some became emotionally dead.

Violation of the rules—most commonly, talking in the cell block or the shop—resulted in the suspension of the only privileges: receiving a weekly ration of chewing tobacco, writing a monthly letter, getting books (primarily religious and historical titles) from the small prison library, and seeing a visitor every eight weeks.

Violators were also often punished by solitary confinement in a windowless dark cell with a stone floor and walls, and no bed or other furniture. It was like being trapped in a tomb. Located in a separate building, "solitary" was also a poorly heated facility where the temperature in the winter often dropped below freezing. And the isolated inmates were restricted to a meager diet—only two ounces of bread and a cup of water each day. Most who went there were starved into submission, but stories also circulated about convicts in "solitary" being beaten, or manacled for days at a time to a "bull ring" (ring bolt) on the wall, forcing them to stand up with raised arms. In fact, during 1874, a disgruntled penitentiary commissioner exposed the brutality of Warden J. W. Wham, who had been fired, by mentioning that in one month "he had chained to the ring-bolt thirty-two men; and some stood there night and day, answering the calls of nature without being let down. . . ." Punishment became a kind of legitimized torture.

There were also random beatings, as untrained, anxiety-ridden keepers struggled to maintain discipline. Of course, most of the brutality never came to public attention, and officials said very little to the press, but an 1874 report mentioned that "charges of inhumanity towards prisoners [had been] preferred against some of the officers. . . ." Those failed to bring any changes, however.

Every year a dozen or more prisoners went insane (although some entered the penitentiary with mental problems, which could only get worse), and for each of them, including Ed Maxwell, it was a place of intense spiritual struggle.

During the 1860s and early 1870s there had been administrative problems at the prison, which had thirteen different wardens in its first thirteen years. When physical punishments, like flogging a convict shackled to a whipping post and placing an inmate in the stocks for many hours day after day, were outlawed after the Civil War, discipline became a challenge, and a spirit of rebellion arose. Some convicts refused to work, violations of the silence rule were common, escape attempts increased (and were often successful), one inmate was stabbed to death in the dining hall, a guard was bludgeoned with a hammer, a deputy warden was killed, and several insurrections occurred.

In response to public concern, Warden Elmer Washburn clamped down on the convicts during his two-year term (1870–72), closing the dining halls and providing meals in the cells (to avoid gatherings), increasing the use of solitary confinement, and even building a "stockade" to separate more than 300 unruly prisoners—often long-term inmates and repeat offenders—from the others. Conditions gradually improved, in regard to safety and security anyway, but he was, in turn, followed by three ineffective wardens in two years—including the brutal J. W. Wham, who wanted to reinstate flogging.

That's when Ed arrived—at a penitentiary that was overcrowded, strictly regulated, and filled with tension. He heard stories about the punishments, the escape attempts, and the insurrections of recent years. One ex-con who had been incarcerated during that era recalled that "the escapes from Joliet Prison of Billy Forrester, Harry Travis, Joe Brown, Mike Kennedy, James Paddock, Josh Compton, Dan McAllister—alias 'Peoria Dan'—and many others, rival in interest the wildest fictions of the novelist." Such escapes were a test of manhood and toughness, and the inmates who succeeded were heroes to those left behind.

The most famous was burglar Billy Forrester, whose numerous tattoos made him one of the best-marked criminals in America. According to one prison official, he had "a Goddess of Liberty on his right arm; an eagle and the Stars and Stripes on the same arm; on his left hip an Indian Queen seated upon the back of a flying eagle; a full-rigged ship on the center of his breast; the coat of arms of the United States on his left arm, and bracelets of red, white, and blue on both wrists." Devoted to expressing his love for American freedom with body images, he also expressed it in another way, by escaping from Joliet three times—the prison record. In the 1870s, Forrester was a legendary figure.

Ed also learned about crime from more experienced convicts who broke the silence rule to talk about their exploits, especially "the art of thieving," as it was called. Most of the Joliet inmates were, in fact, serving time for burglary, robbery, larceny, and horse theft—men who were not sorry for their deeds but proud of them, and who regretted only that they had been caught.

First offenders, like Ed, were known as "fresh fish," and were usually impressed by those who were more experienced, both as criminals and as survivors of the prison struggle. As an 1872 report on the Joliet Penitentiary pointed out, "The young and inexperienced criminal, who is guilty of his first offense, comes in contact day after day with the old offender, who is always ready and anxious to educate him, as only he knows how; thus he becomes familiar with crime, and too often, after a short sentence, leaves the prison a worse and more dangerous man than when he entered the institution." A lawbreaker's violent crimes often came *after* he had served time in prison for a nonviolent offense.

Ed would also have learned some of the convict jargon—that he was serving a "stretch" (one-year sentence) in "stir" (the penitentiary), for committing a "graft" (burglary), and had to mind the "screws" (guards) until he got out. The prison was not a true community but a mere collection of disrespected men, who nevertheless shared common circumstances and attitudes and whose language was an expression of their profound alienation.

Horse stealing was a common, and rather colorful, criminal occupation of the post–Civil War period, and the more experienced practitioners at Joliet would have attracted Ed's interest. One of them, William Howard, from Peoria County, boasted to the other inmates "that he had stolen over 100 animals," according to a prison official. Another one, J. H. Higgins, who had several aliases, had operated "all over the West," and could no doubt tell fascinating stories about his exploits. Yet another inmate, a professional horse thief from southern Illinois, held a kind of unofficial state record for penitentiary terms—at Alton first, and then at Joliet. As one warden commented, without identifying him by name, "He was first sentenced to the state penitentiary in the 40s," and he is "now serving his seventh term for horse stealing, and accepts the vicissitudes of his vocation philosophically. . . ." Many other horse thieves were also serving their third or fourth term—which suggests that powerful psychological factors were driving them too. One must consider what stolen horses symbolized to downtrodden lawbreakers wanting to assert themselves, exhibit manly control, and flee from authority.

Among the inmates, such criminal and prison experience gave the convict who possessed it a certain stature. He was not more of a loser than others, but someone to be admired. He had met other challenges—had succeeded at his chosen profession whenever he could and had survived the rigors of prison when he failed to stay free.

The adoption of an alias was also a mark of criminal experience—and the vast majority of career criminals had one or more. Two of the most experienced horse thieves, "Old Jim" Jones and "Old Bill" Miller, used "Williams" (the second most common alias at Joliet), and Ed Maxwell would soon adopt it as well. The impressionable young inmate, who would later steal horses as Ed "Williams," may have been influenced by the mystique surrounding such older, highly respected figures.

Also, a young horse thief named Henry Williams, sent up from Madison County in November 1873, was killed a month later when he was forcibly immersed in an ice-cold bath as a punishment for not doing enough work. He had complained that his hands were sore and he couldn't move them any faster, but to no avail. An inquest later said that he had a weak heart, which simply gave out, either from "the violent physical struggle" or "the shock [of the] cold bath," but one Joliet newspaper said that he was "literally drowned," for they held his head under water. The Chicago newspapers called it murder, but as in most other cases of inmate abuse, no prison guards were punished.

When Ed arrived, the Williams case was being widely talked about within the prison, fueling the chronic anger of the inmates, who always felt victimized. They deeply identified with Williams, whose death crystallized the awful repression they experienced.

According to one Joliet prisoner of the 1870s, "There are but few [inmates] who will admit the justice of their punishment; the rest are unfortunate. . . ." That is, most of them saw no relationship between their actions and their fate. They were victims, reviled and oppressed by an unjust system. And that common view was surely reinforced by sharing the same daily regimentation, hardship, and psychological abuse, regardless of how more or less severe, or continual, or violent their criminal behavior had been. (Ed had stolen less than $20 worth of clothes.) Of course, that outlook fostered resentment of lawmen, the justice system, and society in general, among the "sad and dejected men" who comprised the bulk of the prison population. And if not viewing themselves as victims of society, they were, at least, regarding themselves as victims of misfortune—often thinking, "There's plenty on the outside worse than me that go free."

The inmates commonly adopted a fatalistic view of life, thus relieving themselves of any responsibility for their situation. As one Joliet "prison poet" of Ed Maxwell's era put it, "I'm jugged [in prison] this early morn/ 'Cause once I happened to be born." This is the polar opposite of the "simply shape your own character" outlook that underlaid the Gospel of Success. Both are extremes—inadequate, misleading views propounded for self-serving reasons.

The mind of an inmate was seldom focused on meaningful change. The issue for the vast majority at Joliet was not how to reform, but how to endure. As another nineteenth-century convict put it, in a couplet of poetic advice, "Brace up, and stand your punishment as gritty as you can,/ And always, try and take your medicine like a man." That was the essential penitentiary philosophy—and it was definitely shared by young Ed Maxwell, for whom masculine identity was an obsession.

During his prison ordeal, Ed probably did not maintain contact with his parents (we know that he did not in his later incarceration). And he had good reason not to: In the face of urgings from them to acknowledge his guilt, repent for his misdeeds, and seek the Lord, he could not maintain the defiant identity that he had started to construct—and the stoic manliness that prison survival demanded. Also, the respect and admiration that he so desperately wanted could not come, then, from David and Susan—to whom he was just an erring lad, lured by the devil to break one of the Ten Commandments and jailed before he was twenty-one.

Small wonder that Ed Maxwell was not reformed by serving time in Joliet Penitentiary. He did learn the shoemaking trade, however, and was an obedient inmate. In fact, he received a one-month reduction in his sentence for "good behavior."

On the morning of his much-longed-for day of release, he was notified that his time would be up at a certain hour and that he should be ready to leave. Later taken to the administrative quarters, he was given a new suit of clothes, his discharge papers, ten dollars in cash, and a railroad ticket to the place he had come from. The warden then bid him good luck and advised him to conduct his life so that he would never come back.

Then the great iron doors swung open and Ed Maxwell was again a free man. It was March 2, 1875, and as he walked to the depot and boarded the train for Macomb, he must have felt pleased that he had survived the rigors of prison life—had showed everyone that he was "up to snuff." But now the question was, how would a young, impoverished ex-con, who craved acceptance and respect but had been rejected and dehumanized, create a satisfying identity in a world that was more anxious than ever to shut him out and keep him down?

5

⟩✦⟨

The Maxwell
Brothers
Become Outlaws

By 1875 the national depression was beginning to have an impact, even in a growing and progressive county seat like Macomb. Local manufacturing was starting to decline, and building had been very slow for some time. As the *Macomb Journal* editor admitted early that year, "Eighteen hundred and seventy-four was a dull year for building in Macomb." Residential construction, especially, had been below its usual brisk level, and tradesmen were struggling to find work.

In the countryside, farmers were still feeling the impact of low crop and livestock prices, which had dropped following the Panic of 1873. Loan foreclosures were rising. As farmers tightened their belts and bought less, shopkeepers in Macomb and the outlying villages were beginning to complain about the "dull times." The editor of the *Macomb Journal* soon summed up the situation in McDonough County: "Times are hard; poverty pinches, and the universal cry is, 'How are we to make both ends meet?'"

It was a difficult time to be dreaming of farm ownership or looking for work.

While Ed was still in prison, the Maxwell family had moved to Taylor County, Iowa. Whether their son's arrest and conviction had contributed to David and Susan's decision to leave McDonough County is unknown. Many folks thought that they had pulled up stakes toward the end of 1874 "to get away from their disgrace," as parents whose oldest son had been labeled a "desperado" and sent to the penitentiary. That may have been a factor, but the Maxwells were also still in quest of land they could own—and the more promising life that would come with it. So were many others. Noting the general tide of emigration from McDonough County in the 1870s, the *Macomb Eagle* editor remarked, "Hard times, low prices for farm produce, and scarcity of money create such a general feeling of dissatisfaction in the minds of many that they break up, sell off [land and livestock], and move to the great and growing West."

In the mid-1870s Taylor County, in southwest Iowa, had less than five thousand people, and Bedford, the county seat, had less than one thousand. So, land was not as expensive as in Illinois. Most of the settlers were from Ohio and Indiana, but some of the more successful farmers were from Pennsylvania, so David probably knew someone who had already settled there and was doing well.

The Maxwells had lived there briefly in 1869, when the opportunity to rent a farm apparently had not materialized. This time, they stayed for most of a year in Taylor County before moving farther west, to Nebraska, late in 1875. But David was still working as a tenant farmer or a hired hand, so they left no record of their lives in southern Iowa.

Ed may have gone west to see them, but if so, he did not stay. He returned to, or remained in, McDonough County, where he probably had a few friends. His religious, socially conservative parents may not have wanted him to join them, fearing a negative impact on their younger sons, especially Lon, who was a teenager.

Like his struggling father, Ed apparently dreamed of farm ownership—at least as his long-term goal. In an interview later that year (1875), he told a reporter, "I wanted to be honest. . . . I wanted to follow my business until I got money enough to buy me a little farm, of 40 or 80 acres, then marry, settle down, and live an honest life. This was my intention and pride." If that *was* his long-term intention, the "business" that he finally decided to follow, in order to get the money for a farm, was theft.

Of course, he knew that working as a hired hand would never provide the income he needed to change his life, even if he could find that kind of job again, and he realized that his shoemaking apprenticeship in the Illinois State Penitentiary would not encourage any shop owner to hire him. The stigma of being an ex-convict would prevent his reintegration into the economic system—at least in western Illinois. So, his culture now failed to provide him with a legitimate means of making his way in the world, or even gaining an acceptable self-image.

It is not surprising that during 1874 and 1875 Ed's dream of having a farm, which showed the impact of his father's long quest and hard struggle, was being superseded by another, more satisfying and attainable dream, that of becoming a noted desperado—a dream that rejected his father's world completely. His underlying psychological problem—a sense of inadequacy and self-contempt—made him expect hostility from others and demanded that his new identity be recognized by all who might otherwise disparage him. Ed's efforts as an outlaw were never essentially about getting money but about what he imagined that he might become—a man to be reckoned with, talked about, and admired.

By the 1870s, Ed had also been exposed to stories that celebrated bold and violent men. Cheap literary periodicals were carrying tales about "Indian warfare, California desperado life, pirates, wild sea adventure, highwaymen, crimes," and other sensational topics, as early sociologist William Graham Sumner pointed out in 1877. And some newspapers also carried similar, if shorter, items of that kind. Back in Lewistown, for example, the *Fulton Democrat* had published a long article that idealized Indian-fighting scout Kit Carson as well as various tales of adventure that portrayed courageous, quick-shooting fictional heroes. The real world of outlaws was romanticized too. In 1873 the *Macomb Journal* carried a thrilling, three-column, front-page story about an Iowa train robbery that portrayed masked bandits, "with a revolver in each hand," who took control of a train, stole money, and galloped off on their horses, and the *Macomb Eagle* printed a historical article about robbers and gunmen on the Illinois-Kentucky border titled "DARK AND BLOODY GROUND." Newspapers were learning to captivate readers with sensationalized accounts, and lawbreaking sometimes took on a kind of glamour because it was so daring.

The James-Younger band of outlaws, in particular, may have influenced Ed. They had become increasingly notorious since 1866, when they had robbed the bank at Liberty, Missouri—the first daylight bank robbery by an organized gang. By the early 1870s, the James and Younger brothers were wanted in several states and had become infamous—and celebrated—the subject of numerous newspaper reports and the focus of endless comment by the public, especially in the Mississippi Valley. The *Macomb Eagle* editor even compared Jesse James, "the celebrated Missouri brigand," to Dick

Turpin, the idealized highwayman of the exciting novel *Rookwood* that went through a dozen editions in the nineteenth century. To Ed, who later mentioned the James and Younger brothers in a letter from prison, their exploits surely seemed more heroic than despicable. After all, they had reasons to oppose the forces that shaped their lives, and they took their risks. They were men who had to be respected. Jesse James and his band may well have nourished Ed's repressed desires for radical freedom, heroic self-assertion, and revenge against the system—and helped to inspire his own quest for self-realization as a daring lawbreaker.

There is also evidence that Ed—like Billy the Kid in New Mexico—was already a reader of dime novels, those short, cheap, action-packed, and sometimes supposedly "true" accounts that celebrated tough, assertive men who were not afraid to be violent—historical figures like Kit Carson and Wild Bill Hickok, and fictional heroes like Seth Jones, who first appeared in 1861, in the best-selling dime novel of all time. Although not a bandit, Jones is a manly denizen of the frontier, rather like James Fenimore Cooper's Leatherstocking, who exhibits self-reliance and courage—traits that Ed admired. And the end of the novel reveals that "Seth Jones" is a dreamed-up identity, an alias, developed by an otherwise more conventional man. Ed Maxwell would do exactly the same.

Although the first and most famous fictional bandit-hero, Deadwood Dick, created by Edward L. Wheeler, did not appear until 1877, Edward Willett's *The Twin Trailers; or the Gamecock of El Paso,* published in 1872, featured courageous frontier brothers, one "fond of hunting and perilous adventure" and the other "wild and dashing, even to recklessness." Other dime novels that Ed might have read featured gunfights and narrow escapes, the kind of manly adventure that he longed for. Of course, the central characters were men to be admired—for their bravery, self-assertion, and skill with guns—so Ed's reading may have provided a fantasy life that soothed his chronic sense of unworthiness.

Interestingly, an 1878 commentator on the new "Boys' Literature" in periodicals (serialized dime novels, which commonly centered on a youth) summarized the typical content by saying that "the boy hero of the tales" often rebels against his father's confining world, reinvents himself as an exemplar of manliness, and has adventures: He "encounters and overcomes men . . . by audacious courage and mean strategy," and he does not hesitate to use "the pistol, the knife." So, the impressionable reader of those stories "fancies himself a sort of hero" too, and he "takes on the morbid passions and propensities of the vicious and the outcasts of society." That may well have been the kind of identity transformation that Ed underwent. It is significant that he would soon blame the start of his outlaw career on the reading of "yellow-covered literature" (pulp fiction).

Whatever was influencing him, by sometime in April 1875 Ed had made a life-shaping decision: He would act to verify his emerging self-image by robbing homes in the countryside. That represented a momentous psychological change because he would no longer pretend to be part of the moral order; he would forge his destiny apart from family and society. And if he still ever dreamed of buying "a little farm" one day and achieving respectability as a landowner, that door soon closed behind him. The forces he would unleash, both within and outside himself, would eventually determine his fate.

Lon was then sixteen, and he must have been thrilled to see again the older brother that he had always admired and probably had written to at the penitentiary. Invited to join Ed, he had a choice to make: either stay in Iowa, working with his perennially struggling father, or go with his brother to share a more exciting and lucrative life outside the law—and show that he was a worthy comrade, a man. Of course, he decided to go.

Sometime in late April, Ed and Lon (the latter using an alias) started burglarizing homes and stealing horses in the countryside northwest of Macomb—the Blandinsville area. That soon led to other exploits, in Hancock County, west of McDonough, and by the time Ed was identified as one of the desperadoes, there was excitement bordering on hysteria in both places.

The most comprehensive account from Hancock County appeared in the *Carthage Republican* on June 11, under a stirring title:

BANDITTI!

Two Desperadoes Make Reprisals
on LaHarpe, Durham, and Pilot Grove
Townships. They Capture La Crosse
and Decline to be Arrested.
The People Greatly Excited.

If Ed had wanted to inspire fear and respect among the rural people who had ignored and devalued him in the past, he was notably successful. One reason for the public anxiety was that the robbers struck in the night— often at occupied farmhouses, whereas most burglars stole from stores, homes, or sheds that had no one inside. The very idea that lawbreakers would come out of the dark, enter a house, and steal valuables while the owners slept and were helpless, unnerved many people. In one case, a man's money and watch "were taken from . . . pants [placed] under his head while he was sleeping," a feat accomplished "by running a hand up the pants leg, which hung over the side of the bed, and cutting the pocket out." That kind of theft was incredibly daring—and the potential for violence if the person awoke was frightening to contemplate.

And in the rural world of the nineteenth century, before electricity, there was no quick way to light up a house inside—and no way at all to banish the darkness outside. The age-old association of darkness with the presence of unknown evil was beginning to play on people's minds. Some began to hear, or see, mysterious horsemen in the night.

The robbers also lived in the wild and moved at random. They were indeed "banditti," as the newspaper said, using the old word for bandits. Their "midnight depredations" had placed several townships "at the mercy of as lawless a set of bandits as ever infested the Old World," as the *Republican* put it, and no one in Hancock County knew where the robbers would show up next. The very fact that they were not associated with one community or township—and were, in fact, outsiders—also made them very difficult to trace or investigate. Some people felt they were the same two men who had committed a robbery in nearby Henderson County, but nobody knew anything for sure.

Any strangers were apt to be under suspicion. In Burnside, north of Carthage, "two men of suspicious appearance" were accused of being the robbers, and then two others were accused as well. All four were held, searched, and interrogated, but were later declared to be simply tramps, "deadbeats" who were in the countryside looking for work.

Meanwhile, the dozen robberies were exhilarating adventures for Ed and Lon, whose freedom of movement and choice of actions gave them a new sense of mastery, or control over their lives, that was the polar opposite of all the routine and restriction they had known. They had transcended the limitations imposed by poverty and disrespect, and they surely began to associate the condition of freedom with life outside the law.

Also, in the village of La Crosse, Ed and Lon, identified as "Maxwell and Post," had drawn their revolvers on a small posse, forcing them to back down, in a sort of shotless gunfight, and then had vanished into the timber. That, too, was a daring act, which fostered a kind of admiration for their boldness—reflected in the phrase "They Capture La Crosse" in the article title.

The robberies continued, and more than a month later, on July 22, the *Macomb Journal* carried a long, comprehensive account of the banditry, focused mainly on McDonough County. It was widely reprinted in the western Illinois region:

A MODERN MURRELL.
THAT BOLD FREEBOOTER MAXWELL.

With a Confederate, He is Making Things
Lively in the Northwest Townships.
A Short Sketch of Some of the Robberies
Charged to the Intrepid Thieves.
$500 Reward for Their Capture and Conviction.

Something near three years ago a farm hand named Maxwell, living in Blandinsville Twp., stole a suit of clothing in the village of that name. . . . For this offense he was sent to the penitentiary. His term of confinement expiring some three or four months ago, he appeared upon the scenes of his former exploits. Soon after his return, several robberies were committed, and it was generally supposed that Maxwell with a confederate by the name of Post were the perpetrators.

These robberies and housebreakings, beginning two or three months since, have been wholesale in number, and of a character showing daring and adroitness. They have been generally confined to Emmet, Blandinsville, Sciota, and Hire townships, of this county, and the sections of Hancock and Henderson [counties] adjoining that district.

The following is the manner of the depredations: A horse was stolen from a stable in Emmet; thence west into Hire a half dozen houses were broken into on the same night, and moneys amounting up into hundreds of dollars were taken. A day or two after, the horse was found somewhere in the vicinity of the last house-breaking. . . . A short time after this, houses were broken into in the vicinity of La Crosse, Hancock County. It is currently reported that Maxwell and his "pal," in open daylight, went boldly into La Crosse [to rob a store], and when officers attempted to arrest them, the [outlaws] drew their revolvers, awed the guardians of the law into submission, and left town at their leisure. This maneuver raised Maxwell in the eyes of the people from a straggling, house-breaking thief to a bold free-booter.

While the action above described was the talk of the community, a couple of horses were stolen from the stable of E. S. Smith, Sciota Township. Four days later the animals were found, badly stove up, in the vicinity of Hamilton, 40 miles west. Houses broken into over in Hancock County during the nights of those days were evidence that "Maxwell was on the move."

The Smith horse-stealing exploit occurred about a month ago. Since that time, quiet has been the order until within the past week, when house-breaking and robbing in that section has revived. A few nights since, the house of Mr. Ferris, near Blandinsville, was broken into, and a small amount of money taken; another gentleman (whose name we did not learn) suffered in like manner to the extent of some $60; Wednesday night last John Isom's house, Hire Twp., was entered, and $22, a pocket book, and papers taken; also, ex-[county board] supervisor Carlisle's house was broken into, Mr. C's pocket book taken from under his pillow and $35 or $40 abstracted, as well as a lot of valuable papers, among which is a note calling for $900. A raid was made on the house of S. B. Davis, who suffered to the tune of $5 in money, as well as his pocket book and papers. On Sunday night the residence of L. English was the victim, and over $50 was the booty. All these houses are in a circuit of four miles. . . .

Since the above was set in type, we learn that on Tuesday night the robbers were again abroad, that attempts were made on the residences of Mrs. Rebecca Hainline and Joseph Kidd, each being ineffectual, as the families were awakened by the noises. The fact is, the people of that section sleep now with one eye open. Great excitement pervades the neighborhood of the daring house-breakings. Parties are out searching for the thieves, lanes are patrolled, and suspicious-looking persons are examined. Times are hot for Maxwell, without a doubt.

If Ed ever read that article, he was surely pleased to be viewed as "A MODERN MURRELL," for John A. Murrell was a legendary desperado of the early Mississippi Valley, the head of a gang that had robbed and killed in the 1830s. As with Jesse James and others, Ed's sense of identity as an outlaw was deeply influenced by the public response to his crimes. In contrast, the alias "Post" protected Lon from identification by lawmen—

and also kept David and Susan from knowing that Ed's corruption of Lon had occurred.

The newspaper report failed to note an important fact: The farmers that Maxwell and his "pal" robbed were all substantial landowners. None of the many tenant farms in the area were visited by the nighttime bandits. By early August, however, the editor had become aware of the social class slant to the robberies, and he quipped, "Out in Emmet, Sciota, Hire, and Blandinsville townships, it is said that those families who haven't been robbed by Maxwell are not admitted to good society." The *Macomb Eagle* alluded to the same social class factor: "Maxwell . . . and Post pounced down upon the farmers in that locality like a pair of fiendish guerillas. . . . The lives of many of the best men in McDonough County have been in peril from these desperate and lawless villains. . . ." By "the best men" the editor clearly meant "the most prosperous men."

Of course, the well-to-do were more likely to have money or valuables worth stealing, but they also represented the social class that Ed, and probably Lon, envied and resented. Some people also recalled that while Ed was being taken to Joliet in 1874, he boasted "that when he returned, he would make it 'lively' for the people in Hire and Blandinsville [townships]"—as if he had a score to settle with at least some of the farm owners in the prosperous area where he had once lived.

In any case, it is clear that the Maxwells had an axe to grind against the social group that dominated the rural world in which they, and their parents, had struggled and failed to rise. Rather like "social bandits" in the Old World, they were "unwilling to bear the traditional burdens of the common man, poverty and meekness," so they revolted against their oppressors. They turned things upside down, looting and intimidating the well-to-do, thereby achieving a measure of revenge. Unlike true social bandits, however, including perhaps Jesse and Frank James, they were not widely admired, and protected, by members of their own social class. They were too alienated for that.

It is also evident that the Maxwells did not steal horses to sell them. They simply stole them to use in their robberies, and then abandoned them and stole some others. That was a wise approach, for county sheriffs and city marshals commonly circulated, by telegraph and letter, descriptions of stolen horses, which often had markings that made them easily identifiable. And it also showed that the exploit itself, not the potential income from it, was the key motivation for the young outlaws. As another noted bandit, Henry Starr, once commented about his own experience in the far West: "Of course, I'm interested in the money . . . but I must admit that there's the lure of life in the open, the rides at night, the spice of danger, the mastery over men. . . . I love it. It is wild adventure." And so it was for the Maxwell desperadoes in that summer of 1875.

Ed and Lon had thrown off the oppressive limitations of poverty and low social status and had ventured into a world of unlimited self-assertion. They were the heroes of a self-created drama—of their own destiny.

As a boy, local historian Quincy Hainline had lived in the northwest part of McDonough County, in Hire Township, where many of the robberies occurred, and he later recalled the local response: "Excitement was running high in the township. We expected every morning to hear of some of our neighbors being found murdered in defense of their homes. It was almost a reign of terror. A meeting was called, and a vigilance committee was formed to patrol the roads. A $500 reward was offered, to kill [them] at sight." The size of that reward—a very respectable year's income in 1875—also reveals the socioeconomic status of the landowners who had been victimized.

Those vigilantes from the Blandinsville area, armed with revolvers and double-barreled shotguns, were indeed intent on taking the bandits "dead or alive," as the Carthage newspaper put it. Even if they captured "Maxwell and Post," as the *Macomb Eagle* reported, "there was talk of lynching them," for the reward would be the same and there would be no chance of escape. Oddly enough, the leader of that vigilante group was Miles Bond, who had killed Provost Marshal William Randolph in a gunfight during the Civil War in order to keep his brother from being arrested for resisting the draft. Very much like Ed, Bond was not much interested in maintaining the law, but he was devoted to using guns and asserting his manliness.

Of course, the sheriffs of Hancock and McDonough counties were also searching for the robbers, as was Constable Henry Wolf of Blandinsville and Deputy Sheriff Benjamin Howard, who also lived there.

But Ed and Lon were hard to track down. Because they were homeless, they completely disappeared between their raids. Also, their hunting treks as boys in the heavily timbered Spoon River and Illinois River country in Fulton County had given them extensive outdoor living experience. They knew how to cook, eat, sleep, and care for horses in the open. They were prepared to live on the run.

People in the northwest section of McDonough County and eastern Hancock County talked of little else as the summer wore on, and there were many rumors of sightings on some road or in some village. Meanwhile, the owners of the Wells Brothers Store in Macomb responded to the heightened anxiety by selling "nickel-plated revolvers" for self-protection—dubbing them "Maxwell Terrifiers"—and they did a brisk business.

But by the time the "Modern Murrell" article appeared, the Maxwells were not even in McDonough County. They had stolen two more horses and fled eastward, to Fulton County, where they could hide out in the dense timber that they had been familiar with in the 1860s. There they hunted for some of their food and practiced shooting with their rifles and revolvers—which they had probably done in McDonough County as well, before they starting raiding houses in the countryside.

In a late August interview, Ed bragged about his accuracy with guns: "Ed informed our reporter that with one of their Spencer rifles, at a distance of 800 to 1,000 yards, he can put five of the seven shots inside the size of a common door, and with his revolver at 100 yards can hit a man ('or the size of a man,' he suddenly said, correcting the expression) four out of five times."

The seven-shot, .50-caliber Spencer rifle had been the most widely used repeating rifle in the Civil War, but it did not have the range that Ed claimed. His revolver was apparently a Colt Navy model, like he used later on, but it was not very accurate at 100 yards. Like Jesse James, Wild Bill Hickok, and some other outlaws and gunfighters, Ed was doing some creative reputation building, but as later events would show, he and Lon were remarkably good with their guns. Indeed, their notion of manhood called for skill with firearms—as well as the willingness to use them.

The Maxwells also continued to steal, at least occasionally. A *Fulton Democrat* article from October 1881 mentions one 1875 incident in which a buggy and set of harness were stolen from a farmer named Alonso Mc-Cally, who lived north of Table Grove. He and a few companions tracked the vehicle into the Spoon River brakes, where they encountered the resting Maxwells, who could not use the buggy in the brush anyway and let him retrieve it. When McCally later returned with a posse and found them again, Ed scared the men off, as he later reported: "When they got within thirty rods of us, I took a revolver in each hand, leaped into the road, and gave a yell. You should have seen those fellows run. . . ." Apparently he did not have to fire any shots.

That episode shows the kind of desperado defiance that had a shaping impact on the identity of the young outlaws. In a sense, Ed and Lon had to both evoke pursuit and withstand confrontation in order to prove themselves. And when they did those things, there was enormous elation, a sense of power over others that temporarily soothed their long-standing frustration and resentment.

Ed and Lon also told McCally's posse that "they would never be taken alive." That remark was also made by Jesse James and Billy the Kid—and by other outlaws who saw themselves in heroic terms. It confirms that the rob-and-hide activity of the Maxwell brothers was an assertion of their outlaw identity. They relished their growing reputation as desperadoes, pursuing self-realization by asserting a kind of superiority over the culture that held them down—not just by breaking the law but by defying the authorities. If lawmen or posses wanted to catch them, they had to be willing to risk a gunfight.

Of course, as their raids continued, Ed and Lon only increased their alienation, distrust of other people, and potential for violence—not to mention their likelihood of being killed. Their outlawry was, in the long run, profoundly self-defeating.

Soon one hundred men were in pursuit of the Maxwell brothers, including Sheriff Waggoner of Lewistown, but always on the move, they were hard to locate. An 1881 account in the *Macomb Journal* summarized their activity in this way, "They established a 'den' in Fulton County, among the Spoon River brakes, from which point they injected raids of robbery. A favorite plan of the brothers was to steal a couple of horses, ride them 75 or 80 miles in a night, then turn the almost dead animals loose. Next night they would burglarize a number of houses, then steal two more horses and strike out for other points." Although the distance they rode stolen horses is exaggerated here, this shows that, in the public mind, the Maxwells (or Maxwell and "Post") were regarded as daring outlaws—hiding in the still-wild places, striking where they pleased, galloping off on stolen horses, and remaining just beyond the reach of the law. That is, in fact, what they had done in McDonough and Hancock counties, so they simply continued that pattern in Fulton—often hiding in thinly settled, wooded townships like Isabel, Waterford, and Liverpool.

Although some of their robberies were undoubtedly not reported in the newspapers, an 1881 article in the *Fulton Democrat* refers to several horse thefts—and mentions the response of Sheriff Waggoner:

TWO DESPERADOES AT LARGE

. . . On Friday night they stole two valuable horses from
Moses Bordner, living two miles east of town. . . . The alarm

---

was raised at once, and Sheriff Waggoner, accompanied by a posse, started out on Sunday morning in pursuit of the horses and thieves. . . . The thieves are two young men, and are described as follows: One is about 22 years old, rather low, heavy set, with a very dark, full beard. The other claimed to be 17, was smooth-faced, of medium stature, lightweight, light complexion. Both seemed to be intelligent, and well dressed. But the thieves are desperadoes, and are well armed.

Fifty dollars each will be paid for the return of the horses, and $50 each for the thieves. . . .

Later

Major Waggoner, Robert Prichard, Mr. Bordner, and others started on the trail of the thieves on Sunday, and tracked them nearly to Peoria. They stole a new saddle at Jacob Maus' place, in Liverpool Twp., and all along their route were firing off their arms. . . . They managed to get through Peoria without being seen by the officers, but were finally tracked by Mr. Prichard to the rope ferry three miles north of the city. Mr. Prichard, and [Officer] Kimsey, of Peoria, found the horses, coming home, at Germantown. The thieves had stolen other horses, and had stripped everything off of Bordner's horses and turned them loose. . . .

It is hardly expected that these desperadoes will be arrested. It would certainly take a hot fight to secure them, for they are armed with a nine-shooting carbine and four navy revolvers.

This reveals that Ed and Lon had been, for a time, in the agricultural and wooded countryside southeast of Lewistown where they had lived as boys. Moses Bordner's substantial farmstead, with its high-quality horses, would have been familiar to them. If David Maxwell had been a tenant farmer on Bordner's acreage during the 1860s, there may have been lingering animosity between the owner and the renter. It is also evident from this report that the Maxwells did not shoot at people but did sometimes fire their revolvers—like cowboys shooting up Dodge City or Abilene. With fast horses and blazing guns, they proclaimed their new identity.

At about the same time, in late July, a series of burglaries occurred in and near communities that were north of Lewistown and west of Peoria. Those nighttime robberies were not explicitly connected with the Maxwells, in the newspapers anyway, but some of them were probably their work, as they rode west of Peoria, staying in the wild areas, to reach the Illinois River ferry north of the city. They crossed into Woodford County, where they had also lived several years earlier, but they apparently remained close to the river.

While that was happening, authorities in McDonough County informed Sheriff Waggoner and others that they were pursuing Ed Maxwell and a man named "Post," and those robbers were indicted in Fulton County for "larceny" (horse theft).

But by that time, at least one law officer, Deputy Sheriff Charles C. Hays of McDonough County, had become convinced that the mysterious figure called "Post" was, in fact, Lon Maxwell. Like so many county sheriffs and city marshals of that era, Hays had no police training, but, like Waggoner, he took great pride in tracking down lawbreakers. Born and raised in Pennsylvania, and a stonecutter by trade, Hays was an admired Civil War veteran. An erect, athletic-looking figure, with dark hair, a flowing mustache, and hazel eyes, he had been a captain in the Seventh Illinois Cavalry—noted for making "Grierson's Raid" through the South, the most famous cavalry venture of the war—before serving as deputy sheriff.

Hays was originally from Canton, so he knew Fulton County as well as the Maxwells. Using telegraph contact with other law officers, and traveling by train to other communities, he doggedly tracked the outlaws, who had eventually secured a skiff and traveled up the Illinois River as far as LaSalle, and then had reversed direction and come down the river, stopping at various towns.

When they arrived at Beardstown on August 18, 1875, the unrelenting lawman was waiting for them. Several newspapers printed extensive accounts of the apprehension of the Maxwells. The *Bushnell Record* provides the most detailed one—based on an interview with Hays:

> Arriving [at Beardstown] on Tuesday, he waited until [the next] morning about nine o'clock. Then, while walking through town he spied the one, Edward, coming from the river. Watching him enter a store, he procured the service of John Husted and Tice Missinham to assist him. . . .
>
> Upon entering the store [Hays] walked up to Maxwell, laid his hand on his right shoulder, seized his right arm, and informed him that he was his prisoner. Immediately his assistants came up, one

seizing his left arm, the other his coat collar in the rear. Maxwell immediately sprang like a tiger. He squirmed, kicked, bit, and did every way he could to escape, and so strong and powerful was he that these three large men could scarcely hinder him from drawing his dirk, or succeed in hand-cuffing him. Finally he was overpowered.

The captain, leaving him in charge of an officer, sought the other [Maxwell]. Traveling in the direction of the river . . . he soon spied the other one sitting in a skiff. He approached, unobserved, and took a survey of the situation. In a moment he decided that it was again necessary to resort to strategy. He slipped back a short distance and secured the assistance of John H. Davis and Thomas Doyle. . . . They landed [a] skiff above him and walked carelessly along as if to pass him. . . . He then hailed them and wanted to know if they wanted to buy a skiff. They did. He invited them to approach and examine his. Davis took the lead, and wading into the water, he cautiously approached toward [Lon's] carbines, which were lying plainly in sight. When near enough, he seized them.

Maxwell immediately drew a revolver. At the same time, Doyle was coming in upon his right. Maxwell fired at him, but luckily the ball only grazed his body, doing no harm. By this time, Captain Hays was in his front, and the other men, one on either side, each had his piece [revolver] leveled at him; and with the assurance that upon further resistance he would be shot, he wisely concluded to surrender.

This was the first actual gunfight involving one of the Maxwells. Fortunately, only one shot was fired before Lon surrendered—knowing that otherwise, with the odds at three to one and his opponents not standing next to one another, he would be gunned down.

Aside from the Spencer rifles, Lon had three revolvers and a half bushel of cartridges. The Maxwells were obviously prepared for the moment when they would put their shooting skill to use in a gunfight that would confirm their identity as desperadoes. What counted with them was a romantic readiness to confront the hostile forces that threatened their hard-won self-esteem, but the great gunfight would not come until the close of their career.

Undoubtedly relishing his status as the heroic law officer who had captured the desperadoes, Hays provided another detailed account for the *Macomb Journal* reporter, and it continued the story beyond the disarming of both men:

On the way up town [from the river], officer Hays told Lon that they had arrested his comrade. "Did he make a row?" asked the young thief, evidently knowing that it was Ed's determination not to be taken without a fierce battle.

When Ed, who was under guard, heard the pistol-shot fired by his brother, he grew terribly excited: "My God," he exclaimed, "they are killing my brother. Let me go to his help."

When brought together, Ed and Lon were visibly relieved, and they admitted what Ed's outcry had already confirmed for Hays: They were not Maxwell and Post, but the Maxwell brothers. As this report also shows, they were deeply bonded desperadoes, prepared to fight for each other and, if necessary, die together.

As Hays soon found out, they were also prepared to escape together. He brought them by train to Bushnell, where he had to keep them overnight at a hotel, for the three of them needed to catch a morning train for Blandinsville, where the brothers would face a preliminary examination in court. A terse newspaper account depicts their escape attempt: "While in the hotel there, although chained together, they made an attempt to escape by running out of doors, and down the street, having, unnoticed, slipped off their boots for this purpose. Hays pulled out after the chaps like a locomotive, however, and caught them after a 75 yards race."

Meanwhile, Hays was celebrated in the *Macomb Journal* as a "courageous, efficient officer" who deserved the thanks of every resident of the county for "searching them out, hunting them down, and effecting their dangerous capture." He was a local hero—and as such, was certain to be elevated from deputy to sheriff at the next election, just two months away.

News of the Maxwells' capture spread like a prairie fire throughout McDonough County and adjacent areas, reaching almost everyone before any of the weekly newspapers could print the story. People came pouring into Macomb to see the notorious desperadoes, who were brought in from Blandinsville by wagon on August 19. According to the *Macomb Journal,* the Maxwells were "more attractive than a circus," as men, women, and children stood along the dusty streets to catch a glimpse of them.

The public was clearly fascinated by such committed, daring lawbreakers, and one newspaper even viewed them as a local version of "The James Boys." That was surely a comparison everyone was making—even though the Missouri bandits focused on stage, train, and bank robberies. The

Maxwells were not just criminals intent on making money outside the law; they had assaulted the very system itself, had opposed the social order—not because they regretted the subjugation of the South, like the James brothers, but because they opposed the subjugation of the Maxwells.

For a time, as men from throughout the county gathered near the square and emotions were running high, local officials even feared that the Maxwells would be "strung up without judge or jury," but better judgment eventually prevailed.

As the public satisfied its massive curiosity and released its long-pent-up anxiety, some were disappointed to find that Ed and Lon were not big, rough-looking specimens of outlaw manhood. The *Journal* reporter was one who shared that response:

> Personally, they do not at all fill the bill of imagination as to how such reckless daredevils ought to look. Ed, the older, is considerably under medium height, weighs 140 pounds, and there is nothing about his looks indicative of fierceness. He has a close-cut beard, talks more than ordinarily intelligent, and affects no bravado. He is probably 28 or 30 years of age. Lon is a queer-looking specimen of a neighborhood terror. He is not over 17 years old, has an effeminate look, and one would judge from his appearance that a sound spanking would be a more efficacious mode of punishment for him than prison bolts and bars. And yet, despite appearances, there is no denying the fact that these two men are a pair of more than ordinary outlaws.

Ed's small stature was the first item of note—as it had been for him throughout his life. He was then only twenty-two years old, so his dark beard gave him an older look. At five feet, five inches, Lon was slightly taller than Ed, but his light brown hair, blue eyes, fair complexion, clean-shaven appearance, and finer features gave him the softer look that more than one observer noted during his outlaw career. If he was sometimes perceived as "effeminate" as a teenager, he too—like his short brother—may have felt that he had to demonstrate his manliness in a world that failed to recognize it.

Whatever the case, Lon was by then as alienated from society as Ed, and it seemed to both men that their bond, as brothers and comrades, was the one sustaining relationship, aside from their struggling parents, in a world of oppressive forces. In the coming years, that bond would become a determining factor in their destiny.

The Great Escape— and Recapture

When the Maxwells were brought in, first to the court in Blandinsville and then to the jail in Macomb, there was considerable talk of lynching— not just because nearby victims of their raids were angry and wanted revenge, but because people feared they would escape. They had little confidence in what the *Macomb Eagle* called "our badly demoralized and dilapidated county jail."

That was, in fact, McDonough County's second jail. The first one had been a two-story log building constructed in 1832 on West Jackson Street, just two blocks from the square. During twenty-four years of use, many prisoners had escaped from it, including two accused murderers—Thomas Morgan, in about 1840, and David Burress, in 1854. Neither man was ever caught. When the railroad came through and the frontier period was over, the log jail was regarded as an outdated structure, unworthy of a progressive county, so in 1856 a new brick jail was built.

Located at the southeast corner of Lafayette and Carroll streets, just beyond the northwest corner of the square, it was a somber-looking, two-story, red-brick structure, with rows of four to five windows on each level, on all sides but the rear. Surrounded by a high board fence, it looked substantial. Inside, the sheriff's office and three large cells were on the ground floor, and quarters for his family or a deputy were upstairs.

Unfortunately, it was not constructed very well—with only a thin metal lining on the cell walls and floor—so prisoners escaped from it as readily as they had from the old log jail. Complete records are lacking, but when Sheriff Jack Lane finished two years in office, late in 1870, and decided to leave law enforcement, the *Journal* editor praised him because "during his entire term . . . not one [prisoner] escaped, this being the first such instance in the history of sheriffs since the erection of the present jail." There had been half a dozen other sheriffs since 1856, so escapes were numerous. Between 1871 and 1875 there were several more, and by then the jail had become the butt of local jokes and derogatory comments.

Sheriff Josephus Venard was determined to end the jailbreak tradition, which had become a sort of challenge to prisoners—prompting more escape attempts where so many had previously succeeded, and making Macomb renowned for the failure of its criminal justice system. An 1876 article in the *Macomb Journal* reflects the ongoing contest of ingenuity and determination that engaged the beleaguered sheriff in the mid-1870s:

THE BEAUTIES OF BEING SHERIFF,

Especially When You Have the Worst Prisoners
And the Poorest Jail in the State.

While [Venard] has been sheriff, it is safe to say that the meanest set of prisoners in all America have fallen to his lot, and he has had the meanest jail in America to keep them in. His two years have been an incessant campaign against desperate men breaking out of the old rickety jail, whose rotten walls invite prisoners to "hack in and crawl out." Catching prisoners in various attempts of escape has been his weekly pastime. He has placed patch upon patch where the iron lining was ripped off the walls; has pulled men from beneath the floor, where they were at work burrowing under the foundation; has snaked them from the vaults [i.e., the septic system]; has arrested them in their bold dashes for the door. His nights have been disturbed by the rasping sound of file and saw, working steadily upon grates or bolts; and he has captured enough tools to equip a brigade of housebreakers. He has been successful in keeping his prisoners, but has been kept mighty busy in doing it. . . .

Despite Venard's vigilance, the public was apprehensive about the incarceration of the Maxwells, "the most desperate outlaws ever confined in the county jail," as the *Journal* later put it. It was as if some ultimate contest were being waged: Would the finest sheriff in recent times be a match for the notorious outlaws? Venard was especially cautious and watchful, and had the assistance of Deputy Sheriff Hays, as well as a new deputy (H. W. Gash), and two other men (former sheriff G. L. Farwell and guard James Blazer) while the desperadoes were in his jail.

Despite those precautions, the incredible—or perhaps, the inevitable—occurred anyway. On the evening of August 28, the most famous jailbreak in McDonough County history took place. The *Macomb Journal* carried the story, an exciting narrative that was widely reprinted, but most people knew the details long before that issue appeared:

ESCAPED!

THE PRISONERS MAKE A RAID
ON THE SHERIFF, OVERPOWER HIM.
Ed Maxwell and Charley Roberts Escape.
The Excitement in Macomb—
The Night Ride after Them—
They Are Still at Large!

Monday evening last, at half past eight o'clock, Sheriff Venard went to lock the prisoners in their cells, as is his usual custom. James Blazer, who is acting as a guard, unlocked and opened the hall door. Captain Venard passed into the hall, where the prisoners are permitted to stay during daytime. Before Blazer could close the door behind the sheriff, Ed Maxwell leaped with the activity of a cat, a distance of eight or ten feet, upon the Sheriff. Instantly Charley Roberts followed up, with Lon Maxwell and one or two other prisoners. Although taken by surprise, the Sheriff grasped the two Maxwells, who for a time he succeeded in holding. But Roberts caught him by the hair with one hand, and with the other blinded him and endeavored to thrust his fingers into Venard's eyes. In this predicament Ed Maxwell broke loose and, with Roberts, dashed for the door. Lon tried to follow, but Venard forced him back into his cell. . . .

When Maxwell and Roberts rushed out of the jail, three or

four men were going along the street in its vicinity—among them, Mayor [Alexander] McLean. That gentleman hearing the noise, looked in the direction of the jail and saw the two prisoners emerge. As soon as [they were] out, Maxwell and Roberts separated, the former running out North Lafayette Street, and the latter striking up East Carroll. His honor took in the situation at once, and gave Maxwell a lusty chase. Maxwell, however, as fleet as a deer, and better acquainted with night locomotion than McLean, eluded his pursuer and vanished up an alley, out of sight. Roberts also made good his escape.

Within five minutes, the affair was known for blocks around, and an excited crowd gathered at the jail. It was supposed that Maxwell, true to his old tricks, would on first opportunity steal a horse, upon which to get away. Acting upon this idea, States Attorney [Crosby F.] Wheat, procured all the saddle horses that could be gotten together, quickly mounted men upon them, and sent them galloping in all directions into the countryside, to awaken the farmers and warn them to watch their stables . . . and at the same time maybe capture Maxwell.

In the meantime telegrams were sent to the various officers in this and adjoining counties—also special dispatches were sent to the Quincy and Chicago papers. Postal cards were printed at this office, giving descriptions of the two men; these were directed to constables, city marshals, and chiefs of police in every city, town, and village within a radius of 50 miles. By midnight the county was thoroughly bulletined.

Among those going into the country were Officer Farwell, Marshall McClintock, and George King of the night police force. Their party went direct to Colchester, from which point Captain Farwell dispatched King, with a man who had been aroused [there], to the country north of Crooked Creek, to warn farmers, while he, with McClintock, kept that neighborhood under close surveillance, thinking that possibly Roberts, who is a citizen of that place, might make his appearance there.

King went as directed, and aroused the people north of the creek, among them Elijah Welch. Welch thinking there was more scare than danger, it appears, paid no heed to the warning, and did not watch. Within two hours after, one of his horses was stolen, and about 8 P.M. Maxwell was seen upon the animal, near J. B. Eakles' [home], four or five miles west of Welch's, riding for dear life.

Up to this writing, no further authentic account of his whereabouts is known. He is hotly pursued, and were it not for the extensive cornfields, which are wildernesses for hiding, and Maxwell's more than usual adroitness and daring, he could not get away. . . .

This lengthy account is an excellent record of criminal pursuit by lawmen in the nineteenth century—when telegraph alerts, postcard descriptions, dispatches to daily newspapers, and mounted posses were important procedures.

The postcard "wanted" notice, immediately printed and mailed by Sheriff Venard, offered $100 for the capture of Ed Maxwell and the same amount for the capture of Charley Roberts, and it provided descriptions of both men: "Ed Maxwell is about 5 feet, 5 inches in height, well built, black hair and black mustache, and had on nothing but shirt, pants, and shoes when he escaped. Charley Roberts is about 5 feet, 10 or 11 inches in height, light complexion, clean shaven, and had on one arm in India ink the picture of a woman in a short dress, holding up a vase of flowers."

Despite such an effort, criminals who left the area were fairly safe because photographs were still seldom available for distribution, communication between law enforcement agencies was irregular, and lawbreakers on the run simply adopted an alias—which Ed Maxwell would soon do.

The daring escape, despite precautions at the jail, helped to make Ed Maxwell a legendary outlaw in central western Illinois, a desperado that people loved to talk about. Like the often violent title character in Louis L'Amour's *Hondo,* he had demonstrated that he was "quick, hard, and dangerous." For weeks after the escape everyone was looking for him—or was afraid that he would suddenly reappear with a gun to steal a horse or rescue his brother.

Local historian Quincy Hainline, who was in his mid-twenties when the great jailbreak occurred, later recalled the local talk about the young desperado. "There were a great many rumors and stories of his getaway," most of which were untrue, he said, and "it was thought that he was making an effort to join the James and Younger boys. . . ." Hainline's comment reveals that the notorious James-Younger gang, which was centered across the river in Missouri, was by 1875 not just a criminal reality but a legendary presence—the ultimate band of desperadoes—in the public mind, so it seemed natural to associate Ed Maxwell with them. The often-repeated legend that Ed and Lon rode with "the James and Younger gang" had its origin in that kind of rumor—which associated them with mythic outlawry, the great oppositional force to the progress of civilization (now that the Indians were gone from the Mississippi Valley or lived on reservations). There is no evidence whatsoever that the Maxwells ever tried to join that notorious gang, but Hainline, who was acquainted with Ed and Lon, was probably correct when he asserted that they "got their inspiration" from those legendary outlaws.

Charley Roberts, a twenty-one-year-old from Colchester, who was being held for horse stealing, was never recaptured, but he was of minor interest.

A month after the jailbreak, on September 28, Lon was tried in Mc-Donough County Circuit Court. He pled guilty to "burglary" (robbing homes) and "larceny" (horse stealing), and was sentenced to two years in the penitentiary. That was a fairly light sentence, for he was still a teenager. Deputy Sheriff Hays took him to Joliet on October 8.

Of course, Ed's escape reduced the reward that Hays collected. He received only half of the $500 posted by local residents, and half of the $200 offered by Sheriff Venard. Hays had caught them both, but only Lon stayed caught, so the other $350 remained available, to prompt lawmen and bounty hunters to find and capture Ed. Hays again tried to locate him, riding through the heavily wooded townships west of Macomb and asking people if they had seen anything, but he had no luck.

As the weeks passed, rumors continued to circulate—that Ed had been seen in some town or other, that he had joined the James gang, and even that "he was arrested for a [new] crime and, under another name, was imprisoned in the Jo Daviess County Jail, from which he also escaped." All of the reports were false.

Ed had, in fact, slipped out of Illinois by crossing the Mississippi River and had drifted north to Minnesota, where he may have worked briefly as a sawmill employee in South Stillwater but certainly worked as a farmhand nearby, in rural Washington County. For a year, nothing was heard about him in Macomb, although he apparently committed robberies elsewhere from time to time.

Then, in September 1876, Sheriff Venard received the following letter from the Stillwater chief of police, Matthew Shortall, inquiring about "a man by the name of Ed Maxwell" who was "considered a desperate character" in that area. The chief's motive was apparent: "Please look the matter up, and let me know if he is wanted, and how much reward, if any, there is for his arrest." Venard replied by telegraph, "Arrest him," and then sent a follow-up letter with a description of Ed, an account of his Illinois crimes, and an indication that there was a $350 reward for his capture.

Shortall was so concerned about the reward money that he did nothing immediately but wrote again to Venard and put his cards on the table: "It has cost me some money to look the matter up, and it will cost me some more to get him; besides, he is a dangerous man to take, and I do not care to go any further in this matter until I am sure of the $350." The investigation had not cost the financially focused Stillwater police chief any money; rather, Ed apparently could not resist trying to impress a few new friends with his outlaw identity, and one of them had passed the word to Shortall—perhaps to secure a share of any reward money. In any case, the chief got the assurance that he wanted: Venard telegraphed again, "Arrest him; I will be responsible [for paying you the reward]." For the Macomb sheriff, a few days of anxious waiting followed, and then Shortall responded by telegraph: "We have arrested Ed Maxwell; come after him."

Located on the St. Croix River, eighteen miles east of St. Paul, Stillwater was a thriving lumber town, despite the national depression. Along the riverbank it had half a dozen sawmills, employing more than 700 men, who took the timber that was floated down in huge rafts by the logging companies and cut it into boards, for shipping out by railroad. Stillwater also had a few flour mills and an agricultural implement factory—but its chief business was lumber. A boomtown by 1876, it had about 7,000 people and was rapidly growing. As people moved in and shops and homes went up, the demand for carpenters exceeded the supply. In 1874 alone, some 140 buildings had been erected.

Although Stillwater was the Washington County seat, with a handsome courthouse on the hilltop back from the river and a nearby jail, the most imposing institution was the state penitentiary located on the north edge of town. Opened in 1858 as a territorial prison, it had only about one hundred inmates in 1876, but that number would double in two years. The most famous inmates that the prison ever received were Cole, Jim, and Bob Younger, who were captured on September 21, 1876, just two weeks after they and the James brothers had attempted to rob the Northfield, Minnesota, bank. They were sentenced to life imprisonment at Stillwater—where the most famous of the brothers, Cole, was often interviewed and written about. He remained a celebrity outlaw.

The Northfield fiasco, which broke up the original James-Younger gang, leaving three of the bandits dead, the Youngers in captivity, and Jesse and Frank wounded, was the news story of the year in the Midwest, and it must have come to Ed's attention. The Stillwater newspapers carried several articles on the failed robbery, the ensuing manhunt, and the imprisoned Younger brothers—whose life-size, head-image photographs, taken after their capture, were even displayed at the local opera house. Ed was surely rooting for the James brothers, who were still on the loose, heading back to Missouri.

Like so many logging towns, Stillwater had saloons—more than a dozen of them by 1876. Fights and assaults were common, contributing to the four or five hundred arrests in a typical year. There was also a good deal of burglary and, in the nearby countryside, horse stealing.

The most noted local law enforcement officers in Washington County were the Shortall brothers. John, who was often called "Jack," had been born in Kilkenny, Ireland, in 1829. He came to Stillwater in 1856 and served two terms as city marshal in the 1860s before becoming the town's first chief of police in 1870. His brother Matthew, always called "Matt," was seventeen years younger and made an even larger impact. A determined-looking man with a dark, flowing mustache, he was appointed chief of police in 1873, at age twenty-seven, and held the position for twenty years. During that time he became known as "one of the best police officers and detectives in this section of the country," according to the *Stillwater Gazette*.

Fortunately, his first encounter with Ed Maxwell was reported in the *Gazette* too. Ed's desire to be "good with a gun" prompted him to buy, or steal, a .44-caliber Henry repeating rifle, and he was practicing with it on August 26 when Shortall confronted him. Their encounter was treated in a seriocomic way by the reporter:

AN UGLY CUSTOMER

On Saturday evening, as Chief-of-Police Shortall was returning from supper he noticed a stranger down by the seabeat shore of Lake St. Croix practicing with a Henry repeating rifle—using a log for a target. The chief gently remonstrated with the stranger, informing him in the most delicate manner possible that such practices were in contravention of certain city ordinances, and that it would become his painful duty to arrest him, did he not forthwith refrain.

The shootist did refrain, and bringing his rifle to bear upon the astonished officer, he stated in language not to be misunderstood that he didn't propose to allow no son of a son to interfere with him or his innocent diversion.

Matt was dumbfounded. He sought in vain for an opening to "run in" on the man, but the fellow kept him covered, with that wicked eye of his glancing along the polished tube. Matt says it was a mighty handsome gun, but he never saw one he disliked the looks of so much as this one. So he left. That's what Matt did—not because he was afraid, but it chanced to occur to him just then that he had an appointment up town.

Probably when he got up town he was the maddest man in Washington County. Taking unto himself the requisite assistance, he returned, but his victim had departed. If the fellow had been visible then, there would have been blood, sure.

During the entire night the search was kept up, but without success. Who the fellow was is a mystery, though some believe he has been here before, and was once employed in Hersey, Bean, & Brown's [saw]mill.

The mill was located in South Stillwater, between the railroad tracks and the river, and Ed may have worked there for a time when he first came to the area. As events later showed, he was apparently familiar with the sawmills along the river.

This reckless act by Ed was, of course, characteristic of him. He felt so intimidated by authority figures that he turned violent whenever someone tried to dominate him. And confrontations with lawmen and posses were a means of asserting his identity as a desperado—which meant, to him, a man who could not be dominated—so he never avoided them. As with the posse confrontations back in Illinois, Ed did not fire a shot. He was not anxious to kill—just ready to defy, to show his manhood, with a gun.

It is interesting to note that Ed was firing a Henry—a sixteen-shot, lever-action repeating rifle, which had far more firepower than the seven-shot Spencer he and Lon had used in Illinois. And it was amazingly accurate at several hundred yards. The Henry was, in fact, an early version of America's most famous rifle, the Winchester, and Ed's practice with it revealed his fascination with the advancing technology of guns.

The encounter at the riverbank was additional motivation for Chief Shortall, who realized that the stranger who had threatened him with a rifle was the same outlaw that he later heard about from an informant.

Ed's arrest occurred on September 30, right after Sheriff Venard responded by telegraph to Shortall's inquiry about the reward. A week later, the *Stillwater Messenger* gave the details:

> Not long after [the confrontation at the riverbank], Matt received a photograph of a man named Ed Maxwell, who had broken jail in Illinois, which said photograph had a striking resemblance to the man who had held Matt at short range. Our chief never likes to allow a lawbreaker to retain even a temporary advantage over him, and never loses a chance to get even. He kept his eye (figuratively speaking) on this fellow, and learning that he was paying his distresses to a young lady in the town of Denmark, he and Deputy Sheriff Holcombe visited the southern part of the county on Saturday, looking for the lover. By the exercise of a little strategy they surrounded a house in which he was, and nabbed him at a moment when he did not have his trusty rifle in his grasp.
>
> He was brought to this city and, waiving an examination, was committed to jail, where he has since been visited by his inamorata, a Miss Stotesbury, who was not at all pleased with the crooked course of their true love.

The identity of the Stotesbury girl remains unknown, but the only marriageable females in that family in the mid-1870s were Bertha, Sarah, and Lucilla, the daughters of widower William Stotesbury, a farmer from Canada who lived in Denmark Township. Ed later told a Macomb reporter that he was "honestly in love with a girl" in Minnesota, so his interest in the young woman was apparently genuine. The folks in McDonough County even heard that he "expressed . . . intended reformation on account of the love he bore some woman," and that was probably true.

His beloved almost certainly knew nothing about him, however, and was probably shocked to discover that he was a wanted man, an outlaw. An item about the arrest in the *Stillwater Gazette* mentions that "[h]e gave his name as 'Ed Williams,' but his name is Ed Maxwell, whose home is in Missouri, and he is a noted southern desperado, for whose capture a reward of $350 has been offered." So the Stotesbury girl surely knew him as "Ed Williams"—and this is the first public mention of the name under which both Ed and Lon would later achieve national notoriety.

The reference to "Missouri" suggests that Ed told people he was from there, rather than Illinois, to avoid any connection with his actual outlaw past. However, that state was legendary as the home of the James gang and other lawbreakers, and a story soon circulated that the mysterious and rather handsome loner "had shot and stabbed a sheriff in Pike County, Missouri" and that he had come to Minnesota "to live down his past career and try to be a better man." While that may be simply folklore, it is likely that Ed spun that yarn to cast a romantic aura around himself, as a desperado who had, and would, defy the authorities. To Ed, there was no point in being a desperado unless people knew it—and changed their way of looking at you.

Little is known about Ed's activities in Minnesota prior to his arrest. A *Macomb Eagle* article indicates that he went back to laboring as a farmhand: "Maxwell . . . at the time of his capture was working on a farm. He had in his possession nearly seven hundred dollars in money, a good horse, and a watch—which is a fair indication that 'farming' pays up that way. . . ." Of course, the reporter was implying that Ed had also been busy as a robber and horse thief. A Stillwater newspaper commented, too, that he "was always flush with money, jewelry, and good clothes."

If he did work briefly at a sawmill or as a farmhand, his work would have been seasonal, and during the winter of 1875–76, he was probably unemployed. He later told a reporter, "I went to Minnesota, where I . . . passed myself off sometimes as a hunter, stopping in a rural neighborhood; then would go out on hunts."

Oddly enough, he also attended a rural school, despite the fact that he was then twenty-two years old. As he said in an interview, "All last winter I went to a country district school; I behaved myself, acted honorably, and learned." That comment supports the notion that Ed's schooling had been interrupted back in Fulton County, when he had to help his destitute family during and after the Civil War. In Minnesota he probably worked as a mill hand and farmhand during the work seasons, and then hunted in the winter, which gave him time for schooling. It is also possible that the Stotesbury daughter he fell in love with was a schoolteacher, who motivated him to continue his education.

In any case, Ed Maxwell's interest in learning suggests that he was a complex figure, intelligent and literate, and in some ways suited to succeed. But he was also hungry for admiration, resentful of authority, and driven to escape his apparent fate as an impoverished hired hand.

Ed was also striving to end his alienation. By the early fall of 1876 he was clearly making friends among the young people in southern Washington County. The *Macomb Eagle* provides a vivid account of his arrest—which did result from betrayal by a friend, who perhaps had heard the "Missouri desperado" story and had contacted Chief Shortall.

On the night of his arrest, the officers surrounded the premises where Maxwell was stopping, but he with other young men was absent, attending a dance. The officers stationed themselves in the barn where Maxwell and the others were to stable their horses on their return—while the faithless friend with the officers was to point out in the darkness the object of their search.

The dancers returned, the critical moment arrived, but the young man who was to do the pointing out was taken with a weakness in the knees and failed to point, and the officers had to go on guess work. The head officer, a very large, muscular man, "made a dive," and luckily got the right man on the first grab. Then commenced a desperate struggle—the hardest, the officer said, he ever engaged in. They finally got Maxwell floored, with the big, fat officer lying across him, while the other officers put the "wristlets" on him, and he was taken to town and put in jail.

Ed later commented, in an interview, that while at the party that day he "had spent a merry time with the girls," and he must have, for the newspaper also reported that "Maxwell was visited at the jail by numerous sympathizing acquaintances, among them several young ladies, and to one of the latter, Ed made a present of his watch."

The young woman to whom he gave the watch was apparently Miss Stotesbury, and according to a later report, he "confided all his misdeeds" to her, and she told him "to serve out such sentence in prison as might be adjudged proper, and she would be true and wait for his return." That situation is psychologically suggestive—placing Ed's beloved in a kind of parental role, as the source of forgiveness and reacceptance, and intimating that his problems were rooted in childhood anxieties about being reaccepted after failing to measure up. Also, the pocket watch that he presented was a nineteenth-century symbol of masculinity and adulthood, as if to say, "Please view me or remember me as a man."

Another report, in the *Stillwater Lumberman,* asserted that Ed and his beloved were actually engaged: "While in the jail here he was visited by a Miss Stotesbury, of Denmark, who is reported to be engaged to marry him, and between [them] a very affecting scene took place at the jail. Her friends assured her that he would not be taken out of the state. . . ." She was apparently in tears at the thought of separation.

The young woman was also surely distraught because she had to decide who Ed really was—the quiet, courteous outsider, the hired hand and hunter, the man anxious for more schooling at age twenty-two, or the Illinois robber, Ed Maxwell, who was perhaps plying his nefarious trade in

Washington County. Had the law caught up with a man on the mend, who was creating a new life for himself, or with a committed desperado that no one, including herself, could change?

The Stotesbury girl may never have known for sure, but if she did vow to remain true while he was in the penitentiary—which accepting his watch may have indicated—she later changed her mind. Ed was extradited to Illinois and never saw her again.

Macomb constable G. L. Farwell had been sent by Sheriff Venard to bring Ed back from Minnesota, and he was surely the source of the *Eagle's* vivid account of Ed's arrest, having heard about it from Shortall. And Farwell undoubtedly told the Stillwater authorities about Ed's lawbreaking and daring escape back in Illinois. Shortall became so concerned about the possibility that Ed might escape from him, perhaps through the effort of his friends, that he and another officer slipped Ed and constable Farwell out of town at night and took them to a distant train depot. After all, his very considerable reward was at stake.

So fearful were McDonough County officials that Ed might again break jail, or that a mob might lynch him, that arrangements were made to hold his trial on the very day Captain Farwell was scheduled to bring him in. Perhaps the speediest criminal trial in Illinois history was soon recounted by the *Macomb Journal:*

QUICK WORK.
FROM JOLLITY TO JOLIET.

Yesterday a Bold Freebooter,
Today a Prison Convict.
Maxwell's Return to Macomb—
His Trial and Sentence.
The Daring Desperado Interviewed
By a Journal Reporter.

... The news that Captain Farwell would come on Saturday morning drew a large crowd to the depot at train time. The train was over an hour behind; the crowd increased, and when the engine came puffing into the depot, bringing the train and prisoner, there were not less than five hundred persons assembled, so curious were they to see Maxwell. The prisoner, strongly ironed, was escorted by officers to the courthouse.

Such a large turnout, and the excited running and push-
ing of some anxious to see him, tended to alarm Maxwell,
who was really apprehensive that he would be mobbed. He
kept close to the officers, and was glad when once inside
the courtroom.

Court was in session. The prisoner was soon arraigned,
and pleading guilty, in less than two hours after arriving in
town he had been sentenced to the penitentiary for two
years on each of three indictments—six [years] in all. After
the sentence, he was conducted to jail. . . .

Ed's response to the turbulent mob is noteworthy. He would ponder this
event, and his fearful reaction, during his years in prison, reflecting on it
until the very presence of the mob became something quite different—a
verification of his identity as an outlaw. Like the bandit hero Deadwood
Dick, in the first of many dime novels about him, Ed was surprised, and
eventually pleased, "that [he] had attained such desperate notoriety."
What people thought of him always mattered.

Because Ed had become an outlaw celebrity in the McDonough County
area, a "Daring Desperado" whose defiance of the law had made him a kind
of dark hero, the ultimate rebel against authority, everything he did and said
was fascinating to the local public. So, he was interviewed at some length
while in jail awaiting his shipment to the penitentiary. For his part, Ed "was
not only willing, but anxious" to tell his story, living up to public expectations by portraying himself as a bold, resourceful desperado—a man who
was, at least periodically, superior to the forces arrayed against him. Ed's
account of his stunning jailbreak a year earlier is a prime example:

Brother Lon and I had talked the matter over for several days.
At last we let Roberts into the secret. None of the rest knew it.

I was in control of the whole matter. I had intended to break out
the night before, but there was no opportunity.

The night of the break, when the sheriff came in, I was sitting,
all prepared to spring; made a remark to the sheriff to throw him
off his guard, then sprang by him. When I got outside the jail, I
ran north two blocks, then west a couple, then took south. I knew
where the timber was, southwest of town, and struck for it.

Once out of sight of my pursuers, instead of running, I walked
leisurely along, putting my hands in my pockets, whistling as I went

out of town. I did not know at the time if either Lon or [Roberts] escaped.

I traveled some 25 miles that night; made the Mississippi the following night, which I crossed on a log. In the meantime, I had gotten an entire change of clothing (I'll not tell you how . . .).

Next day, I struck a train, passed myself off as a strapped brakeman, and thus went to my people in Iowa.

The closing reference to seeing his "people," his family, in Iowa, demonstrates that David and Susan were still living on a tenant farm that fall, somewhere in Taylor County. Of course, they probably did not know about Ed's escape from jail, or even about the recent, dramatic arrest at Beardstown. Were they also unaware that their sons had turned to robbery and horse stealing? There are no records about their contact with people back in McDonough County. In any case, Ed surely did not tell his parents the whole truth, regardless of what they already knew. And that was the last time he ever saw them.

Ed's account of the escape, which he knew would be printed in a local newspaper, shows that he sought the public's admiration, rather like Jesse James, who often identified himself to victims and even wrote occasional newspaper articles describing his criminal exploits.

In the same interview at the McDonough County Jail, the reporter said that Ed "charged his lawless course in life to too much indulging in yellow-covered literature." In short, he was an avid reader of dime novels, which commonly had yellow covers and celebrated men of daring and violence. But was that perceptive self-criticism or an effort to shift some of the blame for his lawbreaking to a much-decried form of popular culture? Perhaps both.

Whatever the case, those cheap, popular paperbacks would soon focus on a few real-life outlaws, including the James gang, Billy the Kid, and the Maxwell brothers. Although Ed never realized it, his career would help to inspire the outlaw hero in American fiction.

Like many other outlaws, Ed did not regard himself as evil or immoral, but simply as more bold and resolute than most men—as if life had only two choices: Be weak and remain the victim of circumstances, or be forceful and, as he said in his story, exercise "control of the whole matter." And as if to emphasize his good character, Ed told the *Macomb Journal* reporter that he had a reputable code of personal conduct: "He does not smoke, drink, or chew, and seldom swears ('never before women or boys,' he says)." All the records about him support that claim.

The reporter was impressed with Ed, and referred to him as "a nice-appearing, pleasant-spoken little fellow, with manly and winning ways." Of course, Ed had also told the reporter what he wanted to hear—that "he had prayed earnestly for strength to keep him in his determination" to abandon "his former course." Indeed, he had "shed tears more than once during the conversation." While it is possible—perhaps likely—that Ed was truly repentant, and anxious to refocus his life, that state of mind proved to be temporary, for his outlaw career never stopped, except when he was incarcerated.

As the reporter was leaving, Ed stated that he would "behave himself when at Joliet," and he asked the reporter "to tell the people that he will in the future live an honest life." As that suggests, the captured outlaw clearly felt that his life was of interest to "the people." He was no longer a nonentity. And he apparently knew "the people" very well—knew that the same meek, struggling, conventional folks who secretly admired his courageous self-assertion as a desperado also wanted to regard him as a man on the mend, a decent sort of fellow who had seen the error of his ways. And perhaps he was such a person, in the fall of 1876. In any case, there was no harm in letting them think so.

But Ed's dramatic escape from jail had been the crowning act of his spiritual rebirth as a desperado, his triumph over social restraint—the jail, the law, the limited world of his father—for the thrilling freedom of self-formation, a new identity in another place. And now he was headed for a longer stay at Illinois State Penitentiary, which promoted alienation and resentment rather than reform, and where, among the convicts, defiance was admired and escapes made men legendary.

David Maxwell, the father of the outlaws, in his Civil War uniform, 1862. (Courtesy of Gary Jacobsen.)

Susan Maxwell, the mother of the outlaws, during the 1880s in Nebraska. (Courtesy of Gary Jacobsen.)

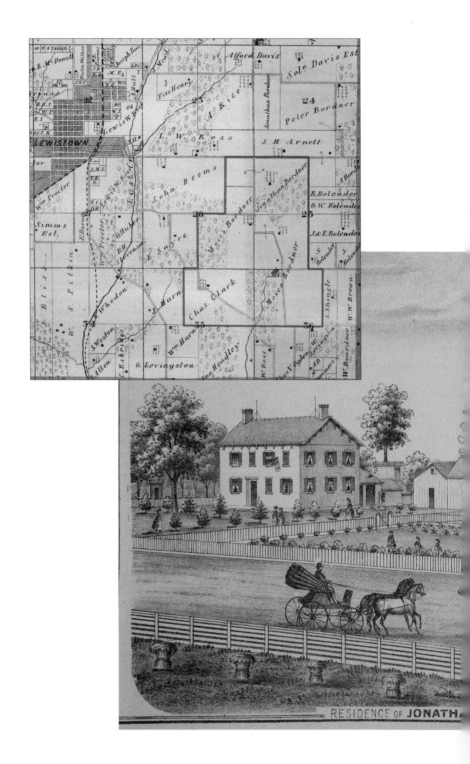

RESIDENCE OF JONATH.

The map [left] shows part of Lewistown Township, southeast of the county seat, where the Maxwell brothers were children during the Civil War. The land owned by Charles Clark and the Bordner brothers is outlined. In the center of that area is the Bordner School, attended by Ed and Lon. (From the 1871 *Atlas Map of Fulton County*.)

Also from the *Atlas* is the lithograph below of the Jonathan Bordner farm, showing the affluence of leading settlers in that neighborhood. The two-story brick farmhouse, built shortly before the Civil War, still stands. The small, two-windowed building just across the yard was probably for hired hands. As this drawing reveals, the possession of many horses symbolized wealth. The Maxwells eventually stole horses from Jonathan's brother, Moses, who had a similar farm.

DNER, SEC. 25, LEWISTON TOWNSHIP

Part of Sec^s 4,5 and 8, Eldorado Town$^{\cdot}$
A BIRDS EYE VIEW ON

Also from the *Atlas*, this lithograph
shows a livestock farm in McDonough
County, illustrating the socioeconomic
difference between wealthy owners, such
as Hicks, and tenants like the Maxwells.
The owner's sizable farmhouse, in the
lower right, is surrounded by a picket
fence and faces a park-like grove of
planted trees, while just above it is a
tenant farmer's small log building, with
a yard planted in vegetable gardens.

The map [opposite] shows McDonough County, west and northwest of Macomb, in the 1870s. The Maxwell tenant farms were probably in Section 4 of Tennessee Township and Section 35 or 36 of Hire Township. The Hicks School, in Section 34, was attended by the Maxwell children. Ed worked as a hired hand southeast of Blandinsville and northwest of Clarksville (now Sciota). (From the 1871 *Atlas Map of McDonough County*.)

Ebenezer Hicks (inset) resided in Section 33 of Hire Township but rented portions of his vast acreage to tenant farmers, including the Maxwells. (*Courtesy of Lawrence M. Kerr.*)

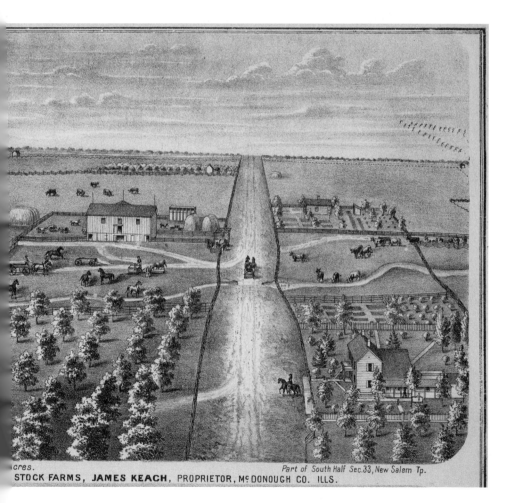

cres.   Part of South Half Sec.33, New Salem Tp.
STOCK FARMS, **JAMES KEACH**, PROPRIETOR, M^cDONOUGH CO. ILLS.

The main street of Blandinsville, where Ed stole some clothing from the Dines Store in 1874, launching his career as a desperado. (From the 1906 *Souvenir of Blandinsville, Illinois*.)

Below: The Splendid McDonough County Courthouse, where the outlaws were tried and convicted—Ed in 1874, Lon in 1875, and Ed again in 1876. (Courtesy of Archives and Special Collections, Western Illinois University Libraries.)

Fulton County sheriff David Waggoner, who pursued the Maxwell brothers in 1875. (Courtesy of John D. Waggoner).

Stillwater, Minnesota, police chief Matthew Shortall, who captured Ed in 1876. (Courtesy of the Washington County, Minn. Historical Society.)

Above is the McDonough County Jail, from which many lawbreakers escaped, including Ed Maxwell in 1875. By the time this photograph was taken in the early 1880s, the building was no longer a jail but had become the Park House Hotel. (Courtesy of Archives and Special Collections, Western Illinois University Libraries.)

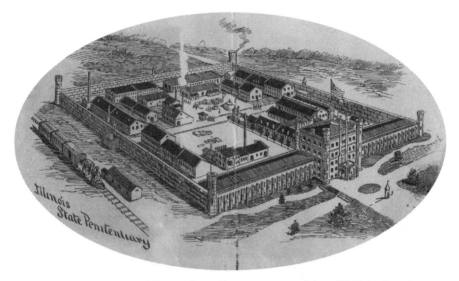

Bird's-eye engraving of Illinois State Penitentiary at Joliet (1860s), showing the cell blocks stretching away from the massive entrance and, within the fifteen-acre enclosure, the stone buildings that housed the various shops. The Chicago, Alton, and St. Louis Railroad is at the left. (Courtesy of the Chicago History Museum [ICHi-51056].)

The penitentiary's boot and shoe shop, where Ed and Lon Maxwell worked during the 1870s. (Courtesy of the American Correctional Association/Illinois Department of Corrections.)

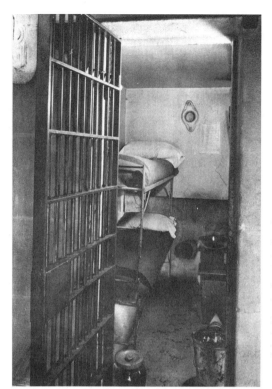

One of the prison's tomb-like cells. Designed for one man, each cell housed two by the later 1870s. A water jug and "slop-bucket" are on the floor. (Courtesy of the Abraham Lincoln Presidential Library.)

Prisoners march in silent lockstep, to or from the shops, under the watchful gaze of a keeper during the late nineteenth century. (Courtesy of the Abraham Lincoln Presidential Library.)

Collage of penitentiary photographs. One of the two huge cell blocks is shown in the center, and below it is the prison's south wall, with the entrance. To the right, above, is an 1878 photograph of outlaw Frank Rande, the most famous inmate of that era. To the left is Rande's half-naked dead body, hanging in his solitary confinement cell (1882). The bottom left image shows inmates mixing in the prison yard, which was only permitted for a few hours on the Fourth of July each year under Warden McClaughry. The lower right image shows women at work in the prison's small female division. (Courtesy of the Abraham Lincoln Presidential Library; from an 1892 book, *Behind the Bars*.)

RANDE THE BANDIT

Warden Robert McClaughry, who
headed the prison for fourteen
years, starting several months after
Ed Maxwell arrived. His efforts to
improve inmate living conditions
and reduce brutal punishments
helped to make him a noted prison
reformer. (Courtesy of the Abraham
Lincoln Presidential Library.)

Ed Maxwell, probably age 27. All known photographs of Ed were taken in the last year of his life, 1881. (Courtesy of John M. Russell.)

Lon Maxwell, at about age 20. Like his brother, he was a nice-looking, polite young man who did not fit the stereotype of the outlaw. (Courtesy of John M. Russell.)

7

✥

Prison Time
and Justice Issues

When Ed Maxwell arrived at the Illinois State Penitentiary on October 9, 1876, the institution was undergoing significant change, and the man behind it all was Warden Robert W. McClaughry, who eventually became one of the best-known criminologists and prison reformers of the nineteenth century.

Oddly enough, McClaughry hailed from the village of Fountain Green in eastern Hancock County, just fifteen miles west of the Maxwell home area in McDonough County, but he belonged to an earlier generation. Born on a farm near that isolated frontier village in 1839, and raised there, he was the son of settlers from New York. Once, when he was barely fourteen, he was "lost in a snowstorm, with his team, on the trackless prairie, and endured a night-long battle with wolves," so he knew the challenges of the frontier—and had the composure to face hostility.

Young McClaughry's country school education was supplemented by studying Latin under the local Presbyterian minister. He later graduated from nearby Monmouth College, in 1860, and then taught Latin there as he pondered his career opportunities. After briefly editing the *Carthage Republican,* at the Hancock County seat, he recruited a company of soldiers for the 118th Illinois Infantry during 1862 and eventually fought near Vicksburg in the Civil War. Elected captain, he was soon promoted to major.

Because of ill health, he spent almost two years working at a Union Army office in Springfield. Afterward, "Major" McClaughry served as Hancock County clerk and pursued business interests in Illinois, Missouri, and Iowa while becoming interested in penal reform.

In July 1874, McClaughry, who had no experience in prison operation, was appointed warden of the troubled Joliet penitentiary, while Ed Maxwell was serving his first term. He immediately began a series of reforms that eventually earned the huge prison a national reputation—and probably the thanks of many inmates.

Among his practical changes were improvements in prison cleanliness, which included mattresses and frequently washed sheets, replacing the straw beds and coarse blankets (changed only twice a year) that had been customary for each cell. McClaughry also strove to improve the cell-block ventilation and the heating system. Moreover, he tore down the huge stockade that had been built four years earlier to contain unruly prisoners.

But the most important change was his development of "a new penology, based on psychological study of the criminal and remedial, instead of purely retributive, punishment," as one newspaper put it. Sidney Wetmore, a Joliet inmate (1874–76) who was imprisoned when the Maxwells were there and who later worked for McClaughry, pointed out in *Behind the Bars at Joliet* that "he also abolished the dark-cell, the 'bull ring,' and other ways of subduing the men, and by a system of privileges granted for good conduct, he greatly improved the condition of affairs left by his predecessors."

Although treatment of the inmates did improve, Wetmore was being overly positive. Some "brutal and capricious punishments" continued, perhaps without McClaughry's knowledge. After all, the prison staff was used to handling the men harshly. In 1878, for example, one black prisoner was repeatedly whipped and, later, killed by a keeper who forcibly gagged him until he couldn't breathe. An investigation, never released to the public, soon turned up many other instances of brutality, especially involving prisoners held in solitary confinement.

In any case, McClaughry had a more enlightened view than his predecessors. He regarded no prisoner as an incorrigible evildoer or brute, and knew that men were enormously influenced by their circumstances, experiences, and opportunities. As Wetmore once said, "Major McClaughry sought to give each inmate an aim in life, and to start him on the road to respectability, with a chance to gain an honest living." With that in mind, he greatly enlarged the prison library, encouraged the development of work skills, hired a prison schoolteacher, and placed a slate and chalk in each cell, so those who wanted to learn could pursue basic studies. He also permitted inmates to receive a weekly newspaper. Ed Maxwell subscribed to the *Macomb Eagle,* the paper that had once labeled him a budding desperado.

In October 1876—the very month that Ed arrived—the *Joliet Signal* summed up McClaughry's impact after two years: "Our ever popular and gentlemanly Warden has by his indefatigable efforts raised the prison to a higher standard of excellence in all its departments than it has ever attained before." Although Illinois State Penitentiary was still a harsh, overly repressive institution, it was better than many other American prisons.

After Ed and Lon left Joliet, McClaughry started photographing new prisoners and initiated the Bertillon method of recording in detail a convict's physical features—both innovative identification procedures. He was later influential in promoting fingerprint identification, which was adapted from British authorities at Scotland Yard. McClaughry was also a prison reformer in Pennsylvania (1888–91), the Chicago superintendent of police during the World's Fair era (1891–94), the warden of the new federal penitentiary at Leavenworth (1899–1913), and the president of the National Prison Association (1899–1903). Joliet was simply the beginning of his remarkable career, which culminated in national acclaim.

Ed and Lon must have been acquainted with the talented prison reformer—a handsome, bearded man, with smiling gray eyes and reddish-brown hair, who had just turned thirty-five when he came to Joliet. He was a parentlike but stern leader who prided himself on knowing many of the convicts personally.

But the young warden was also extremely busy managing an overcrowded institution, which was feeling the economic stress of the 1870s depression. Designed for a thousand inmates, Illinois State Penitentiary had 1,520 males and a few dozen females when Ed arrived in the fall of 1876, and within two years the population briefly hit 1,900—the highest number in the prison's history—before starting to decline as another Illinois prison opened at Chester. Two inmates to a cell was then almost universal throughout the prison.

And despite McClaughry's leadership, the penitentiary was still a tense and turbulent place. Within days of Ed's arrival, for example, six prisoners escaped, only four of whom were eventually recaptured. In the summer of 1877, a "general outbreak" of perhaps two hundred prisoners was narrowly avoided when one inmate leaked the plans to a keeper, and some twenty ringleaders ended up in solitary confinement.

Lon had been processed on October 8, 1875, and was prisoner 9318. As Ed had done in 1874, Lon asserted that he was "temperate" (a nondrinker) but professed no religion, and he listed his occupation as "farmer." He was only seventeen.

In the spring of 1877, six months after Ed had returned to Joliet, McClaughry approved the request of Ed and Lon to become cell mates, a privilege that surely came with good behavior, and could be withdrawn, so they were not troublesome convicts.

In many ways, the Maxwells were typical Joliet prisoners of the 1870s. They were young, and most of the inmates were in their twenties or late teens. A few were as young as fourteen—an improvement from the 1860s, when some boys as young as ten were incarcerated there. Also, like the Maxwells, most were serving sentences for larceny (which included horse stealing), burglary, and robbery. And most inmates had sentences of five years or less. With good behavior, a man serving a five-year sentence could be out in three years and nine months. The majority of the inmates were also serving their first or second term.

Moreover, as one might expect, most of the penitentiary inmates were poor. Their economic struggle, and the social rejection that often went with it, prompted them to disobey the law, and the same factors commonly caused a lack of sympathy for them on the part of their social superiors. As one scholar has put it, "Criminal justice [in the nineteenth century] was the strong arm of the stratification system. It was part of the process that made subordination real."

Also, as the "Convict Register" for 1870–75 reveals, there were many inequities in the prison sentences, which fostered a widespread feeling among the inmates that the justice system was, in fact, unjust. When Ed was at Joliet, there were men serving twenty-five- or thirty-year terms, and even life terms, for murder, while others convicted of the same crime had only one-year sentences.

The most famous Joliet inmate during the 1870s—and perhaps the century—was Frank Rande, a desperado whose real name was Charles C. Scott. Born in Pennsylvania and raised partly in Iowa, he was a short, muscular, and rather handsome man, with dark brown hair, a short full beard, and piercing brown eyes. In the late 1860s he had tramped the country as an itinerant worker before turning to theft, and he was imprisoned for a time at Northern Indiana State Penitentiary. In 1877, following a farmhouse robbery near Gilson, in Knox County, Rande was pursued by a posse, and he shot one man dead and wounded three others. Soon afterward, he killed two other men and wounded two more in a Fayette County gunfight. He was eventually captured at a pawn shop in St. Louis, where he also killed an officer and was himself severely wounded. A famous outlaw by then, Rande was tried in Galesburg and sentenced to life in prison at Joliet.

By the time he arrived, on February 23, 1878, Lon had been released, but Ed surely knew of Rande from the *Macomb Eagle,* which had reported his capture on page one, declaring his crimes "the most daring and desperate deeds of blood that have occurred in the country since the terrible days of the guerilla warfare on the border." Moreover, Rande was already the subject of one hastily written true-crime book, Stephen R. Smith's *A Journalist's Account of the Outlaw Rande,* which had appeared before his trial was even concluded. The front cover featured a photograph of the famous desperado with one pistol in his hand and another tucked into his belt. Like Jesse James, and for that matter, Ed Maxwell, Rande enjoyed his notoriety, and he had the photograph taken so he could sell copies to curious thrill-seekers who came to his trial. On the back of each *carte de visite* copy was a printed inscription: "Frank Rande, the Great Bandit of the West."

Ed may not have met Rande, but he must have heard about him within the penitentiary, for it was full of rumors about his robberies, jailbreaks, and gunfights. One newspaper had referred to him as "The American Brigand," and another had called him "The Brilliant and Daring Bandit of the Wabash," labels that Rande was proud to repeat. Also, both Joliet newspapers carried articles on Rande's conviction and subsequent arrival at the penitentiary. One official there asserted that he was almost as famous as Jesse James, and according to prison rumor, he was "said to have killed altogether sixteen different persons"—an exaggeration, much like the folk mind would also develop to dramatize the deadly gunfighting of Billy the Kid.

Four years after Ed's release, Rande attacked and nearly killed McClaughry's assistant, Deputy Warden James McDonald, and severely wounded a guard by wielding an iron poker in the harness shop. During the fracas that followed, he was bludgeoned and shot, but he survived. A week later, on March 7, 1884, Rande was found hanging in his solitary confinement cell. His death was quickly ruled a suicide, although he had never been suicidal and, after the attack, had been despised by the prison guards. Rande's dead body, hanging half-naked in his cell, was later featured on an Illinois State Penitentiary collage-type postcard—a final testament to his notoriety.

Ed served two years with the self-styled "Great Bandit of the West," and if he ever dreamed of becoming more notorious than Frank Rande, his dream would eventually come true.

During the 1860s and 1870s, a large number of the Joliet Penitentiary inmates sought and received pardons. The public wanted to believe that criminals would change their ways if given the chance, and state officials were anxious to relieve the overcrowding at Joliet—and reduce the costs of incarceration—so pardons were fairly common, even for some criminals who were clearly dangerous.

In Fulton County, for example, Isaac Harris, who lived near Vermont, clubbed a man to death in 1860, was convicted of manslaughter, and was sent to Joliet for fifteen years, but he was pardoned after serving just one year. A few years later, in 1863, two Fulton County men convicted of horse stealing were sentenced to Joliet for five years and were pardoned in 1864 and 1865. Ex-convict John Yarnell, who killed Lewistown Marshal James Goodwin in 1867, was convicted of murder and sentenced to Joliet for fourteen years, but was pardoned only eighteen months later.

Hundreds of similar pardons were granted during the years when the Maxwell brothers lived in Illinois. In his 1876 "Warden's Report," for example, McClaughry indicated that 179 men and three women had been pardoned during the past two years.

One example of the governor's pardon authority that surely came to Ed's attention was the case of outlaw John Tuggle, of McDonough County. Next to the Maxwell brothers, he was the most disturbing and violent desperado in the county's history. A muscular six-footer with uncombed brown hair and piercing gray eyes, he was just seventeen in 1872 when he was first convicted and sentenced to three months in the county jail for horse stealing. He came to widespread public attention in September 1876 when he and his younger brother Charles robbed some stores in their hometown, Industry, about twelve miles south of Macomb. They were soon pursued by a posse, and Charles was arrested, as was Ed Avery, an accomplice who had stored the stolen goods. Shot in the hip during a gun battle with Sheriff Venard, John Tuggle escaped. Several days later, while Tuggle was stopping at a farmhouse near the southern border of the county, three men recognized him and struggled in a long fight to subdue him, eventually shooting him in the head at close range.

Authorities brought in the twice-wounded desperado, who was still virtually unmanageable, according to a *Macomb Journal* report: "He walked around his cell like a caged beast, and swore, and went on in a terrible manner. He said that it was his intention to have killed Higgins and his son, and Robinson [the three who subdued him], and but for the son's shooting him he would have broke loose and killed all of them." During his days on the run, Tuggle told a friend that he had actually been stalking the posse, hoping to kill Sheriff Venard, who had wounded him. It was Tuggle's open defiance of the law, much like Ed Maxwell's, that earned him the labels "outlaw" and "desperado."

The Tuggle brothers were soon convicted of burglary. John, the instigator of their lawbreaking, was sentenced to six years and Charles to four, at Joliet. Avery received a shorter sentence. According to a Macomb newspaper account, the older, more violent Tuggle swore that he would kill Sheriff Venard as soon as he got out.

Ed Maxwell would have been well aware of those three violent lawbreakers, for they were jailed with him and their cases came up in the same circuit court term. In fact, Sheriff Venard took them to the penitentiary along with Ed on October 9, 1876.

During that period of time, John Tuggle and Ed may have realized that they had much in common—aside from the fact that they were the same age. The older son of a poor tenant farmer who had served in the Civil War, John was orphaned at eleven, "leaving him in the hands of strangers," as one report said, and he was valued primarily for his capacity to work. For him, too, life must have seemed bleak and unpromising. Alienated, frustrated, and rebellious, he had drawn his "kind hearted, fair haired," and emotionally dependent younger brother into lawbreaking, much like Ed had done with Lon.

Charles Tuggle died in prison, on June 6, 1878, and two years later, people who had known John since childhood organized an effort to secure a pardon for him, which was granted on October 8, 1880, while Ed was still at Joliet. Then Tuggle returned to McDonough County, where he supposedly stalked ex-Sheriff Venard and soon shot two men on the street in Colchester. Sent back to Joliet for six years, he died there in 1885.

The prevalence of pardons also contributed to the eruption of lynching in some counties after the Civil War. In Tazewell County, along the Illinois River east of Peoria, public anger over easy pardons contributed to the lynching of Bill Berry, leader of the infamous Berry gang of horse thieves and robbers, on August 1, 1869. He had been indicted as an accessory to the murder of Deputy Sheriff Henry Pratt—even though he had not been involved but simply headed the gang—and no one wanted him to serve just a short sentence, which would probably result from conviction-and-pardon. Other members of the gang who were later convicted as accessories were sent to Joliet, but were pardoned in the mid-1870s—much to the dismay of local residents.

In October 1875, in Mason County, just south of Tazewell, another lynching occurred that was explicitly related to the pardon issue. A well-known horse thief and robber named Beurope Pemberton, who had served two terms in the state penitentiary, was seized by "a vigilance committee" and hanged for horse stealing "even though no evidence was brought forward to convict him." A Bloomington newspaper account, titled "LYNCH LAW IN ILLINOIS," summed up the underlying reason for the mob violence: "Mason and Tazewell counties have never punished severely a criminal—except by mob law—but that he has been freed by the governor in a short time after his sentence; and so the citizens boldly proclaim that Lynch law is the only law in Mason County, and in Tazewell County things are no better. . . ." The *Havana Republican* made a similar comment on the Pemberton lynching: "This is the fault of mock [i.e., inept, unjust] trials, and more than all else, of Executive Pardons. It is next to impossible to convict anybody of a high crime, and difficult to insure the execution of a sentence when it is passed. No wonder Lynch law and mob violence prevail."

If lawbreakers as violent as John Tuggle and Isaac Berry, and as committed to crime as Beurope Pemberton, could get pardons, it is not surprising that many, if not most, inmates at Joliet in the 1870s made some effort to secure one. The 1872 committee report on conditions at the penitentiary commented that "[t]he facilities for obtaining pardons . . . have been such that [a pardon] has become the great central thought in the mind of the convict from the time of his conviction; this is the subject of the majority of their letters. . . ." And that was true of the Maxwell brothers.

Three of their prison letters found their way into the *Macomb Journal,* and all three are focused on obtaining a pardon for Ed, who had a much longer sentence than Lon. The earliest one, addressed to a farmer near Blandinsville who had been robbed by the Maxwells, appeared on March 22, 1877, under a title that implies the editor's skepticism about Ed's reformation:

"OUR ED,"
WHICH REFERS TO MAXWELL,
THE FREE-BOOTER.
A Letter from Him to One of
Our County Citizens.

Joliet, Ill., March 4, '77

To Mr. John B. Isom, Blandinsville, Ill.:

Dear Friend: I, this beautiful Sabbath morning, take the pleasure of writing to you, hoping that this will find yourself and family and friends enjoying the best of health, and prospering, as this leaves me the same and, most of all, a better man, with a fixed purpose to be one hereafter; and I sincerely hope that you and Mr. Carlisle, and all others who know me, will forgive me for all my cruel and unjust acts, toward you and all others, that I have committed, and that you will not feel too hard on me for what I have done, even though I could not blame any of you if you did. . . .

And, Mr. Isom, many a bitter tear I have shed in my lonely cell for my past conduct toward my fellow men, and the distress and grief I have caused my poor mother and father, who even now do not know where I am, for I fear to tell them, for it might be the means of my losing poor mother, whose health is not good, for I know she would take it to heart very much to know that her two sons were here, and me for so long a term, who ought to be at home helping them instead of being here. My brother gets letters from home, and that is the way I get to hear from them.

But then, how often do we regret a wrong after it is committed. Yet, if I could recall any past conduct, willingly would I have done so long before now. But, as it is, I shall try to do better hereafter. That Bible, that you and Mr. G. W. Hainline gave me as a present, I still have, and every night, after my work is done, I read a chapter in it—not for appearances, but for my own good—and I pray to Him, giver of all good and perfect gifts, who we must all look to in time of need. I care not who makes fun of me for it.

I see the error of my ways. If I had not got into bad company I would not be where I am. It appears that at just the time I needed good associates, I fell in with bad ones, and from little [bad deeds] to worse, have come to the Penitentiary. I sincerely hope that all the young men who were once my associates will take care and shun all bad company, for we are all led astray ere we "swear off" [bad company].

I am in the shoe shop, siding boots, and do from 18 to 14 pair per day. My brother is lasting [i.e., shaping the upper portion of] shoes. He is working in another shop, and I cannot get to speak to him. I see him about every day at a distance. I never look at him but what I think of my past conduct, and it makes me feel very wretched indeed. We get to go to church [together] every other Sunday.

There are a great many of us here together—about 1,850 in all—and a great many of them are pardoned and quite a number have had their sentences lessened by the Governor of the State, and I often wish I hadn't acted as I did, and then I might have had friends to help me too, in time of need. But I still hope that you will have mercy on me for once, and Mr. Isom, if I should get my lawyer to try to get my sentence shortened, would you and Mr. Carlisle be willing to sign it to help me? I don't think I deserve a pardon, so will not ask for one. I would like to have my time lessened, so I could do some good for myself and others, and not have to spend the best years of my life in here. I would promise faithfully to do what was right hereafter, both Lon and I. Please talk to Mr. Carlisle for me and ask him to forgive me for what I have done, and [ask] if he will help me in this. I do not want any of you to think that I hold any malice against any of you at all for anything.

If you see Mr. Samuel Cullum, give him my best respects, as also to all other inquiring friends. I hope to hear from you soon. . . .

I remain your true and sincere friend.

E. Maxwell

This carefully crafted letter touches a variety of topics designed to arouse the sympathy and support of Isom, from Ed's appeal for forgiveness and claim of spiritual reformation, to his frequent prayers to God and Bible reading—and even his need to reconnect with his ailing mother and his cruel separation from Lon. Clearly, the Bible given to Ed by John Isom and G. W. Hainline had prompted Ed to approach Isom as a person who might be persuaded to help. Both men were prosperous farmers in northwest Hire Township, a few miles east of Blandinsville, where Ed had worked as a hired hand. J. E. Carlisle, also mentioned by Ed, owned a farm nearby. They all lived in the rural neighborhood between Blandinsville and Sciota where Ed had become known—and where he later raided farmhouses. ("Samuel Cullum," apparently the newspaper's error in transcription for Samuel Pullam, refers to a neighbor in southern Hire Township, near the David Maxwell tenant farm.)

Of course, the letter was designed to challenge Isom, and other Christians who might read it, to live up to the ideal of forgiveness—and to act on their belief that God could, in fact, reform a lawbreaker like Ed. Although the letter may reflect aspects of Ed's spiritual struggle in prison, it is so carefully contrived to achieve a desired impact that it seems more self-serving than repentant. Ed casts himself into the socially approved role, so common in

Christian storytelling, of the youth who fell into "bad company" and was led astray, but who now sees, as his trite comment says, "the error of my ways." But Ed's claim that others led him astray is puzzling because he never identifies those "associates" or says anything specific about them. And he later tells Isom that he has no friends to help him.

Another compelling self-image, bound to evoke a positive response, is that of the Bible-reading convict, struggling to reform himself, who is ridiculed by other inmates for doing so. "I care not who makes fun of me for it," he says—but everything we know about Ed suggests that he would have been driven to fit in at the penitentiary, to be regarded as "up to snuff" by the other inmates. For so many incarcerated men, prison life was an outward performance, designed to evoke the appearance of reformation, and that was probably what Ed was enacting in his letter—which he knew would also be read by prison officials before it was mailed.

The most touching part of Ed's letter is his reference to separation from Lon, the one person with whom he had a deep bond. If he did feel "very wretched" when he saw Lon at a distance in the shoemaking shop, perhaps he reflected that, in Lon's case, he himself was the "bad company" who had led his younger brother astray.

In any case, the letter was effective enough to prompt a response from Isom (which does not survive), saying that he would help, which in turn caused Ed to write him again. This time he signed both his name and Lon's, for Warden McClaughry had just given permission for the brothers to "cell" together:

> I. S. P., Joliet, Ill.
> May 13, 1877
>
> Mr. [John B.] Isom.
>
> Dear Friend: I received your very kind and welcome letter and was exceedingly glad to hear from you. Lon and I are both well and sincerely hope that this will find you and your family and all friends enjoying the same blessing. I am very thankful to you indeed for offering to help me in my present position, after I have so wrongfully misused you. My mind was greatly relieved to hear that the good people of McDonough County do not feel so unforgiving toward me as I supposed. I truly feel very sorry for my past conduct, and if ever I am forgiven and helped from here, I will try and do right in the future, for this has learned me a lesson, if I did have to pay dearly for it. . . .

Lon and I are celling together now. I have plenty of time to talk to him. He thinks we acted foolishly in doing what we did, and perhaps it was the best thing that could have happened to us, in getting here right in the start [of our outlaw career], for if we had gone on much longer, we would have been as bad as the Younger brothers and the James boys. In one or two months longer we would, no doubt, have tackled a bank. But I am glad we never got that far along, for as you say, we often dash down in an instant what it will take years to build up. . . .

All the means [money] that I have got to go on is what [my lawyer] Tunnicliff has. . . . If he is willing to undertake to help me, [for] what [money] he has of mine, and get your kind assistance, and Mr. Carlisle's and Mr. Pullam's, I feel assured of a commutation of my present position, but if he does not, then I can do nothing more, unless Lon can collect what is due me in Minnesota. . . .

You spoke of sending us something to read. We would be very thankful if you would send books, or some good Sunday school papers, and we will take good care of them and send them back again.

I will close now for the present, while we remain your true and faithful friends.

Ed and Lon Maxwell

Surely the most revealing comment in this letter is Ed's view of himself and Lon as potential rivals to the "Younger brothers and the James boys." Although he was trying to make Isom believe that a truly notorious outlaw career had been stopped just in time, the remark shows that Ed was well aware of those famous desperadoes—who were, in fact, identity models for him, if not for Lon as well. While Ed may have been seeking a pardon to continue his quest for outlaw notoriety, he may have been reassessing things, too, and reaching out to see if reintegration with society was even possible. A pardon effort, showing at least some sympathetic interest in him, would have kept that possibility open.

That the Maxwell brothers were sharing the same cell by the spring of 1877 was also important to their destiny, for that allowed Ed to continue his impact—perhaps his domination—of Lon, who was still only eighteen. If Ed's deepest motivation was to end his sense of inadequacy and, per-haps, shame as an undersized, impoverished failure by shaping a Jesse James–like identity as a daring desperado, Lon's motivation throughout his life was clearly to be a comrade, and an equal, to his older brother, who had been his role model, and perhaps his protector, throughout his childhood and youth. A sensitive, mild-mannered youngster who might strike others as effeminate would be likely to need the acceptance and protection that Ed, who really did love him, always provided.

Realizing that Lon would soon be released, Ed mentioned in the letter that his brother might "collect what is due me [for work] in Minnesota," revealing that they had discussed that errand for Lon. Ed had also surely told him about his adventures while on the run for more than a year, and about the logging boom and money flowing in the north. It is not surprising that Lon eventually went there.

Before his release, Lon also wrote a letter aimed at obtaining a pardon for Ed. It was addressed to C. C. Hays, who had arrested them and had succeeded Josephus Venard as the sheriff of McDonough County. Hays did not respond, so Lon wrote a second time, on his nineteenth birthday, and that letter was printed on page one of the *Macomb Journal,* on June 28, 1877. In it, the teenage outlaw asserts that Ed "is sincerely repentant of his past conduct," wants to "live the life of a quiet, inoffensive citizen," and "will lead a better life hereafter." Then he asks the sheriff to help by "having several of the most influential men of McDonough County ready to sign a pardon [request] for him."

Sheriff Hays probably did not respond to Lon's second letter either, and he surely did not act to seek a pardon for Ed. Neither did lawyer Damon G. Tunnicliff. The McDonough County authorities knew that Ed could be dangerous, and if he were released early and then returned to robbery and defiance of the law, they would feel partly responsible. Hays may have been cordial to young Lon at the jail, which probably prompted the teenage lawbreaker to write him, but the sheriff also recalled his fierce struggle with Ed in Beardstown and the attempted escape at Bushnell, so he was surely glad the more notorious older brother was imprisoned.

Besides, by 1877 Sheriff Hays was having his own problems. Because of the frequent and embarrassing prisoner escapes in McDonough County, officials had constructed a new jail in 1876. Located two blocks west of the square, on Jackson Street, near the old log "calaboose" that was still serving as Macomb's city jail, it was an imposing, two-story, red-brick structure that had an office, twenty-four small cells, a dining hall, bathrooms, and eight rooms for the sheriff's family. Built at a cost of $26,000, it seemed an impregnable fortress of law and order.

Several prisoners were transferred to the new jail on November 27, 1876, and in January Hays moved in with his family—a wife and two children.

At the same time, community leaders proudly showed the formidable new facility to visiting law officers, undoubtedly pleased that their town was finally transcending its reputation as the jailbreak capital of western Illinois.

Unfortunately, the long tradition of local escapes and the challenge of the modern, much-celebrated facility were too strong for some prisoners to resist. There were two jailbreak attempts in December, and then, on the evening of February 2, 1877, four men did escape. Those prisoners were never recaptured, and the reputation of Sheriff Hays slipped into an irreversible decline. This escape occurred only weeks before Lon sent his first letter asking Hays to help get a pardon for Ed, the county's most notorious criminal and jailbreaker.

In the next year or so, three more jailbreaks occurred while Hays was sheriff, so the former hero of the 1875 Maxwell manhunt was increasingly criticized for being negligent—and was, in fact, censured by the county's Board of Supervisors, who also hired a jailer to assist him. The *Macomb Independent* concluded that "the escape of prisoners has made the Hays administration a disgraceful one." At the same time, the imposing new jail had become "a laughing stock in all the neighboring counties," as the *Macomb Eagle* put it.

Things got even worse for Hays in September 1878. The embarrassed, anxiety-ridden sheriff discharged his revolver to intimidate a prisoner and accidentally killed a seventeen-year-old youth in another cell who was being held for attempted burglary. That occurred at an unfortunate time for Hays because he was up for reelection. In November the hero-turned-embarrassment was soundly defeated, and as one local commentator put it, "he was so chagrined and disgusted [that] he disposed of his possessions and moved to one of the Dakotas. . . ."

The new sheriff was Winslow Taylor, a former shopkeeper from Industry whose father had served as sheriff in the 1850s. But he had no better luck than his predecessor. On March 1, 1879, no less than seven prisoners escaped from the new jail, including Zack Wilson, a gun-toting, small-time desperado who was awaiting trial, on a change of venue from Hancock County, for killing a man named Thomas McDonald in a gunfight at nearby Plymouth in August 1876. A hastily organized posse tracked down six of the escapees, but Wilson was never recaptured.

In several other cases, killers in the county were apprehended and brought to trial but were not convicted. As the editor of the *Macomb*

Journal remarked after one of those trials, "It has grown into a proverb that 'a man cannot be convicted of murder in McDonough.' . . ." And in 1879 the *Macomb Eagle* editor summed up the public view: "The frequent cold-blooded murders in this part of Illinois, and the trickery of lawyers and perjury of witnesses, who save the necks of the very worst villains, [are] not calculated to satisfy the people, who clamor for justice and for the punishment of crime."

Beyond that, horse stealing was on the rise in McDonough County, partly because the breeding of horses had emerged as a major enterprise since the war, increasing both the value and the number of available animals, and partly because the continuing hard times brought more tramps and other outsiders into the area. And few of the thieves were being caught. As the *Macomb Eagle* said in the summer of 1877, "Horse thieves are doing a thriving business in some parts of the county."

It is not surprising that at least two Anti–Horse Thief Association (AHTA) chapters were organized in McDonough County to help protect rural people from "horse thieves, house thieves [robbers], tramps, and cut-throats," who had become "so bold and numerous in this vicinity that the law-abiding citizens were almost compelled to take the law into their own hands," as one chapter leader put it. In some other counties, Anti–Horse Thief Associations even asserted the right "to hang a culprit on the most convenient limb." By 1880, Illinois had well over one hundred AHTA chapters—and the state headquarters for those groups was at Bushnell, just fifteen miles from Macomb.

Small wonder that as the troubled and violent 1870s drew to a close, McDonough County residents did not respond to the pleas of the Maxwell brothers for initiating a pardon effort for Ed, the young robber and horse thief, the dangerous desperado, despite the fact that pardon requests of all kinds were commonly granted by the governor. The public's lack of interest, except perhaps for the kindly Mr. Isom, probably further embittered Ed, who felt, at least much of the time, that people were uncaring and oppositional to him anyway. As he spent his long, hard, pointless days in the penitentiary—that dungeon of alienation, deprivation, and despair—he was surely reminded that the cards were always stacked in favor of people with some social standing, with connections in the place where they lived. In that way, Ed's prison experience validated his identity as an outsider— and made him psychologically prepared to again defy them all.

8

Lon's Struggle to Go Straight

Lon was released from the penitentiary on July 8, 1877, shortly after his nineteenth birthday. His "good behavior" had resulted in a three-month reduction of his two-year sentence. Like Ed in 1875, he was given ten dollars, a train ticket to Macomb, and a new suit of clothes—but his was a less institutional-looking outfit, designed to help a newly released man avoid being pegged immediately as an ex-con. That was another of Warden McClaughry's reforms.

It is likely that Lon stopped in Macomb only long enough to buy a ticket for Nebraska. He knew that his parents were homesteading on the prairie in the south-central part of the state. By rail, he could travel to Omaha, then west along the Platte River to Hastings, and then he could walk southwest for twenty miles to their sod house.

Nebraska was a new state, established in 1867, and like Kansas it was attracting large numbers of settlers during the 1870s. In the two years following Lon's release, 100,000 new settlers arrived, many of them no doubt attracted by the glowing reports of fertile, well-watered prairie land (especially east of the 100th meridian) that was ideal for growing grain or raising livestock. And it was available for nothing but a registration fee, plus some hard work, under the provisions of the Homestead Act.

The Maxwells had settled in Adams County, which was composed largely of gently rolling prairie lying just south of the wide but shallow Platte River. From 1848 to 1871, the most well-known place in that region was Fort Kearney, located in what later became Kearney County, just west of Adams. That noted military post, two hundred miles west of Omaha, protected nearby settlers from the Indians and guarded wagon trains and stagecoaches that moved along the great Platte River Road, extending across Nebraska to the Missouri River. During the pre–Civil War period, the fort was often called "the gateway to the Great Plains."

Adams County was organized right after the fort was discontinued, in December 1871. At that time it had only twenty-nine voters and their families, but by 1880, it would have 10,235 residents, including the Maxwells. Throughout the 1870s, canvass-topped prairie schooners, bringing in more settlers, were a common sight, and the new railroad was a marvel, launching an era of massive cultural transformation.

In 1875 David Maxwell entered a claim on a 160-acre homestead in Logan Township, in the sparsely inhabited southwest corner of the county. The closest hamlet was a place called Osco, several miles west, in Kearney County. A post office had been established there in 1875, and probably only a few sod houses were already built in that vicinity when David and Susan arrived. Because they received their mail at Osco, the Maxwells were sometimes misidentified in the newspapers as residents of Kearney County. Osco did not develop into a small village until the 1880s, and Logan Township had no communities, so there may have been no school for the Maxwell children to attend, at least for awhile.

After some two dozen years as late-coming tenant farmers, who had always arrived after the first settlers had established themselves and land prices had gone up, David and Susan Maxwell had finally ventured onto the raw frontier. They were among the original settlers in Adams County, and the land was free—if they could stick it out.

Like so many other homesteaders, the Maxwells immediately constructed a sod house—a habitation that had certain drawbacks, including dirt floors and walls, and trickles of muddy water that came through the roof during heavy rains. It was also difficult to keep insects and even snakes out of a "soddie," and it was always dark inside, simply because the walls were so thick and there were few windows. But that unique kind of building was remarkably cool in summer and was almost impervious to the cold wind that characterized the Nebraska winters.

Whatever its shortcomings, their sod house was the first place that David and Susan Maxwell ever owned, and surrounded as it was by land they were acquiring, it surely symbolized the more promising life that had eluded them for so long.

During their early years of struggle, along with the arduous task of establishing a farm, the Maxwells were also faced with a variety of hazards—including prairie fires, blizzards, and rattlesnakes. But the most pressing problem for most Nebraska homesteaders was a lack of fuel on the almost treeless plains, and many youngsters—no doubt George, John, and Jimmie Maxwell among them—were assigned the chore of gathering buffalo chips, which burned well if they remained dry.

David proved his claim and received his deed early in 1880. Fortunately, a brief newspaper article about the Maxwell family appeared less than two years later, in the *Hastings Nebraskan,* after the exploits of Ed and Lon had drawn national attention:

THE MAXWELLS

... They live on a homestead near Osco, Kearney County, Nebraska, in a neatly built sod house, 18 x 25 feet, with a shingled roof and board floors. Everything about the premises denotes thrift and industry.

There are three boys younger than Ed and Lon, and they are sprightly lads, with no trace of the desperado or daredevil in their appearance. All the members of the family stand well in the estimation of their neighbors, the father being superintendent of a Sunday school in his vicinity. The mother and sister are among the most respected ladies in the neighborhood. ...

The shingled roof and wooden floor of their sod house were probably improvements that David had added when he had the time and the money.

The 1881 article on the Maxwells mentions only three sons, but David and Susan had four small boys when they arrived. Their deepest tragedy came in 1879, when seven-year-old Jimmie died. The *Juniata Herald,* published in a frontier village a few miles west of Hastings, carried his brief obituary: "Died.—At the residence of David D. Maxwell, in Adams Co., Neb., March 23, 1879, James D., son of David D. and Susan Maxwell, aged seven years, three months, and eight days. Jimmie was loved by all who knew him, but his play days are over, his feet are still. He sleeps under the flowers of Nebraska." The article does not indicate what caused Jimmie's death, but in that winter there was a bad diphtheria epidemic that killed many children.

The brief 1881 article on the Maxwells also mentions only one sister. That was Flora, age nineteen. Alice was twenty-four, and she had been married for five years, to William E. Thorne, the elected surveyor of nearby Webster County. Flora, who did not marry until 1891, apparently left home soon after Jimmie's death, perhaps to live with her sister, who already had two children, or to work as a domestic helper—much like Antonia Shimerda in Willa Cather's famous Nebraska novel, *My Antonia.*

The 1880 federal census for Silver Lake Precinct, Logan Township, Adams County, Nebraska, lists only David, Susan, and their remaining sons: George, age fourteen; John, age eleven, and Charles ("Gabe"), age six. David was then forty-eight and was slowing down, showing the impact of an arduous life of tenant farming, repeated moving, military service, and homesteading. He was apparently also still affected by his long sickness as a Union soldier, which Susan mentioned in a letter written sometime during the 1870s. She was forty-seven.

The short article on the Maxwell family also provides information—undoubtedly from David—about Lon's effort to live an honest life in a world far from Ed's influence: "During the season of 1878, Lon worked a farm near Silver Lake, and raised over eight hundred bushels of wheat. He sold his grain and came to Illinois in the fall, but returned to Nebraska in the spring of 1879, and purchased eighty acres of land near Macon in Franklin County. He then went to northern Wisconsin, as the father believes, with the honest intention of earning money to pay for the land." Lon had probably helped his father during 1877, then rented land nearby. Why he visited Illinois after the 1878 harvest is unknown, but he probably wanted to see Ed. A Joliet inmate could have one visitor every eight weeks, but it is unlikely that his brother ever had any. When Lon was ready to leave the penitentiary in 1877, he had probably promised to return for a visit after he was settled.

Franklin County bounded Kearney County on the south, so Lon was hoping to establish a farm not far from his parents. He bought a parcel of land as soon as he came of age, in June 1879. Whatever his future plans may have been, it is clear that in the years immediately following his release from prison, Lon was a hardworking prairie farmer.

At that time, Adams County had about 80,000 acres of undulating prairie land under cultivation. Wheat was the dominant crop, but farmers also raised oats, corn, rye, barley, and flax. It was a booming agricultural area.

Hastings, a dusty and rather drab collection of plain wooden shops and small homes located on the divide between the Little Blue River and the Platte, was the county seat. Laid out in 1872, it had some thirty businesses within the first year, and the Burlington and Missouri River Railroad, which had just arrived, was the primary reason. By 1880 three more railroads also stopped at the upstart community, which had 3,000 people, and it was a major grain and livestock shipping point in southern Nebraska. Because of increasing prominence, Hastings became the Adams County seat in 1878. It replaced nearby Juniata, which had served that function for eight years, and to which David and Susan Maxwell always related more closely.

The south-central part of Nebraska, along the Platte River, had its own law-and-order problems. Webster County, just south of Adams, was home to a band of thieves that robbed the county treasury at Knoxville, Iowa, in October 1876. Soon afterward, one of the leaders was identified at Hastings and was chased out of town by the deputy sheriff and his posse with their guns blazing. During the later 1870s, Doc Middleton and his gang of horse thieves were notorious in the state, and there were also many less-noted robbers. For that reason, vigilante movements were common. In Logan Township, where the Maxwells lived, fear of depredations by thieves prompted the formation of a "Vigilante Committee" in 1878, and lawbreakers were threatened with retaliation by lynch law.

There were, in fact, a number of Nebraska lynchings—including this one, tersely noted in the *Grand Island Times* on April 14, 1881: "A desperado named Reddy McDonald, one of a group of sixteen thrown into jail at Sidney, Neb., was detected in a plot to escape, and was hung on a tree in the courthouse yard." The vigilantes who killed that desperado had been operating since 1875. In Adams County, the fatal shooting of a homesteader by a robber who stole his mules soon led to an arrest, and the killer was jailed at Hastings. A lynch mob immediately formed and tried to storm the jail, but the sheriff managed to remove the prisoner through a window and spirit him away to a jail in another county. The fortunate lawbreaker was later convicted and imprisoned. Small wonder that as the 1880s began, there was considerable controversy over the presence of mob violence in a state that was trying to shed its "wild frontier" image.

Ed had undoubtedly told Lon about the booming lumber industry up north, between the St. Croix River on the Minnesota-Wisconsin border and Wisconsin's Chippewa River Valley, sixty miles to the east. So, that's where he went, seeking work. That lush, green wilderness, stretching for hundreds of square miles, would be the setting for the Maxwells' emergence as nationally famous desperadoes.

On his way there, Lon stopped at Stillwater, where Ed had been arrested in 1876, and, according to a local newspaper, he "got the fine Winchester rifle which [Chief] Shortall had secured at the time of the capture." Whether he tried to obtain the back pay that Ed felt he had coming from some local agency, perhaps the Stillwater Lumber Company, is unknown.

Western Wisconsin had been a fabulous timber region since before the Civil War, when massive log rafts—"cribs" of cut trees, roped together, extending perhaps 150 feet wide and 500 feet long—were already being floated down the Mississippi River for eventual sale at St. Louis. At that time, perhaps one-sixth of all the pine forests in America grew along a single river, the Chippewa, which flowed south for some two hundred miles in the western part of the state before running into the Mississippi just below Lake Pepin.

At the lower end of the river's course, it passed through the northern part of Pepin County and then flowed along its eastern border. Within that small, irregular-shaped county, which had been established in 1858, the Chippewa had several tributaries—the Cranberry, Fall, Dutch, and Bear creeks on its east side, and the Eau Galle River, the Red Cedar River, and seven more creeks on its west side.

Many sawmills operated along the bigger streams, cutting logs into lumber, shingles, lath, and pickets. In 1880 the Durand newspaper reported, "The lumber manufacture of the various mills in the Chippewa Valley this year will reach 230,000,000 feet of lumber; 60,000,000 lath, and 70,000,000 shingles, with about the same [70,000,000] amount of pickets." But that output was topped by the board feet of uncut logs. During the later nineteenth century, vast numbers of them were sent down the Eau Galle River, the Red Cedar River, and other streams to the Chippewa. And just below Durand, that major river had a secondary channel, fifteen miles long, called Beef Slough, which became a major "log boom" (or storage) area where cut timber was sorted and kept for later shipping on the Mississippi. In the year that Lon arrived, 1879, some 250 million board feet of lumber was floated down the Chippewa River as logs, most of it coming through the boom at Beef Slough. That amount rose to 300 million board feet the following year—and even that was doubled by 1885.

Much of the logging was done in the colder months by lumberjacks at camps scattered through the vast forests. In 1880, the *Dunn County News,* at nearby Menomonie, reported that "the Mississippi Logging Company has about 40 camps on the Chippewa River, and has already contracted for nearly 115,000,000 feet of logs"—and there were several other companies with logging camps in operation.

In the spring, after the ice melted, crews struggled to move the logs down the Chippewa, bound into huge rafts and directed by towboats like the *Iowa City* and the *Artemus Lamb,* and that work continued through the warm weather. Hundreds of men, especially from Pepin County and, just to the north, Dunn County, were involved. Many others worked in the dozens of sawmills located along the rivers.

Everything else in western Wisconsin was related to the timber enterprise and the challenge of logging, and that hard, sometimes dangerous work in remote areas produced a culture dominated by tough, determined, little-educated, but fiercely egalitarian men. Among them, it was not the land that a man owned but the work he could do that gave him stature— even though the mill owners dominated the economic environment and were the only figures, aside from community businessmen, likely to rise in social status.

The Chippewa Valley was a world apart from everything Lon had ever known, in the agricultural counties farther south, and perhaps that was part of its appeal for him—a very young man, anxious to prove himself.

In 1870 Pepin County had 4,659 people, and it grew, slowly but steadily, to 6,188 by 1880. There were about ten villages and hamlets, the most important of which was Durand, the county seat, which had almost a thousand people by 1875.

Founded in 1856, Durand was located on the eastern shore of the Chippewa River, near the mouth of Bear Creek. The landscape stretching to the east was mixed prairie and woodland—with oak, maple, ash, basswood, butternut, and elm trees—but to the west, across the river, was a vast rugged forest of tree-covered hills, small valleys, and winding streams. A pole ferry across the river was started in 1857, and that was followed a few years later by a horse-operated one.

In those early days the town was dependent on river traffic—keelboats like the *Dutch Lady* and small steamboats like the *Belle of Pepin*—but by 1860 it had dirt roads and was reached by a stagecoach line. The townspeople dreamed of a railroad connection, and worked toward it, but Durand never had one until after the Maxwell brothers had created the most exciting, and disturbing, episode of local history. Because it had no depot, the town also had no telegraph. At the close of the 1870s, it was still a remote place.

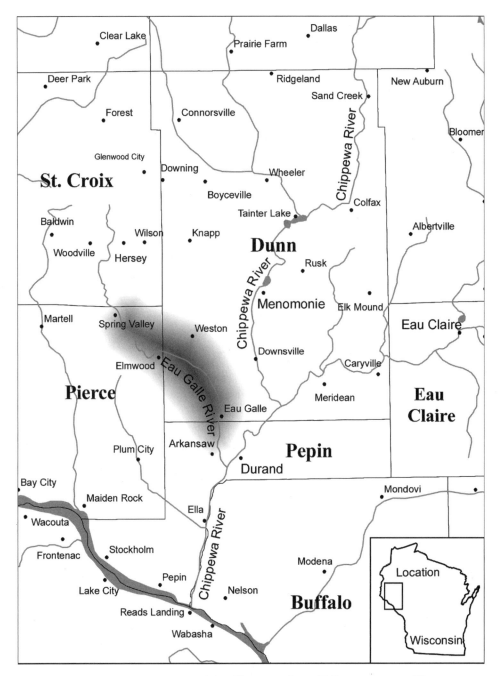

Dunn and Pepin counties, and the Chippewa River Valley, in western Wisconsin. The shadowed area, known as the Eau Galle woods, was the initial focus of the 1881 manhunt for the Maxwell brothers.

Durand had more than a dozen wooden shops, three churches, and a large, two-story schoolhouse, but its most imposing structure was the Pepin County Courthouse, a handsome, Greek Revival–style, white-frame building located a few blocks from the river. Erected in 1874, it was thirty-six feet wide and forty-two feet long, and was graced by tall windows on all sides. In the front, it had four columns supporting a full-width portico, topped by a huge, louvered cupola. The courtroom was on the second floor, and various county offices were below. Like all courthouses, it symbolized the county's commitment to law and order.

The grounds of the stately Pepin County Courthouse would provide the setting for the climactic scene of the Maxwell saga.

Lon did not work right away as a logger, but he was part of the vast lumber industry. He went to the hamlet of Hersey, located in western St. Croix County, about thirty miles northwest of Durand and fifteen miles west of Menomonie. A community of 340 people by 1880, it was little more than a log-processing place spawned by the lumber boom. In that year, some twenty-five million pounds of wood—mostly lumber, shingles, and lath—were shipped out on the local railroad, so there was abundant hard work for able-bodied men to do, although much of it was seasonal, done in the winter.

Three sawmills and a post office had been established during the 1870s, and the village was finally platted in 1878. According to an early description, "The streets are regularly laid out, but on account of the numerous [tree] stumps, locomotion through them is by devious ways." On the outskirts of the village, the primeval forest was retreating, attacked in the cold weather by hundreds of saws and axes. By 1880, shortly after Lon arrived, Hersey had five stores, two livery stables, a blacksmith shop, a hotel, a grain elevator—and ten saloons. Like many other lumber towns, it was a place where loggers caroused on Saturday nights.

An 1881 *History of Northern Wisconsin* describes the sawmill where Lon was employed for most of a year, starting in late 1879: "E. S. Austin is the proprietor of a mill for the manufacture of soft and hard lumber. It has a circular saw which turns out from forty to fifty-five thousand feet a day. Fifty thousand shingles and twelve thousand lath are the product of a day. . . ." A prominent lumber baron, Austin was president of the St. Croix Land and Lumber Company and had a hand in several other business ventures in western Wisconsin.

While he worked at the Austin sawmill, Lon boarded at the home of a German immigrant named Ed Wolf. A twenty-six-year-old who also worked at the Austin mill, his occupation was "sawing shingles," according to the 1880 census. Wolf's household included an eighteen-year-old wife, an infant son, two teenage girls (who assisted with duties at the boardinghouse), and four boarders: Charley Wolf, age twenty-four; Lou Green, age twenty-eight; Andrew Nelson, age seventeen, and Lon Williams, age twenty. All four of those men worked at "making shingles."

The census reveals that Lon had adopted the same alias that Ed had used in Minnesota. It also lists his place of birth, and that of his parents, as "Illinois," revealing that Lon had concocted a false background, which many ex-convicts felt compelled to do in order to escape their past. His listed age is also inaccurate: He was twenty-two in June.

The Wolf brothers were, in fact, Lon's reason for coming to Hersey. According to a later newspaper item, "Lon Williams had written to his brother Edward his intention to go to Hersey, Wis., where he had a friend. . . ." Ed Wolf later commented that he and his brothers had been "acquainted with the Williams brothers upward of ten years"—which meant that Ed and Charley Wolf knew they were the Maxwell brothers and that Lon was an ex-convict living under an alias. Surely Ed Wolf had told Lon about an available job cutting shingles in Hersey and had offered him the opportunity of boarding with them.

Apart from his work experience at the Austin sawmill, Lon's early activities in Hersey are unknown. One later newspaper report, in the *St. Paul Pioneer Press,* characterized that period of his life in the worst possible terms:

> Lon Williams has been known at Hersey, Knapp, and Menomonie for at least two years, and while he has ostensibly been working, he has been in deviltries of various kinds. He has associated with the very worst class of people. . . . It is a fact that depredations and outrages have been committed and traced directly to Lon Williams, which have now been made public. He had worked in sawmills and wagon shops, and last winter [1881] had a contract to get out cord wood for a Hersey firm, but he was never known to be steady and reliable at a job. . . .

This is almost surely untrue. The vague nature of Lon's "deviltries of various kinds" and "depredations and outrages" suggests that the reporter was simply doing some creative development of his story. There was, in fact, a great tendency for newspapermen to provide titillating accounts of the Maxwell background once the brothers had become infamous. Another account of Lon's life asserted that, while in Hersey, he "occasionally drank rather freely," and after Ed showed up, "the brothers were seen in saloons." But reliable sources—people who knew Lon—indicate that he, like Ed, never drank or hung out in saloons. Furthermore, he was apparently never in trouble with the authorities until after his brother arrived, and those who actually knew Lon liked him.

Far more reliable is the comment of Ed Wolf, Lon's landlord, who knew him very well and simply summed up his early life in Hersey by saying, "Lon Williams, when he came to this town, went to work in a shingle mill here and boarded at my house, and behaved like a gentleman all of the time he was here, until his brother Ed came."

Sometime in late 1879 or early 1880 Lon met a pretty teenager named Fannie Hussey, who was then living in Hersey. Little is known about her, but she played a crucial role in the destiny of the Maxwell brothers.

Fannie was born in Wisconsin on March 17, 1864, to W. E. (probably "William") and Bridget Hussey. He was from New York, and Bridget was an Irish immigrant whose maiden name was Stuart. The Husseys also had an older daughter, born early in 1862, but she died at age seven. Apparently, Fannie's father died in the mid-1860s as well, but the exact time and place remain unknown.

The Hussey family lived for some years in Waubeek Township, a sparsely populated area four miles north of Durand. In 1880 it had only 214 people. The township was bounded on the north by Dunn County, on the east and southeast by the Chippewa River, and on the west by the Eau Galle River and Waterville Township. A tributary of the Chippewa, the Eau Galle flowed through dense forest, which stretched away to the north and west, becoming part of a vast timber belt in Dunn and Pierce counties.

The 1870 census for Waubeek Township, in Pepin County, finds Bridget— who was then thirty-six—already remarried to William Thompson, a farmer who hailed from New York. They lived on a farm just west of the Eau Galle River, near the boundary of Waterville Township. Thompson had also lost a spouse, in 1866, and he apparently had two daughters by that first marriage. He and Bridget, who commonly went by her middle name, Catherine, were married in 1867. The same census also indicates that Fannie, who was then six, had a twin brother named William. The Thompsons also had two small sons, Stewart and Russell, so their family was a "yours, mine, and ours" situation.

Bridget and her children, and perhaps her new husband as well, attended the Methodist church at Arkansaw, a few miles south of the Thompson farm. Located along the curving Arkansaw Creek, where a small valley featured high bluffs and outcroppings of limestone, the village had a flour mill, a dozen shops, a school, two churches, a hotel, an entertainment hall, and a furniture factory during the 1870s. Arkansaw had a few hundred people by 1880 and thought of itself as a rival to Durand.

The 1880 census indicates that the Thompsons had moved twenty miles north, to Hersey, in the northwestern part of St. Croix County. William then listed his occupation as "mason," but he also owned a sawmill back at Waubeek, where there was an important log boom that provided a constant supply of timber. By that year William's daughters had apparently left home, and Fannie's twin brother is not in the census either, for whatever reason. The Thompsons also had a third son, Allen, who was just three years old.

A sometimes unreliable newspaper source asserts that Lon met Fannie at a dance held at nearby Knapp on New Year's Eve 1880. That is possible, for he was a light-brown-haired, blue-eyed, and well-built young man whose handsome features would have made him attractive to young ladies. Living in a community for the first time in his life, as opposed to being on a farm, he was apparently becoming more outgoing, and he did not have Ed as a ready substitute for other social interaction. But the 1880 census for Hersey lists the Ed Wolf household, where Lon boarded, almost immediately before the William Thompson household, so Lon and Fannie were surely neighbors.

Another newspaper report indicates that the Thompsons, while living at Hersey from time to time, also maintained their farm at Waubeek, so Lon's interest in Fannie increasingly prompted him to visit the northwest corner of Pepin County: "Lon Williams made the acquaintance of the girl he married, Fanny Huzzy [*sic*], while at Hersey, and his frequent trips to her stepfather's [farm]house, Mr. Thompson's, offered him an opportunity to become acquainted not only with the forests, but the farmers residing in that country [near Waubeek]." In any case, Lon and Fannie commenced a courtship that led to marriage over the Fourth of July weekend, 1880.

According to a local newspaper, there was a grand celebration in Hersey on that Fourth of July—featuring a thirty-gun volley at sunrise, a morning parade, a huge procession to the picnic grounds, a patriotic speech, a reading of the Declaration of Independence, a picnic lunch, an afternoon dance, a shooting exhibition, and a "grand ball" in the evening. Drawing some 2,000 people, it was called "the largest gathering ever" in the Hersey area by the newspaper that described it.

The speaker of the day was Rev. David Downer, of the Arkansaw Methodist Church, who "delivered an oration which was simply magnificent." It was his church that Bridget Thompson and her children had attended in Arkansaw for many years. Surprisingly, the thirty-four-year-old minister was also a crack shot with a rifle: "At 3 o'clock Mr. Downer interested the boys by exhibiting his skill in the use of a repeating rifle, among others, breaking 14 glass balls in 15 successive shots with the rifle, and firing 15 shots in 11 seconds, each shot striking within a circle of 6 inches at a distance of 4 rods." Perhaps his shooting skill helped to attract Lon, who knew him and liked him—and who could shoot like that too.

According to a letter by the Hersey correspondent for the nearby *Hudson Star and Times,* "Five weddings occurred in our village on the 3rd and 5th." One of those was the wedding of Lon Williams and Fannie Hussey. No official marriage record survives, but a newspaper account published in July 1881 comments that "Parson Downer, of Arkansaw . . . officiated at the marriage of Alonzo Williams and Fanny Huzzy [*sic*], a beautiful girl of Christian character, about a year ago. . . ." They probably took advantage of Downer's plans to be in Hersey over the Fourth of July weekend, to arrange for the ceremony.

Since Lon had been living under the alias that had been used first by Ed, "Williams" became Fannie's new name too. By then, Lon had probably abandoned his plan of returning to Nebraska, where his real name and criminal past would have been revealed. Fannie apparently did not know that her handsome, likeable, hardworking husband had a prison record back in Illinois. And by late 1880, she was pregnant.

It is tempting to infer that Lon had indeed decided to change his life, had put his outlaw identity behind him, and was committed to living an honest life. After years of alienation as a desperado, a convict, and a frontier tenant farmer, he was clearly striving to belong, and he must have found in his relationship with Fannie an outlet for the soft, emotional side of himself—which he had repressed while growing up, so he could be tough enough to merit Ed's approval and be his comrade. And he surely felt pleased that in a culture where men substantially outnumbered women, he had attracted and won a delightful girl who was regarded as "a real looker," a beauty.

After the wedding, Lon and Fannie settled down in Hersey. One later newspaper report, by a correspondent who had looked into Lon's past, commented that "all accounts [by local residents] agree that the devotion of this young married and mated pair was unusually marked, on every occasion of their appearance in public together, and [was] exceedingly demonstrative in their home." They apparently lived with the Thompsons until the latter moved back to Waubeek, after which Lon and Fannie may have continued to use the Thompson residence in Hersey, at least for a time.

For some reason, Lon stopped cutting shingles at the Austin sawmill. He may have worked for some months in the nearby village of Knapp— perhaps as a store clerk, as one source indicates. But it is clear that he was seeking more promising work—a job with some kind of future. In the fall of 1880 he became a logger, working to produce cord wood, on a contract basis, for Wilson, Van Vliet, and Company, a Hersey firm. As he later said in a brief interview, "When I got married and settled down in Hersey, I intended to lead an honorable and upright life. I took a contract for cutting cord-wood, and worked faithfully. . . ." There was more money in being a logger than in working at a sawmill, and Lon probably needed to make that change in order to support a family.

Unfortunately, in February 1881 Lon was injured on the job. While swinging a razor-sharp, double-edged axe, he cut his right foot severely. He soon lost his second toe, which was amputated in Hersey by Menomonie physician E. O. Baker. Lon was laid up for several days and walked with pain for some months, the injury being slow to heal.

There must have been severe economic strain on Lon at that point, for he was still a very young man, with limited financial resources and a child on the way. He was also a newcomer to the north woods, with few friends, and his family was far away in Nebraska—where he could not return without revealing his true identity and penitentiary past to a young wife that he both idealized and truly loved.

9

The Wisconsin Desperadoes

The fateful year for the Maxwell brothers was 1881, and it began with Ed's release from prison. Having completed his six-year sentence by serving only four years and three months—with time off for good behavior—Ed was set free on January 21. Despite the claims made in his 1877 letters and the assurances that he had probably given to Warden McClaughry on the day he got out, he was not reformed.

The rigors of prison life notwithstanding, Ed was apparently in good physical condition. Perhaps as an effort to shake off his clean-shaven convict appearance and make a more refined impression, he started wearing a black mustache and a goatee. More than one newspaper later reported that he was "good looking," and no one would have guessed that the striking, intelligent, twenty-seven-year-old man had served two terms in the penitentiary.

Of course, Ed received a train ticket to Macomb, and he probably stopped there, if only to get, or attempt to get, the money that he had possessed when he was arrested, which was supposedly being held for him by his lawyer, Damon G. Tunnicliff. Whether or not Ed was successful, he did not stay in town. It was, after all, the dead of winter, when the cold, barren landscape, with its windblown, isolated farms, seemed to reject any hope of meaningful work and social acceptance. No one in McDonough County needed or wanted him, and he knew it.

Ed realized, of course, that his parents were homesteading in Nebraska, and he had at one time considered going there. But according to a later newspaper report, Lon had written to Ed at the penitentiary, advising him that Nebraska would be "unhealthy"—surely because of the vigilante violence there. In any case, Lon was now in Wisconsin. So Ed's first objective, undoubtedly, was to see his brother, to determine if he still had a partner, a comrade, a sidekick with whom he could make a name for himself as a desperado.

Lon's response to Ed's arrival must have been mixed. He was, of course, glad to see the brother who had been his protector, his mentor, and his companion in earlier years, but his life now had a different focus and his future lay with Fannie and the world of logging—or so he thought.

One newspaper source mentions that Ed "assisted Lon with his wood-cutting job"—at least for a time. The foot wound that had occurred just before or just after Ed arrived might have made Lon temporarily dependent upon his brother's assistance, and thus more susceptible to his entreaties about continuing their career as robbers—or at least cooperating briefly when Ed turned to robbery. A much later, retrospective source indicates that Ed began stealing horses and keeping them temporarily at the farm owned by Fannie's stepfather, William Thompson, where Lon and Fannie frequently stayed, but that often unreliable account may be based only on assumptions about Ed's probable activities or on local storytelling. In any case, that source also suggests how difficult it might have been for Lon, who truly needed help, to avoid involvement with Ed, who was not making an effort to go straight.

One thing is clear: The brothers started spending time together when Lon wasn't working, and that apparently included practicing with guns. A *Chicago Times* correspondent, who interviewed mill hands and others at Hersey after the Maxwells had become notorious, filed the following report:

> I could fill a column with the marvelous shots both brothers made in sport of this kind last spring. Among the many items in my rough notes are the following: At a distance of forty paces Lon would shoot off a revolver in each hand, hitting together a couple of sweet potatoes tossed up by the hands of a person seated on the ground. At eight rods [132 feet] Ed would knock an oyster can off a fence post with a shot from his right-hand revolver, and before

it reached the earth, would put a ball through it from the "navy" in his left hand. Coming up the railroad track together at one time, they drew two revolvers each, and at a distance of sixteen rods [264 feet] sighted a mark on a log at one side of the track. Walking leisurely along, they put twenty-four shots from a couple of pairs of Colt navy sixes within the space covered by the palms of one's two hands. Also, one of the brothers would hold in his hand a clay pipe, and the other, at twelve yards, would break the bowl. This shot required a steadiness of aim rarely reached with a revolver.

The Colt Navy revolver was a .36-caliber handgun, firing six shots. Used extensively by Union soldiers and sailors during the Civil War, it was later common in the West and was the favorite revolver of many gunfighters, including Wild Bill Hickok.

The Maxwells also practiced with Winchester repeating rifles. According to a later report, those were the 1876 model, a .44-caliber, lever-action rifle that could fire sixteen shots in rapid succession. It used powerful centerline cartridges that had a much longer range and greater impact than bullets from earlier repeating rifles. Apparently, Ed and Lon practiced not just for accuracy but also for speed, eventually learning to fire their deadly rifles "from the hip, with an aim few shots [i.e., shooters] are sure of from the shoulder."

As their frequent practice with revolvers and rifles suggests, and their willingness to show others what they could do reveals, they sought opportunities to display their uncommon skill with those icons of manliness. For Ed, remarkable shooting brought the kind of respect and admiration that he craved.

But Lon's struggle to release his long-suppressed emotional life—the inner project that had marked his relationship with Fannie—was surely halted, his feelings forced back under the fierce control of masculine bravado. In a deep sense, his astounding rapid-fire marksmanship, which could make the world stay away, if necessary, was aimed at his own heart. Logger Lon Williams was turning back into Lon Maxwell, the desperado.

The earliest Maxwell brothers robbery in the north woods, of which there is any record, occurred on April 13, 1881. Ed probably knew from his 1876 residence in Washington County, Minnesota, that the store at the St. Croix Lumber Company on the riverfront in South Stillwater often had money overnight, so he and Lon rode over there, spent a day or two, and burglarized it. A local newspaper estimated their haul at $500.

One source mentions that "parties in South Stillwater" knew Ed, so he may have worked for that lumber company back in 1876. If so, he may have felt that he had wages coming that he had not received because he was apprehended by Chief Shortall and returned to Macomb. Was that the "money owed him in Minnesota" which he had told Lon about? Perhaps, but Ed may simply have decided that the lumber company store, thirty-five miles from Hersey, was an easy mark.

Unfortunately for the Maxwells, Ed "Williams" had been recognized when in Stillwater the day before the robbery, and the authorities soon learned that the Williams brothers were living in Hersey. The *St. Paul Pioneer Press* provided an account of the subsequent attempt to arrest them made by St. Croix County Sheriff Joseph Kelly, a forty-six-year-old farmer and Civil War veteran who had been serving as a lawman for less than a year:

> [Kelly] had a hair-lifting encounter . . . at the village of Hersey.
> . . . He had been sent there [by train] with a warrant for the two brothers, on a charge of burglarizing the store of the St. Croix Lumber Company, at Baytown [South Stillwater]. No sooner had he reached their residence than each of them appeared, with drawn revolvers, and ordered him to leave the premises forthwith or suffer the penalty with his life. Mr. Kelly, and the head of the Baytown store, thinking discretion to be the better part of valor, instantly retraced their steps, with a view of . . . raising a posse for their capture, but this was absolutely impossible, as the whole village was in mortal terror of the desperadoes.
>
> They had lived there off and on for five or six months, did little or no work, brandished firearms with the freedom of a Guy Fawkes, and shot with the accuracy of a Bogardus. They gave people to understand that they would be friendly to those who were friendly to them and a terror to those who attempted to interfere. . . .
>
> Naturally enough, therefore, the people did not care to join a posse against them, and Sheriff Kelly retired to Hudson [the county seat] for aid, while the robbers made a break for the forests.

The article concludes by adding that when Sheriff Kelly and the store manager had first arrived in Hersey, "they were met by [the Maxwells] with four loaded revolvers and were driven clear to the depot and out of town"—a violent encounter indeed.

But there is a less dramatic version of this story. An August 1881 account by Ed Wolf, of Hersey, corrects the newspaper's tendency to heighten the desperado-like behavior of the Maxwells:

They were here [living together] about three months when they drove Sheriff Kelly off. They did not follow him to the depot; they simply pointed revolvers at him, and his partner, and told them to get [away], which they did, and they stayed at the depot till train time—while the two Williams boys shouldered their Winchesters and a little sack with provisions and coolly walked out of town.

All these things are highly embellished when reported by your [*Pioneer Press*] correspondent. The Williamses never went around this town brandishing firearms and intimidating all the inhabitants, as reported in the *Pioneer Press.*

Of course, as a friend of the Maxwells and Lon's landlord, Ed Wolf had an interest in keeping newspaper accounts of the outlaw brothers from becoming too overblown and alarming. In fact, by the time this critique of the St. Paul newspaper coverage appeared, he and his brothers had been accused, by false rumor, of abetting the Maxwells.

It is evident, however, that once the story of driving off Sheriff Kelly had started to circulate, it was dramatized in the telling, and that kind of embellished version is what the *Pioneer Press* reported. Another newspaper article about the episode, dated April 29, asserted, "The people of Hersey . . . would be only too glad to have [the Williams brothers] brought to justice" because "the cracking of Peters' safe last winter, and numerous other burglaries, have been quietly credited up to them. . . ." There is no evidence that Ed and Lon committed other local robberies, and Lon would have been very unlikely to do so in the village where he and Fannie lived, socialized, and were well-liked—and where he had been long laid up with a foot injury. Of course, Ed may have done some burglarizing on his own, but this newspaper comment also clearly shows that as soon as notoriety had come to the Maxwells, any unsolved robberies were associated with them in the public mind, as folks wondered and speculated about the lives of such daring and dangerous men.

In any case, the Stillwater robbery had the crucial result of making Ed and Lon, once again, outlaws sought by the authorities. They were on the run in the Chippewa Valley, and Lon was forced to remain apart from Fannie. What she was told by Lon is unknown, but some weeks after Ed arrived, perhaps in March, she had left Hersey to stay with her mother and stepfather in Waubeek—probably because Lon realized that he could not provide for her with his foot injury, and because she was in the later months of her pregnancy and wanted the baby delivered at her mother's.

Also, Hersey was then struggling with a horrific diphtheria epidemic that would last through the summer, taking at least a dozen lives—including Albert Wolf, the teenage brother of Lon's landlord, Ed Wolf—and there was much talk about the unhealthfulness of the town.

Perhaps Lon simply told Fannie that with his brother's help he would find suitable work, away from Hersey, as the warmer weather was coming on. If he eventually told her of the encounter with Sheriff Kelly, he might have claimed that he had not known in advance of Ed's plans to rob the lumber company store, or that Ed had pleaded for his help with the burglary because he was owed money there. And in any case, now they needed to hide out until things blew over.

A brief, untitled article that appeared in Durand's *Pepin County Courier* reveals that, after the encounter with Sheriff Kelly at Hersey, the Maxwells did hide out for a time in the Waubeek area, surely to make it possible for Lon to visit Fannie, and then they stole a skiff and went down the Chippewa River to the Mississippi. It also warned the public that "[t]hey were heavily armed and claimed that they cannot be captured alive."

Traveling by river in a rowboat to avoid capture was, of course, reminiscent of their exploit in 1875 on the Illinois River. Their effort to be "heavily armed" and their public assertion that they "cannot be taken alive" also reflected that earlier episode. These similarities suggest that they wanted to replay their failed 1875 escape by river, to reclaim their prison-damaged identity as desperadoes. And once again, that identity was clearly dependent upon notoriety. For Ed especially, life was not worth living if the public failed to view him with a certain awe, and that meant exhibiting defiance of authorities. But that also guaranteed hot pursuit and increased the likelihood of violent confrontation and eventual capture or death.

The short newspaper item about Ed and Lon also reveals that they were being pursued by Undersheriff Miletus Knight of Pepin County, who would play a significant role in their destiny. Knight and the marshal of Durand had become involved surely because Sheriff Kelly of St. Croix County had alerted nearby lawmen of the standoff at Hersey, and word had reached Knight that the outlaws had been seen north of Durand.

Born in 1838 and raised in Allegany County, New York, Miletus Knight had come west to Wisconsin in 1850. After homesteading and teaching school in Eau Claire County, he had served in the Thirtieth Wisconsin Infantry during the Civil War. Then he moved to adjacent Pepin County and operated a store in Arkansaw, where he also sold insurance and real estate. By 1878 he was the local postmaster. A successful and popular man, with a distinguished look and a better education than most, he served as assistant sergeant at arms in the Wisconsin legislature during the late 1870s. Elected Pepin County clerk in 1879, he moved again, to Durand. By then he wore rimless glasses and sported a waxed mustache, which gave him an officious look. A temperance advocate, he led the local Good Templars lodge and was prominent in several other organizations. When his friend A. F. Peterson was elected sheriff, Knight agreed to serve as "undersheriff," or deputy. Viewed by some as pompous and moralistic, he also worked hard at the job.

The Maxwell brothers succeeded in escaping from Undersheriff Knight—and, in fact, continued down the Mississippi River to Henderson County, Illinois, just above McDonough, where they abandoned the stolen skiff and started traveling on foot through the wooded countryside. An article in the *Oquawka Spectator,* which does not identify them, reveals that they soon returned to horse stealing. They took a bay gelding and a brown mare from well-to-do livestock raiser John Evans Jr., who lived near Decorra, several miles east of the Mississippi River. After stealing saddles as well, they rode south and east, heading for McDonough County. A $300 reward was posted.

This exploit in Henderson County also had an unanticipated but momentous impact on the Maxwell brothers: It put yet another sheriff on their trail—an intrepid bloodhound of a man whose pursuit would eventually drive them from Illinois, and whose effort to publicize their "wanted" status would trigger a dramatic showdown back in Wisconsin.

Sheriff James O. Anderson was born in the western part of Warren County—which later became Henderson County—in 1845, on a farm in Stronghurst Township that had been developed by his grandfather, who had received the land as a military bounty for his service in the War of 1812. Anderson was, then, deeply rooted in the county that he served and felt he had a personal stake in the preservation of order. Like so many other lawmen, he viewed theft, murder, and other misdeeds as threats to the foundation upon which society precariously rested, so he was committed to bringing criminals to justice.

Anderson attended nearby Monmouth College, where he enlisted in the 138th Illinois Infantry and fought in the Civil War. He participated in several battles and loved the military life, so after his discharge in 1864 he reenlisted in the Twenty-eighth Illinois Infantry. He was a sergeant. After the war ended, he continued in the military, serving along the Mexican border.

Anderson was then a farmer for several years, but like so many other successful and heroic Civil War soldiers, he gradually drifted into police work. In 1876 he was elected sheriff of Henderson County, so he was well aware of the Maxwell brothers because of the publicity surrounding Ed's capture and conviction during that year. A muscular man with light-brown hair and a thin, drooping mustache, Anderson was a popular and effective lawman, serving as sheriff until 1886. Later elected to the Illinois General Assembly, he was also appointed sergeant at arms of the state senate.

In July 1881 Sheriff Anderson was interviewed by a reporter for the *St. Paul Pioneer Press,* and he provided information about tracking the Maxwell brothers in central Illinois, upon which the following account was based:

> On May 30th the brothers turned up in Henderson County, Illinois, where in the night they stole two horses, one a bay gelding, the other a brown mare. They rode to Colchester, reaching there on Wednesday, and thence proceeded to Macomb, where they stole a single-top buggy from the stable of Hon. W. H. Neece, the lawyer who prosecuted Lon when he was sent to Joliet. After going 25 miles through the woods, the buggy was run into a stump and ruined. . . .
>
> They then went to Smithfield on the horses' backs and camped in the woods until Friday morning [June 3], when a boy discovered them. They tried to intimidate him and then said they were out hunting. The boy later gave the alarm, and Sheriff Anderson was telegraphed.
>
> He took the track and followed them across the Illinois River, just above Peoria, where they crossed Saturday night and stopped in a schoolhouse [near Ten Mile], putting the horses in a coal shed. An alarm was given by a man who saw the horses sticking their heads out of the shed. An investigation was made, and the schoolhouse was found locked. A trustee unlocked the door, and on entering, [the group of investigators] was confronted by two revolvers. The crowd withdrew without further invitation, and the robbers quietly mounted their horses and rode away. They went about three miles and then doubled back, an old trick of theirs, passing Sheriff Anderson and his posse in the woods.
>
> The trail was not discovered for ten days, when it was found that the thieves had actually returned to Washburn, where they were known. Anderson was notified that they had been seen in Woodford [County], and on getting there, found they had gone north.

Satisfied that they were coming to Wisconsin, Sheriff Anderson sent telegrams and postal cards to all sections, including Hersey, where he knew they had lived, and also to Arkansaw and Durand.

During most of the two-week chase, Sheriff Anderson did not realize that the horse thieves he was after were the notorious Maxwell brothers. A letter that he sent from Peoria to his wife shortly after Ed and Lon had pulled their guns at the schoolhouse and eluded his posse reflects his determination to bring in the two still-unrecognized men: "I have been going night and day since I left home, and I don't expect much rest until I catch the thieves. They were seen passing Secor, thirty miles east of here, last night." He also asserts, "They are regular desperadoes; have drawn their guns on several persons, but . . . I am using the [telegraph] wires, and think I will get them soon." As that reveals, too, he alerted nearby sheriffs, so once again the remarkable David Waggoner of Fulton County was on their trail, as were lawmen in Woodford and McLean counties. But, as in 1875, the young desperadoes simply outran their pursuers.

It was surely when he arrived at Washburn only to discover that his quarry had gone north that Anderson learned from local residents who the horse thieves were. Then he sent out postcards describing the Maxwell brothers—which eventually led to the gunfight that made them feared throughout the upper Mississippi Valley and notorious across the country.

It is clear from the record of their 1881 visit to Illinois that the Maxwells had no meaningful place to go. If they had crossed the Mississippi River after leaving Wisconsin, they would have escaped their fate. But instead, they returned to McDonough County, Fulton County, and Woodford County, where they had once lived. This, too, suggests that psychological needs were driving them. They wanted to reinvent themselves and somehow mitigate the disrespect that they had experienced in those now-hostile places. Stealing the buggy of a noted and wealthy lawyer, when they could have continued to travel by horseback, suggests again their resentment of well-to-do people and their desire for social standing. The David Maxwell family never owned a buggy. That Neece had prosecuted Lon in 1875 only made the venture more satisfying. And Ed and Lon surely wanted to reclaim their shattered identity as desperadoes who could not be caught.

The return to Wisconsin's Chippewa Valley was undoubtedly urged by Lon. His absence from Fannie had stretched into three weeks, and he surely wanted to check on her condition—as well as perhaps tell her what his plans were for the future. He didn't have many choices: Move away with her when she and the baby were ready to travel? Hide out for a while, perhaps near his parents in Nebraska, and return for his family later? As a letter would soon reveal, he was already distraught over his separation from Fannie.

Wisconsin had no significance for Ed.

How the Maxwells returned to Wisconsin is not clear. They had little or no money, for a Peoria newspaper article mentioned that before crossing the Illinois River at the well-known rope ferry a few miles above the city, they "went to a farmhouse this side of Blue Town [in Peoria County], giving up a silver watch for something to eat." But they still had the two Henderson County horses, which were not recovered until later, in Wisconsin. Because they had no money, Ed and Lon resorted to burglarizing farmhouses for food. Months later, Ed recalled one such episode, which almost cost him his life, when an old farmer awoke and fired a revolver at him.

Somewhere during their journey they apparently stole another horse and a buggy. The article in the *St. Paul Pioneer Press* that depicted their escape across central Illinois also mentioned their arrival in the Waubeek area—with that horse and buggy: "When the robbers reached this vicinity they had a new top buggy and led one horse. The buggy was found in the woods with a bullet hole in the back of the box. . . . The horse was left at the house of Mrs. Sands [near the Thompson home], where officer Knight found it and took it. The [Maxwell] boys called for it afterwards. That would have been the time to have taken them." The bullet hole in "the back of the box" suggests that someone had shot at them while they were escaping with the buggy, but no details of that theft have ever surfaced.

The closing comment in this article implies that while searching for the outlaws in Waubeek Township, Miletus Knight had bungled an opportunity to capture them. But in fact, he had done a good deal more than that.

When Lon showed up at the Thompson home, his mother-in-law had tragic news: Fannie was dead. She had died in childbirth, and to make matters worse, their baby was stillborn. Bridget also told him that shortly before her death, Undersheriff Knight, with the assistance of Marshal William Seeley of Durand, had shown up at the Thompson home one evening "with a warrant for the arrest of the Williamses." Fannie, whose life had spiraled into a nightmare of anxiety as her pregnancy neared full term and her husband was being hunted by the law, apparently became overwrought by the sudden appearance of the armed lawmen, who demanded to search the premises and questioned them concerning the whereabouts of Lon and his brother. And of course, Knight probably told the Thompsons more about Lon's true background in the process.

By late May, Ed and Lon's criminal past in Illinois had caught up with them, probably because of communications from Sheriff Anderson, who had finally identified the horse thieves he was tracking. On May 27, for example, the Hersey correspondent for the *Hudson Star and Times* was referring to "the notorious Williams, or Maxwell, boys," and stories were circulating that they had "skipped for Montana" or some other place that was legendary for its outlawry. As that suggests, the very notion that "Williams" was an alias added a certain outlaw stature to Ed and Lon: They were mysterious men who were not what they claimed to be, so their developing story was even more engrossing for the Wisconsin public.

By then, Fannie must have realized that she had married a desperado and that the family life she had dreamed of was no longer possible. Even visits from Lon would now be a perilous undertaking for him. And questions surely arose. Could she still love Lon Maxwell, who had undoubtedly hidden much from her, and had married her under a false name? Would he ever change? And what would be best for the baby? The enormous stress on Fannie triggered premature contractions, resulting in many hours of suffering and her eventual death, despite the efforts of two physicians called in by the Thompsons.

By the time Lon learned of her death, the funeral was already over and the most recent issue of the *Pepin County Courier,* appearing on June 17, had printed her obituary: "Died.—In Waubeek, June 15th, 1881, Fannie Thompson, Mrs. Williams by marriage, the only daughter of Mrs. William Thompson. She died at six in the evening, but in the morning of life. Every means was used to save her life, but failed. God has suffered it [to happen]—it therefore must be well, and we submit with patience though it gives us pain. Funeral at the M. E. Church in Arkansaw, attended by a large circle of friends. Sermon by Elder Downer; text, John 14:3." As her Pepin County death record reveals, "Fanny (Hussey) Williams" had never taken her stepfather's name—the obituary was incorrect—and she had died of "puerperal convulsions." A lovely and widely admired young woman who had made the mistake of falling in love with an outlaw, she was only seventeen years old.

Two days after Fannie's death, Parson Downer conducted her funeral service, and according to one sometimes unreliable source, he "recounted brief portions of the sad story of her wedded life." Whether or not he did that, he was surely struck by the powerful forces that sometimes shape human lives, and that had, in less than a year, turned the happy marriage of a promising young couple into a nightmare of anxiety, separation, and death.

Fannie was buried at the small, isolated Waubeek Prairie Cemetery, a mile or so east of the Thompson home.

Lon's effort to change his life had crashed. He supposedly wrote a regretful letter to his father-in-law on June 28 indicating that he still wanted to reform, but it has not survived. A correspondent for the *Chicago Times,* who soon investigated the Maxwells, depicted a deeply troubled young man, convinced that his one opportunity to mend his life was gone:

> Lon was strangely affected by the news of his wife's death, which he was inclined to attribute in a measure to the unskillful treatment of the physicians attending her—Drs. Smith and Morgan. He was also incensed at [Undersheriff] Knight and [Marshal] Seeley, who visited Thompson's house with a warrant for the arrest of the Williamses, during their absence, while Lon's wife was in a delicate condition. Lon talked freely with a number of friends at Hersey of his wife's death and his own probable future. He seemed to feel that the only incentive in his life to reform had gone, and forever, and [he] looked ahead to fighting his way along a rough road. But for his brother Ed's joining his desperate fortunes to him, despite his unwillingness to abandon the new life he had entered on with his marriage, he said that "things would not have turned against me this way." But now that he was "in for it," he expressed a resolute determination to play a high hand. He remarked repeatedly that Ed and he would shoot at sight whenever and wherever they were interfered with. . . .

While newspaper reports on the Maxwells often mixed rumor with fact, this interview-based account is probably accurate. Among other things, it suggests that Lon's deepest struggle was between his drive for self-realization ("fighting his way along a rough road") and his deterministic view that "things" outside of himself governed his life. He was a man with limited self-confidence, easily manipulated by the older brother who was, in fact, the agent of his destiny.

Lon also poured out his distraught feelings in a letter addressed to Reverend Downer, which was hand-delivered by a boy enlisted as a courier. The most sincere and revealing document by either of the Maxwells, it leaves no doubt that Lon was devastated by the loss of Fannie and was struggling with severe psychological issues:

Sunday Night, June 26, 1881

Mr. Downer, Sir:

I have been wanting to speak with you ever since I came back, and not having the opportunity, I will have to transfer my thoughts to paper.

I want to say this (although it isn't much)—that what few of the neighbors and acquaintances of mine that respected me in the least when I was first married, I want to keep their respect. I know at the present time that I have very few sympathizing friends. The majority doubtless say, "I pitied his wife, but *him*—let him go to the dogs." Now as far as I am concerned . . . what the folks say about me I don't care so much for as this: The talk was started that I married Fannie with the intentions of leaving her. I want to say that no man was ever more honest in his dealing with or profession to a woman than I was with her.

Circumstances placed me in such a position that I could hear nothing of the way things were agoing up here [in Wisconsin] until I finally came up. But too late. She was dead. Oh, this has been a terrible shock to me, although few would believe it. They doubtless say this: "He is glad of it." But Mr. Downer, you had better buried me than her, for I now am a ruined man. My life is wrecked and I care no more for it. I was always alone in the world untill I got her, and now I stand alone again, with nothing to live for and no object in view. It almost sets me crazy when I hear of anyone saying, "He intended to leave her in the spring anyway." But Mr. Downer, if my word is good for anything, believe what I have said.

It can now make no difference to me what people say, only it seems as though I had ought to say [these comments] for her sake but not my own. I know she was too good a woman for me. I knew it [before], but still, I knew as well how to appreciate her as anyone could, and now that she is dead I want to clear her memory of every chance of reproach—because she was as innocent as any angel could be.

And now, Mr. Downer, she has been torn from me. It might have been the will of God, but I think it was the doings of men, and my desire to retaliate is fearful strong. Nothing but respect for her holds me back. But now if they come for me again, I won't run from them. I have nothing to keep out of their way for now. When Fannie was alive, I kept out of their way for her sake, but now they have done all they could; they have driven me away from her, and I'll never see her again now. All they can do is to come and take my life; they can do it easy if they know how. Mr. Downer, my life is so wrecked that I almost want them to come on to me, [so] that they can see what a desperate wreck they have left.

Now, Mr. Downer, I simply tell you all this because I know you to be a man of principle. I mean this just for yourself, and if justice were done me, no charge would be brought against me. I merely wanted to help my brother, and that ruined me.

If it is not asking too much of you, I wish you would pray for me. A petition to God from someone, it seems, would do me good, for I can't do it myself. Farewell.

Respectfully,

L. D. Williams

One of the most revealing documents by an American outlaw, the letter starts by emphasizing Lon's recent struggle for "respect"—the social condition that both Ed and himself were so often denied as the sons of an impoverished tenant farmer moving from place to place in hard times. Lon realized, too, that his once-concealed past (as an outlaw and convict) was now shaping the public perception of his motives: He must have been simply a bad man who had "married Fannie with the intention of leaving her." Lon was fighting against the negative social construction of his identity, and he desperately wanted someone—at least Reverend Downer, whom he admired—to understand that his intentions with respect to her were always honorable.

The ultimate importance of Fannie is also evident. She was more than a perfect wife; she was a spiritual presence—"as innocent as any angel could be"—someone who was obviously helping him reorient his life, express himself emotionally, find something to live for, and create a new identity. Hence, her death left him "a ruined man."

Lon's chronic sense of alienation—also a problem for Ed—is equally explicit: "I was always alone in the world untill I got her, and now I stand alone again. . . ." It was precisely his alienation—and perhaps his fear of being abandoned, stemming from the Fulton County years when David was gone and Susan was preoccupied with outside work—that made him so easily manipulated by the one person he had always bonded with: his older brother. As the letter's closing reveals, he even felt alienated from God, perhaps by spiritual inactivity, and thus was incapable of approaching Him for help.

It is evident that Lon was undergoing an immense spiritual struggle in the days following Fannie's death. His comment, "She has been torn from me," reveals that he was seeking to blame some agency for the tragedy—God sometimes, but more commonly "the doings of men." Like Ed—and, for that matter, like Billy the Kid and other outlaws—he had a deep conviction that the world of men, the impersonal, uncaring social system, had always been unfair to him. And now, once again, he was a victim: "*They* have done all *they* could; *they* have driven me away from her. . . . All *they* can do now is come and take my life. . . . I almost want *them* to come on to me, [so] that *they* can see what a desperate wreck *they* have left." He was clearly blaming the lawmen who had kept them apart and, in the case of Undersheriff Knight and Marshal Seeley, had apparently contributed to her death and the loss of their child as well.

No wonder he had a strong desire "to retaliate," which was temporarily held in check only by his "respect for her"—his deep-down realization that any violence from him would betray the very impact that Fannie had been making on his life. Like a number of later western novel and film heroes whose families were damaged or destroyed by others, Lon felt that he had justification for violent revenge—although the loss of his family was, at most, an unintentional result of the action of local authorities.

Of course, Lon was ignoring his own responsibility for the crimes committed when he was with Ed, saying at the close of the letter, "if justice were done me, no charge would be brought against me." What he evidently meant was that his motive was not to get something for himself by lawbreaking, but rather to help his brother (who had always been there for him) either retrieve money that Ed felt was owed to him or simply steal money that would give Ed the chance for a new start in a society hostile to ex-cons. And then, of course, when they were identified and pursued, things spiraled out of control, and the stolen skiff, horses, buggies, and harness were a matter of self-preservation as they tried to elude the authorities.

In any case, it is clear that Fannie had been having an enormous impact on Lon at a crucial time in his life. She loved him, so he wanted to change, to live up to her expectation—by controlling the forces that still lurked in his outlaw-forged, prison-damaged identity. But now she was gone and he was left with Ed, a very different spiritual influence—and a committed desperado.

Bridget Thompson apparently liked Lon and did not blame him for what had happened. An article in the Durand newspaper reveals that they were together at Hersey, mutually concerned with seeing to Fannie's belongings, after her death:

> Speaking of the history of Lon Williams at Hersey, an old, highly respected neighbor of his says that Lon stole quietly into town . . . with his mother-in-law, Mrs. Thompson, for the purpose of getting some household effects left by his wife. . . . In the conversation [with the neighbor] Lon said: "When I got married and settled down in Hersey I intended to lead an honorable and upright life. I took a contract for cutting cord wood and worked faithfully till my brother arrived from prison and put hell into me. I would give all of St. Croix County to be back where I was last winter, but the game is up. My wife is dead. We are fugitives from justice, and we have made up our minds never to be taken alive."

Lon's brief remarks here are also very revealing and support the self-analysis in his letter to Reverend Downer. A tragically alienated figure with a chronic lack of self-esteem, he had been poised between two forces—the young wife who was clearly healing his anxieties and prompting him to live "an honorable and upright life," creating a positive future for them both, and his brother, an almost demonic figure from his troubled past who "arrived from prison and put hell into me."

But now the good spiritual force was dead, and since rejecting Ed would mean embracing complete alienation—an unthinkable course for Lon—he rebonded with his brother: "*We* are fugitives from justice, and *we* have made up *our* minds never to be taken alive." Once again, as in Illinois, the Maxwells' dread of apprehension exceeded their fear of death, and it did so because capture and confinement would deny or diminish their identity as defiant outlaws, while death—or dying as desperadoes—would not. The Maxwells had indeed become very dangerous.

As the brief conversation at Hersey also reveals, after Fannie's death, Ed's psychological need to be a desperado, and his barely concealed death wish (to validate his bold, manly stature by dying in defiance of the authorities) deeply impacted Lon, who was hopelessly bound to his troubled brother. Alienated and distraught to the point of being suicidal, the younger Maxwell accepted, once again, the only meaningful identity that was being held out to him, even though it could only lead to further alienation—and perhaps eventual violent death. When he said "the game is up. My wife is dead. We are fugitives," he acknowledged that a bridge of no return had been crossed: He had no future that he could imagine, except as his brother's companion, a hunted outcast. His quest to change his life, to belong, had failed.

The Maxwell brothers were both doomed by psychological forces that they could not withstand.

As Ed later reported, Lon was completely distraught over Fannie's death, so they soon visited her freshly turned grave at the isolated Waubeek Prairie Cemetery. "We spent all the night in the graveyard," Ed said, "with Lon cryin' over her grave." Surely fighting his own demons in the profound and threatening darkness, Lon was, "by morning . . . ready to kill hisself [*sic*]."

While the two fugitives were hiding in the Eau Galle woods, they visited her grave several times so Lon could grieve and feel close to Fannie. The young desperado surely blamed himself, at least from time to time, for the loss of his "angel," but among his many psychological issues was the thought that her death was avoidable, that it might have been prevented with competent medical attention—as Ed later said in an interview:

> We never went near her grave that he did not sit there for an hour. Of course, I'd go with him for company, and once I had to keep guard with a cocked rifle.
>
> I heard Lon say once, "What did they [the doctors] take a quart of blood from my wife for?" And another time, when I asked him for his knife to cut a hole in a strap, I looked up in time to see his eyes glaring at me like a tiger, and his knife in his hand ready to strike. I called to him, and he drew his hand across his eyes and sighed, and then said, "Is that you, Ed? I thought it was one of them doctors."

That strange episode perhaps also reflected Lon's repressed animosity toward Ed—which he may have channeled toward the physicians. He appeared to sense that Ed was the cause of his ruined life, but he could not hate the person who was vital to his identity, so he hated the doctors instead.

While hiding in the woods, Ed and Lon probably had the cooperation of Bridget Thompson, who could easily have supplied them with food. And they surely wondered what to do next.

It is unlikely that they committed other robberies, but they may have. A September article in the *LaCrosse Daily News* asserts that in late June they stole two horses "from a farmer living about three miles from River Falls," were pursued by Pierce County lawmen to "the woods near the town of Cady in St. Croix County," and, when fired upon, "abandoned their horses and escaped into the darkness." But since those horse thieves were not clearly identified by their pursuers, that episode may have been mistakenly attributed to the Maxwells after the gunfight at Durand had made them notorious in western Wisconsin. Also, the *Chicago Times* reported that on June 30 Ed and Lon had been seen in Menomonie shortly before a jewelry store was robbed—and implied that they must have done it—but the actual perpetrator of that theft was later caught, tried, and convicted.

Those reports were, in fact, the beginning of what would soon become a torrent of rumor and folklore that would expand and confuse the Maxwell saga for many years.

The Gunfight at Durand

The summer of 1881 was a time of rising anxiety across the country, partly fueled by weeks of hot, dry weather in June and early July, which led to a searing drought that spread eastward from the Great Plains, creeping back across the Mississippi River to the farms of that more well-settled part of the West, still struggling to recover from the depression of the 1870s. In late June, a spectacular new comet, first seen by astronomers but soon visible to the naked eye from twilight till dawn, stunned the American public. Viewers often "felt abashed to find ourselves in the presence of the stranger, who [appeared] before us, unannounced," as one small-town newspaper put it. Of course, anxious and superstitious people soon proclaimed the mysterious visitor a portent of something calamitous that would soon occur.

A few days later, on July 2, President Garfield was shot in the back at the Baltimore and Potomac Railroad depot in Washington, D.C. His attacker was a disappointed office seeker named Charles Guiteau, whose plea for a consul appointment had been repeatedly rejected and whose growing irrationality was manifested as God's voice, telling him to kill the president for the good of America.

As doctors struggled to save the stricken leader, who had two serious bullet wounds, they issued frequent bulletins that were by turns hopeful or gloomy, and the American people kept a long, nerve-wracking vigil, anxiously and repeatedly searching their local newspapers for the latest word on the "President's Condition." Days would turn into weeks, and weeks into months, before the tragic end would finally come, in mid-September.

By then, some people were calling 1881 "The Bloody Comet Year," when "the old notion about the baleful influence of comets had some sort of justification," as one newspaper put it. For other reasons, too, 1881 would be a year of memorable violence, and from early July through December the nation would be tense with concern about the issue of law and order.

On Sunday, July 10, there was record-breaking heat throughout the Mississippi Valley, as the temperature soared to over 100 degrees and fatalities were reported everywhere, from Kansas City to Cincinnati. On the evening of that frightful day, it was still hot in Wisconsin's Chippewa Valley when Ed and Lon Maxwell emerged from their hiding place in the Eau Galle forest and headed south along the river to Durand. At the riverbank just west of town they encountered ferry owner Frank Goodrich and inquired about the location of the Pepin County Jail and the whereabouts of Undersheriff Miletus Knight. Then Frank's brother William ferried the two strangers across the Chippewa. He may have suspected that they were the much-sought "Williams" brothers, but even if he didn't, he could not help but notice that they were armed with Winchester repeating rifles and under their loose-hanging shirttails were bulges that looked like revolvers. So, after they got off the ferry and walked into the town, Goodrich notified the authorities.

As the Maxwell story evolved, the public mind often contributed dramatic facets to it, and that was surely true with regard to their ascribed motive for coming into Durand. The most widely repeated view was that Lon's anger at the two lawmen who had searched the Thompson home and the two doctors who had failed to save Fannie caused him to plan multiple murders, and Ed then joined with him to carry out that violent revenge. An item from the *Milwaukee Sentinel,* which appeared more than two weeks after the gunfight, presents that view:

THE OUTLAWS

Menomonie, July 25. There are no new developments.
. . . Meanwhile, the gossip in regard to the outlaws is rife
. . . and all manner of stories are in circulation. . . .

Parson Downer, of Arkansaw, near Menomonie, who officiated at the marriage of Alonzo Williams to Fanny Huzzy
[*sic*], a beautiful girl of Christian character, about a year
ago, and preached her funeral sermon a few weeks since, is
among the pursuers. . . . He believes Alonzo Williams to be
a man of good impulses. He is free from the use of intoxicat-
ing liquors and not given to profane language, but has been
misled by his brother Edward. It was through some scrape
[the South Stillwater robbery] into which Edward enticed
him that he was a fugitive from justice when his wife died,
an event which has embittered his life.

Coupled with this was a belief, which was stimulated by
his friends, that his wife's life might have been saved had
the doctors who attended her so willed it. He brooded over
these circumstances until nearly crazed, and wrote to Rev.
Downer concerning it. This circumstance snapped the last
cord that bound him to anything like an upright life, and
when he and his brother met the Colemans in the streets of
Durand, they were on a mission to murder Drs. Smith and
Morgan, who had attended his wife, and two officials, Knight
and Seeley, who had offended the grief-stricken man in the
discharge of their duty. . . .

While the article suggests, at first glance, that Reverend Downer was
the source of the assertion that the Maxwell brothers intended to kill
everyone who may have had some responsibility for Fannie's death, the
closing sentence actually contradicts Downer's assessment of Lon as an
essentially decent man manipulated by his brother. The statement of motive was, in fact, an addition by the correspondent, who was admittedly
hearing "all manner of stories" that were circulating about the Maxwells.
A planned mass murder of retribution was a motive that would surely
fascinate newspaper readers, so that is what he repeated.

Another version of this asserts that "Lon Williams told Mrs. Thompson,
his mother-in-law, that he was going to Durand to kill four men—officers
Knight and Seeley, who had offended him in the official discharge of their
duty, and Drs. Smith and Morgan, who attended his wife at her confinement and whom he insisted might have saved her life. . . ." But it seems
very unlikely that he would have told his churchgoing mother-in-law that
he was about to commit mass murder—especially since she had called in

those doctors and had told him about the upsetting search of the premises by Undersheriff Knight and Marshal Seeley. She would have felt the need to stop him and would have reminded him that killing four men was no way to demonstrate Fannie's impact on him or honor her memory.

What surely happened was that Lon's anger at the doctors for not saving his wife and at the lawmen for searching the Thompson home and causing Fannie great emotional stress was simply elevated in the public mind to a dramatic intention—multiple murder in Durand.

A much later newspaper item, reporting an interview with Ed shortly before his death, provides the Maxwells' actual motive: "Our idea was to get to Sheriff Knight's house that night, catch him in bed, get the drop on him, and make him take us to where the horse he captured from us was concealed." This confession of violent purpose, so typical of Ed, is supported by everything that we know about the Maxwells: Ed planned the Durand exploit and, as usual, Lon went along with it. None of their outlaw activities was ever instigated by Lon, nor did their actions prior to the gunfight suggest that they were interested in murdering local physicians and lawmen.

Ed's desire to force Undersheriff Knight to return the stolen horse that he had confiscated was, of course, a crazy intention—even though the bay stallion from the Evans farm was a first-rate steed. It would have been much safer and easier to simply steal another horse at some remote farmstead. But Ed's confrontations with, and escapes from, lawmen and posses were always driven by his need to validate his identity as a desperado—to show that he was not a helpless victim of the social order, a man shamed by his inadequacy, but a revenger—and nothing would soothe the damage done to his self-image by Knight's confiscation of the horse like boldly stealing it back. Other comments by Ed reveal that he also did not have much respect for Knight, viewing him as "an old granny" who lacked the courage to confront them, so Ed was apparently convinced that it wouldn't take much to intimidate him and secure the horse.

That was the problem with creating an identity as a desperado: You always had to live up to it, no matter how dangerous the situation might be. Ed refused to abandon his assertive, radically free outlaw identity, even when maintaining it was reckless and sure to bring a violent confrontation with the law.

As the plan to steal back the horse also suggests, Ed was unconsciously seeking some kind of consummation, some exploit that would permanently seal his transcendence of the subjugated-son-turned-worthless-farmhand identity that had humiliated him. In his mind, the Durand exploit would diminish the impact of his troubled past.

Lon surely did resent the intrusion of Undersheriff Knight and Marshal Seeley at the Thompson home shortly before Fannie died, but that only made Ed's risky venture easier to go along with. Miletus Knight could have come to represent for Lon all the impersonal forces that had been arrayed against him.

Searching for Miletus Knight, the Maxwell brothers met, by accident, the Coleman brothers, who symbolized law and order in the Chippewa Valley. That is why the gunfight resonated so deeply with people in the region and the state: The Maxwells attacked the foundation of civilized society in western Wisconsin.

The Coleman family had come west from Long Island, New York, and lived for many years in Bloomington, Illinois, where father Henry Coleman was a successful blacksmith and implement maker. Charles Coleman was born there in 1841 and moved with his parents to Maxville Prairie in Buffalo County, just south of Durand, in 1857.

During the Civil War, Charles enlisted in the Tenth Wisconsin Infantry— the regiment later famous for having a bald eagle named "Old Abe" for a mascot—and he was wounded at the Battle of Perryville, Kentucky, on October 8, 1862. He was struck in the forehead by a rifle ball, which not only ended his military career but caused him to have blinding headaches and occasional seizures for the rest of his life.

After the war, Charles moved to Durand, where he was a recognized hero and a very well-liked man. Although the lingering impact of his wound made it difficult for him to work, he was a blacksmith, and he also served for several years in the part-time post of undersheriff. He must have done well as a lawman, for he eventually served a two-year term (1877–78) as the sheriff of Pepin County. During that time he arrested several horse thieves, and he once survived a brutal fight with a man in his custody. As his friend and neighbor Miletus Knight once put it, "Charlie was shot through the head once or twice while in the army, but he is not easily handled." Socially, he was very active in the Pepin County veterans' organization, as was Knight.

Milton Coleman was a much younger man. Born in Bloomington in 1856, he was still an infant when his parents moved to Wisconsin. After his father's death in 1869, he remained with his mother, and together they moved to Menomonie in 1875. He was appointed undersheriff of Dunn County by Sheriff T. J. George in January 1879, and after serving for two years, was reappointed to the post by George's successor, Sheriff Sever Severson. Regarded as a very capable officer, although only twenty-five years old, Milton apparently admired his older brother Charles and was anxious to prove himself as a lawman.

The earliest newspaper account of the gunfight was a *Pepin County Courier* extra—a small broadside issued on Monday morning, July 11. It carried a single article, which was printed to alert the community to the awful act of violence. "HORRIBLE MURDER! AT DURAND!" it proclaimed; "Chas. and Milton Coleman Shot Dead by the Williams Brothers." The report includes a brief account of the gunfight and vague physical descriptions of Ed and Lon, who are simply regarded as "desperadoes . . . who have been prowling about this part of the state." It adds that they had often disguised themselves with "false whiskers and hair"—an untrue comment surely based on conflicting descriptions of them.

The most complete of several newspaper accounts of the gunfight at Durand appeared several days later, in Menomonie's *Dunn County News,* and it begins by explaining why Milton Coleman happened to be in Durand on that fateful day:

A DOUBLE MURDER!

One of the most shocking tragedies occurred in . . . Durand last Sunday evening, that ever took place in the Chippewa Valley. About half-past eight on that evening, Milton A. Coleman, Undersheriff of Dunn County, and his brother, Charles G. Coleman, Deputy Sheriff of Pepin County, were shot dead by two desperadoes, Alonzo and Ed Williams, while attempting their arrest. . . .

On arriving at Durand, Sunday evening, it was learned that the Williams brothers had crossed the river in a skiff, about five o'clock in the afternoon, just above the village and were lurking in the vicinity. Milton put [a thief he had caught] in the Durand Jail and, accompanied by his brother Charles, started out to capture them. Several citizens who knew their mission told the officers not to run so great a risk in attempting to capture, without assistance, two such desperate men, armed to the teeth with revolvers and Winchester rifles, and urged them to take a posse of armed men along. But they declined assistance and went on alone, armed with revolvers and double-barreled shotguns, loaded with small shot.

They proceeded up the street leading to the Eau Claire road, inquiring of parties, as they went along, if they had seen any armed persons. Arriving at the house of a man named [J. T.] Dorchester, they again stopped and made similar inquiries of a couple of boys who were on the porch. The boys had seen no such persons, and came to the gate [of the picket fence]. It was now in the dark of the evening, between half-past eight and nine o'clock. While they stood there talking, Milton looked down the street toward the village and saw two men walking side by side, coming towards them, close to the fence by which they were standing. Charles was talking to the boys when his brother said, "Hush! There they are now." The Colemans cocked their guns and the men continued to approach leisurely. Milton stood near the fence, and Charles stepped about six feet from the fence and two or three feet to the rear of his brother. Both had their guns at "ready," and when the two men approaching them were within five or six paces, Milton brought his gun to his shoulder, leveled it on Alonzo Williams, and said, "You are my—"

He never finished the sentence, for at that instant [Lon] Williams fired, and the fatal ball passed through his neck, breaking it, and severing the veins and arteries in its course. Almost at the same instant Milton fired and fell dead. A second shot from the desperado grazed Milton's left cheek as he was falling. After firing his second shot, Alonzo turned and ran back down the street to the corner where they were first seen.

During this fatal and bloody duel between Milton Coleman and Alonzo Williams, another [duel], equally bloody and equally fatal, was being fought by Charles Coleman and Ed Williams by their sides. They exchanged shots almost instantaneously. Coleman received a fatal shot, the ball entering his body just below the heart. He staggered several steps toward the middle of the street, Williams firing shot after shot in rapid succession. Coleman at last sank on one knee and fired a second time, then fell and almost instantly expired. He was struck twice—one shot taking effect in the body and the other in the arm near the shoulder, crushing the bone. It is not known whether Ed Williams, his antagonist, was wounded or not. Ed fired five or six shots, then turned and walked deliberately away and joined his brother near the corner of the fence. The two ruffians then made good their escape.

The only witnesses to this awful tragedy were two boys who stood at the gate, and from the oldest, a lad of about fourteen, the details above narrated were received. He stood inside the gate, the Colemans a few feet to his right and the Williams a few feet to his left. . . . It is evident, however, that he is mistaken about the rifles. Each of them doubtless had a Winchester rifle, but it is plain they did their bloody work with the revolver. It is well-known that a Winchester cannot be fired a second time without throwing out an empty shell. . . .

The rapid succession of shots ringing out in the still night air aroused the people in the vicinity, and they rushed quickly to the scene. Both brothers were found dead where they fell—Milton near the fence and Charles near the center of the street. The hat of Alonzo Williams—a low, round-crowned black hat with a band of crepe around it—was picked up near where he stood during the shooting. Spots of blood were found on the boards of the fence for several feet, which is pretty conclusive proof that he was at least slightly wounded. . . .

The two-story home of brickyard owner James T. Dorchester, in front of which the gunfight occurred, was on the northeastern outskirts of the village, where the road from Durand (Prospect Street) forked, one branch leading east past the village cemetery, to Mondovi, and the other going northeast, across Bear Creek, to Eau Claire.

The *Dunn County News* account is wrong in two respects. First of all, Charles Coleman was not a current deputy sheriff of Pepin County. He was simply a former sheriff who had been enlisted by his brother to help with the arrest. But the symbolic meaning of the tragedy was the same: The Maxwells had murdered the defenders of law and order in two counties. Also, Ed and Lon had, in fact, used their Winchester repeating rifles, firing them from the hip, as they had no doubt practiced doing time and again in recent months. One of the discharged shells was later found. They did not draw their revolvers. And Ed did not fire "shot after shot." When Charles fired a second time, down on one knee, Ed responded again, as he later pointed out: "[He] gave me the other barrel, then I fired again, and he fell clear down. That was all I fired at him. . . ."

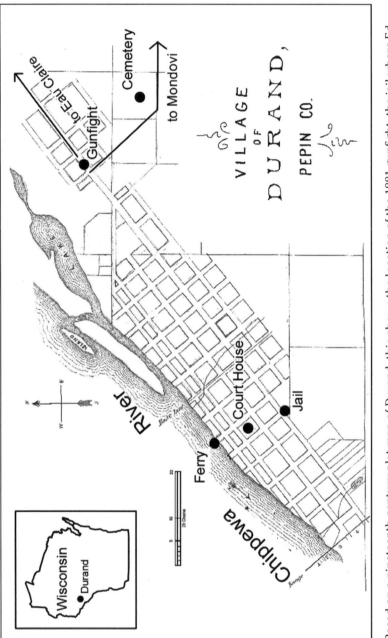

Based on a nineteenth-century plat map of Durand, this shows the location of the 1881 gunfight, the jail where Ed was later held, and the courthouse where he was lynched.

The band of crepe around the crown of Lon's hat was, of course, a sign that he was mourning for Fannie, who had been dead for twenty-five days when the gunfight occurred. As it suggests, and his letter to Reverend Downer confirms, her death contributed to his readiness, or perhaps eagerness, for such a violent encounter.

Several months later, Ed provided an overview of the gunfight during a statement at the courthouse in Durand, and a newspaperman for the *Wisconsin State Journal,* published in Madison, reported it:

> We killed the Coleman boys in self-defense, but didn't know them from Adam. We were sitting in the grove uptown when we saw them pass us. They had guns with them, and looked around often, as if searching for something. We knew there was no game about there, and that they wouldn't go hunting on Sunday if there was, so we knew they were after us, and [we] kept a sharp lookout. When they got past us, they started to run. Then we got over the fence and followed them up the road, thinking we were being surrounded and caught in a trap. We had not gone far before we met them, and the one nearest the fence [Milton] fired first, his shot hitting Lon in the face and arm. Charley fired at me, and me at him a second later. His shot struck my arm, and he fell to my bullet, but got on his knee and fired again. Lon had shot the other one before that, and both men were down. Then we turned and run.

The two accounts differ on the crucial matter of who shot first. The Menomonie newspaper report claimed that Lon had fired while Milton Coleman was speaking to him, and Ed bluntly stated that the younger Coleman had fired first. What probably happened was that, a second after Milton Coleman raised his shotgun to his shoulder, Lon fired his Winchester from the hip, and both shots were virtually simultaneous. Lon's bullet severed the undersheriff's jugular vein and spinal cord—as the inquest later showed—making it impossible for him to fire in response. Another account, in the Durand newspaper, was correct when it asserted, "He [Milton] must have been dead before he fell, but fired one barrel of his gun almost at the same instant that Lon Williams fired the shot which killed him." And after all, Milton's shotgun blast did hit Lon in the arm, shoulder, and face—a shot too effective to be made by him after Lon's bullet had ripped through his neck. Lon may not have fired a second shot, for no discharged shell from his rifle was ever found—and Lon had been severely wounded.

In the other duel, it is more likely that Ed's rifle bullet reached Charles Coleman's lower chest before the ex-sheriff fired his shotgun, for the discharge substantially missed Ed, some of the bird shot merely hitting Ed's arm as Charles staggered in the street, dropped to his knees, and fired again, while being shot a second time by Ed. That final bullet "hit his right arm close to the shoulder, crushing the bone into a hundred pieces," according to the Durand newspaper.

In any case, it is clear that the double gunfight was an accidental encounter for the Maxwells, who had nothing against the Coleman brothers and no idea who they had killed—or even whether they were lawmen, posse members, or bounty hunters—until they later read about it in a newspaper. When Ed claimed that the killings were in "self-defense," he was invoking a code that had been acknowledged time and again in Fulton and McDonough counties—and was still common throughout the Mississippi Valley: If a man pulled a gun on you, it was your right to defend yourself by shooting him dead. You had no obligation to submit to his threat. To Ed and Lon, the gunfight was an act of necessary violence, a defense of their manhood and perhaps their lives. And no account of the gunfight at Durand ever claimed that the Colemans had identified themselves as lawmen. Charles clearly had no badge, and whether Milton's was visible is unknown.

On a deeper level, however, the gunfight was anything but accidental or merely an act of self-defense. The Maxwells' severe alienation and psychological need to defy authority in order to maintain their identity as desperadoes meant that some violent encounter with lawmen was inevitable. It could have happened with Sheriff Waggoner in the Spoon River brakes, or Deputy Sheriff Hays at Beardstown, or Sheriff Venard's posse after the Macomb jailbreak, or Chief Shortall's posse near Stillwater, or Sheriff Kelly and his one-man posse at Hersey, or Sheriff Anderson's posse in central Illinois, or with Undersheriff Knight and Marshal Seeley near Waubeek, but instead, it happened when the Coleman brothers sought them at Durand.

Charles and Milton Coleman were men of good character and great courage, but while the shocked and bereaved public celebrated them as fallen heroes, their motivations were never closely examined. The gunfight was, in a sense, precipitated by young Milton Coleman, a dedicated lawman who recruited his war-damaged but more experienced older brother to hunt down the outlaws. First appointed undersheriff at the incredibly young age of twenty-two, and only twenty-five when he died, Milton was obviously intent on a law enforcement career, but was just as obviously an inexperienced young man. He represented the youthful, post–Civil War generation, raised on tales of heroism but without the mature judgment that came with military discipline and battle experience—or with many years of work as a lawman.

In fact, during 1879 Milton had traveled extensively in the exciting far West, as a young man looking for adventure might—"roughing it among hunters, scouts, miners, and frontiersmen," as the *Menomonie Times* put it. Anxious for a chance to serve as undersheriff, which would come just after he returned, he must have been aware of legendary lawman Wild Bill Hickok, formerly of Dodge City, who had been killed at Deadwood in 1876, and he may have heard of Dodge City's subsequent marshal, Ed Masterson (brother of Bat), who had been shot dead in 1878. Elsewhere, lawmen were searching for colorful outlaws like stage robber Black Bart, who operated in California, and gunfighter Billy the Kid, who was notorious in New Mexico.

In short, Milton Coleman may have had a romanticized view of western lawmen—who faced gunfighters and other outlaws in the states and territories he traveled through—very much like Ed Maxwell had a romanticized view of desperadoes. If so, that would explain why he rejected the counsel of those in Durand who advised him to raise a posse before searching the town, shotgun in hand, for the Maxwells. Moreover, there is other evidence that he was warned to be cautious, as an article in the *St. Paul Pioneer Press* pointed out:

> "Go prepared. They are desperadoes and will resist arrest." These words were written in red on a postal card found on the body of Milton Coleman after he was murdered by one of the Williams brothers at Durand, on Monday evening, July 10th. The card found was soaked in the blood of the victim, but clearly legible on it, written in black ink, was the description of the two desperate characters who were wanted in Henderson County, Ill., for horse stealing. The card was signed by J. O. Anderson, sheriff of Henderson County. It was this simple message that directed the two brave Colemans to their deaths.

Milton was a courageous young lawman, but stalking desperadoes that he knew (from the ferryman) had Winchester repeating rifles, while he and his brother were armed only with shotguns that fired bird shot, was foolhardy. Had the Maxwells intended to shoot them down, they could have done so, in perfect safety, from hundreds of feet away.

As the postcard in Milton's pocket also suggests, he and his brother Charles were perhaps enticed to make the arrest by themselves because Sheriff Anderson was offering a reward for the capture of the Maxwells. Both men were in need of money.

It was the "wanted" postcard that also led to the immediate notification of Anderson. He then traveled by train to Wisconsin and was in Durand by Wednesday morning, July 13, to participate in the manhunt and, if possible, retrieve the stolen horses.

Newspaper coverage of the dramatic gunfight was extensive in the Midwest. The reaction in western Wisconsin was typified by the front-page article in the *Hudson Star and Times* on July 15, which referred to the Maxwells as "TWO HELL-HOUNDS" and asserted that "A Vigilance Committee Is on Their Track." Indeed, a sizable and growing posse was already searching for the desperadoes, who had crossed the Chippewa River after the gunfight and headed north into the rugged forest along the Eau Galle River. Strictly speaking, the searchers were not a vigilante group bent on circumventing the law, but among them were men with lynching on their minds.

The chief exponent of lynching was W. H. Huntington, editor of the *Pepin County Courier.* A distinguished-looking thirty-two-year-old man, who wore glasses, sported a mustache, and smoked a pipe, Huntington had a family background in Vermont and New York. He had edited the *Durand Times* from 1873 to 1876, then had sold that newspaper to enter the livery business, but he had not done well, and so established the *Courier* in 1877. A staunch Republican and a leader in the Odd Fellows and other organizations, he regarded many of the poor, forest-dwelling folks as riffraff and celebrated businessmen like himself. When the gunfight occurred, he was a candidate for state assemblyman, and later that summer, he bought Durand's only hotel, the Ecklor House.

Huntington tended to approve and encourage mob violence. In 1878, for example, when a man named William Chase, accused of murder at Chippewa Falls, escaped from a lynch mob only to be recaptured by lawmen, Huntington recommended that "the mob again take his case in hand" to provide the punishment that Chase deserved.

On Friday, July 15, Huntington printed a five-column story on the Durand gunfight and its aftermath, under the headline "SAD TRAGEDY." Included in its long subtitle was a comment likely to encourage pursuit: "The Assassins Still at Large! $1,700 Reward!" Toward the close of his stirring report, Huntington asserted that "Lynch law is *sometimes* justifiable," clearly implying that this was one of those times.

Back in Macomb, Illinois, the local newspapers began to follow the dramatic case, reprinting articles from many sources, for a horrified and fascinated readership. The first of those pieces, in the July 14 *Macomb Journal,* was titled "THOSE BAD MEN: The Maxwells' Bloody Work." One detailed report of the gunfight, reprinted from the pages of the *St. Paul Pioneer Press,* had the lurid title "BROTHERS OF BLOOD."

The story was also big news in larger cities. The *Milwaukee Daily Sentinel* printed a long article on page one, and the *Chicago Tribune* began its extensive coverage of the gunfight and the manhunt with a lengthy report as well.

In Madison, the *Wisconsin State Journal* reported that the Williams brothers were members of "the James and Younger band of outlaws," thus elevating them to legendary stature and circulating folklore that would spread widely through the newspapers and remain in the public mind for decades. Ed Maxwell would have been thrilled.

The quick association with the James-Younger gang, the ultimate American outlaws, resulted partly from the ultimacy of their act, killing two lawmen from two counties in a single gunfight, and partly from the mystique of outlaw brotherhood that had arisen with the notorious Reno brothers and had continued with the James and Younger brothers, and now included the two Maxwells, the "BROTHERS OF BLOOD."

Meanwhile, back in Durand, an inquest was held on July 11 "over the bodies of Charles Coleman and Milton Coleman, now lying dead at the house of Mr. [Martin] Maxwell [a brother-in-law of the Colemans, unrelated to the outlaws]." Local folks gathered there and reported what they knew. Very few knew anything for certain, despite the fact that a newspaper correspondent asserted that "the murder was the theme of conversation in every household; and on the street many men can be seen discussing the various phases of the murder. . . ." Interestingly, William and Bridget Thompson were summoned by Justice of the Peace A. C. Hammond "to give evidence"—undoubtedly about any contact they may have had with Ed and Lon prior to the gunfight. They also provided accurate descriptions of the two desperadoes. Testimony convinced the inquest jurors, who were led by newspaperman W. H. Huntington, that the Maxwells, locally known as Ed and Lon Williams, were the killers of the Coleman brothers.

Two days after the gunfight, a double funeral for the Coleman brothers was held at Durand. The *Pepin County Courier* gave an account of that huge ceremony, "the largest ever held in this locality," and the separate one for

Milton in Menomonie, as well as the burial. A *Menomonie Times* account of the ceremony for Milton mentioned that "the funeral cortege from Durand entered the streets of Menomonie with the tolling of bells," and "the remains were taken to the courthouse and placed in the hall; the casket [was] opened, and the people looked on the unconscious face of their defender; and then the sad procession—the largest funeral procession ever seen in Menomonie—wound its way to Evergreen Cemetery. . . ."

On the day of the Coleman funerals, all of the businesses in Durand and Menomonie were closed and flags were flown at half-mast. Members of the Durand Masonic Lodge wore crepe armbands for the Charles Coleman ceremony—and kept those on for a month afterward, as a token of remembrance. Local people wanted those sacrificed lives to be held sacred. And in both towns, the entire occasion prompted an upwelling of strong feelings on the issue of law and order, which lasted through the fall.

The grave of Milton Coleman, in Menomonie, was eventually marked by a marble headstone, which simply said that he had died on July 10, 1881, at age twenty-five. Nothing was explained, and no tribute was expressed. But his brother's grave, in Forest Hill Cemetery at Durand, eventually received a limestone marker that said, beneath his birth and death dates, "He died at his post."

While the sentiment behind that inscription is understandable, the sad truth was that Charles Coleman had no post—as many townspeople knew. In the *Pepin County Courier* extra that broke the news about the deadly gunfight, editor Huntington—himself a public official of the local court—stated things accurately: "Charles Coleman, of this village, and Milton Coleman, Deputy Sheriff of Dunn County, were shot and instantly killed. . . ." Charles had no law enforcement position, or it would have been mentioned. In a later issue, Huntington explained that because of his Civil War wound to the head, "he was unable to engage in active business for the past two or three years, and his government pension of $24 per month has been the main support of himself and family." But now even that would cease, leaving "his bereaved and almost helpless family left in very straitened circumstances." The jobless war hero had, in fact, seven children, and although no one outside of the family knew it yet, his wife was again pregnant. His posthumous child, a son, would be named Charles Milton Coleman to honor both of the fallen brothers.

A group of lodge brothers and other men who had known him started a memorial fund to help support his destitute widow and children. Many local residents contributed to that effort—while others searched for the men who killed him.

Milton Coleman's situation also contributed to the public determination to find and punish the killers. He was the chief support of his widowed mother, with whom he still lived, and he was also engaged to be married in the early fall to Miss Rosa Nott, a highly regarded Menomonie school-teacher. Each woman was devastated by her loss.

The killing of two popular brothers, both well-known as lawmen and one admired as a war hero, seemed like an assault on family and community and patriotism, as well as law and order. The regional public's deep sense of cultural violation fostered a temporary strengthening of social bonds that transcended socioeconomic differences. No wonder the grief and outrage of the family and friends of the Coleman brothers was so readily shared by people up and down the Chippewa River Valley. The spirit of vengeance soon arose in the hearts of shopkeepers and mill hands, trades-men and lumberjacks, who muttered about "what ought to be done" to the killers.

Meanwhile, the slain brothers were celebrated, and idealized, in the lo-cal newspapers. The *Pepin County Courier* described Charles as "a model of Christian manhood, a brave, true, strong soul; a lofty patriot; a kind, generous, unselfish man—whose only enemy was evil," and who had died "with undaunted courage, fighting foes of mankind." The *Dunn County News* called Milton "a man of exemplary character and sterling integrity, who won the friendship and esteem of all by his quiet manners, genial ways, and strict devotion to duty."

In the Durand newspaper a poetic tribute called "Sweet Be Their Rest" depicted them as heroes who fell "at duty's post" and are mourned by a distraught populace that will soon "avenge the loss of those who weep." It is clear that many of those who pursued the Maxwells were, in fact, on a mission of vengeance. As the nearby *Barron County News* put it, a few days after the gunfight, "A posse started in hot pursuit," but "the excitement in Menomonie and Durand is terrible, and if the villains are captured by their present pursuers, it is likely that no jury will ever try them." A dispatch from Menomonie to the *Wisconsin State Journal* at Madison agreed: "If [the Maxwells] are caught, there is every reason to believe they will be lynched." And a report from Eau Claire, printed in the *St. Paul Pioneer Press,* was more explicit: "The excited men will probably riddle their carcasses with bullets . . . if [they are] captured."

Like wolves on the frontier, the Maxwell brothers had become symbolic—a vicious, threatening presence, inherently opposed to civilized society, that simply had to be hunted down and eliminated. Of course, that public mind-set prevented any serious reflection on the American social forces that had laid the groundwork for the gunfight, and it distanced people from the reality that men who had shot down public officials in the street were, in fact, much like themselves—not opponents of, but products of, American culture in the West.

Although wounded, Ed and Lon had a good start, for they apparently hid in the woods near the Durand Cemetery until sunset, then circled around the village to the Chippewa River, stole a boat, and crossed over in the dark. Because Durand had no railroad, it also had no telegraph office, so word was slow in getting out. No active pursuit was launched until Monday at about noon, when Deputy Sheriff E. L. Doolittle brought down thirty men from Dunn County to comb the Eau Galle woods, and Sheriff A. F. Peterson gathered a small posse of Pepin County volunteers, crossed the Chippewa, and headed northwest into the same area.

Those men would soon be joined by hundreds of others—all of them anxious to avenge the deaths of two men they knew and admired. In a stirring headline, the *Chicago Times* soon called them what they were: "THE BLOOD AVENGERS." Like the vigilantes in Walter Van Tilburg Clark's *The Ox-Bow Incident,* they had already condemned their prey and were anxious to prove themselves—and to repress their own fear and self-doubt—by participating in a grim, thrilling, manly display of violence.

11

The Great Manhunt

At the time of the Durand gunfight, the great days of the James gang were coming to an end, although Jesse and Frank remained at large. In that anxiety-ridden summer of 1881, the gang robbed two more trains—their final holdups—but since the disastrous Northfield raid five years earlier, the James brothers had spent most of their time hiding, under assumed names, from the lawmen and detectives who were quietly pursuing them. The end of their long career as desperadoes would finally come in 1882.

The big outlaw story during the first half of 1881 concerned Billy the Kid. A New Mexico cattle rustler, horse thief, and gunfighter, he had come to regional attention in 1880, and then in April 1881 he was convicted of killing Lincoln County sheriff William Brady. He gained national notoriety when he broke jail on April 28, killing two deputies in the process. Rewards totaling $1,500 were posted for him, and the new Lincoln County sheriff, Pat Garrett, relentlessly tracked him. On the night of July 14, Garrett shot him dead, and that too was national news. The *New York Times,* for example, reported the outlaw's fate in a page-five article.

At that same time, however, a much more spectacular manhunt, also for sheriff killers, was just getting started in the Mississippi Valley. It would soon involve one of the largest posses ever assembled to pursue outlaws, and eventually many other posses and lawmen in several states, becoming in fact the biggest manhunt for outlaws in American history. It would also generate a vast amount of newspaper copy, becoming as well the most extensively reported outlaw pursuit. The James gang prompted many more articles during their long career, but no single episode of lawbreaking and escape—not even the disastrous bank raid at Northfield, Minnesota, and the subsequent manhunt for those infamous outlaws—generated such thorough newspaper coverage. The nature and extent of the coverage, in fact, had an impact on the size and continuation of the Maxwell pursuit.

The search for Ed and Lon was soon focused on the Eau Galle woods, a thinly inhabited wilderness in the northwest part of Pepin County, north of Arkansaw, which stretched away along the Eau Galle River into nearby Dunn and Pierce counties. As one writer who saw the area in 1881 said, it was a region of "bold bluffs, crowned with chaplets of tall timber," and "ridges covered with a thick growth of trees and tangly brush," and it had "ravines, choked up with an impenetrable mass of scrubby forest," as well as occasionally "stony-sided chasms" and "streams of all sorts." The *St. Paul Pioneer Press* correspondent, who also saw the terrain, summed up the challenge it posed for the lawmen and posse members: "I cannot imagine a country better suited for a hiding place, or one which presents so many difficulties to the pursuers." Like the landscape in many a western movie, it symbolized "the wild," the uncivilized, and it promised a kind of ultimate test for men who were willing to join the manhunt.

The authorities knew that Lon's in-laws lived on the edge of that rugged expanse of virgin timber, just west of the Eau Galle River and a few miles south of a lumber mill hamlet called Eau Galle, so they were determined to search there first.

Moreover, Ed and Lon had been spotted. On the day after the gunfight a woman reported seeing two armed men in that area. "One man carried both guns," she said, "and the other had his hand bandaged."

The Maxwells were on foot, for both were wounded—Lon more severely—and they were not in shape to steal and ride horses. The Eau Galle country was not a place for horses anyway. It was too rugged, and, as Ed and Lon knew, the horses would leave a trail that was easy to follow.

Sheriff Peterson left Undersheriff Knight in charge of his office at Durand and took his posse of a few dozen men out of town to the northwest, "distributing them into small squads which were scattered through the woods between Durand and [the hamlet of] Eau Galle," as the *Chicago Times* soon reported, "and he divided his time between the temporary camping-places of those parties, [which were] on picket and guard duty."

Peterson was a young man—a smooth-shaven twenty-six-year-old whose blonde hair and blue eyes betrayed his Swedish background—and this was his first opportunity to "grasp . . . the widest possible scope of what were the duties, the dangers, and the responsibilities and cares of his office," as a newspaper said. In short, he was inexperienced. In thinly populated Pepin County, which had only 6,188 people in 1880, the sheriff's duties were usually light and were often confined to delivering notices for civil cases and keeping the county seat orderly on Saturday nights.

A more experienced man was Dunn County's ex-sheriff E. L. Doolittle, of Menomonie, a graying, bearded fifty-five year old who had been in the Thirty-seventh Wisconsin Infantry during the Civil War. He had quickly risen from private to sergeant and, toward the end of the war, had been commissioned as a lieutenant. He knew how to manage a sizable group of men. Wounded at the Battle of Petersburg, he had been captured by rebel soldiers. Eventually paroled, he returned home, recuperated for several months, and then returned to the battlefield. After the war, he was a widely admired hero, serving as "colonel" (or commander) of the Dunn County Old Veterans Association. During the late 1860s he had been appointed undersheriff, and then in 1871 and 1872 he had served as sheriff. Dunn County then had about ten thousand people but was rapidly growing, and the sheriff was fairly busy with criminal cases, especially robbery and assault. Doolittle later served as undersheriff while the elected position of sheriff was passed around to others, and, according to one source, he developed "the reputation of always getting his man." Deputized by Sheriff Sever Severson, an inexperienced lawman who remained in Menomonie, Doolittle started southwest to the Eau Galle forest with a posse of thirty men, which soon grew much larger. Within a few days he was in charge of the manhunt, leading volunteers from "Hersey, Knapp, Menomonie, Durand, Dunnville, and all the adjacent towns," as the *Wisconsin State Journal* soon reported.

Because the Eau Galle forest was connected with the vast wilds of western Wisconsin, extending south and west to the Mississippi River, west and northwest to the St. Croix River, and north to Lake Superior, Doolittle knew that if the outlaws escaped from the Pepin County area, an army would not be able to find them.

An early report to the *Chicago Tribune,* on Tuesday, July 12, indicates that some 150 volunteers had already joined the search, and it also asserts, "There are rumors that the vigilantes met their men [the outlaws] early in the evening, and that a pitched battle was in progress, but the news could not be confirmed. . . ." As that reveals, rumors started flying almost immediately. Very few of them were true, including this one.

Another false report, providing what the public deeply wanted to hear— that the desperadoes would soon be killed—was published on the front page of the *St. Paul Pioneer Press.* The article title conveys the essential story:

CORNERED IN A COOLEY.

The Fugitive Williams Brothers Surrounded
by Their Pursuers in the Town of Eau Galle.
But with Their Four Winchester Rifles
and Stock of Revolvers,
They Will Fight to the Last.
Supposition that the Desperadoes Will Be
Tortured to Death if Captured Alive. . . .

As this rumor reveals, people clearly expected the Maxwells to be lynched—and the public mind was already starting to shape their story. Evident here is the foundation for their later emergence as outlaw heroes in dime novels. Pursued by a huge posse, they were defiant fugitives who would surely "Fight to the Last." The constant threat of death from an ever-growing band of vengeful pursuers, together with their dogged resistance, was elevating them to a kind of heroic status.

The Springfield, Illinois, newspaper even carried an article titled "Three Hundred Men Afraid to Tackle the Williams Brothers." It reported that the Doolittle posse had trapped the infamous outlaws in the Eau Galle woods but were waiting for the state militia so as to avoid loss of life. Equally folkloric, that report also reveals the public perception of the Maxwells as uncommonly dangerous desperadoes.

Aside from the widespread desire to bring in, or lynch, the killers of two popular lawmen, another factor that helped to swell the ranks of the posse was the reward money that was soon posted. On July 12 Wisconsin Governor William E. Smith proclaimed a $500 reward for the arrest of the Maxwells, and that was soon matched by $500 rewards offered by Dunn and Pepin counties. Henderson County, where the brothers were still wanted for horse theft, added $200. The $1,700 total was an enormous reward for that era. And it would eventually go higher.

Another factor that helped to draw men into the posse was the opportunity to participate in a grand, exciting manhunt. A number of them were Civil War veterans—"old soldiers," as one newspaper called them—who relished the chance to once again pack their guns, ride their horses, camp in the wild, and prove themselves in a dangerous, military-style operation.

The early efforts of ex-sheriff Doolittle and his posse were soon chronicled in the Menomonie newspaper, which reported that camps had been established at a schoolhouse near the mouth of Knight's Creek and at a deserted mill on Missouri Creek. The posse's headquarters were at the hamlet of Eau Galle, between the two camps. As the report indicated, "From these points scouting parties were sent out each day, to find some trace of the fugitives. At night pickets were placed at various points to keep a constant watch on roads and paths. . . ." The article also passed along "various rumors and reports of the outlaws having been seen," including these:

> Monday, July [11], about 9 a.m., two men seen by Mrs. Pericol and her boy; same evening, about seven o'clock, the two men were seen by a young man at the ford three miles above Eau Galle; . . . same evening about ten o'clock Dr. J. R. Branch, one of the guards stationed at the old school-house near the mouth of Knight's Creek, saw two men approach and shot at them without effect; Wednesday, two men were seen in the bushes by a woman who was picking cherries about eighty rods west of the Pine Tavern. . . . Saturday morning two men were seen by John Adsit entering the woods near Jack Allen's place in Waubeek; the same night, about midnight, two men were seen by Chas. Wenzel as he was crossing a field on his way home. Sunday afternoon, two boys of Truman Smith met two men in the road answering to the description of the outlaws. . . .

Unfortunately, some of the reported sightings were simply cases of mistaken identity, but the fumbled effort at the country school was an actual encounter with the Maxwells.

Lon was severely wounded and Ed was also bleeding from a scattering of shot holes, mostly in his arm. Ed later reported that he took some sixty lead shot out of his brother and bathed Lon's wounds in creek water to help him recover.

Moving primarily at night, they trudged on through the mosquito-infested darkness, then tried to sleep in the daytime. During their flight they often had no food, one time for as long as three and a half days, and they could only slake their thirst when they encountered a stream. As the days passed, they became increasingly thin and filthy, their beards overgrown, hair unkempt, clothes tattered. Hunger, thirst, pain, fear, and exhaustion—

in the stifling midsummer heat—combined to make their experience on the run a nightmarish struggle for survival.

Among the tales that arose during the manhunt was the story of an encounter between the Maxwells and "one of the armed scouts" in the massive posse. The fugitives stopped the lone horseman and "asked how many sheriffs . . . were hunting through the country after them," and when the scout replied that he did not know, they ordered him "to tell their pursuers that they were waiting there . . . to have the whole crowd come and arrest them." Of course, when the scout returned with a large party of men, they had vanished.

Printed in the *Eau Claire Free Press* as a report from the manhunt, this was in fact a folk tale that illustrated the confrontational boldness of the great desperadoes as well as their ability to elude the huge posse of lawmen and vigilantes. Those factors obviously fascinated the public.

The posse continued to grow, and some of its members were mentioned in the newspapers. An article in the *Wisconsin State Journal* reported that "E. C. and Henry Coleman, brothers of the victims, joined the chase yesterday [on July 14]." The older one, Edward, was the general manager of the Bailey Manufacturing Company at Knapp, near Hersey. Henry, just twenty-two years old, had lived with his slain brother Milton and his mother in Menomonie. Fearing that they too might be killed, their mother apparently begged them not to join the manhunt, but both of them felt obligated to do so.

Another man who felt that he should join the huge posse was Reverend Downer, who must have undergone a crisis of conscience when he learned of the double killing. On the one hand, he had known Lon well and realized from the letter that he was a troubled young man, but on the other hand, more lives were potentially at stake, and Downer was the finest marksman in Pepin County—the only one who might be a match for the Maxwells. He decided that he would go, and would shoot the outlaw brothers if he had to—but only "from fear of what they might do hereafter if they escape," as he told a reporter. He was surely hoping that violence of any kind could be avoided.

During that first week or so, the main posse swelled to four or five hundred men, and it became difficult for Deputy Sheriff Doolittle to manage them all, even though he had the assistance of Sheriff Peterson as well as the help of Sheriff Anderson of Henderson County. The men were moved around in large units, partly for control purposes and partly because the leaders were afraid that the Maxwells would confront, and annihilate, any small group of pursuers that encountered them.

Sheriff Peterson was soon replaced by his undersheriff, Miletus Knight, who was no doubt itching to get involved. After all, Peterson barely knew the dead brothers, but Knight had no closer friend in Durand than his neighbor Charley Coleman, with whom he had often swapped stories about the war.

Other lawmen also got involved. Sheriff Kelly of St. Croix County joined the manhunt, although not in connection with Doolittle's huge posse, as the *Hudson Star and Times* soon indicated: "While the main force has been on vigilance duty in Eau Galle, Sheriff Kelly has been doing what he could towards sending men to picket the outskirts of St. Croix County, to prevent escape [to the West] or aid from abettors."

The *Wisconsin State Journal* reported that yet another lawman did join Doolittle's force: ex-sheriff D. C. Whipple of Eau Claire (a town just east of Menomonie). He was described as "an old and experienced detective, who has with him a squad of about forty resolute citizens of Eau Claire County."

The same article that mentioned the arrival of Whipple and his group also indicated that the Maxwell brothers had been joined by two other outlaws, "horse thieves that had eluded the sheriff of Pierce County, near Brookville," but that proved to be just another false rumor. The Maxwells always acted, and traveled, alone.

The *Wisconsin State Journal* also indicated that members of the posse had intimidated Bridget Thompson, and had located two photographs of Lon, "one [side view] representing him neatly dressed, wearing chin whiskers and a mustache," and another "representing him in everyday clothing with a full view of the face."

A photograph of Ed was also eventually located, and those images of the brothers were copied and distributed to many sheriffs, marshals, and police chiefs in Wisconsin, Minnesota, and Illinois. They also became the basis for newspaper sketches that appeared in September. In Durand, copies of the photographs were placed on display at the post office, and an enterprising "photograph artist" who saw a business opportunity in what had become the foremost news story in Pepin County history began selling "photographs of the Notorious Williams Brothers" at his studio.

But the distribution and circulation of those images, as well as the printing of verbal descriptions, only contributed to the torrent of inaccurate reports that complicated the great manhunt, as many a passing glimpse of two unknown men was elevated in someone's mind to a recognition of the Maxwells. In fact, conflicting reports from different places so confused the posse that, for a few days, they were convinced that "there are four men instead of two who are fleeing from justice . . . in separate parties."

No newspaper played a larger role in covering the manhunt than the *St. Paul Pioneer Press*. Anxious to excite readers, it actually printed a sketch of "Edward Maxwell, alias Williams," with a rifle in his hands and a revolver in his holster, on page one, as an illustration for the July 25 issue, but it was simply an artist's rendering of what the noted desperado supposedly looked like. That lithograph was part of a three-column, page-one article with an incredibly extensive title:

RED LETTER RECORD.

History of the Williams Brothers,
Who are being Hunted Down
in the Wilds of Wisconsin.
Their Career of Crimes, from Fulton
County, Ill., to the Forests of
the Badger State.
From Petty Thefts in Illinois
To Deliberate and Cold Blooded Murder
In the Northwest.
The Elder Brother, by Birth and
Breeding a Bad Man,
the Evil Genius of the Family.
Ed Escapes from the Penitentiary
and Involves Lon in the
Meshes of the Law.
The Influence of a Worthy Woman
Restrained, but Could Not Control
the Evil Element.
A Letter from Lon to Parson Downer,
Wherein He Laments
the Loss of His Wife,
Tells the Sad Story of His Misspent Life,
and Vows Vengeance on His Enemies.

This lengthy headline shows the effort of one reporter, and the public mind, to shape the Maxwell saga into a dramatic story—about the transformation of petty thieves into defiant outlaws and the impact of an "Evil Genius" upon his younger brother. That view would later be elaborated into a book-length account of the desperadoes.

This article also refers to interviews with Sheriff Anderson and Undersheriff Knight, and those point to another notable aspect of the manhunt—eyewitness news reporting. Both the *St. Paul Pioneer Press* and the *Chicago Times* printed dispatches from a correspondent traveling with the searchers, to cover the unfolding events, and those dispatches were widely reprinted and used as sources by other newspapers.

"THE WISCONSIN HUNT," a July 21 report from the *Pioneer Press* correspondent at the scene, reveals many problems that impeded the search, including incredibly rough, wooded terrain; undisciplined men in a posse of fluctuating size; poor communication among the camps; very humid, sometimes rainy weather; and incessant rumors of outlaw sightings. The author of that report, Edward Johnstone, became increasingly devoted to covering the Maxwell story.

A July 22 article in the *Pepin County Courier* also reveals the difficulty of separating factual information from the ever-mounting number of rumors:

THE SEARCH!
STILL UNSUCCESSFUL!

The Assassins Still in the
Eau Galle Woods.

Of the many rumors flying in regard to the movements of the murderers and facts obtained by the party in pursuit, about one report in a dozen has some foundation in fact—the remainder are pure inventions or exaggerations. We have visited the "seat of war" nearly every day since the search began and know that the following reports are correct:

On Wednesday of last week a steer was found which the Williams boys had killed and cut out a large portion of the ham and built a fire on the spot and cooked the meat. . . .

The report that they had visited houses and obtained provisions at the end of a revolver is an invention—at least, the officers in charge can find no house that has been visited.

It is also well settled that the murderers went into Adsit's woods early last Saturday morning, and at the time the woods were surrounded and thoroughly searched, they were

---

> hid down on the Chippewa bottoms. After dark they took the
> back track, and at about eleven o'clock Saturday night [they]
> were seen by a young man about 40 rods from Perry Treat's
> saloon. . . . It is known that they have been accompanied a
> part of the time by one man, and the leaders know pretty
> well who that man is. . . .

The editor of the *Pepin County Courier* was trying to sort out the truth, but he was not always successful. After going without food for more than three days, the Maxwells did kill a steer, but as Ed later stated, by then they were not used to having food in their stomachs so the meat made them sick. The fugitives were, in fact, headed southwest, through "the Chippewa bottoms," toward a wide stretch of the Mississippi River known as Lake Pepin, but they were never accompanied by anyone. A man named Charles Scott, whom they knew, was arrested and briefly held as an accomplice, but he was just the victim of rumor. Any friend of the Maxwell brothers was automatically under suspicion.

In fact, as the manhunt floundered, some local leaders became convinced that the fugitives were being helped by sympathizers who lived deep in the woods. That was just a reflection of class prejudice, for those who lived in such remote areas were usually poor and often reclusive, and were sometimes regarded as antagonistic to society at the county seats—hence, likely to aid the outlaws. Editor Huntington, who shared that prejudice, was convinced that the Maxwells had many "assistants in the woods"—and even threatened them all with lynching.

A late July article in the *St. Paul Pioneer Press* also stated that several rumors centered on the Wolf brothers of Hersey, who had supposedly taken the Maxwells in, or had given them food, or had supplied them with ammunition. Those rumors eventually prompted Ed Wolf to write a July 30 letter to the editor of that newspaper, disavowing any involvement with the desperadoes.

The most common rumors were reports that the Maxwells "had been seen somewhere." The *Eau Claire News,* for example, carried the following report in mid-July: "All sorts of rumors have been current here for several days. Somebody at Round Hill claimed to have seen the desperadoes go down the [Chippewa] river in a skiff on Sunday night. Another rumor said that George Hays, a Wabasha liveryman, met them near Plainview on the

Rochester road, on Monday evening. . . ." Likewise, the *Wisconsin State Journal* carried a number of reported sightings, including this one from the area near Lake Pepin on the Mississippi River: "Thomas Ricket, proprietor of a grist mill ten miles north of Maiden Rock, Wis., reports having seen two men, each with a gun in hand, approach the bridge from the east and near his mill," and when they saw him, "they retreated to the protection of the thick underbrush, but not until Mr. Ricket fully identified them as the desperadoes, the Williams brothers, as per the newspaper descriptions of them." This may have been one of the few actual sightings of the fugitives, but the very lack of significant developments "from the front" (the search party) made reported sightings from anywhere in the great forest of central-western Wisconsin seem credible.

Some rumors about the Maxwells were more exciting. For example, the Eau Claire newspaper also reported that the outlaws had been tracked to a remote cabin near the village of Knapp, where they were surrounded, and that shots had been fired, but like the earlier story that pursuers had cornered them, it was completely false. A kind of folk tale, it was obviously created unconsciously in response to what the public most deeply wanted to hear—that the desperadoes were being dealt with and all the anxiety would soon be over. Likewise, the *Pepin County Courier* reported that Ed Maxwell had been spotted, and fired upon, along a road west of Durand, but had escaped. Although excited posse members had fired a few shots at someone, that was a case of mistaken identity.

Disappointed that the search was not yet successful, and bored by the monotony of camp life, many of the posse volunteers began heading home. What had been at least four hundred men soon became several dozen. But on July 25 the manhunt took a new direction when Governor Smith ordered a Menomonie militia company, the Ludington Guard, to proceed to the front and aid with the pursuit.

The forty-three-man cavalry unit was under the command of Captain T. J. (Thomas Jefferson) George, a colorful figure known as "Old Buckskin." As one reporter soon said, the captain had "served with gallantry in the Civil War"—and he could "tell a capital story and sing a good song." Sporting a long, curly, brown beard, he loved the camaraderie of military life and enjoyed using firearms. He was also a two-term former sheriff of Dunn County, and he had hired Milton Coleman as undersheriff in 1879.

Of course, the coming of the cavalry increased the military nature of the manhunt, which had already employed camps, commanders, squads, pickets, and scouting parties, as lawmen drew upon their Civil War experience to organize the huge effort. "THE PITILESS PURSUIT," as one newspaper headline called it, had been renewed.

Smelling an even bigger story, the *Chicago Times* sent a special correspondent to accompany the cavalry unit and issue periodic reports. He soon did so—from the Old Schoolhouse Camp (July 25), Camp Cady (July 26), and the Maple Springs Camp (July 27 and 28). Along with descriptions of the rough terrain and camp areas, he also repeated various rumors about the outlaws, including the discredited story that the Wolf brothers had supplied them with food and ammunition. He also described some forest dwellers, including one old woman who stoutly declared, "You fellers will never ketch them 'ere boys. They be too smart for ye"—and who was sure those "human tigers" would kill anyone they encountered. She clearly admired the daring desperadoes, who struggled alone against an army of manhunters. Of course, that view was not otherwise expressed in newspapers but would later inspire dime novels about the Maxwell brothers.

That same correspondent's reports—some of which were published in the *New York Times* and the *Washington Post*—included descriptions of several pursuers, including Sheriff Anderson, who felt indirectly responsible for the gunfight, since one of his reward postcards had been found on Milton Coleman's body. But no pursuer was more fascinating to the reading public than a western scout known as Buffalo Charlie:

> Maple Springs Camp, Dunn Co., Wis., July 28—New life has been infused into the pursuit of the Williams brothers by the arrival of eight Indian scouts and thirty bloodhounds, employed out west by the United States government. The scouts are headed by Buffalo Charlie. . . .
>
> Buffalo Charlie's parents, brothers, and sisters were killed by Indians over six years ago, since which time he has given his whole heart to his work of tracking redskins and fugitives from justice generally. The trail of the outlaws will be taken up in the vicinity of Doolittle's camp, and the scouts will go ahead with the entire pack of bloodhounds, starting such a hunt as was never witnessed in the big woods before. . . .

With the arrival of that Indian fighter and scout, it seemed that the far West had come to rescue the posse from impending failure. The other scouts, including a certain Yellowstone Kelly, and the bloodhounds had not actually arrived yet, but Charlie assured everyone that they were coming.

In a subsequent report, the correspondent described the frontier scout's tracking skills:

> . . . Buffalo Charlie was no fool. His familiarity with woodcraft has been proved by his movements in the brush and timber. His knowledge of signs and sounds is great and thorough, beyond dispute.
>
> He would stoop down and show the track of a man's foot where the faint traces of it were invisible to the eyes of his companions, until they followed his words as he revealed to them the art of the practiced scout. Charlie's knowledge of the Yellowstone country, or persons and places in Dakota and Montana, and of dates and Indian campaigns, further strengthen the belief that he has been . . . what he represents himself to be—an Indian scout of the plains.

Charlie, a well-built six-footer, seemed to embody heroic manliness, and he immediately led a party of ten men on a scouting foray that kept them out until the next morning.

Meanwhile, because of an Associated Press dispatch that was derived from material in the *Chicago Times,* various newspapers around the country soon reflected the exciting notion that Buffalo Charlie had come to assist with the floundering manhunt. A denizen of the Wild West, he would surely be a match for the outlaws, or so many people hoped.

Unfortunately, Buffalo Charlie, that colorful scout of the plains who seemed to be just what the posse needed, was also an old tale teller who no longer knew or cared where the truth left off. Another report by the *Chicago Times* correspondent soon revealed that Charlie had gulled the entire corps of volunteers—and the reporters:

> Camp Cady, Pierce County, Wis., July 29, via Menomonie, Wis., July 30—Buffalo Charlie's fellow scouts and thirty bloodhounds failing to come, and his movements taking a suspicious turn, he was put under arrest by Capt. Doolittle this morning. . . . He says that he is known out west by the various names of Buffalo Charlie, Charlie Lewis, and Yellowstone [Kelly]. He . . . is strongly suspected of complicity with the Williams brothers, to whose assistance he is believed to have come as a spy. . . .
>
> According to his own story, as revised to date, Buffalo Charlie has not been in regular government employment since 1878. He says he has done occasional scouting since, in the summer, and hunted buffalo in the winter. Evidently he has been working his

way, for the past two months, up the river to St. Paul, hiring out
as a cook in hotels along the route. . . .

As this reveals, "Yellowstone Kelly," the other noted scout who was
supposedly coming, turned out to be a second imaginative self-image developed by Charlie, who employed his western scouting and hunting background—however limited that may have been—to personify "the West,"
rather like the famous Buffalo Bill Cody was already doing with the help of
Ned Buntline and others. Even the name "Buffalo Charlie," as well as the
light-colored mustache and goatee that he sported, suggests that Buffalo
Bill had inspired the poor, yarn-spinning drifter. In any case, public disil-
lusionment with him was expressed as far away as the *Washington Post*.

Buffalo Charlie—soon nicknamed "Bogus Charlie"—was threatened with
lynching and ended up in the Dunn County Jail at Menomonie, accused of
aiding the Maxwells. In reality, his only purpose was to get a little attention and, perhaps, some food. But his ruse had exposed the manhunters'
deep yearning to see themselves, too, as exemplars of manliness, akin to
the "Buffalo Bill"–type of figure who had awed and inspired them.

The disclosure of Charlie's yarn-spinning, and the fact that he took in
everyone for a time, accelerated the growing public disenchantment with
the great north woods manhunt, which had begun with heroic self-confidence and was ending with ignominious failure. In southeast Minnesota
the *Wabasha Herald* criticized the posse leaders for being unwise: "Buffalo
Charlie was the last straw. . . . Several sheriffs, numerous detectives, lots of
constables [i.e., marshals], and five or six companies of militia were taken
in by a hungry tramp who has told large stories to big ears. No wonder
that they have had plenty of hunting but have failed to bag the game."

The *Milwaukee Sentinel* and *Wisconsin State Journal* printed a more thorough critique of the operation, pointing to the less-than-heroic approach
of the sheriffs and their volunteers: "The fact of the matter is, the pursuers
have stood in mortal fear of the outlaws, and have tried to capture them by
moving about in vast bodies which the pursued had no difficulty whatever
in detecting, and finally in escaping." The same article also revealed that
the manhunt had been hampered by "a series of petty jealousies among
the leaders of the pursuing party." And there was, in fact, conflict over
who should direct the effort. Ex-sheriff Doolittle commanded the largest
force of men at one time, but the killings had taken place outside of his
Dunn County jurisdiction, and he was no longer the sheriff there anyway,
so when the Ludington Guard arrived, Sheriff Peterson and Undersheriff

Knight wanted that militia unit to report to them, rather than Doolittle, even though the cavalrymen were from Dunn County.

The prevalence of rumors, often eagerly spread by the press, and the general lack of communication among the camps and squads of men had also hindered the operation. As late as July 28 there was a sensational rumor that "ex-Sheriff Doolittle and two companions had been killed by the Williams brothers in the Eau Galle woods." That was reported in several newspapers before Doolittle could refute the story.

On July 31 the Ludington Guard, which had accomplished nothing at considerable expense, was ordered out of the forest, and during the following week the remaining posse volunteers left for home. Mostly young men, they were anxious to return to work as well as tired of monotonous guard duty and endless searching in the "Terribly Torrid Weather" (as the Durand newspaper put it), which had already killed hundreds of people in the Mississippi Valley.

In a very apt article title, the *Chicago Times* referred to them all as "TIRED OUT AND TRICKED," and declared that the great pursuit had been "Abandoned by the Amateur Blood-Seekers." The desperadoes had escaped.

As the search dissolved in western Wisconsin, Undersheriff Knight and the two surviving Coleman brothers "sent thousands of letters, postal cards, and photographs to all parts of the country," as one newspaper reported, and they continued to follow leads, as did Deputy Sheriff Doolittle of Dunn County.

That effort, coupled with reports that the Maxwells had escaped from "the big woods," generated even more rumors about the outlaws, which came in from anxiety-ridden communities across the state—including nearby places like Menomonie and Eau Claire and more distant communities like Palmyra and Genesee (near Milwaukee). Sheriffs and small posses responded to those rumors.

In the other direction, stories started to come in from across the Mississippi River. One account asserted, for example, that the Maxwell brothers had ventured into "Frank Werner's saloon" in downtown St. Paul, and "each had two revolvers in a belt strapped around his waist." Another report claimed that they had been in Wabasha, along the Mississippi River, and yet another one said they had been seen in Sauk Rapids, hurrying to catch a ride on a freight train.

Some jittery people no longer cared if they saw two men at all. A "perfectly reliable man" near Princeton, Minnesota, east of St. Cloud, swore that he had seen Lon, who "pretended to be looking for work," and authorities in New Ulm, west of Mankato, notified Sheriff Peterson that they had captured Ed. The marshal at Princeton soon realized that the man thought to be Lon was simply a tramp, and Sheriff Peterson, who traveled to New Ulm, discovered that the man in custody there was also just "a tramp, who had stolen some harness." Obviously, by late summer any out-of-work drifter in the upper Mississippi Valley was likely to be mistaken for one of the Maxwell brothers.

Faced with these and other reports, the *Milwaukee Sentinel* summarized the confusing situation, in an August 6 article titled "UBIQUITOUS SCOUNDRELS": "Stories continue to circulate . . . that the Williams brothers have been seen in nearly every town in northern and southern Wisconsin and Minnesota." Because they had so thoroughly vanished, the outlaws had become a presence in the public mind, affirmed by every mysterious figure who turned up anywhere.

There were also reported sightings in other states, especially along the big river. An August 7 communication to the *St. Paul Pioneer Press* from a man in New Albin, Iowa, asserted that two suspicious-looking strangers seen there were "without any doubt . . . the Williams brothers," and a small posse was after them. The *Press* concluded that they were "undoubtedly the men who were seen at several points along the Mississippi last week, and the week before," but their identity was not yet firmly established. Lawmen were alerted at Lansing, Marquette, Dubuque, and other places in eastern Iowa.

Anxiety gripped some communities. On August 12 one central Illinois newspaper reported, "It is believed the [Maxwell] boys have got away by means of some kind of water craft on the Mississippi River," and "It is hoped that the officers at Burlington, Keokuk, Warsaw, and other points will keep a sharp lookout for the desperadoes, as they will surely try to make for the woods in central Illinois." In short, the outlaws were probably returning to their old haunts.

That the Maxwells may have fled downriver once again was also considered by Sheriff Anderson as he returned by riverboat to Henderson County, inquiring along the way about the infamous fugitives. In an article about his return, the *Oquawka Spectator* stated, "At LaCrosse, on his way down the river, Sheriff Anderson learned that parties had seen two men fully armed with guns and revolvers, who were coming down in a skiff, and who represented themselves as trappers, but are believed to be the veritable outlaws—the Maxwells."

Anderson decided to stay on the case, by remaining in touch with Deputy Sheriff Doolittle, sending inquiries to other lawmen, and inquiring as he came downriver, even though he had recovered the two horses stolen from the Evans farm in his county. More than anything in his life, he wanted to be the man who caught the desperadoes. Still feeling indirectly responsible for the Wisconsin tragedy, Anderson also started raising money in Henderson County for the destitute family of Civil War hero Charles Coleman.

As the hot August days slowly passed, the Maxwell story faded from the newspapers, but like the summer haze it was still spreading and drifting through the cities, towns, and rural areas of the region as people shared what they knew, or thought they knew, about the famous outlaws. And it would soon appear in the press again, as another gunfight with lawmen erupted in an equally remote region of the Mississippi Valley and numerous other posses joined the great manhunt.

12

⚛

Another Gunfight—
and the Renewed
Manhunt

September 19 finally brought the long-feared national tragedy: President Garfield died, at his cottage in Elberon, New Jersey, of inflammation brought on by the gunshot wounds of July 2. Newspapers across the country draped the columns of their headline story in heavy black borders and provided details about the stricken leader's last day, the medical complications that caused his death, and the funeral preparations.

Afterward, for many days, both city and small-town newspapers were filled with long accounts of the funeral, tributes to the fallen leader, biographical sketches of Garfield's life, and bulletins on the new president, Chester A. Arthur. Memorial services were held in thousands of communities, which were often jammed with mourners who came in from the countryside to participate in the outpouring of grief and to share the sense of national loss.

There was also renewed interest in the president's attacker—now his assassin—Charles Guiteau, who was in jail awaiting trial. As someone who had killed the living symbol of American democracy, he became the focus of enormous public hatred. A sergeant in the military unit assigned to guard him, a man distraught over Guiteau's evil deed, tried to shoot him in his cell—the first of three attempts on the prisoner's life that fall—and many Americans approved that effort. Also, the authorities were treating him as "a prisoner already condemned and sentenced," as one dispatch from Washington, D.C., put it, although Guiteau was not even indicted until early October.

The whole issue of law and order would stir the nation's mind through the fall of 1881. It was a bad time to be wanted for killing lawmen, and reports of the Maxwell manhunt often shared the front page with articles on the president's assassin.

Because of the enormous newspaper coverage in July and August, people in Illinois were well aware of the killings at Durand and the huge manhunt for the Maxwells. For example, on August 4, the *Pike County Democrat,* at Pittsfield, ran a front-page story on "THE WISCONSIN OUTLAWS," summarizing the gunfight and the pursuit, and emphasizing the threat posed by the killers to lawmen and posse members: "The pursuers are satisfied that unless extreme caution enables them to approach the outlaws while they are asleep or overcome with exhaustion, one or more of [the pursuers] will fall victims to their unerring rifles." The same article asserted that "the most knowing hunters [i.e., pursuers] say that chances are, the murderers are now on their way safely down the Mississippi, and one or two stories that have come up the river, of two men being seen here and there, give woof and warp to the story."

Just below Pike County is Calhoun. A hilly, heavily wooded expanse located where the Illinois and Mississippi rivers converge, it is forty-five miles from north to south but not more than eight miles wide except at the northern end, where the two great, muddy streams are farther apart. Calhoun County is river bluff country, looking rather like southwestern Wisconsin, and in the nineteenth century it was an isolated place. The big rivers that bordered it, except on the north, prevented the county from being reached by stagecoach and railroad lines, so outsiders seldom came there. Most of the local people liked it that way.

During the Civil War there was considerable local discord, theft, and violence. As a Chicago newspaper article reported, Calhoun County's isolated bluffs "made a capital place for bushwhackers and horse thieves." One longtime resident later recalled that men claiming to be Southern sympathizers "came over from Missouri and made raids in Calhoun," but often they were just highwaymen "in the stealing and robbing business for the booty there was in it." And typically, after they came, robbed, and vanished, "[local] citizens would gather the next day and try to hunt them down."

Residents fought among themselves as well. When Union soldiers returned on furlough early in 1864, civil conflict erupted, culminating in a "disgraceful affray" at Hardin, the county seat, between local Peace Democrats, or "Copperheads," and soldiers: "A Copperhead cheered for Jeff Davis, and was promptly shot down by a soldier. The Copperheads then gathered and hung three soldiers and shot three others dead." Afterward, vigilantes organized to apprehend the killers, who were of course protected by their friends. Because of such episodes during the war, Hardin became a deeply divided, violent place, with many things to hide.

The Civil War animosity in Calhoun County was slow to heal. There was lingering mistrust among local residents, which combined with the depression of the 1870s to inhibit economic development.

By 1880 the county had less than a dozen small villages and hamlets—mostly impoverished places like Bachtown (pop. 197), Hamburg (pop. 115), and Brussels (pop. 106). Even Hardin, on the Illinois River, had only 300 people. It was the smallest county seat in Illinois. The poor folks who lived in the countryside were commonly subsistence farmers and fruit growers. In the entire state their county was the only one that did not have a single bank or hotel, and like Pepin County, it had just one weekly newspaper and no telegraph office.

For men on the run, it was a great place to hide.

By mid-September there was a story circulating that the Maxwell brothers had been seen near the village of Newport, so Calhoun County Sheriff John Lammy was riding through that area trying to find their trail. Forty-one years old, Lammy had emigrated from County Tyrone, in northern Ireland, with his parents in 1849. His mother had died in 1851, when he was eleven, but his father was a prosperous farmer. In his youth Lammy had worked as a farmhand near the village of Hamburg and then was a schoolteacher in two country districts and in Hardin.

Lammy looked very Irish. Of medium build, he had a pale complexion, hazel eyes, and wavy red hair, as well as a bushy mustache. He was a smiling, affable fellow, ready to befriend anyone. Unlike so many lawmen of his era, he had not served in the Civil War, so he was able to avoid the animosity that engulfed many local residents.

Apparently having some college education, Lammy founded the *Calhoun Herald* in 1872 and edited it for a year so before selling it. In 1874 he was elected sheriff, and while in that position he also served as president of the Hardin Village Board of Trustees. One of his crowning moments in that position came when he read his own brief history of early days in the county at a public gathering to mark the nation's centennial in 1876. From then on, he was a kind of symbolic figure—the spokesman for Calhoun County's pioneer heritage.

Reelected as county sheriff three times, but still unmarried at forty-one, Lammy lived in a two-room apartment above the county jail, and he devoted himself to his job. A man of genial disposition and kindly ways, he also related warmly to the people who lived in the villages and the countryside, becoming perhaps "the most popular man in Calhoun County," as one newspaper soon characterized him.

One of Lammy's friends was Sheriff E. W. Blades of Pike County, an affable, intelligent, and enterprising forty-seven-year-old from Delaware who had come west in 1856 and was a successful grocer in Pittsfield when he wasn't busy as the county's chief lawman. In 1881 Blades was serving his second two-year term as sheriff.

On Sunday, September 25, Lammy and Blades responded to rumors that the Maxwell brothers were hiding nearby and to a report by Pike County Deputy Sheriff George Roberts that he had identified the outlaws during a chance encounter while hunting, and the result was another killing that was reported throughout the Mississippi Valley. A few days later, in a long article titled "A SAD CALAMITY," the *Pike County Democrat* provided a reasonably thorough account of what had led up to it:

> It has been known for some time that the Maxwell boys, alias the Williams brothers, who murdered officers sent to arrest them for horse stealing in Wisconsin . . . were in Calhoun County, making Bay Island on the Mississippi their headquarters, but most of the time ranging through that county and the lower part of this [Pike], going at all times heavily armed and at all times alert against any attempt to take them.
>
> Last week Deputy Sheriff George W. Roberts, who resides in Pearl, while out with his little boy hunting squirrels, came upon them in the woods and had quite a lengthy conversation with them—he, although recognizing them from photographs in his possession, giving no token of that knowledge. Immediately upon his arrival [in town], he telegraphed to Sheriff Blades about the meeting. . . .
>
> Being fully satisfied from information gathered that [the Maxwells] would be found on the west side of Calhoun in the vicinity of Mozier's Landing, [Blades] telegraphed back for a posse to meet him at Belleview last Friday night at 12 o'clock. In response, August

Simpkins, H. M. Chitwood, and James Hayes—all of this place—
and Loren Huntley, of Barry, armed themselves and, leaving here
shortly after dark, proceeded to the place of rendezvous.

Just what occurred during Saturday we have not learned, but
Sunday morning the Pike County posse under Sheriff Blades, with
which were also Deputy Roberts, Mike Fisher, and Austin Henry of
this county, met Sheriff John Lammy, with his deputies Churchman
and McNabb, and perhaps others, also bent on the capture of the
outlaws. . . .

Lammy was shot dead and two others were wounded near the western
edge of the county, about fifteen miles northwest of Hardin, in a field surrounded by woods and divided by a sluggish stream called Fox Creek.
The lawmen who were with Lammy soon contributed their own accounts
of the tragedy. A report by Sheriff Blades, which appeared in the *Missouri
Republican* in St. Louis, provided an exciting account of the gunfight:

We divided our forces into two parties. Sheriff Lammy went
southeast with his, and I northeast with mine. We were to make a
circuit and meet a couple of miles east.

It was about noon, the men say, that Lammy called his force to
a halt for a conference as to whether or not it would be better to
subdivide his force. While they were discussing matters, Jim Hayes,
one of my posse who was with him, saw a man at the lower side
of Lawrence Roth's wheat field with a gun. They were about two
miles north of Hamburg and between that town and the creek.

Sheriff Lammy and Deputy Churchman mounted their horses and
rode around, to head off the man with the gun, telling the others
to cut across the field on foot. . . . Lammy and his deputy went up
the creek and got around east of the man with the gun and then
started back west. They could not see anything for some time, and
then they came suddenly upon a man sitting on a log not thirty feet
away. The man had a gun across his lap, and there was another man
lying behind the log, but the officers didn't see him then.

Lammy jumped off his horse, raised his revolver, and told the
man to surrender. It was Alonzo Williams with the gun. He threw
up his hands—but to aim his gun at the sheriff, and the latter immediately fired. Alonzo did not drop as expected. In fact, it was
hardly possible that he was hit at all, for he took quick aim at the
sheriff and sent a bullet through his head. Lammy was killed so
quick that he didn't feel it. The shooting then began all round.

One man a quarter of a mile away says that he counted 31 shots, but I think there were only 21. Churchman fired seven shots. He emptied his revolver, but unfortunately was not a good shot and did not bring down his man.

But there were two men, for Ed Maxwell (or Williams) had sprung to his feet at the first shot, and had joined his brother in the fight, using a revolver with terrible effect. He shot Churchman in both legs, his intention seemingly being to disable him only. . . .

McNabb rushed into the fight . . . and after he had fired one shot, Alonzo called on him to throw up his revolver. He didn't want to hit him, he said, and wouldn't if he would surrender. McNabb said that he would keep on firing till one of them fell. He fired twice in succession, when Alonzo sent a bullet through his right shoulder, and that put an end to the shooting.

The murderers jumped on the horses of Lammy and Churchman and rode away at a gallop. One of them had no shoe or stocking on one foot, but we could not find the missing articles on the ground. . . .

Of course, the posse knew that Lon had injured his right foot, which still bothered him, and that he often went without a shoe or boot. In fact, he had been without shoes and had an apparent gunshot wound on his right hand when Deputy Roberts had seen the Maxwells in the woods.

An eyewitness account later published by Deputy Sheriff John Churchman asserted that he and Deputy Frank McNabb had initiated the gunfight and were wounded first, and that Sheriff Lammy came along moments later and was shot in the head while dashing for cover. Churchman's version was apparently more accurate in that respect, but it was also an effort to portray himself as a heroic man of action:

At this moment [Lon] Maxwell jumped up, leveled his gun on McNabb, and ordered him to get down off of his horse. I immediately jumped off my pony and hitched it [to a tree]. By this time Maxwell had made McNabb get off his horse and was cursing him, and ordering him to come up to him, swearing that he would blow his brains out if he did not. I hollered at McNabb not to do it but to "shoot the son of a bitch." Fearing that he would shoot McNabb, I leveled my pistol at [Maxwell's] head and fired. Maxwell then turned and fired at me. McNabb, taking advantage of the interval, got behind a tree and fired at Maxwell. . . . I [had] opened the fight to save McNabb's life.

Churchman, a thirty-five-year-old insurance agent, and McNabb, a twenty-four-year-old schoolteacher, did not identify themselves as law officers, nor did they indicate that they were part of a larger posse surrounding the area. Of course, the former's outcry and opening gun shot surely convinced the outlaws that they must shoot back or die.

Churchman's account was an effort to celebrate his own role in the gunfight, especially since many wondered why he had emptied his gun at the desperadoes and had never hit either of them. If he had been wounded early in the fray, as he claimed, Churchman might not be held responsible for failing to shoot the Maxwells. And if he had fired first to save McNabb's life, he would not be blamed for starting the gunfight that might have been avoided.

Authorities soon checked at Bay Island, near Hamburg, where rumor said the Maxwell brothers were hiding out, and found that "for three weeks they [had] stayed with a fisherman named Charleton, at his hut on [the] island" and had "furnished most of the provisions needed at the hut during their stay," so the poor, solitary river rat was sorry to see them leave. They apparently did not trust the fisherman, for they took his rifle and revolver, but when they left, on the Sunday of the gunfight, they returned them to him. According to the *Missouri Republican,* Charleton "now has many stories to relate about his guests."

After the gunfight, an early newspaper report indicated that the Maxwells "have been located in the vicinity of Pecan Island, near the mouth of the Illinois, and still have their skiff with them." The sheriffs of St. Charles County, Missouri, and Madison County, Illinois, formed posses to patrol both sides of the river. And because the desperadoes were in a boat, apparently headed downriver, Sheriff Blades went to St. Louis to secure the assistance of professional lawmen there. A September 27 dispatch that was carried in many newspapers, including the *Milwaukee Sentinel,* describes the rising tension in the St. Louis area because the Maxwells were thought to be in a stolen skiff "making their way down the river" with several posses in hot pursuit: "They [the Maxwells] may pass here before morning, as the night is very dark. A drizzling rain is falling . . . but the country is alive on both sides [of the Mississippi]." The Maxwells had become a threatening presence, not precisely located but advancing toward the city.

The *Missouri Republican* in St. Louis began giving extensive coverage to the manhunt, including a September 28 article that shouted, "THEY ARE COMING! The Maxwell Desperadoes in a Skiff on the Mississippi." It included sketches of Ed and Lon, based on Wisconsin photographs, "to make every person familiar with their faces." It also pointed out that Ed now "has chin whiskers as well as a mustache" and Lon "now has a mustache and a goatee"—as the drawings showed—for Deputy Roberts had noted the additional facial hair when he had talked with them in the woods.

Sheriff Blades recruited the St. Louis chief of police, Ferdinand B. Kennett, and several detectives, who together formed the most capable, experienced posse that had yet pursued the Maxwell brothers, and they traveled back up the Mississippi by tugboat, planning to encounter the desperadoes on or off the river. An account of the unusual riverboat posse was soon provided by the *Alton Telegraph:*

THE MAXWELL BROTHERS.
Hunting the Desperadoes.

The sheriffs, police, and other authorities in all this part of the country are on the lookout for the Williams, alias Maxwell, brothers, Lon and Ed, the Wisconsin desperadoes. . . .

Marshal Reilly, of this city [Alton], received a dispatch from Chief of Police Kennett, of St. Louis, Tuesday, stating that the desperadoes were seen passing Cape au Gris, about 40 miles above here on the Mississippi, at 11 o'clock Tuesday in a skiff, and asking him to be on the lookout.

Chief Kennett arrived here at 8 o'clock this morning on the tug *Susie Hazard,* accompanied by Sheriff Blades, of Pike County, and detectives O'Neill, Eggs, Steward, Desmond, and Willow, all brave determined men, well armed and prepared to take their lives in their hands in an attempt to arrest the murderers. As the tug has a draft of 8 feet, 3 inches, it was considered impolitic to take that craft any farther, and Capt. L'argent's propeller *Truant* was engaged to take the party as far as Cape au Gris. . . .

It is supposed that the Maxwells are trying to make their escape down the river, and rumors prevail that they may be hidden among the ravines and bluffs above this city. They are desperate men, armed with two revolvers each, and an eighteen-shot, breech-loading Winchester rifle between them, and as they are good marksmen, it will be no child's play to apprehend them. . . .

A tall, slim, balding man, with dark hair and a wispy mustache, Kennett had just taken over as chief of the 450-man St. Louis Police Department in April, and he was anxious to prove himself by demonstrating his ability in a major manhunt. Despite the reputation of the Maxwells, Kennett was confident: "The chief says he is sure of bagging his game," according to a St. Louis reporter who interviewed him. He assured the public that he would soon take the desperadoes, dead or alive.

The small riverboat, loaded with armed lawmen and towing a skiff, left Alton on September 28 and cruised up to Grafton, where the posse stayed overnight. On Thursday morning a half dozen militiamen from the Grafton Guards joined them, and the *Truant* continued to Point Landing, ten miles farther upriver. Along the way, many shallows and sloughs were explored by skiff, and occasional short excursions were made along the shore, but no one saw the outlaws. Local folks encountered by the posse often had opinions about where "they must have gone." Another Alton newspaper article stated that "from the many reports and rumors that prevailed, it was evident that the outlaws had left the vicinity of the river and had taken to the woods in Missouri."

A telegraphic dispatch from a St. Louis newspaper correspondent soon indicated that the new focus of the manhunt was Lincoln County, Missouri, and that "Sheriff Blades, of Pike County, Ill., is in that county with a large posse." Chief of Police Kennett and a squad of "eight or ten policemen and detectives" were also there, and the sheriffs of both Lincoln and St. Charles counties led posses that were involved as well.

The prevailing theory was that the Maxwells were traveling across the state "with a view of getting to the Indian Territory." In short, they were escaping to the West, where they could vanish into a less well-established culture that was not focused, as the whole upper Mississippi Valley seemed to be, on pursuing the Maxwell brothers.

The huge publicity surrounding the Illinois-Missouri phase of the manhunt created a certain hysteria, similar to what had arisen in Wisconsin. In and around Calhoun County, people were "greatly alarmed and terrorized because of the belief that these outlaws are at large," according to a September 28 report. One anxiety-ridden Pike County village even offered an additional reward for their apprehension.

All of that, in turn, led to wild rumors and even false arrests. For example, a September 29 newspaper dispatch titled "CAUGHT: Men Captured at St. Louis Who Are Supposed to Be the Williams Brothers," depicted the arrest of two heavily armed young men who "came from Wisconsin" and "were hiding in the bushes on the riverbank in the northern suburbs." The story was widely reprinted but was soon discredited. The two young men did not resemble the sketches of the outlaws.

Reports soon came in that "the Maxwell boys had been seen" in Cape-au-Gris, Hannibal, Foley, and rural Ralls County, Missouri, as well as Alton, Belleview, Detroit (in Pike County), East St. Louis, and "a dozen" other places in Illinois. The newspaper drawings had, in fact, simply made the manhunt more challenging, as many regional residents soon connected those images with any two strangers who broke the law, acted suspiciously, carried rifles, or simply passed through the area.

When the pursuit in Lincoln County had come to nothing by early October, authorities felt they had been mistaken about the overland route and began to realize that, once again, the Maxwells had escaped. And no one was even sure which direction they had gone. That, too, was front-page news in many newspapers, including the *Milwaukee Sentinel,* which printed a four-column story about the desperadoes, illustrated with the St. Louis sketches, under the stirring title "REVOLVER RULE," subtitled "The Notorious Williams Brothers Give Missouri Authorities the Slip." The article mentioned that "a large number of armed men are still after the Maxwells," but "there is little hope that the outlaws will be captured." It also asserted that the Maxwells had burglarized a store in Nebo, a hamlet in Pike County. There was never any reliable evidence to connect them with that robbery, however, so the report merely shows that they were being associated with any and all mysterious robberies that had recently occurred along the Illinois-Missouri border.

It is clear that the gunfighting reputation of the Maxwells impeded the pursuit. Many volunteers—one report said "500 men," but perhaps three hundred is closer—had joined the various Illinois and Missouri posses, but most did not plan to get too close to their quarry. Newspaper exaggerations about the desperadoes did not help. One account that appeared in both Chicago and Milwaukee newspapers stated that "each [of the outlaws] was equipped with an eighteen-shot rifle and from five to seven revolvers"—an exaggeration that raised them to the level of super-outlaws, who could gun down an entire posse. Another report, printed in the *Chicago Times,* claimed that some locals had talked with the Maxwells, and that "Lon, who killed Lammy, showed a wound in his left arm where a 32-calibre [revolver] ball had passed through it, and he ridiculed the weapons that the Calhounites carried."

Maxwell folklore even gave them the most dangerous outlaw comrades:

"Reports are that the James boys are with the Williams Gang," said an article in the widely circulated *Chicago Times.* The very notion that America's most notorious outlaws *had joined the Maxwells* reveals the infusion of mythic outlaw ultimacy into the unfolding Maxwell saga by the fall of 1881.

Indeed, stories of all sorts began circulating, and a few of them made it into the newspapers. As in Wisconsin, rumors that the Maxwells "had been seen" somewhere came from many sources, especially after the authorities had admitted that they did not know where the outlaws were. One of the most convincing reports was this dispatch, which appeared in the *Milwaukee Sentinel* on October 4: "A special from Clarksville, in Pike County, Mo., says that the steamer *Dora* arrived there last night and brings the intelligence that the Maxwells are known to be on Bay Island, in the Mississippi River, about four miles from Hamburg. A posse went out from Hardin, Ill., to get them."

Another dispatch, from Pittsfield, said that the outlaws had returned to the wooded hills of Calhoun County and that "three different posses are organized [there] to take the field tonight." But none of those posses encountered the outlaws.

On October 4, the *Chicago Tribune* reported that the desperadoes had been seen many times "roaming around in Calhoun County," where "one of their recent exploits was to ride into a small village saloon and order drinks for a crowd of loafers" and then promptly ride away while "no one attempted to molest them." That was simply a localized version of a folk tale about them that had originated during the manhunt in Wisconsin—a tale suggesting that they were appreciated, and perhaps feared, by Calhoun County folks. And the underlying purpose of the story was the same in both places—to suggest why the authorities had been unable to apprehend them.

Reports about the outlaws came in from other counties as well. One St. Louis resident who had been hunting near Carlinville, Illinois, claimed that on October 9 he was accosted in the woods by two armed men who took his gun, held him captive, and refused to identify themselves—but they answered to the description of the Maxwell brothers. The man later escaped and then returned with a posse "to search the woods for the Williams boys," who had vanished in the meantime. Yet another report came from Alton, where "A Mysterious Stranger," who was well-armed and "seemed greatly interested in the Maxwell, alias Williams, brothers," took a ferry across the river there, pulled a gun on the boatman, and vanished into the woods on the Missouri shore. The assumption that he was one of the desperadoes resulted in yet another posse in pursuit.

By the fall of 1881, only the long-notorious James brothers had been sought by more posses in more places than Ed and Lon Maxwell, who had temporarily topped those Missouri desperadoes in public fascination. After all, they were not just robbers but gunmen, wanted for killing sheriffs in two states. As one newspaper headline put it: "THE MAXWELL DESPERADOES: Still Killing the Faithful Officers of the Law."

The mythic allure of their identity as sheriff killers may also have encouraged imitators. In Iowa, for example, when petty thieves known as "the Mercer boys" shot dead a deputy sheriff in November, one newspaper reported that they were "emulous of the red-handed record of the Williams brothers."

As dozens of contradictory reports flowed in to the authorities and several posses continued the fascinating search, Illinois Governor Shelby M. Cullom offered a new reward: "$500, for the capture of the notorious Williams brothers, who recently turned up in Pike County and killed the sheriff of Calhoun County . . . besides wounding two of the posse." The reward money for the Maxwell brothers then totaled $2,200—a bigger sum than for any other outlaws except Jesse and Frank James.

While that gave further incentive to lawmen and posse members, their work was, at the same time, hampered by bad weather. After another long dry spell in the upper Mississippi Valley, a tornado swept through western Illinois on September 24, causing extensive damage in Quincy and destroying the village of Camden. For many days "the telegraph lines were down in all directions," according to a Chicago newspaper, and there was no communication with Calhoun County except by mail.

Then heavy rain began to fall on September 30—with terrible thunderstorms in some areas—and it lasted for five days. Outlaw trails became difficult if not impossible to follow, and pursuit on horseback became a miserable struggle rather than high adventure. By October 4, Wisconsin and Illinois newspapers were talking about "the alarming rise in rivers and streams" and "a general deluge of farming lands in the vicinities of the rivers." The Wisconsin River, the Rock River, the Illinois River, and many smaller streams reached very high levels, and the Mississippi River was soon above flood stage. Local authorities had to focus their attention on helping flood victims and on repairing washed-out roads and bridges.

The streams receded for about two weeks, and then a second deluge occurred, lasting three days, and the Mississippi Valley rivers and creeks surged to record levels. As the *Milwaukee Sentinel* reported on October 18, in a front-page story titled "DELUGED: Disastrous Results of the Recent

Great Fall of Rain," the damage was considerable "along the Wisconsin, Fox, Chippewa, Rock, Mississippi, and other rivers . . . and the waters are still rising. . . ." Many people were calling it "the greatest flood ever known" during the autumn season. Within a week or so, the Mississippi River was more than ten miles wide in some areas, and the *Alton Telegraph* soon reported that "the destruction on both sides of the river is incalculable."

Because of the widespread devastation, the second phase of the great manhunt for the Maxwell brothers was essentially over. But the search continued. Occasional reports that they were seen somewhere came in throughout the fall to authorities in both Wisconsin and Illinois. Other posses and lawmen became involved, and arrests of men thought to be the Maxwells continued in Milwaukee, St. Louis, and other places.

Back in Calhoun County, there was enormous praise for Sheriff Lammy, whose funeral on September 26 had been attended by "the largest concourse of citizens ever assembled in Hardin." Hundreds of mourners slowly followed his coffin up the steep dirt road to the hilltop cemetery that overlooked the village and, beyond it to the east, the Illinois River. The local court soon passed an official resolution, celebrating him as "an honored, brave, and . . . able officer," who was "stricken down by assassins and outlaws from another state, who were seeking to make an asylum of our law-abiding community of this county. . . ." As that comment reveals, local residents knew little or nothing about the Fulton County and McDonough County background of the desperadoes, associating them primarily with Wisconsin, where they had come to regionwide—indeed, national—attention.

A story circulated about Lammy—that when he was informed about the presence of the Maxwell brothers in his county, he knew that pursuit would be dangerous, but said to some friends, "The people of this county have repeatedly elected me to the office [of sheriff], and it is as little as I can do to risk my life for them." True or not, it was the kind of story that people liked to tell about a local hero.

Other stories about Lammy also circulated after his death: that he would loan impoverished people money to pay their property taxes rather than serve foreclosures, and that he personally saw to it that underprivileged children in Calhoun County received a Christmas gift every year. Those are probably folk tales or exaggerations based on single episodes, which were developed after his death by residents of a very poor county who wanted to celebrate a hero who had exemplified concern for people like them. Nevertheless, Lammy was clearly a fine man.

During the next several months, residents of Calhoun County contributed more than $1,000 for an imposing monument, a thirteen-foot-tall marble shaft that was erected at Lammy's gravesite in the cemetery at Hardin. It proclaimed that he was "KILLED While in Discharge of His Duty as Sheriff." Of course, those same people talked about lynching the desperadoes who had gunned down their defender, if they could only find them.

Because Sheriff Blades and his men were not involved in the gunfight, there was anger at them among some residents of Calhoun County. A nearby newspaper reported that "the citizens of Calhoun County are greatly incensed against Blades and the Pike County posse; they claim [that] if [Blades and his men] had shown half the bravery of Lammy, McNabb, and Churchman, the murderers would have been killed, not Lammy." The chief complainer was James McNabb, editor of the *Calhoun Herald*—and also the county's superintendent of schools—whose twin brother had been wounded in the gunfight. But his animosity against the tired and frustrated Pike County sheriff was fueled by the newspaper report of Deputy John Churchman, who strove to avoid criticism for starting the gunfight by affixing the blame on others: "Now all the bad management in the whole affair was from the cowardly action of [Blades' men], with the shotguns, not supporting us, for if they had come promptly to our aid, we would have captured the outlaws, and brave Lammy would not have been killed. . . ."

Blades was stung by the criticism, and despite his respect for a dead hero, he felt obliged to respond. In an October 13 letter to the *Pike County Democrat,* he asserted that the attempted capture by Lammy and his men had been unwise: "The general understanding was that the arrest should not be attempted until a sufficient force should be brought into position and ready to fire at a given signal if they (the desperadoes) should refuse to surrender," and "Had this plan been carried out, the capture of the outlaws would have been secure, but its violation cost the life of a brave man and an honored citizen, and the escape of the desperadoes. . . ." It was a sad but true comment on the Calhoun County tragedy. Lammy and his two deputies initiated the gunfight when they should have waited for the rest of the posse, who were too far away to participate in the sudden battle. After all, they had been searching for the Maxwell brothers, who were renowned marksmen with rifles and revolvers. As Charles and Milton Coleman had also learned, in the moment they died, you can't expect to beat the Maxwells in a gunfight.

With the killing of the Coleman brothers and Sheriff Lammy, and the wounding of Churchman and McNabb, the Maxwells had become legendary gunfighters—the only ones who ever achieved real fame through gunfights east of the Mississippi River. Articles about them had by then appeared, or would soon appear, in major newspapers in Atlanta, New York, Philadelphia, Washington, D.C., and other cities.

In the Mississippi Valley, the *Chicago Tribune* alone carried thirty articles on the Maxwell brothers during 1881, versus fourteen on the James gang, and the *Chicago Times* (even more widely circulated) carried more than fifty. Dozens of items also appeared in the daily papers of St. Paul, Milwaukee, and St. Louis. In a front-page story about the killing of Sheriff Lammy, the *Missouri Republican* proclaimed the new preeminence of the Maxwell outlaws: "THE JAMES BOYS AND THE DESPERADO RANDE ECLIPSED AT LAST." If the brothers-against-brothers gunfight at Durand had made the Maxwells notorious, their escape against incredible odds had elevated them to the stature of outlaw heroes—men whose motives were dark but whose defiance and courage were the stuff of legend. As the *Dunn County News* put it, "The Williams' escape . . . is a matter of wonder, and is more romantic than the long journey of the James brothers after their bloody exploit [the Northfield raid] in Minnesota."

It is not surprising that during the second half of 1881, the sensationalistic *National Police Gazette,* published in New York, carried half a dozen articles on Ed and Lon, most of them illustrated with woodcuts. One of those reports began by asserting their preeminent notoriety: "No criminals have attracted a larger share of public attention than the Williams brothers. . . ."

And with all that notoriety came increasing amounts of exaggeration and folklore. One newspaper, for example, asserted in late October that the Maxwell brothers had "committed a number of murders" in Illinois and Missouri.

Although it is doubtful that Ed and Lon ever knew quite how notorious they were, the outlaw brothers had in any case achieved their goal of autonomous, and celebrated, existence in defiance of the social order. But ironically, they were still just desperate movers across an inhospitable cultural landscape—a nightmarish extension of their early life—with no real hope of ever being anything else. And their violent career was about to close.

13

Ed's Capture and Lon's Escape

As the fall of 1881 continued, so did America's massive struggle with the issue of law and order. In Arizona Territory, a hot, dusty boomtown called Tombstone gained national notoriety on October 26 with the gunfight at the O.K. Corral. Three enemies of the Earp brothers were killed, and Virgil Earp (the new marshal), Morgan Earp, and Doc Holliday were wounded. Only the later-renowned Wyatt Earp was unscathed.

Was the now-famous gunfight a justifiable police action against men who had defied local authority in Tombstone—as several western films would later portray it—or a lynching by gunfire of troublesome cowboys who had threatened violence, or simply an act of vengeance by the Earps and Holliday, who hated the men they shot? After all, sixteen-year-old Billy Clanton had raised his hands and announced, "I do not want to fight," but he was shot down anyway, and another Earp opponent killed at the corral, Tom McLaury, did not even have a gun. No wonder Virgil Earp was relieved of his job as marshal and the popularity of the Earps in Tombstone sharply declined. In fact, "a hastily organized 'Citizens' Safety Committee' turned against the Earps and made it clear that any such future [gunfighting] action on their part would result in an immediate public hanging." But that threat of lynching did not stop the violence. In the months that followed, the Earps and their enemies engaged in a bloody vendetta, in which Morgan Earp was killed, Virgil was wounded, and Wyatt then killed two men that he blamed for those shootings—as well as another man that he just happened to run across—and then went into hiding.

Meanwhile, other states and territories in the West continued to have shootings and lynchings at an alarming rate.

In the Mississippi Valley, which was striving to curb western-style outlawry and disorder, authorities were still hunting for the James brothers, whose many robberies had also resulted in at least half a dozen murders, and for the sheriff-killing Maxwell brothers, whose bloody defiance of law and order epitomized the meaning of "desperado." Many people in Missouri were not inclined to report sightings or rumors of the James brothers, who were hiding out near Independence, but descriptions and images of the Maxwells had recently been seen by hundreds of thousands of people in several states where no one admired them or wanted to shield them from the law, so reported sightings of them continued to come in.

The pursuit of the Maxwell brothers took a new turn on October 25, when the *Milwaukee Sentinel* reported that Lon had been jailed in that city. The story was still sketchy at that point, but a man who claimed to be William Kuhl from central Illinois had been arrested on October 23 and was being held for identification.

A follow-up article the next day revealed the growing certainty that the man was Lon, as well as the difficulty of identifying criminals before the advent of fingerprinting:

DREAD SUSPENSE.

Officials Awaiting Someone to Fully
Identify the Supposed Lon Williams.
Story of the Detention of the Suspected
Party, Who was Disguised as a Tramp.
The Chain of Circumstantial Evidence
Closing around the Alleged Murderer.

... Deputy Sheriff [James] Greding met the suspected man on the 3rd of last month, from which time to the 23rd of that month he constantly shadowed him, each day finding some new reason to suspect him as one of the Williams brothers. The stranger's appearance in every particular agreed with the description the officer had in his possession. ... The officer immediately took him into custody. ...

Lon Williams having reportedly suffered amputation of one of his toes . . . it was observed that one of the stranger's toes had been subjected to surgical treatment. . . . Lon Williams had a scar diagonally across his left hand, which mark was not wanting in the suspected man. Subsequently, an examination by Dr. Allen revealed the scar of a bullet wound . . . on the prisoner's shoulder, which . . . Lon Williams bears.

Among the persons who visited this city to identify the man were Sheriff Severson, of Dunn County, and Dr. Baker, of Hersey. . . . The talk of the physician added to the suspicion of the officers here. He said, "[I] wouldn't care for Ed, but I'd like to see Lon go scott free."

Detective Matteson, of Peoria, an acquaintance of William Kuhl, visited the suspected man and failed to identify him as Kuhl. . . .

Dr. E. O. Baker was acquainted with Lon and had amputated the second toe on his right foot, so Milwaukee authorities should have determined, from his comments, whether the man calling himself William Kuhl was really Lon Maxwell. But somehow they didn't. The apparent reason was that those city police officials did not trust the small-town physician, who was clearly sympathetic to Lon.

Also, Kuhl claimed to be from Woodford County, where the Maxwells had once lived, and that gave rise to the notion that "William Kuhl" was simply another alias adopted by one of the fugitives.

Moreover, on October 31 both of the surviving Coleman brothers and Undersheriff Miletus Knight arrived in Milwaukee, and they positively identified the arrested man as Lon Maxwell. Although he had never seen the Maxwells up close, Knight had talked to several people who knew Ed and Lon, and he had studied their photographs, which he carried with him, so he viewed himself as the indispensable identifier of the desperadoes. A self-righteous man who never questioned his own actions or admitted his fallibility, Knight reportedly claimed that he "can not be mistaken." And young Henry Coleman, now a Dunn County deputy sheriff, had apparently been acquainted with Lon in the Menomonie-Hersey area, where he had hunted and fished with him—or so he claimed. That was good enough for the *Milwaukee Sentinel,* which printed a November 1 report titled "FULLY IDENTIFIED," flatly claiming, "The Mild-Mannered Peorian Proven to Be Lon Williams, the Desperado."

The *National Police Gazette* soon carried an article on the controversy, illustrated with a woodcut of the accused desperado showing his foot to a room full of investigators, in a vain effort to disprove the dead-certain identifications by Miletus Knight and the Coleman brothers.

Another story about the identification process, which got as far as the November 1 *Washington Post,* asserted that during the interview Henry Coleman wanted to kill Lon on the spot: "Coleman drew a large Navy revolver and leveled it at the prisoner, but the deputy sheriff restrained him from shooting." That dramatic account may have been folklore.

Despite the apparently firm identification of Lon, Sheriff John Rugee of Milwaukee County hesitated to release the prisoner to the authorities from Pepin and Dunn counties. The man calling himself William Kuhl continued to deny that he was the notorious desperado, claiming that he was just an itinerant worker from central Illinois, and Rugee wanted him "thoroughly identified before he is taken to the scene of that terrible Coleman tragedy and placed in the dangerous position of being attacked by a mob. . . ." In short, the cautious lawman feared a lynching—an especially heinous act of public violence if the victim was somehow not Lon Williams after all.

The *Sentinel* article of November 1 broke even more startling news: "Sheriff Rugee's deputies had had both of the men known as the Williams brothers in custody, and one of the fellows [Ed] was released through the sheer stupidity of the jail authorities. . . . That [other] man was in better condition and had in his possession two revolvers and about $80 in money. . . ." Described to the Coleman brothers, "Kuhl's companion" was soon identified as "the desperado known as Ed Williams."

Embarrassed Milwaukee authorities began searching for Ed, who "has not been seen since the day of his release," according to the newspaper, and Sheriff Rugee was under even more pressure to surrender Lon to Pepin County officials.

On Wednesday, November 2, the suspect identified as Lon was released to Miletus Knight and a posse of twelve men, who took him by train to Menomonie. On Thursday morning, the outlaw was placed in the Dunn County Jail—and put under heavy guard, for fear of a lynch mob.

Unfortunately for Miletus Knight, the Coleman brothers, and the Milwaukee police, the identification of William Kuhl as Lon Maxwell soon fell apart. On November 3 Lon's father-in-law, Bill Thompson, visited the Menomonie jail and flatly asserted "that the man in custody was not Lon Williams." Thompson's motive may have been questioned, but others would soon agree or at least express reservations. Two days later, the embarrassed *Milwaukee Sentinel* reported the view of local residents in the Menomonie-Hersey area—that the prisoner was not the famous desperado: "Dr. Baker avers that he amputated, back of the second joint, the second toe of Lon Williams, in a drug store at Hersey," and "The druggist who was present at the operation, and who has the toe in alcohol, and other witnesses who were there, say this man is not Lon Williams." Kuhl was also taken to Durand, where local people also failed to identify him as Lon. The district attorneys of Dunn and Pepin counties were reportedly so upset by the weakening of the identification that they threatened to prosecute Kuhl anyway, to determine in court if he was somehow associated with the Coleman killings. Later, when witnesses stepped forth to affirm that Kuhl was in Illinois at the time of the Durand gunfight, they quietly dropped that approach.

William Kuhl was finally released on November 7 after spending two horrific weeks in jail—at a time when he was ill and should have been in a hospital—simply because he had a strong facial resemblance to Lon Maxwell. Later in the month, newspapers reported that Kuhl was filing suit against the Milwaukee County authorities for false imprisonment and other violations of his rights. He sued for $25,000 and was eventually awarded $5,300.

While Kuhl was in jail at Menomonie and Durand, many newspapers carried a bulletin from St. Louis indicating that lawmen there had apparently arrested the outlaws. That, too, had damaged the claim by Wisconsin authorities that William Kuhl was actually Lon, and as soon as the mistaken arrest of Kuhl was apparent, Miletus Knight was planning to help with the identification in St. Louis. But before he could get there, it was clear that those prisoners were not Ed and Lon either. Unlike Kuhl, those two men were not tramps who had been out of touch with friends and relatives for years, and they soon proved who they were.

Early November was a frustrating time for Miletus Knight, who had begun to view himself as the chief authority on, and principal identifier of, the Maxwells, but had badly blundered in the Kuhl case. He probably began to wonder whether his strategy of blanketing the Mississippi Valley with descriptions and lithographs of the outlaws would work after all. Then, a few days later, he received a telegram from Sheriff Joseph Kilian of Hall County, Nebraska, that sounded very promising: "Edward Maxwell was captured after a hard struggle. Alonso [*sic*] got away." Kilian's certainty was encouraging, so the undersheriff wired back that he would arrive at Grand Island, the county seat, on the first available train.

On November 10, the *Grand Island Times* described the capture in a detailed article that had also been sent as a dispatch to major newspapers in the Mississippi Valley. The exciting struggle and gunfight between the outlaws and the four-man posse led by the sheriff was itself the best evidence that the multistate manhunt for the Maxwell brothers had finally paid off:

A MURDERER CAPTURED.

Ed Maxwell, alias Ed Williams,
A Wisconsin Murderer, Captured
By Sheriff Kilian, and Lon Maxwell,
His Brother, Still at Large. . . .

Grand Island, Neb., Nov. 9, 1881—Last Monday evening [November 7], Sheriff Kilian, of Hall County, received information from Chris Staal, a constable in Merrick County . . . that there were two suspicious characters at the house of a neighboring farmer named William Niedfeldt [two miles southeast of Grand Island], and from knowledge obtained from a Milwaukee paper it was supposed they were the notorious Maxwell brothers, alias Williams, wanted in Wisconsin. . . .

The sheriff was at the time engaged with an orchestra, playing for a dance at Liederkranz Hall, and while tooting on his B flat, laid his plans for the arrest. About four o'clock in the morning he called to his assistance his informer, Chris Staal, [as well as] Ludwig Schultz . . . and August Nitsch, a young cigarmaker of this city. They armed themselves with revolvers and double-barrelled shotguns, and proceeded at once to Niedfeldt's house, reaching there about five o'clock, and under the pretense of being goose hunters, had his wife prepare breakfast for them.

There being but two rooms to the house, Kilian and his posse were shown into the one where the two brothers had their bed on the floor. They were on the alert and in the act of arising when the officers of the law arrived. . . . Their Winchester rifles were within easy reach of the bed, while each had a pair of revolvers under his pillow. The compliments of the morning were passed and a general run of conversation entered into between Kilian and the brothers, who claimed to be from Hastings . . . and also on a goose hunt. They were asked questions about the town and persons living there, which they were unable to answer. . . .

The [Maxwell] boys dressed themselves quietly, always

keeping within reach of their guns, and a close watch upon the actions of the pretended goose hunters. As they were dressing, Kilian noticed that Lon Williams, the younger of the two, who had lost the second toe on his right foot, put his stockings on with his feet under the bed clothing. After finishing dressing, Ed Williams took up a position near the corner of the room, with his right hand on his Winchester, while Lon left his arms and hat and coat, and walked leisurely out of the kitchen door, and towards the barn. This changed Kilian's plans, and he concluded to take Ed while Lon was out of doors . . . and have only one to contend with at a time. Kilian deliberately walked up to Ed and said, "I want you," whereupon Ed made a move to bring up his gun. Kilian grabbed him around both arms, floored him, and took the gun away from him while Nitsch covered him with a shotgun, and in a twinkling he was secured and bound.

When [Ed] saw that the jig was up as far as he was concerned, he warned his brother of the impending danger by a series of yells. Kilian, fearing that the latter would take warning and escape, stepped outside the kitchen door. . . . Lon having heard the signals given by his brother, came running around the corner of the house, when he was immediately confronted by Kilian's revolver and commanded to halt. The answer was a shot from [Lon's] revolver, aimed at the sheriff, who saw the movement and was fortunate enough to dodge it and get into the kitchen, immediately closing the door and partially stepping to one side, with his foot against the door. Lon came up and gave it a kick, expecting that it would fly wide open and enable him to "get in his work" with his revolver. It only opened about three inches, however, when he found himself looking to the muzzle of Nitsch's shotgun. He then jumped around the corner of the house again and went to a window but a few feet away. This had been anticipated by Nitsch, and when Lon attempted to raise his revolver to shoot through the glass, the former had a fine bead on his head and pulled both triggers—but each cartridge failed to explode.

This seemed to satisfy Lon that further attempts to rescue his brother would prove futile, and with proper regard for his own hide, he gave it up as a bad job. This was the last seen of him. . . .

> The sheriff and his party then loaded their prisoner into
> a lumber wagon and started for Grand Island, and by 8:30
> he was in prison. . . .

A later report added that Lon had shot twice at the sheriff, the second time by firing through the kitchen door while Kilian kept it closed with his foot.

The story was carried in the *New York Times* and other newspapers across the country. In the *Philadelphia Evening Telegraph,* it was a front-page article titled "RUNNING DOWN WESTERN OUTLAWS," and in the *Chicago Times* it was the criminal news headline item, "'DOWNING' A DEMON: The Capture of a Man . . . Believed to Be One of the Williams Desperadoes." One widely reprinted account that first appeared in the *Hastings Gazette-Journal* was tersely titled "THE SHERIFF KILLERS." That was, in fact, the essence of the Maxwells' public identity.

Many of the newspapers celebrated Sheriff Kilian. A German immigrant, he had just become a naturalized citizen when the Civil War broke out. He served in the Ninth Ohio Infantry for sixteen months, and then moved to Davenport, Iowa, where he enlisted in the Seventh Iowa Cavalry. In 1864 his regiment was assigned to Fort Kearney to help quell an Indian uprising, and after his tour of duty ended in 1866, Kilian decided to settle in nearby Grand Island. The Hall County seat, Grand Island was incorporated in 1872, and the courthouse, which included jail cells, was constructed the following year. The town boomed in the late 1870s, and by 1880 it had 3,000 people, including a number of German immigrants. A good-natured, popular man, Kilian worked in various shops during the 1860s and 1870s, and was both a deputy sheriff and the director of the Grand Island Band. Elected sheriff in 1877, he was then thirty-nine years old. By the time he made the arrest that brought him widespread acclaim, he was an experienced lawman. A reporter for the *Wisconsin State Journal* interviewed Kilian shortly after Ed's capture and described him: "He is a German, about five feet eight inches in height, [with] dark eyes, a full black beard and mustache, a good, substantial carriage, [and] a figure neither large nor small, but of sufficient stoutness to denote at least average strength or more, an open countenance, and an outspoken, genial demeanor. . . ."

For his heroic achievement, Kilian soon received one half of the reward money that had been offered in Wisconsin and Illinois for the arrest of the Maxwell brothers.

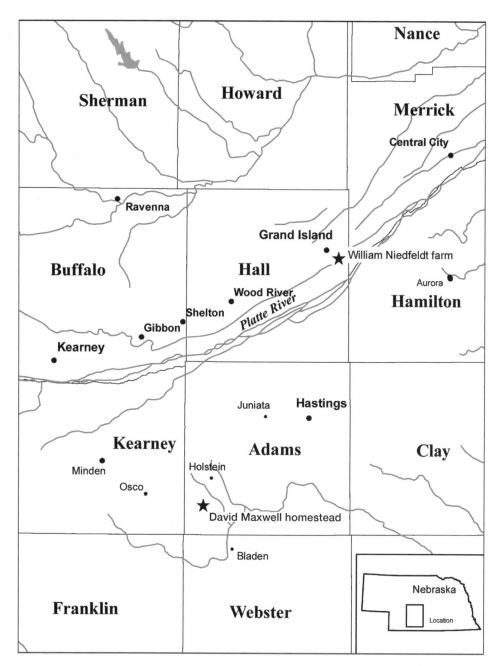

Part of south-central Nebraska, showing the locations of the Maxwell homestead in Adams County and the Niedfeldt farm, where Ed was captured.

When Ed arrived at the Hall County Jail on Tuesday morning, November 8, he was booked as "William Edward Maxwell, alias Williams," who was "a fugitive from justice." He was held there for seven days under heavy guard while positive identification was being made and extradition papers were being processed. Although questioned more than once, he said very little. Sometime during his first night in jail he tried to pick the lock on his cell, but was discovered.

Two days later, Miletus Knight and the Coleman brothers arrived, and according to a local newspaper, they "interviewed the prisoner, who they pronounced to be Ed Maxwell, beyond a doubt." Actually, it wasn't that simple. Stung by his mistaken identification of William Kuhl as Lon, Knight wanted a photograph taken of the captive, which he could then send to prison officials at Joliet. According to the *Pepin County Courier,* Ed resisted the process until "Undersheriff Knight then told him that they proposed to have his photograph, dead or alive. He then allowed his photograph to be taken with his long hair uncut and his face unshaved." He was then shaved and had a haircut, and was photographed again. That image showed "a good-looking man . . . with an intelligent and determined expression," and it was sent to the Illinois State Penitentiary. On November 15 the prison authorities replied by telegram: "The picture, though poor, is unmistakably that of Edward Maxwell."

While that process was going on, Knight tried to fool Ed into disclosing his identity and incriminating himself by a procedure that completely violated his civil rights. Realizing that Ed would not recognize the Coleman brothers, he introduced Henry as a young lawyer from Omaha offering his services. But the ruse did not succeed: "All of importance that Williams did say was that he thought he was suspected of being one of the Williams boys from Wisconsin, and that if he (Coleman) could only succeed in getting him just two steps outside the jail, and put his Winchester into his hands, he would fear neither God nor the devil, and he (Coleman) would be well paid for his service."

The authorities in Illinois—Sheriff Anderson, Sheriff Blades, and others—were also interested in the apparent capture in Nebraska, but they let the Wisconsin lawmen take the lead in identifying Ed and returning him for trial because the latter had circulated the descriptions and images that had led to the arrest.

The first of several newspaper interviews of Ed also took place at the jail in Grand Island. Reprinted in the November 17 *Macomb Journal* and in other newspapers, it indicates the enormous public interest in his capture.

Reporting that "this section of the country is wild with excitement over Ed Williams," the article also reveals Ed's inner tension as someone who craved notoriety but was afraid to disclose his identity.

> "At what place had your home been prior to coming to Nebraska?"
>
> "I prefer not to answer."
>
> "Was your partner a relative or merely a friend?"
>
> "An acquaintance." . . .
>
> "You were accused of horse stealing; was it true?"
>
> "We had no horses with us, nor [were there] any in Nebraska that I had ever taken."
>
> "If you were innocent, why had you so desperately resisted arrest?"
>
> "Well, a man might be fearing arrest for a crime of minor importance, and possibly for crimes he was not guilty of." . . .
>
> "Would it not be better to suffer the extent of the law for a slight crime than to deliberately shoot a man down who might be attempting the arrest?"
>
> "Well, it's a bad thing to shoot a man, and I wouldn't want to do it unless I thought I had call to—but after a man had been in prison and had gotten out, and everybody gave him the cold shoulder—that was not pleasant." . . .
>
> "What arms has your partner with him now?"
>
> "Two large navy revolvers, and he is the best shot with a rifle or a revolver that I ever saw. In shooting at a mark, I have seen him do things that I thought impossible for any man to do."
>
> "Did you yourself resist arrest?"
>
> "I had done all I could to prevent it, and if I had had more room, and not been taken by surprise, somebody would have gotten hurt. I would never have been taken if I had had the least intimation of the object of my captors and been out of doors. I would have defied them all." . . .

The interview reveals Ed's pent-up bitterness against all those who had given him a "cold shoulder"—that is, had showed no respect for him and had prevented him from belonging—and suggests that when he defied authority with his guns, he was somehow striking back at those who had devalued him and had prolonged his alienation. Moreover, his terse expression of bravado, "I would have defied them all," crystallizes the heroic identity that he had constructed, and to which he wanted to remain faithful despite his incarceration. The captive desperado was indeed Ed Maxwell.

His false claim that his comrade was just "an acquaintance" was obviously an effort to protect Lon so the authorities would not be sure who they were searching for. But of course, they were already certain about Lon's identity.

That people in Nebraska were "wild with excitement" over Ed's capture, and that thrill-seekers were trying to get in to see him, reveals his impact as a dark hero. He had become a compelling expression of drives deeply hidden in many homesteaders—a man opposed to constraint, resentful of authority, tired of anonymous toil, and bent on a dangerous path of self-realization that rejected traditional social codes. One newspaper would even call him "as fearless a desperado as was ever brought prominently before the public." And yet the newspaper correspondent who interviewed him admitted that, despite his reputation, Ed was "gentlemanly in his demeanor—a man who would create a favorable impression among strangers." In a certain sense, he was just like other decent men but was more overtly resistant to social restraint.

The interview at Grand Island concludes with a comment on how and why the Maxwells had come to central Nebraska: "The two brothers came west on a freight train last Monday, and when near Lockwood Station, five miles east of here, jumped off the train while [it was] in motion. Their father, David Maxwell, resides at Osco, Kearney County, this state, and it is supposed that the boys came west to make a visit." Actually, David and Susan lived in Adams County, east of Osco, but the assumption was otherwise correct. As Ed later told a reporter, "[W]e both wanted to see the old man very badly." Lon had last seen him in 1879, but Ed had not seen him since 1875.

The very fact that the Maxwells were intending to visit their parents despite the obvious risk of being caught is also psychologically suggestive. On one level they wanted to escape the limited social and economic world of their parents and clearly rejected some of their values, and on another, Ed and Lon still wanted to relate to them—especially to David, from whom they had become increasingly alienated by their own actions. Prodigal sons indeed.

Another reason for holding Ed at Grand Island for an entire week was the expectation that Lon would soon be caught, and both outlaws could then be returned together to Wisconsin. As soon as Sheriff Kilian had placed Ed in jail, he led a posse in pursuit of Lon. When Henry Coleman arrived, he joined that group, which scoured the countryside around Grand Island.

Much of the landscape was still covered with tallgrass prairie, where a fugitive could easily hide. Several other posses in nearby counties soon joined the manhunt, which scoured the Platte Valley area. Of course, Adams County authorities were involved because many felt that Lon would seek help from David and Susan, who lived less than forty miles southwest of Grand Island.

A November 11 dispatch from Nebraska to the *St. Louis Globe-Democrat* reflected a sighting of Lon and expressed confidence in his capture:

> The party that has been out searching for Lon reports having found traces of him near Aurora, Hamilton County, twenty-five miles from here. He was seen by a farmer and had on a brown duck hunting jacket. He had no arms that were visible, but while conversing with the farmer, he kept his right hand in the bosom of his coat, where he doubtless had a revolver, ready to use upon the slightest indication of hostile demonstration. . . .
>
> Another posse left in search of Lon today at noon. The whole country is up in arms, and the prospects for his capture are good.

Another dispatch revealed that, while near Aurora, Lon had "sent a boy into a store to buy some articles of food for himself." However, the posse that soon arrived there "lost the trail," according to a later report from that small town. About all that anyone could say, by late in the week, was that Lon was apparently heading east, perhaps back through familiar country, when he was last seen.

As he fled through the still-empty places of early Nebraska, moving on doggedly and desperately in the cold November nights, one wonders if Lon ever reflected on the double misfire of August Nitsch's shotgun, the fateful "click-click" that had allowed him to be once again a man on the run, instead of a corpse.

By the time Miletus Knight and the Coleman brothers finally took Ed from the jail on November 15, to start the long trip back to Pepin County, the search for Lon had lost its focus. As the *Grand Island Times* reported, "Several posses who have been out after Alonzo Maxwell think they were close upon him at times, but in every case he managed to elude them. Some are of the opinion that he left the country [i.e., the area] at once after the arrest of his brother, while others think he is still in this vicinity." No one knew where to look, and the searchers were becoming discouraged.

The failure of the Nebraska manhunt was blamed on both the rugged, empty terrain and the supposed assistance Lon was receiving from friends.

A dispatch from Omaha to the *Chicago Tribune,* for example, asserted that he was apparently hiding in Kearney County, in "a region of sand hills, offering numerous hiding places, and he is probably fed by friends, who also keep him informed of the whereabouts of the pursuers."

As in western Wisconsin, the fruitless, well-publicized search also prompted various reports that Lon "had been seen" somewhere. One that made the newspapers concerned a young stranger who showed up in Grand Island one night. He "had a very vicious look," told some people he was a criminal, and "talked a great deal about the Williams boys"— precisely what Lon would not have done.

Soon the *National Police Gazette* carried an article that printed a wood-cut illustration of Lon, based on a recent photograph, hoping that the general public might assist the manhunters. But most of the *Gazette*'s readers were not located in the West, so that didn't help, except to increase Lon's notoriety.

With Ed's capture and Lon's escape, the outlaw career of the Maxwell brothers had reached a decisive climax. One was securely jailed and the other was being hunted—and might not function as a bandit without the brother who had always incited their criminal exploits. But the destiny of Ed and Lon was still unfolding, and both of them would, in different ways, suffer the harsh fate of a desperado.

Miletus Knight, the Durand under-sheriff who pursued the Maxwells in western Wisconsin, sent photographic "Wanted" postcards of them to lawmen in several states, and brought Ed back from Nebraska. (Courtesy of the Pepin County Historical Society.)

James O. Anderson, the Henderson County sheriff who pursued the Maxwells across central Illinois, sent "Wanted" postcard descriptions of them to other lawmen, and participated in the great manhunt. (Courtesy of the Abraham Lincoln Presidential Library.)

A street in Durand (1880s), showing the still-frontierish look of the town where the gunfight occurred. (Courtesy of the Pepin County Historical Society.)

Charles Coleman, the ex-sheriff of Pepin County who was killed by Ed Maxwell in the famous brothers-against-brothers gunfight. (Courtesy of the Pepin County Historical Society.)

Milton Coleman, the undersheriff of Dunn County, who was killed by Lon Maxwell in the gunfight. (Courtesy of John M. Russell.)

W. H. Huntington, editor of the *Pepin County Courier*, who encouraged lynching, witnessed the lynching of Ed Maxwell, and praised the men who did it. (Courtesy of the Pepin County Historical Society.)

Dunn County ex-sheriff E. L. Doolittle, who headed the massive posse that searched for the Maxwells in western Wisconsin. (Courtesy of the Dunn County Historical Society.)

Below: Three officers of the Ludington Guard, the cavalry militia unit that pursued the Maxwells. Seated is T. J. George, nicknamed "Old Buckskin," who is holding a repeating rifle and wearing an ammunition belt. (Courtesy of the Dunn County Historical Society.)

Sheriff John Lammy of Calhoun County, whose death in a gunfight led to extensive pursuit of the Maxwells in Illinois and Missouri. (Courtesy of the Calhoun County Historical Society.)

Lammy's tall gravestone, celebrating him as a hero "KILLED While in Discharge of His Duty as Sheriff," is located in the cemetery at Hardin, Illinois. (Photographed by the author.)

Sheriff Joseph Kilian of Hall County, Nebraska, who captured Ed on November 8, 1881, near Grand Island, and then pursued Lon with a posse for several days. (Courtesy of Gene Q. Watson.)

Below left: A photograph of Ed taken at Grand Island, for sending to officials at Joliet prison for positive identification. Ed resisted the process but complied when threatened. (Courtesy of the Pepin County Historical Society.)

Also, a photograph of Lon that was probably taken at the time he was married (July 1880) or in early 1881. He was twenty-two. (Courtesy of the Pepin County Historical Society.)

The Dunn County Courthouse, where Milton Coleman's body was on view after the gunfight, and where Ed Maxwell was displayed to, and interrogated by, the public shortly before his death at Durand. (Courtesy of the Dunn County Historical Society.)

The Pepin County Courthouse, where Ed was arraigned on November 19, before being lynched from an oak tree standing just outside this image, to the left. Near the courthouse is the Pepin County Jail, where Ed was held before his death. (Courtesy of the Pepin County Historical Society.)

LYNCH LAW IN WISCONSIN.

IN THE COURT ROOM.

THE HANGING.

THE MURDER OF MAXWELL.

A Cowardly and Brutal Taking Off.

Maxwell by making a rush at him. Part of the crowd surged in between him and the officers, who were easily crowded to one side, and others seized Maxwell, over whose head a noosed rope was quickly dropped, and he was half dragged, hay

On November 21, 1881, the *Stillwater Daily Sun* printed these two imaginative sketches of the lynching of Ed Maxwell, as part of a front-page story that severely condemned the mob violence. The *Sun's* report was part of national newspaper coverage, which included two front-page articles in the *New York Times*. (Courtesy of the Wisconsin Historical Society.)

The cover of *The Boys of New York* for December 31, 1881, just weeks after Ed was lynched, announcing the start of *The Williams Brothers; or, A Thousand-Mile Chase*, the first work of pulp fiction about the Maxwells. The woodcut depicts them in a canoe, making their escape by plunging over a waterfall on the Chippewa River. The Chippewa had no such waterfalls, nor did the Maxwells ever escape in a canoe.

"DOUBLE QUICK, THE KING HARPOONER; or, The Wonder of the Whalers," By ALBERT J. BOOTH,

NEXT WEEK!

THE BOYS of NEW YORK

A PAPER FOR YOUNG AMERICANS

Vol. VII.   NEW YORK, JANUARY 7, 1882.   No. 884

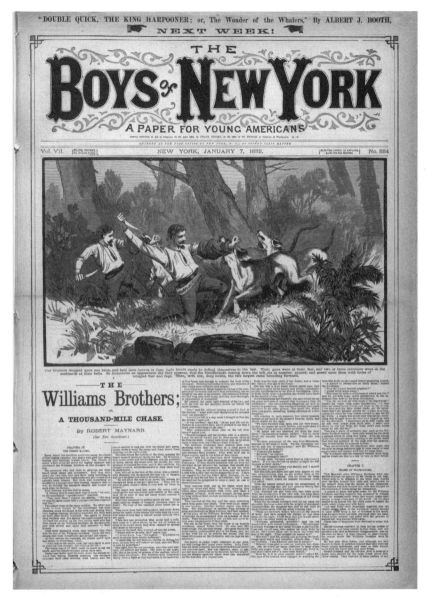

THE Williams Brothers;
or,
A THOUSAND-MILE CHASE.

By ROBERT MAYNARD.

(Our New Contributor.)

The second installment of *The Williams Brothers; or, A Thousand-Mile Chase*, in *The Boys of New York*. Dated January 7, 1882, it features a woodcut showing Ed and Lon fighting off a pack of vicious bloodhounds. By then thousands of readers were hooked on the saga of America's heroic outlaw fugitives, fleeing for their lives through the wilds of the Mississippi Valley, which ran for an incredible thirty-eight installments in a trilogy of action-packed, serialized short novels.

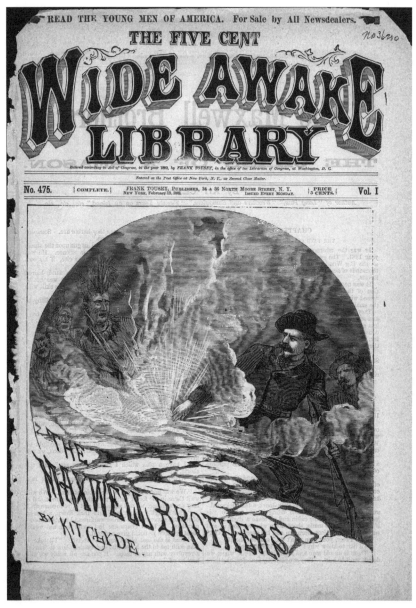

The cover of *The Maxwell Brothers* by Kit Clyde, in a dime novel series called *The Five Cent Wide Awake Library*. Dated February 13, 1882, it is the only pulp fiction about the Maxwells that does not use their alias, "Williams." The woodcut on the cover shows Ed setting off a powder charge to create a huge smokescreen, which allows the outlaws to escape from pursuing Indians.

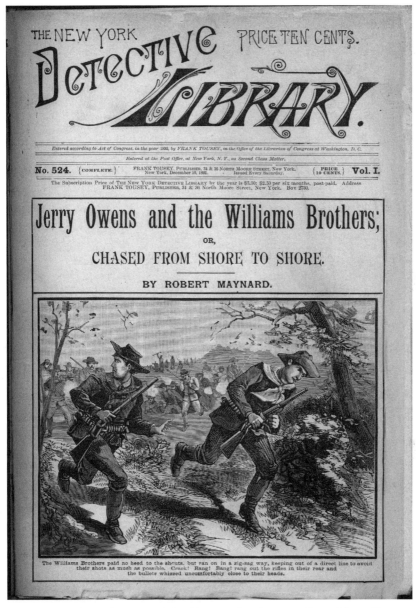

The cover of *Jerry Owens and the Williams Brothers; or, Chased from Shore to Shore,* an 1892 dime novel in *The New York Detective Library.* The woodcut on the cover shows Ed and Lon fleeing from a massive posse. The intrepid young detective, Jerry Owens, is their chief pursuer in all three of the 1890s "Williams Brothers" dime novels, the final appearances of the Maxwells in pulp fiction.

The broken and weathered gravestone of Fannie, "beloved wife of Alonzo Maxwell," who lies buried in the still-remote Waubeek Prairie Cemetery northwest of Durand. The inscribed letter-in-stone to "Dear Fannie" is barely visible at the bottom. The marker symbolizes their tragic love and the enduring mystery of Lon's fate. (Courtesy of Don and Jane Rahman, School District of Durand, Wis., Web site.)

14

The Desperado
and the Public

Some of the most notorious nineteenth-century outlaws, such as Sam Bass (d. 1878), Billy the Kid (d. 1881), and Jesse James (d. 1882), had a complex relationship with the public, which saw in them competing aspects of American cultural life: the appeal of individualism and the presence of disorder; the excitement of wild adventure and the threat of violence; the nobility of courage and the persistence of evil. In the unforgettably turbulent year of 1881, Ed Maxwell was also one of those figures, and his death would come midway between Billy's and Jesse's, as nationally known outlaws seemed to be finally meeting their end in notably violent ways.

Ed's status as an outlaw celebrity, a kind of dark hero of self-assertion, was reinforced at every stop on the way to Pepin County. And it was evident from his interviews that he was determined to play his chosen role to the violent finish that he often sensed was coming.

His legs shackled and his arms handcuffed, Ed was taken on the Union Pacific Railroad to Omaha, where a crowd met the train to see the famous outlaw, and he was held overnight in the Douglas County Jail. A local newspaper printed a lengthy story about "MAXWELL, THE MURDERER" and proclaimed that the two Maxwells "have their equals only in the James brothers."

Ed was not allowed to give an interview, but his brief comments to Miletus Knight on the way to the jail were noted by a reporter: "As he was going up Farnham Street, he said, 'I've seen this town before. Me and my pard were here a little while ago.' When he reached the jail, he stated that they [he and Lon] had walked by there and looked the place over." Ed's use of the uncommon term "pard" (for "partner") suggests the influence of dime novel slang, as in the 1874 title *Hurricane Bill; or, Mustang Sam and His "Pard," a Romance of the Evil Land* by Joseph E. Badger, Jr.

Ed's extradition from Nebraska also involved a poignant missed opportunity to see his father, who had naturally heard of the arrest. Because Ed was at first trying to conceal his identity, he rejected the chance to see his father—and then he regretted it:

> Just as the party was leaving Grand Island for Omaha, [Undersheriff] Knight received a telegram from Hastings, Neb., from David Maxwell, the father of Ed, requesting him [Knight] to wait another day, as he wanted to come to Grand Island and see his son. The dispatch was shown to the prisoner, who said that the man was not his father. Later, Ed asked Knight to stop . . . in Omaha and telegraph his father to meet him there, as he would like to see the old man. The prisoner, however, was taken next morning to Wisconsin. . . .

Why did Ed change his mind? Of course, he at first did not want to admit that he was Ed Maxwell, hoping that Nebraska authorities could not connect him with the killings in Wisconsin. And there was also the troubled bond with David, the demanding, religious father who had subjected him to a childhood of poverty, insecurity, and anxiety—the father whose world he had rejected by escaping into a defiant outlaw identity. As he knew from his experience in Macomb seven years earlier, it would have been tough to face the old man in a jail cell. But if Ed did somehow long for his father's understanding, the desire to see him—perhaps for the last time—probably became overwhelming.

According to another, later report, Ed was also concerned about Lon and wanted to pass words of caution to him by way of their father. He finally resorted to a letter: "Henry Coleman succeeded in getting a letter Ed wrote to his father from the jail in [Omaha], which is evidently intended for Lon's perusal as advice is contained therein not to trust himself to Bill Thompson, the stepfather of Lon's late wife, as Thompson 'would give you away sure.'" The letter not only typifies Ed's concern for his brother;

it also suggests that Lon may have indicated to Ed his intention to return to Wisconsin, where his beloved Fannie was buried.

The only public comment about the Maxwell family at the time of Ed's capture was a brief item in the *Hastings Gazette-Journal* written by a stringer who reported on southern Adams County—and probably knew David and Susan: "The parents of the Maxwell boys, one of whom was captured at Grand Island recently, live in Silver Lake Precinct," and "this blow falls with terrible effect upon them in their advanced years." David and Susan were, in fact, only in their late forties, but dire poverty, unrelenting hard work, and perpetual frustration had surely aged them considerably.

The next stop for the celebrity outlaw was St. Paul. A reporter for the *Stillwater Daily Sun* depicted the scene at the depot during that two-hour wait for the next train to western Wisconsin, and briefly spoke with Ed:

ED MAXWELL.

His Reception in St. Paul.

. . . Yesterday, Sheriff Knight of Pepin County, two of the Coleman boys, and the Sheriff of [Hall] County, Nebraska brought Ed Maxwell, the noted murderer and criminal, through St. Paul on the C., St. P., M. & O. Railway. There were over a thousand people at the depot, who pushed and jostled each other with an eagerness and persistence worthy of a better cause, to catch a glimpse of this noted character.

The prisoner was brought into the Main Depot, escorted by four men mentioned above, heavily shackled, both arms and legs. The mob that followed compelled the officers to lock themselves with the prisoner in a small room until the train started for Menomonie, to which place they were to take the prisoner. At 1:45 they pushed themselves with the prisoner through a mass of seething humanity to the cars, when it seemed as if the crowd would hang on, and accompany the prisoner to his destination.

The prisoner is a mild-looking man, and would never be taken for the desperado he has proved himself to be. . . . We asked Maxwell if he thought they had the right man, and he replied that he "thought not, but [he] was fearful that they would hang him when they reached their destination." . . .

Among the crowd in St. Paul was Stillwater Police Chief Matthew Shortall, who had arrested Ed in 1876. He, too, could identify Ed, and he was no doubt also anxious to meet Sheriff Kilian, whose reward would be much larger than the one he had received from Macomb officials five years earlier.

While in St. Paul, Ed was recognized by others as well, and as soon as concealing his identity was no longer possible, he openly admitted that he was the notorious desperado. Then he provided a remarkable interview for a local newspaperman named Edward R. Johnstone, who was writing for the *St. Paul Pioneer Press.* A shorter version of this vivid item, titled "A NOTORIOUS WESTERN RUFFIAN," appeared on page one of the *New York Times:*

MAXWELL IN MANACLES.

The Notorious Desperado Passes through
St. Paul, on His Way to the Scene of
His Last Crime. . . .
A Large Crowd Feast Their Hungry Eyes
Upon the Chained Murderer—
How He Looks and Acts. . . .

. . . The officers were supplied with Winchester rifles beside their small arms, and kept close watch on their prisoner, who, as he stepped from the train, was the target at which thousands of pairs of eyes were aimed. Many of the spectators had evidently expected to see a savage, ferocious-looking monster, and therefore, there was a general expression of disappointment when there appeared to the public gaze a trim, compactly built little man, with black hair, chin whiskers, and mustache, neatly dressed in a new suit of black store clothes, with a slouch hat, whose whole appearance was quiet and subdued, and whose undeniably good looks could not but make a favorable impression.

He looked anything but the daredevil and murderer he has won the notoriety of being; and such expressions as "He don't look so terrible, does he?" and "Why, he's not such a villainous-looking fellow, is he?" were heard on all sides. . . .

If any doubt had been wanting of the villain's identity, however, it was speedily furnished, for as Maxwell stepped

---

from the car, E. C. Austin, a well-known lumberman of Hersey, extended his hand to Maxwell, with "How are you, Ed?" "How do you do, Mr. Austin," said Maxwell.

Mr. Austin said to a reporter that he knew Ed Maxwell, and there was no doubt about his identity. "His brother Lon worked for me for a long time. It made my blood run cold to shake hands with a murderer, but I wanted him to know that he was recognized."

A young man named Eastman, of Denmark, on tiptoes in the crowd to get a sight of the prisoner, said, as soon as he caught sight of him: "That's Ed Maxwell! I have seen him many times. . . ."

Followed by the curious crowd, the officers led Maxwell into the depot, and hence into the men's waiting room. Ed was given a seat in the corner, and his guards and he were attacked by a frantic mob of sightseers. For a few minutes all was hubbub and confusion, and it was difficult for the reporters to get near the prisoner or his keepers. . . . During all the excitement Maxwell was cool and unperturbable. . . . After a few minutes conversation with the *Pioneer Press* reporter, he was taken into the parcel room, where he was less liable to the annoyance of the crowd. Here his handcuffs were removed, and he partook freely of a lunch. . . .

He never once, throughout all the time he was at the depot, showed the slightest trace of any feeling of contrition or regret for what he had done. His only expression of regret was when speaking of his capture; he said that if he could only have got to his gun, he would not have been in his present plight. . . . As he said this, his brown eyes flashed fire, and his looks indicated, more than words could well do, the resolution and determination of the man.

Asked whether he considered himself justified in the killing of the Coleman brothers, he said that was a question he would not answer. . . . Later on, he claimed that he and Lon were obliged to do the deed in self-defense—that the Colemans' lives were nothing to him, as compared to his own. He talked in the most matter of fact way about the shedding of human blood. When asked if he believed in murder, he looked fiercely at his questioner and said, "Did you ever hear of the Williams boys firing upon anyone unless they were first attacked?" . . .

Sheriff Knight informed the *Pioneer Press* reporter that the Maxwell brothers were in the Eau Galle woods but a week, while the search was kept up for nearly a month. They made their way to the Mississippi River, traveling at night, and crossed at Lone Rock, where they secured a boat. The river was low, and though Ed says his hands were swollen so that he could hardly lift them, they managed to propel the boat by means of some [wooden] shingles.

"It was certain death behind and liberty in front, and I would have rowed the boat if it had torn my hand off to have done it. I knew that our pursuers would look for us up in the woods, or up and down the river, so I determined to strike out at once for the prairie, where there was more room to shoot. The longest time we were ever without food was eighty-five hours. For the first twenty-four hours of that time we suffered intensely, but after that the pangs of hunger gradually died away. We had no friends in the woods to help us, as has been so often stated."

To illustrate Ed Maxwell's deficiency in moral sense, it is only necessary to repeat the idea of his wonderful forbearance in resisting the temptation to shoot a man who was riding within range of his gun, while he was in the Eau Galle woods: "Why, I could have put a bullet in him in a minute; but you see, I didn't want to commit a murder, so I lay down and let him go by."

When asked if he was not afraid to go back to Menomonie, he gave his questioner a look full in the face and said, "I do not fear anything. I am prepared for the worst. I have to die sometime. We all have to do that, and as long as one is prepared, it matters little when death comes. If I have to die [now], I will do it like a man." . . .

He talked like a man who had nerved himself for the worst, and was prepared to meet his fate. There was little of the braggadocio manner about him. . . .

Ed says that they never went south at all, and denies that he and his "partner," as he calls Lon, were the parties who killed a sheriff and wounded and routed his posse near St. Louis in [September]. . . .

Ed speaks fluently and in an earnest manner. What was singular in a man of his reputation, during the whole of the hubbub and excitement yesterday . . . was [that] he did not utter an oath, an imprecation, or a vulgar word. He took the attention of the crowd very quietly, looking everyone who gazed at him square in the eyes, and never cowering or flinching from the curiosity of the masses. "All this fuss is annoying," he said, "but it can't be helped." . . .

This remarkable crowd scene and interview explicitly raises the issue of Ed's moral character. Although he was clearly respectful of others while captured, and was cooperative and sincere in responding to questions—more so than many people would have been in his position—he lacked "any feeling of contrition or regret" for the Durand gunfight. He felt that his actions were "justified." As that reveals, Ed had embraced the radical individualism of a gunfighter: Whatever he did, whether it was good or bad for the public, he felt that he had a right to be left alone, unhampered in his exercise of personal liberty, and if accosted by anyone, he had a right to be violent. He also said the same thing to Ed Coleman, brother of the dead lawmen, on the train to St. Paul, and Coleman later reported that in a letter to the *Eau Claire Free Press:* "He further stated that he would not allow any man's life to stand between him and liberty. And that he would shoot anyone who attempted to interfere with his business." That was the essence of his code, which would later be shared by many a hero in western novels and films—and is nowhere more clearly expressed than in John Wayne's final film, *The Shootist,* focused on the last days of an aging gunfighter, John Book. It is, then, an assertive code that would eventually be admired by millions of Americans, even though it is not rooted in a sense of right and wrong (or social responsibility) but merely in an individual's sense of who he wants to be.

Ed's remark about "dying like a man" revealed again his deep anxiety about being regarded as a man, which had been a psychological issue for him since his teenage years. (Surely that same issue prompted the violent behavior of many other outlaw gunmen, including John Wesley Hardin, Ben Thompson, and Billy the Kid, who started shooting men as teenagers.) And Ed apparently realized that facing death, perhaps at the hands of a lynch mob, would be the ultimate test of his chosen identity as a defiant desperado. In a sense, he had willed this final challenge, and he was prepared to confront his fate.

Ed's comments on facing death might have come, too, from gunfighter John Book: "I have to die sometime. We all have to do that, and as long as one is prepared, it matters little when death comes. If I have to die [now],

I will do it like a man." What Ed meant by being "prepared" was, simply, having come to terms with his destiny—having fully embraced the role of the defiant outsider, the desperado, which gave his life meaning. He realized that he was bound by the choices he had made—but at least he had escaped the intolerable confines of shame and disregard. In that spiritual sense, he was a free man, confident that his chosen identity would see him through, even when facing "the worst."

Because of the gunfight at Durand and the horrific survival test that followed—with "certain death behind [them] and liberty in front," as he put it—Ed had achieved a sense of authenticity, a conviction that he had become what he was meant to be: He was an outlaw who could defy them all, who could face the threat of death from sheriffs in the street and an army of pursuers, and still function with courage and self-control "like a man." Hence, he spoke with a sense of quiet confidence, "looking everyone who gazed at him square in the eyes."

It is evident too that Ed's sense of having become what he had intended was symbolized by "his new suit of black store clothes, with a slouch hat." That dark outfit expressed the confident, and perhaps mysterious, identity of a man to be reckoned with, a man of courageous defiance who had slowly materialized during the seven years since a frustrated and disrespected hired hand had stolen one or two suits of clothes from the Dines Store in Blandinsville.

As all of this suggests, Ed had a complex, layered character. He clearly exhibited sincerity, respect, and self-control, for example, but those values obviously challenged the public's social construction of his identity as a "desperado," a thoroughly evil public enemy, a savage "monster." Terms like "outlaw" and "desperado" were, in fact, simplistic substitutes for psychological comprehension.

Of course, Ed's assertion that he and Lon had never gone south and had not killed Sheriff Lammy was stunning—especially to the people of Calhoun and Pike counties. The Maxwells had supposedly been recognized by Deputy George Roberts of Pike County from photographs, and besides, who else could shoot like them and would not hesitate to kill a lawman? Even the killing of Lammy, with a single bullet to the head, fired by the quick-drawing man identified as Lon, was virtually identical to the way Lon had killed Milton Coleman. And the posse had reported that one of the desperadoes in Calhoun County "had no shoe or stocking on one foot," and Lon wore only one shoe, with either a sock or a moccasin on the other foot, for many months after his injury and toe amputation. The

Maxwells also had previous experience escaping by skiff—down the Illinois River—so that seemed like something they would do.

But Ed was commonly glad to tell the public about his deeds as a desperado, yet he denied that one. Moreover, he later described the severe gunshot wounds suffered by Lon and himself, which made it likely that they would head for their parents' homestead for help, rather than down the Mississippi. The *Wisconsin State Journal* soon reported on the severity of their wounds, which Ed had mentioned to Henry Coleman while on the train to Menomonie: "Ed's arm was badly riddled with shot, and Lon's arms, shoulder, and head received nearly the full charge from Milt Coleman's gun. Ed says he picked out over sixty shot from Lon's wound. Their arms were soon badly swollen, and for a long time it seemed certain that Lon would be obliged to submit to an amputation; but both finally got the better of their wounds, which slowly healed. Ed still bears the scars received in that affray."

But if Ed was telling the truth, who then killed Sheriff Lammy and wounded his deputies? About four weeks after that shooting, a bank was robbed at the village of Fieldon, in Jersey County, just across the Illinois River from Calhoun County, and the perpetrators were recognized as Charles Clay and John Burress, two young men who were newcomers to the area. In an October 20 article on the robbery, the *Jersey County Democrat* reported that they "have been around Fieldon ever since Sheriff Lammy was killed, and have been regarded as suspicious characters." Despite what that comment suggests, no one suspected that they were the men who had killed Lammy and wounded his deputies. And because that tragic gunfight was flatly blamed on the Maxwells, Clay and Burress simply remained in nearby Jersey County—where they later robbed the Fieldon bank. When authorities did finally pursue them for that holdup, they quickly departed from Jersey County.

Then, as the *Chicago Times* reported, the legendary status of the Maxwells still had an impact on the investigation, for "the conviction [arose], in the minds of the people, that these men, Clay and Burress, [were] the Maxwell or Williams brothers, to a certainty." That incredible misidentification apparently occurred because Charles Clay and John Burress were roughly the same size as Ed and Lon Maxwell—and oddly enough, one of them was "a little lame about one ankle." Like Lon, he left a distinctive footprint. No wonder the men known locally as "Clay" and "Burress" seemed to be the notorious desperadoes, employing aliases while hiding out in the area.

It is likely that Lammy's posse, searching for the Maxwell brothers, encountered Clay and Burress, who thought the sheriff and his men were trying to apprehend them for a train robbery that they had recently committed, so one of them pulled a gun on Deputy McNabb, and when the anxiety-ridden Deputy Churchman started shooting, they opened fire to avoid capture. Being professional outlaws, they too were good with their guns.

So, the massive continuation of the 1881 manhunt in Illinois and Missouri, involving more than a dozen posses, was simply the most fabulous example of the public tendency to blame the notorious Maxwell brothers for any and all mysterious crimes when they were on the loose. The only truth that it reveals about the sheriff-killing desperadoes is their huge significance for the American public—to the point where they had become a delusion.

Edward Johnstone of the *Pioneer Press* boarded the train at St. Paul, and then spoke with Ed at some length during the long trip to Menomonie. As a result, the desperado and the newspaperman became well acquainted. While Johnstone was intrigued by the polite, talkative outlaw, Ed apparently enjoyed conversing with a man of roughly his own age who seemed genuinely interested in him.

Born in Utica, New York, and educated at Dickinson College in Pennsylvania, Johnstone was a thirty-year-old reporter who had worked for a short time in Peoria before coming to St. Paul. Hence, he knew about Fulton and Woodford counties, where Ed had grown up. A talented writer who was on the rise in journalism, he would later edit newspapers in New York and Cleveland. Five years earlier, in 1876, he had covered the famous Northfield, Minnesota, raid and the subsequent manhunt for members of the James gang. During that assignment, he had interviewed Cole, Jim, and Bob Younger, who had been captured near Madelia. No doubt Ed was fascinated to hear about those notorious desperadoes from a man who had actually met them.

Johnstone's coverage of the Ed Maxwell story would soon spark controversy in Pepin County—and also do much to bring the outlaw brothers to national attention and help to inspire the dime novels that made Ed and Lon even more well known.

As the train carrying Ed Maxwell rolled across eastern Minnesota and western Wisconsin, telegraph messages alerted communities along the way, and "crowds thronged the various stations," as one report said, hoping to get a glimpse of the famous desperado. One Wisconsin newspaper also soon commented that "there seemed to be a disposition with some, while Ed Williams was on his route, to make a hero of him." Not that anyone praised his record as an outlaw, but some surely admired his daring and determination. After all, he and Lon had survived one of the most talked-about gunfights in the history of the Mississippi Valley—perhaps second only to the Northfield ambush of the James gang—and were still accused of killing Sheriff Lammy in the Calhoun County gunfight. They had also eluded one of the largest posses ever assembled to pursue American outlaws, and many others, in a spectacular manhunt that eventually extended into six states—and was still continuing for Lon.

When the train finally got to Menomonie on a chilly Thursday afternoon, November 17, Johnstone filed an interview report for the *Pioneer Press:*

TALKING ON THE CARS

I sat in the same seat with the manacled prisoner, from St. Paul to here, and until we reached Hudson he conversed glibly and smoothly. After that point was passed, he lost a trifle of his easy confidence, though at no time did he show any sign of fear.

At Hersey . . . he was recognized by scores of people, and told me without any hesitation the names of the various men who called out, "That's him!" or "How are you, Ed?" as he went through the pantomime of hand-shaking with his ironed hands jingling heavily.

He has dropped all pretense that he is not the much-hunted Maxwell, alias Williams, and has told me point blank that he and his brother Lon shot the Colemans, though he stoutly asserts that they killed them in self-defense. . . .

I tried to get Ed to confess that he had been in Illinois lately, but this he positively denies. . . .

Being asked as to how he came to be taken, Ed said with a frown, "They took us unawares. If I could have reached my rifle when I was wrestling on the floor with the sheriff and his man, there would have been a couple of corpses in that house. . . .

Ed claims that Lon did the right thing to get away, but [Henry] Coleman says he [Ed] feels a little bitter about what he once called "Lon's desertion."

Ed's disarming, almost childlike sincerity contrasted with his apparent willingness to kill. His expression of regret thàt he could not manage to shoot down two more lawmen could only damage his position with the authorities, but it reveals how much Ed needed to assert his chosen identity as a defiant desperado, an identity that had been compromised by his capture. With that stunning comment he was countering the perception that he was a powerless, ineffectual man—which was his very purpose for being an outlaw. He was not weak, not unmanly; they had simply taken him by surprise.

The closing comment about Lon reveals that Ed was at first very troubled by the fact that his brother had failed to rescue him. That seemed like a violation of their outlaw bond, their commitment to fight to the death for each other. But Ed apparently concluded, after some reflection, that Lon had done his best, and it was better that at least one of them had escaped.

Ed's brief stay in Menomonie was covered by several newspapers. The November 18 *Wisconsin State Journal* provided the best account of his arrival, mentioning that "[a] large but orderly crowd had assembled at the depot in Menomonie, yesterday, to get a glimpse of the desperado when the train came in," and when it did, "the prisoner, heavily ironed, hand and foot, was taken from the cars to the bus [i.e., carriage] standing near and driven at once to the jail." It also added that "Maxwell fears a lynching party. . . ."

A front-page item in the November 18 *Milwaukee Sentinel* depicted the Menomonie Jail and reflected the incessant rumors that a lynch mob was forming:

AT HOME:
THE CAPTURED BANDIT.

. . . The jail is a brick building with the sheriff's residence on the ground floor and the jail on the second story. There are four compartments in the jail, which are separated from each other by strong walls. Two of the rooms are not fitted with cells; the other two . . . contain each a corridor, with three cells. All the cells are lined with boiler iron and have barred windows. . . .

The mysterious movements of the friends of the murdered sheriffs tonight gave rise to the rumor that the prisoner will be taken from the jail and hung.

Yet another dispatch to the *Sentinel* reflected the same cause for alarm: "Small squads of citizens are congregating at Menomonie, which undoubtedly means that [Ed's] days are numbered. It is thought that a mob is being formed to lynch him."

By then, almost everyone who knew anything about the murder, the manhunt, and the capture anticipated mob violence. As the *Wisconsin State Journal* put it, "Grave fears of lynching" bothered the Menomonie authorities. However, Edward Johnstone said in a dispatch from there, "People here talk freely about how much they would enjoy seeing [Maxwell] hanged," but "In Durand, if anywhere, an attempt at lynching will be made."

Johnstone was granted another interview with Ed in the Dunn County Jail that evening, and then he telegraphed a lengthy report from the local depot. His "Menomonie interview" with Ed appeared the following day in several newspapers, including the *Chicago Tribune:*

INTERESTING INTERVIEW WITH ED MAXWELL, ALIAS WILLIAMS, NOW IN JAIL AT MENOMONIE, WIS.

Menomonie, Wis., Nov. 17—. . . Maxwell is a small and rather good-looking man, and does not appear to act like the blood-stained desperado that he is. In an interview with your correspondent this evening, he conversed gladly and smoothly. . . .

"Do you acknowledge the killing of the Coleman brothers?"

"Yes, sir, but it was done in self-defense."

"Did you know who the men were before you shot?"

"We thought it was Sheriff Knight and a deputy, and we wanted to see him."

"How long were you in the Eau Galle woods?"

"About five days."

"Have you any objection to giving me an account of your flight after the killing?"

"None whatever, sir. Immediately after the shooting we crossed the Chippewa River in a skiff we found on the bank, using a shingle and fence board for paddles. We both were wounded, myself in the right arm, hand, and shoulder; Lon in the arm, breast, and face, his arm being so badly hurt and

---

swollen that at times he would be crazy with pain, and twice drew a knife on me.

After crossing the Chippewa we pursued a westerly course, traveling by night and lying still during the day. We were eighty-five hours without enough food to make anyone a decent meal. . . .

We crossed the Mississippi near Maiden Rock . . . in a batou which we found on the bank. It seemed to us as though Providence helped us get away as we did, in the crippled condition we were in. . . ."

"Did you have any help in your flight?"

"None whatever, to use a strong phrase. We had been away so much that we were afraid to trust anyone."

"What do you think the chances are for Lon's capture?"

"I don't know, but," he added significantly, "he is a good shot."

Ed's reiteration that the Coleman killings were in "self-defense" reminds us that, aside from his obvious meaning—that he had a right to oppose force with counterforce—the gunfight was, more deeply, a defense of the bold, defiant outlaw identity that he had constructed to keep from feeling shamed as a man of no value. The Maxwells' desperate and demanding flight from the massive posse was, of course, also a validation of that identity, so Ed was glad to recount their remarkable escape.

It is interesting, too, that he felt "Providence helped us get away," as if they were oppressed, struggling victims that God naturally responded to. Ed did not think of himself as a perpetrator of homicide, pursued by righteous avengers. Like so many violent men—and perhaps, like all people—he possessed an enormous capacity for self-justification.

Aside from his guilt before the law, however, which most people realized but Ed stoutly denied, he could not escape moral responsibility for killing Charles Coleman. Although he did not plan to shoot down the ex-sheriff, Ed's outlaw self was his own creation, and in choosing to be defiant and threatening—however prompted by inner drives and provoked by his social circumstances—he had precipitated the violent confrontation. Ed's decision to shoot anyone who tried to stop him was made long before the gunfight at Durand, and influenced by his brother, Lon had made exactly the same decision.

Another version of that Menomonie interview, which appeared in the *St.*

Paul Pioneer Press and other newspapers, includes Ed's remark that he and Lon "were suffering so terribly from their wounds that the days seemed weeks in length," and that "every moment they heard, in fancy, the ring of a rifle or the whiz of a bullet." In short, for many days they lived in great pain and constant fear. They experienced the horrific underside of their romantically conceived role as desperadoes—the grim reality of physical and psychological suffering that would later be denied or minimized in western books and films with outlaw heroes.

Asked by Johnstone at the end of the interview if he was telling the truth, Ed also remarked, "I don't lie, sir. I guess I haven't a great while [to live] in this world, and I don't want to add lying to my other sins." As that suggests, and other interviews also demonstrate, the "Notorious Desperado" was easy to relate to. Aside from his need for admiration, which prompted frank comments on what he had done, Ed also yearned for sympathetic companions, so he often spoke as if he were confiding to a potential friend, hoping for some understanding and appreciation.

On Friday morning, November 18, Ed was interviewed at the jail by a reporter for the *Dunn County News.* The latter printed a lengthy summary of Ed's remarks, including some details of their escape from the Wisconsin manhunters that are not reflected elsewhere:

> After the shooting, the Williamses went around the village and reached the Chippewa below the town. Here they found an old skiff and crossed the river, then passed up the Eau Galle, avoiding the roads as much as possible, and reached the spot where their horse and buggy were concealed in the woods, about daybreak. They had some extra clothing in the buggy, and they made a change, hiding their blood-soaked clothes under a log. . . .
>
> While in the woods they frequently saw squads of the pursuing party, and at one time three men on horseback rode so near to them that they thought surely they would be seen. They covered two of the men with their Winchesters, and Ed now recognizes his man to have been Henry Coleman. He even began to press the trigger, when Lon whispered, "Don't shoot; we can slip away from them." Lowering their rifles, they crawled back out of sight and the horsemen passed by. . . .
>
> They were ten days slowly working their way southward to the Mississippi, traveling always in the night. One evening they passed through Plum City and finally reached Maiden Rock, where they

found an old boat and crossed Lake Pepin to the Minnesota side. . . . It was not till some time after they had reached Minnesota that they found out what they had done, by reading a newspaper. . . .

Like Johnstone, this reporter also found it hard to reconcile the outlaw's reputed "bold and desperate character" with his very civil demeanor: "He is prepossessing in appearance, gentlemanly in address, easy and self-possessed in conversation." Ed's combination of aggressive and respectful qualities suggests that he had learned, during his highly stressful upbringing, to repress his frustrations—and to play very well the role of a polite, self-controlled, obliging person. But the early result of that effort—struggle and failure, shame and disregard—had eventually become intolerable, leading to crimes that were acts of rebellion and escape, as well as pleas for respect and admiration. Yet Ed's more quiet, conventional side also remained, despite his outlaw career.

Other comments by Edward Johnstone, who spent more time with Ed during his final days than anyone else, support this assessment of his character:

> During the hours of desultory chat that the reporter had with Maxwell, many incidents of his adventurous life were recounted by the latter, in a style which, if terse, was graphic, and differed entirely from the conventional braggadocio style indulged in by Big Nosed George [Parrott] and scoundrels of that ilk. In fact, nothing seemed to disgust the man more than loud talk of any kind, and he said frequently that profanity was as useless as whisky drinking or running after lewd women. . . .
>
> In short, it seemed to all who talked with Maxwell, at all connectedly, that he had taken the [more gentlemanly] robbers of ye olden time as prototypes, and had modulated his voice to softest accents in order not only to keep up the role, but as well, to surprise those who expected to meet a blatant man, full of strange oaths and lewd remembrances.

The self-controlled, respectful, obliging young man was the real Ed Maxwell too, just as the defiant, self-assertive outlaw was, but people wanted to acknowledge only the violent desperado. Viewing him, largely through sensational newspaper accounts and rumors, as a man completely unlike themselves, it would be easy to kill him—and they would never have to reflect on the culture and circumstances that produced him.

Ed's willingness to admit and describe the killings at Durand seemed, to some readers, like an invitation for a lynch mob, as an editorial in the *Milwaukee Sentinel* soon pointed out: "Ed Maxwell appears to have thought violent death as desirable as life imprisonment. The confession of his identity [and deed] to the Dunn County people can hardly be explained upon any other theory. . . ." That was as close as anyone came to realizing that Ed did, in fact, have a need to die in just that way, defiantly resisting the social forces around him, to validate his identity.

On the morning of November 18, the authorities were anxious to move Ed on to Durand for the preliminary court hearing, but before they did so, he was exhibited to the public at the Dunn County Courthouse for three hours and then was confronted by the mother of the slain Coleman brothers. The shackled and doomed desperado had become a kind of thrilling spectacle, like the prisoner at a public execution, even though he had yet to be indicted, much less tried. Viewed by people as a monster of violence, he was dehumanized by their massive curiosity and hate.

That strange and exciting scene was also depicted by Edward Johnstone, whose article appeared in the *Pioneer Press* on November 20:

HIS LONG JOURNEY ENDED

. . . Inside the building a scene almost unprecedented in criminal annals was being enacted. The county board, which was then in session at Menomonie, had made a formal request that Maxwell be brought into the large courtroom and exhibited to the multitude. This was done without a dissenting word, and for three hours, the manacled man stood there, as nearly every man, woman, and child [in the county] filed past him.

His composure never left him for a moment, and the only sign he gave of appreciation for his position was a half sneering smile, which would at times betray itself beneath his mustache to the close observer. He answered all the questions put to him, and there were many, with a uniform courtesy and in a voice whose modulations were persuasive, if not convincing.

About 10 o'clock Mrs. Coleman, mother of the murdered men, was brought in, and confronted the accused murderer. The old lady bore up bravely, though tears suffused her eyes and her voice trembled slightly as she said, "How could you kill my boys?"

In the softest of tones and the most feeling of accents, Maxwell replied, "I am truly sorry that I did so. I did not know them at all. We were not after them. Our idea was to get to Sheriff Knight's house that night, catch him in his bed, get the drop on him, and make him take us to where the horse he captured from us was concealed. He would have gone, I am sure, but if he hadn't, he'd have had to die."

It certainly did not soothe the anguish of Mrs. Coleman to know that her sons were not victims of premeditated murder, and yet Ed clearly and directly answered the question she had asked. Charles and Milton were killed in an unplanned gunfight, and to Ed and Lon, they were simply lawmen or posse members who had pulled guns on them. His expression of regret for the deaths showed his sympathy for the bereaved woman, an aging mother much like his own, who was, in an emotional sense, another victim of the tragic encounter. But while Ed regretted the consequence of the gunfight, he showed no true repentance, no desire to not repeat the deed. He failed to realize his responsibility for what had happened at Durand—partly because he did not comprehend the inner forces that were driving him, forces he should have resisted.

Of course, Ed's admission of their real purpose, which might have included the murder of Undersheriff Miletus Knight, did him no good either. A way of asserting that he was resolute of purpose and ready for violence, it reflected Ed's chronic longing for public esteem—and his occasional slide into immature bravado. He did not seem to realize that killing Knight—which he probably never anticipated having to do—would have contradicted his claim, made in the St. Paul interview, that "the Williams boys [never fired on anyone] unless they were first attacked."

In any case, all the attention in place after place—which had climaxed with the long public exhibition at Menomonie—must have convinced Ed that he had succeeded in his quest to establish a heroic, defiant public identity. He was no longer someone who didn't matter.

Why the Menomonie authorities felt that either the "exhibition" of Ed to the local multitude or the "interview" with Mrs. Coleman was necessary is not known, but both revealed the public fascination with the notorious desperado. If he could not be tried in Dunn County, he could at least be confronted, and hated, there—even if that was a dangerous self-indulgence likely to incite a lynch mob.

Of course, many people felt that a lynching would probably take place in Pepin County, where the gunfight had occurred. Ed did too, but he was determined to live up to his chosen role as a desperado. He apparently realized that, for him, death at the hands of someone, or some mob, was a kind of inevitability—and perhaps even a necessity, offering a strange kind of self-fulfillment. After all, facing it, composed and defiant, was the supreme form of heroism, the undeniable mark of a man—according to the American myth of manliness, which had such an impact on Ed's identity. As he had said in another interview, "Those who have led such a life as I have, expect death every moment, and when my time comes, I shall not squeal, for I am prepared to die game."

He surely was, and horrific though it might be, lynching was perhaps easier for Ed to contemplate than endless years at a Wisconsin penitentiary. From that nightmarish world of disrespect and dehumanization, now looming on the horizon, death would be the ultimate escape.

15

The Lynching at Durand

In the fall of 1881 almost everybody in America hated Charles Guiteau, and officials were concerned that he would "perish by mob violence" if the public could get access to him. Unable to lynch the presidential slayer, people in towns across the country expressed their desire for vengeance symbolically, by hanging and burning him in effigy. As one Illinois newspaper reported in late September, "The ball was started in Deadwood [Dakota Territory] on Tuesday, where the hanging and burning was done with the wildest excitement; a like demonstration took place on the same evening in Chicago, and another in Wheaton, Ill." The symbolic lynchings continued for many days—perhaps more commonly in Illinois than elsewhere because Guiteau had been born and raised in Freeport, near the Wisconsin border.

One additional cause of public outrage was the insanity plea used by Guiteau's lawyer, George Scovill, who was also his brother-in-law and, incidentally, a resident of Waukesha County, Wisconsin. He not only disclosed to the press Guiteau's strange beliefs—the most notorious being that God had directed him to kill the president—but pointed out that some of the slayer's relatives had also experienced mental problems, and that as a child he had lost his mother at age seven and had been repeatedly beaten by his intensely religious father simply because he had a speech impediment. According to one newspaper report, some family members felt that he was "a downright lunatic," and several years before the assassination, "a physician stated, after examination, that he was unfit to be at large." Guiteau was, in fact, mentally unbalanced, but the idea that such a plea, if accepted by the jury, would save him from the gallows was exasperating, even intolerable, to many Americans. As the editor of the *Canton Register* in Fulton County put it, "When a man is sane enough to plan and carry out a dastardly, cold-blooded murder, that man is sane enough to hang. It is high time that the 'mad men' in this country were given plainly to understand that sane people have some rights which lunatics are bound to respect."

As that commentary suggests, the newfangled insanity plea seemed to contradict the all-important tenet of personal responsibility, which was central to the moral vision of most Americans. How could evil be opposed and justice be asserted if perpetrators were not held accountable?

Also, many people felt that society could be protected only by severely punishing offenders, not by understanding their problems or helping them. In short, public anxiety often made the comprehension of a lawbreaker, and compassionate treatment of him, virtually impossible. An article in the *Pepin County Courier,* for example, declared that Guiteau was simply "a thoroughly bad man," and thus he deserved the "vengeance" that "good citizens" should administer to such "hyenas of society."

As those terms also suggest, most people maintained a mythic, polarized view of their relationship to violent lawbreakers: us "good citizens" versus those thoroughly evil "hyenas of society," who are not at all like us. In fact, some commentators, such as the editor of the *Peoria Transcript,* declared that Guiteau was "a natural-born criminal," a man "whose moral nature was essentially vicious and perverted." If that was true, however, in what sense could Guiteau be held responsible for his actions, being the victim of a vicious, inherently evil nature that he did not choose to have?

The public's mythic view also held the "good citizens" blameless for any and all violence in their culture, while licensing them to exact "vengeance" on those who broke the law to prey upon them. And that vengeance was often expressed by lynching. Of course, deep down, there was a relationship between the society that perpetuated such a mind-set and the prevalence of violent crime.

Ironically, even Ed Maxwell shared the general outrage at Guiteau's assassination of the president. While in jail at Menomonie, he told Edward Johnstone, "That was a cowardly act of Guiteau's, and you bet I'd like to have a shot at him from my Winchester. I wouldn't miss him . . . and I wouldn't wound him slightly either. Guess if I got away from here and killed Guiteau, the whole neighborhood wouldn't turn out and hunt me through the woods." Guiteau's attack on the unarmed president had offended Ed's sense of masculine integrity and courage. Shooting armed men who confronted you was one thing—an act of self-defense and a demonstration of manliness—but a surprise attack on an unarmed man was "cowardly" and deserved lynching with a bullet. In more ways than one, Ed Maxwell reflected commonly held American values.

He also clearly saw that the degree of public outrage at some killer commonly depended on the popularity of the dead man. Although he did not realize it, the more a victim symbolized society itself, the more likely it was that the victim's killer would become a scapegoat for violent drives within the American people—drives born of anxiety, guilt, and fear.

Fueling the emotional involvement in the Guiteau case was the public realization that America was experiencing a crime wave. Major newspapers were, in fact, printing columns with titles like "Criminalities," "Deeds of Darkness," and "Ways of the Wicked" that tersely summarized significant crimes committed across the country. The *Chicago Tribune* staff started publishing annual statistics on American murders; although undoubtedly incomplete, their total for 1881 hit 1,266—only to reach 1,467 a year later.

Disturbed by what they read, many Americans believed that swift, certain punishment was the only way to control the problem. An early November editorial in the *Canton Register* reflected that widespread public view:

> The general growth of crime everywhere throughout our nation cannot be gainsaid. There must be a cause for this increase. Is it in the laws? No. The law is clear. . . . Is it because our people are becoming ignorant? No. The standard of intelligence was never higher. . . . Is it because men are naturally more wicked than they used to be? No, because the disposition of men was always to do evil. . . . We must attribute it to a lack of respect for the law, arising from a failure on the part of the proper officers to execute the same. The only power to subdue crime is fear. . . .

Of course, that commentator did not consider the impact of violence-provoking cultural myths, the Civil War experience, social inequities, counterproductive penitentiaries, destabilizing westward movement, and sheer poverty on the "growth of crime" in America. Like so many, he wanted to "subdue crime" without dealing with, or even recognizing, the causes of it. Instead, he simply asserted that the justice system wasn't effective enough—and made a good point despite his shallow comprehension of the issue.

People felt that violent criminals in particular often went unpunished—because of poor law enforcement or juries unwilling to convict—and they were right. Moreover, when convictions did occur, the sentences were light. As the *Tribune* pointed out, for 1882, "in our own city . . . footpads and sluggers pursue their violent calling with almost perfect impunity," and of Chicago's fifty-four murders that year, "only one [killer] was hanged, the majority of the others [who were convicted] being sent to the penitentiary for short terms."

Like the granting of pardons, that unfortunate circumstance led to a widespread reliance on lynch law. When the *Tribune* first started providing annual statistics on lynching (the extralegal killing of accused lawbreakers) for 1882, it reported 117 cases, a listing that was surely incomplete. Even before that, a thoughtful letter to the *Tribune* in the fall of 1881 pointed out that "'Lynched' . . . is a very common headline in the news columns of the daily journals," especially because of its prevalence in the frontier states and territories and in the South.

And he was correct. In 1881, for example, there were lynchings in almost every state and territory in the far West—Colorado, New Mexico, Arizona, and others. Although murder was the leading provocation, sometimes the crime was just cattle rustling or horse stealing, as in the following short item from the November 10 *Tribune:*

TWO COWBOYS HANGED BY A MOB

Tucson, A.T., Nov. 9—Bill Littenbern and Sandy King, two members of a noted cowboy gang, were recently arrested for dealing in stolen stock and taken to Shakespeare for trial. At about 2 o'clock this morning, over a dozen masked men went to the jail where the two men were confined, seized the guard, and hung the cowboys to a joist until dead.

As this reveals, the term "cowboy" still had negative associations in the 1880s. To many it simply meant "a low-class Western ruffian." Cattle*men* were respected, but cow*boys* were not. The former were owners; the latter were simply workers—little-respected hired hands whom vigilantes could kill without significantly upsetting the public.

Of course, lynching was also common in the South, where criminals—and sometimes just unfortunate blacks—were lynched from North Carolina to Arkansas in most years, including 1881. Surely many of those acts were not reported in newspapers.

States in the upper Mississippi Valley, which wanted to outgrow their habit of mob violence, continued to have lynchings as well. An 1881 Wisconsin newspaper article summed up the situation in several states, mentioning recent examples in Minnesota, Iowa, Nebraska, and Ohio. The author neglected to mention Michigan, where in September 1881 "a mob of forty half-breed French barbarians" battered down the jail door in Menominee, lynched two brothers by clubbing them to death, and then dragged their corpses through the streets. Illinois also had lynchings in recent years—at Cairo, Carbondale, Columbia, Chicago, Ipava, Murphysboro, Olney, Salem, Winchester, and other communities. Indiana also had some, and Missouri had a great many. Small wonder that the *Quincy Daily Herald* had pointed out in 1878, "The custom in American communities of summarily executing a criminal without waiting for the law's delay is becoming a very general one," and "the instances are rare when the parties to the lynching are ever punished, or even arrested, and as a rule, public sentiment sustains the deed and shields the actors in it."

Aside from racially charged situations, in which black men were accused of raping, killing, or otherwise assaulting whites, killing a lawman was the most certain way to incite a lynch mob. Strangely enough, in the very year that Ed Maxwell started his outlaw career, a thief named David Hardy, who had been raised in McDonough County—and was, like Ed, the son of a tenant farmer—was lynched in Missouri for killing a constable who was trying to arrest him. Similar lynchings occurred every year, including 1881. In Carthage, Missouri, for example, during that summer, three men were lynched for complicity in the murder of a deputy sheriff.

That lynching in such cases often had strong popular support is revealed by the sensationalized title of an October 2, 1881, *Chicago Tribune* report on an Illinois incident:

LYNCHED.

The People of Bloomington, Ill.
Turned into Howling Madmen.
Cold-blooded Murder of the Jailer

by a Horsethief.
An Extraordinary Sensation Produced
in the City by the Deed.
The Jail Immediately Attacked
by a Crowd of 5,000 People.
The Doors Battered in by the Mob
After an Hour's Determined Effort.
The Horsethief and Murderer
Dragged Out and Strung Up.
Hilarious Satisfaction of Men,
Women and Children at the Spectacle.

Before the Bloomington lynching, some members of the mob supposedly had said, "This [shooting of the jailer] comes from the failure of our courts to punish crime. He [the killer] ought to be hung!" And after hanging the prisoner from a nearby maple tree in full view of the Bloomington police, the mob leaders were never tried for their act of "popular vengeance." Even the *Tribune* seemed to excuse the deed, commenting on the incident by stating, "There is too much law quibbling and too little justice for murderers. . . ."

A few days after the Bloomington incident, the editors of the *Milwaukee Sentinel* commented on the issue of lynching—and told its neighbor to the south what needed to be done to curb that kind of violence: "If the State of Illinois wishes to suppress mob law, it has only to see that its statute laws are enforced. By this means, the state can be taken out of the category of frontier communities and placed in that group of states governed by the principles of law and justice." In short, Illinois needed to learn from the morally superior state of Wisconsin, where presumably lynchings no longer occurred.

The latter did have a better record than most states, although there had been some incidents over the years, including a double lynching at Stevens Point in 1875 when a mob hanged two brothers who had killed the Portage County sheriff.

But the *Sentinel*'s gloating commentary came in early October, and by mid-November the most notorious regional desperado of the era, aside from the James brothers, was being brought back to Pepin County to stand trial where the justice system could not possibly slake the public thirst for revenge—for in Wisconsin the death penalty had been abolished in 1853.

On Friday, November 18, Ed was put into a buggy and, under heavy guard, was taken over the rough road that led south twenty miles to Durand. Surely everyone in the party, which included officials from two counties, was apprehensive about mob violence as the group headed for the town where the whole episode had started.

It had been unseasonably cold and the Chippewa River was full of thin, floating ice when the lawmen and their captive reached the west bank, across from Durand. Sheriff Kilian, Undersheriff Knight, and Deputy Sheriff Henry Coleman placed Ed into a boat, and they were rowed across to the east shore, where a crowd of people were waiting to see the noted desperado. According to a newspaper report, there was "an occasional threatening remark" directed to Ed as the group walked up the river bank and into the center of town.

The jail was not quite two blocks southeast of the courthouse. Constructed in 1871 and 1872, it was a two-story, white frame building that looked like a house but had iron bars on the windows. One reporter described it as "a flimsy, insecure structure throughout." Ed was to be there only overnight because, as the Durand newspaper editor put it, "our jail would not hold a vagrant—much less a desperado like Williams." Ed was placed in the largest cell, containing a comfortable bed, two chairs, a table, and a stove.

On that Friday night Ed was interviewed once again by Johnstone, who was staying with the sensational story that was allowing him to make extra money by sending dispatches to newspapers in Madison, Chicago, and other places. During the long train ride to Menomonie, or perhaps at the Dunn County Jail, Ed had asked the young newspaperman if he would write his life story, and Johnstone had agreed to do so if Ed would provide the information.

Sensing that his outlaw career was over and that he might soon be lynched, Ed apparently realized that a story about his life was another kind of escape—the fulfillment of his longed-for identity as a desperado and the ultimate defeat of those forces that had always devalued him. So, he was anxious to respond to Johnstone's questions and get the process under way.

No complete life story ever appeared, partly because Ed did not live long enough to provide the information, but the interview at Durand— one of the most remarkable memoirs by an American outlaw—was soon published in several newspapers, including the *Chicago Tribune:*

A DEAD MAN'S TALE.

A Reporter's Interview with
Ed Maxwell in the Durand Jail.

. . . Many local stories [folkloric accounts] were exploded by Maxwell, who answered questions [from the authorities] freely and straightforwardly. . . . He was seemingly anxious to begin his life [story], and whispered to Henry Coleman to turn the crowd out as soon as he could and leave me in there, as he wanted to talk uninterruptedly. Coleman therefore about 9 o'clock cleared the room of all but [Deputy Sheriff] Carpenter and myself.

The scene was a strange one. I threw myself down on the bed. Maxwell dragged his chair close to the side of it and rested his handcuffs on the edge. Coleman leaned at the foot, where he could listen, and Carpenter was tipped back in a chair in the farther corner. . . .

"Tell me of your travels after you crossed the Mississippi at Maiden Rock," I said.

"Well, we went due westerly, or maybe a little north of west, and got out [of the deep woods] near Breckenridge. We traveled mostly nights, but some daytimes, and as we were skillful burglars . . . we didn't have much trouble in getting all we wanted to eat. If there was any money handy, of course we took that, but we let horses alone. To take them would kick up too much hullabaloo to suit us just then.

We saw a good many people, but didn't have to make any bluffs. If we saw any men coming, we threw our rifles into the long grass, and sometimes crouched there ourselves. . . .

At last we got into a heavily wooded country, where there was lots of lakes—more than I ever saw anywhere before. One of the biggest was called Leech Lake, and on its banks we camped for a long time, hunting and fishing.

We did not have a bad time till Lon got the fever. He was terribly sick with it for two weeks, and I thought he was going to die lots of times, but I pulled him through.

I tell you, Lon's all broke up, and it's not his hard time, but his grief for his wife that's done it. She was a mighty nice girl, and her death nearly drove Lon crazy. . . .

The fact is, we suffered so with our wounds, and traveled so much at night and in such out-of-the-way places . . . that

I got kind of mixed up about localities. I guess it must have been along about the first of October when we struck south and headed for Sioux City. . . . When we got to Sioux City we skirted the town and struck for the railroad south of it.

We partly walked and partly stole rides on freight trains to Omaha. . . . We walked right through the principal streets of Omaha, and I carried the guns while Lon lugged the blankets. No one noticed us at all. They are used to [men with] Winchesters. . . .

I never suspected Kilian at the farmhouse where [I] was captured. . . . I think Lon did all he could to help me. He's a mighty good shot, but he missed Kilian because he came on him in a hurry, and it was the dark of the morning. . . ."

"See here, Ed, aren't you telling me a good many crooked stories? Weren't you and Lon in Illinois lately?" I asked this with a little nervousness as to the way he would take it, but he raised his handcuffs lightly, looked me straight in the eyes, as he always does when talking, and resting the irons on my breast, said solemnly,

"As sure as you feel the weight of these on you, so sure am I telling you the truth. You asked me yesterday if Lon or I killed the sheriff of Calhoun County. I don't know where that county is. I haven't been in Illinois since the Coleman affair, and I never knew about the racket there until I read it in a paper after I was captured."

I believed the man then, and I believe him now. He dropped his solemn mood in a moment and said,

"Speaking of Illinois, you saw the crowd at the St. Paul Depot, didn't you? Well, that wasn't a patching to the gang that met me at Macomb, Ill., when I was captured there. I had no idea until then what a desperate reputation I had. The whole country turned out to see the great moral show, just as they did at Menomonie," he said jocosely, and went on in the same strain:

"Lon and I had a good deal of fun in Illinois. Near Smithfield once we stole a couple of horses, and got some harness and a buggy from another barn [and were pursued]. . . . When they got within thirty rods of us, I took a revolver in each hand, leaped into the road, and gave a yell. You should have seen those fellow run. . . . We did that sort of thing so often with sheriffs and officers that we began to think that we couldn't be captured and that we were the only brave men in the world.

No, it was not reading dime novels or such stuff that started us on the road [of outlawry]. It was just as I've told you—our luck in standing off so many who had a right to be brave."

Speaking of his life, Ed said: "Why, when you write up that book, I'll tell you more adventures than you ever dreamed of—how I've been shot at, and how I've shot at folks—never unless they attacked me first though. . . .

I look upon my life as if it were a profession. I believe in religion—believe in it hard—but I'd rather have my Winchester."

Ed's interview was an exercise in self-celebration, but for all that, it was revealing. Clearly, the high points in his life were the times when he commanded respect or attention from others—whether as a captured desperado or a fearless lawbreaker with a gun. Like so many people with chronic low self-esteem, he changed to the opposite condition—a feeling that he was invincible—when violent feats and public attention allowed him to repress his unworthiness. As his recounting of the Smithfield incident shows, Ed had recast his life into a myth of spiritual rebirth through courageous defiance. More accurately, perhaps, he had escaped from a hated identity through self-idealization.

His closing comment, too, is revealing. Ed had been taught by his parents to employ religion to deal with life's problems, but that encouraged self-blame and fostered a sense of unworthiness that he could not tolerate. The opposite response was to assert himself—to reach for his Winchester, the very symbol of his identity as a desperado.

Ed did not deny "reading dime novels"—which he had admitted doing seven years earlier—but he denied that they had prompted his outlaw career, and that was surely truthful in the sense that they did not provide lawbreaking role models for him. Outlaw heroes did not emerge until 1877, when the tremendously popular fictional bandit Deadwood Dick first appeared—and Ed was already serving his second term at Joliet. Although he never knew it, the first dime novels based on real desperadoes—which were focused on Jesse James (June 1881) and Billy the Kid (August 1881)—had just been published, and within two months there would be the first dime novel on the Maxwells.

But Ed was clearly influenced by the popular culture of legend and folklore that depicted, and sometimes celebrated, the James gang, whom he had known about for years and had mentioned in his letter from prison. His comment that he and Lon once felt they "couldn't be captured" suggests that they hoped for the kind of notoriety-without-arrest that marked the much-fabled James boys.

Again Ed denied the killing of Sheriff Lammy, but his account of traveling across Minnesota did seem vague and a bit confused. Although Johnstone clearly believed him, the editor of the *Pepin County Courier*, W. H. Huntington, who had also interviewed Ed earlier that evening, did not. He felt that Ed's story "was partly true and partly false," and he flatly told his readers that Ed and Lon had surely gone "down the river instead of across Minnesota and . . . did the shooting in Illinois." Their differing response to Ed's account occurred largely because Johnstone had come to admire the bold, resolute, risk-taking desperado, so willing to speak his mind, even though he regarded him as a dangerous man, while Huntington simply saw Ed as an evil, self-serving criminal, a man without conscience, who would of course lie about his deeds to avoid additional public outrage. The views of the two newspapermen illustrate the competing public visions of the outlaw in American culture.

Ed also told Edward Johnstone a bit more about their experience in Minnesota, including their struggle to obtain fresh clothes: "We didn't get along at all [for clothes] while we were around Leech Lake, and we were the sorriest scarecrows you ever saw. We had torn up all the lighter parts of our clothes to make bandages for our wounds, and keeping those bandages wet cured us in the end." But he added, "When we started south we got some clothes—a coat, two vests, and a pair of pants—and afterwards we found some shirts and stockings in a house we burgled for food."

Leech Lake was a remote area in central northern Minnesota, a hundred miles west of Duluth and a few hundred miles northeast of Nebraska, their eventual destination. Had they remained there, hunting and fishing, their fate might have been different.

Johnstone also met with Ed the following morning (Saturday, November 19) at his jail cell. Of course, Ed's world had become a vivid realization of the social circumstance that had prompted him to become an outlaw: He felt surrounded by impersonal social forces. And because he had no one that he could trust or confide in, Ed reached out to the young newspaperman who had shown an interest in him and would, hopefully, one day tell his story. Johnstone later filed a report on their final conversation:

This morning between 9 and 10 o'clock [Ed] sent for your correspondent, who, arriving at the cell he left the evening before, found a gaping crowd peering through the bars, and in the cell proper several persons were talking to Ed, whose shackles had been taken off, so that he might walk up and down, and relieve his limbs of their numbness. He took your correspondent into a corner, and said, "I haven't any friends here. I guess I haven't many anywhere. But you don't seem particularly hostile, and I would like to ask you what you think about my waiving an examination. They told me I was to be examined at 9 o'clock this morning, but now I hear that the district attorney says he won't be ready until 2 o'clock this afternoon. I guess if I waive a hearing, he won't have much to get ready for. What do you think about it?"

Your correspondent then told him [apparently agreeing], and he said, "I've made up my mind then, but will make a statement about the murder before I leave the courtroom."

We had some further conversation . . . [and Ed joked], "There will be a big crowd at the examination today. You stand at the door and sell tickets, and be sure you divvy [with me] on the square."

In another account, Johnstone reported one more statement that Ed made, either on that morning or the night before. The captured desperado had been pacing back and forth in his cell, and he suddenly stopped, turned to Johnstone, and said,

"You don't think I'm walking about because I'm nervous, do you? I never felt less like it in my life. I don't feel a bit afraid. And really, this is honest: It is a sort of relief to be captured and be free from that everlasting hunted feeling, that glancing at every fellow with one eye, while you look at your pistol with the other. I was getting mighty tired of that sort of thing, though of course I fought hard against being taken. Now I know I am in a ticklish place. I know that as well or better than you do, but I don't believe they can rightfully convict me, for I shot in self-defense. . . ."

Ed's closing comment about pleading "self-defense" shows the impact on him of murder trials in Fulton and McDonough counties, where men who had killed someone often made that plea and were acquitted. Even when the victim was a law officer, as in the killing of William Randolph by the Bond brothers in Blandinsville, a jury could be swayed by that plea. But Ed was insisting on a standard of right and wrong—the natural law of self-defense—that had been stretched in those cases to excuse any resistance to authority, and that approach was being replaced by the socially sanctioned practice of yielding to officers, whenever and however they confronted a man.

And Ed was, in a sense, fantasizing, dreaming that what had worked now and again for defendants who had some measure of public sympathy would somehow work for him—the outsider, the desperado.

Of course, Ed was clearly lying about not being nervous. He was filled with anxiety about the lynch mob that everyone anticipated, but he wanted to appear unafraid. Facing death without showing fear, and hence, dying on his own terms, was an important mode of self-expression for Ed—an assertion of his intense drive for control over his life, and over society's perception of him, which had arisen during his teenage years of drifting and disrespect and had become built in to his adult identity. Now the ultimate test of his manhood had finally come, and he did not want to blow it.

Outside on the snow-covered grounds of the courthouse and the jail, people were already gathering. By noon, two hours before the arraignment was to start, some five hundred people were milling around, sharing what they knew and how they felt about the killings, the manhunt, and the desperado.

The fate that had been stalking Ed ever since he had pulled a gun and made his first escape on horseback early in 1874 finally caught up with him that afternoon. Edward Johnstone provided a vivid description of the scene at the courthouse just prior to the lynching on that cold, blustery day, November 19, 1881:

THE STORY OF AN EYE-WITNESS

. . . [The courthouse at Durand] is surrounded by a large yard, in which are several small and one large tree—one with a projecting limb reaching toward the walls of the building.

When I reached the yard, I found a number of people there, all talking about Maxwell, and all waiting patiently, though it was far from warm and there were several inches of snow on the ground, for a sight of the prisoner when he should be brought out for his preliminary hearing. Most of them gathered there seemed like farmers or lumbermen from out of town, and there was a fair sprinkle of women and children.

As the crowd augmented, and 2 o'clock came, the courtroom upstairs . . . was crowded to suffocation, as Maxwell, cool and collected as he was yesterday when he landed from a skiff in the midst of a crowd on the river bank, and not showing the faintest trace of nervousness, was led through the aisle between deputies Knight and Coleman. The crowd surged and pushed to get a better sight of him, and threats grew from mutterings to menaces, but he flinched not a whit and stood before Justice [W. B.] Dyer and [Court Clerk W. H.] Huntington as unconcernedly as if he had been on the bench and they in the dock. . . .

Actually, Johnstone had not witnessed the court proceeding, nor did he see the lynching that followed it. He had apparently gone to Menomonie to file his morning story by telegraph, and everything occurred while he was gone, so he created the scene by fictionalizing, based on what he knew of the setting and of Ed. His account did show, however, that he clearly admired Ed—and for precisely the same reasons that many other Americans admired desperadoes: He was unafraid and in control, even when he was facing hostility.

The largest inside space in all of Pepin County, the courtroom was forty-two feet long and thirty-six feet wide, with several eight-foot windows on each of the longer sides, and three more on the far end, opposite the door, where the judge sat impassively in his black robe. Wayne B. Dyer was an inexperienced justice of the peace. A sixty-eight-year-old Wisconsin pioneer, he had been a log cabin settler, an early tavern owner, a Civil War veteran, and over the years an avid deer hunter—having killed some 600 by his own count. He was not elected justice of the peace until the late 1870s. Dyer was apparently unconcerned about the threat of lynching—and never issued an order relating to the prisoner's safety or attempted to control the crowd at the courthouse. The rows of wooden chairs in front of him had been filled for more than an hour before he arrived, and around them, crowded against the walls, were other spectators who had come later, and had packed themselves together for the privilege of seeing and hearing the notorious desperado.

Johnstone went on to report that after pleading not guilty, Ed made a statement to the court about the Coleman gunfight—which he quotes—but in fact, Ed had changed his mind and had never made any statement. Johnstone had simply used the statement that Ed had made to the Coleman relatives in Menomonie, assuming that it would be similar. Johnstone also asserted that Ed was grabbed by a howling mob in the courtroom and, as women shrieked, was dragged out of the building amid cries of "Hang him! Choke him! Burn him!" His final depiction of Ed was unforgettable: "I caught one glimpse of his face as he was going down the stairs. It was pale as marble, but his eyes glared defiance, and every look betokened his agonizing wish, 'If I but had my Winchester and a second's freedom. . . .'"

But that wasn't what happened either. Like so many others, Johnstone could not resist the urge to make an exciting, powerful story from raw materials provided by the Maxwell saga, and the lynching was, after all, the climactic event—and he had missed it. His account has importance, however, because it was widely reprinted in the newspapers and later became the basis for dime novel and true crime accounts of the lynching.

What really happened was exciting enough, as revealed in an account by editor Huntington of the *Pepin County Courier,* who had served as the court clerk and had seen it all. Because the newspaper was a weekly, his report did not appear until November 25.

LYNCHED!

The Fate of Ed Williams.

. . . Saturday afternoon the prisoner was brought before Justice W. B. Dyer, in the courtroom. The house was crowded with men, women, and children from nearly all parts of this and adjoining counties, anxious to get a view of the notorious criminal. He gave his name as William E. Maxwell, and to the charge as read by the justice, entered a plea of "not guilty." He also waived an examination and was committed for trial.

Without delay the officers started to conduct the prisoner back to jail. Just as the prisoner, in the charge of Sheriff Peterson, Deputy Knight, Deputy H. Coleman of Dunn County, Sheriff Kilian of Grand Island, Neb., Marshal Seeley, and [Deputy] Thomas Garvin, reached the bottom of the stairs, one [man] cried, "Hang the s—n of a b—h," and a dozen or more determined men tackled the officers. A man with a noose dodged in the door and soon had it over the murderer's head, with a regular "hangman's knot" under the left ear. The officers made a desperate resistance, but were overpowered by superior numbers and were hurried down the hall away from their prisoner.

Maxwell fought like a tiger, but he fought without his favorite weapons, against men as determined as himself, and in less time that it takes to write these lines, the rope was securely 'round his neck, a cry from the leader of "haul away" [was heard], and the rope tightened with a jerk that landed Maxwell on the porch outside the building; another jerk and he reached the ground, from where he was dragged to an old oak tree east of the courthouse, and quickly suspended 30 feet in the air, with his handcuffs still on and a heavy pair of shackles hanging from his left foot.

As soon as they could possibly get to him (about 15 minutes) the officers cut down and took charge of the body, which was afterwards interred in the Potter's field of our cemetery.

While Huntington's account is accurate, it is brief and omits details that he either did not glean from other eyewitnesses or suppressed because he did not want to foster a negative public response to the lynching. A less well-known report by a visitor to Durand, which appeared in the *Eau Claire Free Press,* is more detailed and dramatic:

STILL ANOTHER ACCOUNT

I was passing by the courthouse, on the 19th, at about 2:15. Williams' preliminary examination was supposed to be going on in the upper story, which was jammed with a crowd of 200 or 300 men, women, and children. . . .

Had they looked from the north windows, out upon a sturdy oak tree about 150 feet from the building, they would have seen a rope hanging from a bough projecting about thirty feet above the ground. The end of the rope, which dangled from the bough, was in the hands of a knot of men waiting and listening under the tree. The rope—which was 300 feet long—passed around the corner of the building to the portico in front, and the other end, with a running noose, was in the hands of another knot of men who were waiting to do their part. All was quiet. . . .

Soon the sound of crowding steps was heard inside the building. Williams had waived examination. Court had adjourned. [Under]Sheriff Knight and his assistants were leading Williams downstairs to go to the jail, and the crowd was following. The men under the tree got themselves ready to pull their end. The men on the portico who held the noose end of the rope were watching for their prey. The front door opened, and a pistol shot from the crowd inside was heard.

Williams came forth, his hands shackled together and one
foot free from his iron bonds to allow motion. Like a flash
the noose was around his neck. The men at the tree started
to run with the rope. It pulled taut around Williams' throat
in a second, and shackled as he was, he was jerked from
his feet and fell on his back with a dull thud, his head being
wedged against one of the pillars around which the taut rope
passed. A few jerks and his insensible body, with a great livid
bruise on the right temple, rolled down the steps, slid along
the ground towards the tree, and rose in the air a corpse.
Not a spasm—not a convulsion—of his form was seen. The
rope was fastened, and the lynchers mixed with the crowd,
which had given a yell as the body went up.

The officers, in the meantime, were not heard from. The
crowd, which was noisy and excited, increased . . . to over
500, and not a word of sympathy or regret for the fate of
Williams was heard.

As that account reveals, Ed was unconscious from being jerked off his
feet and repeatedly yanked against a column of the portico, until his fallen
body finally broke free and was pulled across the lawn and up the dark,
leafless tree to hang from a long heavy limb, his arms still handcuffed and
a chain dangling from one leg. By then, his head was surely drooped over,
and he was either dead or nearly so.

Watching among the "noisy and excited" crowd that had cheered for the
lynchers were the widow of Charles Coleman and several other Coleman
relatives. Whether they had known of the plans in advance has never
been disclosed.

The eyewitness from Eau Claire stayed around long enough to report
what the authorities did when it was all over: "After the body had hung
about twenty minutes, some officers ventured to cut it down. It was taken
into the courthouse [where a hurried inquest was held], and at 4:30 it was
buried in the potter's field."

He also added comments about the behavior of the crowd: "As the body
was being removed, the rope was pounced upon and cut to pieces by
relic hunters. The gathering then slowly dispersed, discussing the matter
noisily, and with increased excitement." As they headed home to tell the
story, it is doubtful that any of the perpetrators or witnesses realized that
a huge controversy was about to erupt.

The highly visible daylight lynching, repeatedly predicted and socially approved, was the final public appearance of a man who, like Jesse James, had remained true to the Platonic conception of himself—to borrow a phrase from *The Great Gatsby*—however much that dreamed-up identity had placed him at odds with the law in several states.

Ed Maxwell was a deeply American desperado.

16

The Lynching
Controversy and
Durand's Fate

The lynching of Ed Maxwell, "the notorious desperado," was reported in newspapers all over the country, from the *Boston Post* to the *San Francisco Chronicle,* and as the dramatically violent year of 1881 came to a close, that act of mob vengeance in a remote north woods village provoked widespread comment on the issue of law and order. The traumatic murder of the president, the attempts to kill his assassin, and the much-discussed trial of Guiteau had laid the emotional groundwork for the discussion, but Americans were finally confronting a deeply disturbing aspect of their culture.

On November 20, the lynching was front-page news in the *New York Times*. The detailed report appeared under a terse but graphic title that implied the reader's familiarity with the story of the famous sheriff killers:

ED WILLIAMS LYNCHED.
DRAGGED FROM THE COURTHOUSE
AND PUT TO DEATH.

A Mob's Revenge for the Murder
of the Coleman Brothers. . . .

On the following day, the story was front-page news again, as the *Times* printed more on Ed's adventurous outlaw career, under a book-like title: "A WESTERN BANDIT'S FATE: Ed Williams's Many Crimes and Tragic Death. . . ." Both articles were based on dispatches by Edward Johnstone, thus carrying his inaccuracies to a national audience.

Back in McDonough County, Johnstone's reports were reprinted in the *Macomb Journal* from the pages of the *St. Louis Globe-Democrat,* under a localized title: "SNUFFED OUT AT LAST: Ed Maxwell, Whose Criminal Career Began in This County, Closes It at a Rope's End. . . ."

The *Chicago Tribune* also carried a three-column story about the lynching, written by Johnstone but given a lengthy, sensationalized title by the *Tribune* editor:

JUSTICE.

The Red-Handed Desperado
Lynched at Durand Yesterday.
Confession of the Outlaw,
That He Killed One of the Colemans.
A Rope Thrown Over His Neck
during the Preliminary Examination.
The Villain Dragged Down the Stairs
and into the Courtyard.
His Body Hanged to a Tree. . . .
The Desperate Murderer Died
as He Had Lived, Without Fear.
Without Mercy for His Victims,
He Asked None for Himself. . . .
A Record of the Many Bloody Acts
Which Made Ed and Lon Williams
Infamous.

Of course, the opening word of this long headline raised the essential issue: Was such mob violence somehow an acceptable form of "justice"—in this case, or in any case?

Johnstone's account included an overview of the Maxwells' background and outlaw career that was sometimes wildly inaccurate. He asserted that the Maxwell family had come to Fulton County as "refugees" displaced by the war, had moved to Washburn in 1874, and had lived for a time in Lexington in McLean County. Obviously, he had never discussed the family background with Ed. Showing the common tendency to localize and magnify an exciting story, he also reported that Ed had been "imprisoned in the Stillwater Penitentiary," only thirty miles away, while Lon had been "associated with the worst class of people [in Hersey], and many crimes there have been traced to him."

Johnstone did provide an exciting story of the lynching, however—presenting Ed as a bold and fearless man, who "did not flinch" but "glared defiance" at the mob that attacked him, thereby earning a certain respect. He concluded, "Maxwell died as he had lived, a desperate man, but endowed with an amount of physical courage rare indeed, and filled with a restless energy that preferred crime to inaction." Ed would have loved it.

Johnstone's report for the *Tribune* was simply a variation of his dispatches to newspapers in New York, St. Louis, and other places. In the *Milwaukee Sentinel* version, for example, Ed is depicted as a man who expected to die with his boots on—convinced "that he would suffer death by mob violence," but he remained "as gritty as ever" while "his end was approaching."

Partly through Johnstone's dispatches, Ed had become a widely known outlaw hero, an exemplar of daring and defiance, for a national readership. People wanted to know more about him—and his still-pursued brother. So, folklore continued to spread, and as the Maxwells' career was being recounted, their story was starting to take on a life of its own, ready to be reinterpreted in the dime novels that would soon start to appear.

There was also widespread disagreement about exactly what had happened when Ed was killed—even among those who were at the Durand courthouse. As the *Stillwater Daily Sun* editor commented a week later, "Every witness of the hanging of Maxwell, thus far heard, tells a story entirely varying from all of the others, except in the one feature, that all agree that Maxwell was hung."

Of course, residents of Pepin County especially disliked the celebration of Ed as an outlaw hero in Johnstone's account. But they had even greater reasons for dismay. A November 22 dispatch by him, which was printed in Chicago, Milwaukee, and other cities, asserted that "the body of Ed Maxwell was cut down after hanging about half an hour, and an inquest was held, with the following verdict: 'Came to his death by falling from the courthouse steps and breaking his neck.'" In short, the mob action was covered up by the authorities in Durand.

That triggered an angry response by the editor of the *Pepin County Courier,* who not only asserted that Johnstone had left town before the lynching but denounced him as "an unmitigated, d—n liar," whose account was inaccurate in several respects, including the inquest report. Moreover, in a blatant effort to label an outsider as the source of trouble, Huntington claimed that the *Pioneer Press* reporter had tried "to excite the citizens to take the law into their own hands, and spent most of his time in saloons, trying to stir up a mob—so that he could get the glory of writing it all up for his paper."

That charge seems very unlikely, although Johnstone had surely asked local residents about the potential for a lynching and was undoubtedly dismayed that it had come after he had left town. In any case, the people of Pepin County certainly did not need encouragement from an out-of-town newspaper reporter to lynch Ed Maxwell. Their mob action had been approved in advance by Huntington.

Moreover, there was essential truth in Johnstone's account of the inquest—although he was guilty either of taking too literally someone's cynical, joking report to him or of imagining the inquest jury's exact words. In fact, the inquest judge and the jury (which may have included members of the lynch mob) had completely failed to do their duty. Hastily brought together, they called no witnesses to testify that a mob had lynched Ed Maxwell and asserted nothing at all about the cause of his death. The judge's report provides clear evidence of a cover-up:

INQUEST UPON THE VIEW OF THE DEAD BODY OF EDWARD MAXWELL

I hereby certify that upon receiving notice that the body of Edward Maxwell was found dead at the town of Durand on the 19th day of Nov., 1881, I issued my precept—to Undersheriff M. Knight—to summon, forthwith, six good and lawful men of Pepin County to appear before me at the courthouse in said town of Durand to inquire upon the view of the body of Edward Maxwell, there lying dead, how and by what means he came to his death.

Summons returned by Sheriff Knight, with Philo Barton, Philo Goodrich, Geo. Hutchinson, Geo. Tarrant, W. B. Atkins, and J. Van Norman duly summoned as jurymen.

Upon view of the body, and upon advice, I believed an inquest not necessary and therefore caused the body to be buried in the Potter's Field in the village cemetery of the town of Durand. . . .

Nov. 19, 1881.
A. W. Hammond, Justice of the Peace

Of course, the inquest's failure to even indicate that Ed had been lynched eliminated the need for indicting members of the mob, many of whom were known to local authorities. Miletus Knight was certainly in on the cover-up, since he had witnessed the lynching and knew at least some of the men responsible. He had also chosen the jurors, who were hardly "good and lawful men" in that they clearly provided the "advice" that subverted the proceedings: Leave this case alone; assert nothing at all.

Knight later tried to exculpate himself by providing his own account of the lynching for the *Wisconsin State Journal.* The undersheriff asserted that he and five other officers "did all in our power to prevent the hanging" but were "overpowered." And then, like editor Huntington, he essentially praised the lynchers for doing it right, like good men should: "It was done by the best citizens of this and adjoining counties, in broad daylight, and without . . . the influence of liquor." Of course, if he knew that it was done by "the best citizens," who were they? Why did he not arrest them, or at least investigate, as soon as he was not "overpowered"?

A few days later, at Madison, while collecting part of the reward money for capturing Ed, Sheriff Kilian was interviewed by a *Chicago Tribune* reporter regarding the lynching. He was with Miletus Knight and the other officers who were shoved aside by the mob, and he indicated that "none of the mob were masked" and that in Durand "no effort is being made to bring the lynchers to [justice] for their lawless act." Very few residents in Pepin County wanted local people divided against themselves in a lynch mob trial, and most of them supported the mob's action anyway.

In a little-known report on the lynching sent to Governor Smith, Sheriff A. F. Peterson said that he was astonished at the widespread approval of the act: "I have not yet heard one [person] openly condemn the deed . . . and many openly justify [it], commonly on the ground that Maxwell steadily persisted [to say] that when he was out of this, he would kill Undersheriff Knight, Sheriff Kilian, and others who have been active in his pursuit and arrest." While Peterson may have heard that comment, it was surely folklore that arose to help justify the mob murder. Ed had one opportunity after another to threaten revenge in his interviews, but never did—nor would a shackled and handcuffed man, headed for prison, be a threat to anyone. Peterson was claiming that the lynching was, if not quite justifiable, at least understandable, and he also blamed other "authorities of the county" for taking no steps "towards punishing the lynchers." Although he was the sheriff, he excused himself, saying, "I reside at Stockholm and am but little acquainted with the citizens of Durand. . . ."

One resident who had witnessed the lynching, and who opposed both it and the cover-up, caused a huge stir when he wrote an anonymous letter to the *St. Paul Pioneer Press,* asserting that the mob had "murdered Ed Williams in cold blood," with the collusion of local authorities, and that the governor should step in to enforce the law. Furthermore, he threatened that if the mob members were not punished, he and other avengers would "burn the county seat—the courthouse, the jail, and every building in the village of Durand that shelters one of the alleged mob."

The warning letter closed with a reference to Lon, asserting that he "is now on the road to Durand," where he may be killed, too, but "he will not be the only dead man there on that day." Of course, that comment raised speculation that the frightening letter, signed by someone calling himself the "Voice of Justice," was written by a friend of the Maxwells, who knew that Lon would retaliate, regardless of the risk, and many people took it seriously. The *Chicago Times* reflected that "Lon Maxwell . . . may not be unreasonably expected to reappear on the scene" where his brother had been lynched, and might indeed settle the score by burning their whole town. People felt that he would make a formidable avenger.

Soon afterward, the "Voice of Justice" letter was widely reprinted, appearing, for example, in the *Chicago Tribune,* the *New York Times,* and the *Washington Post.*

Regardless of who wrote it, that letter prompted enormous anxiety in Pepin County. Not only the mob of "blood avengers" but the huge number of people who had seen them, or knew who they were, worried and wondered about what the ultimate consequences of the lynching would be.

Another protest came in the form of a poetic broadside, called *Murder, Murder, Public Murder!* which was posted around town. It satirized the lynchers—and those who approved the violence—as illustrated by these two stanzas:

> O, it was a glorious sight!
> You ought to have been there,
> To see this piece of bleeding clay
> Suspended in the air.
> Strangled, dead and bleeding,
> We hung him up so high,

While each pious lady shouted,
"I'm so glad to see him die!"

You know, we weren't a bit afraid;
He was manacled at last.
Sheriff Kilian of Nebraska
Had made him sure and fast.
So, you see, there was no danger,
Not any in the least.
O, we had a jolly time—
And a jolly, ghoulish feast!

As the poem reveals, mob violence unleashes inner drives that are inherently immoral. Someone else's suffering and death becomes emotionally gratifying, even "a jolly time."

But editor Huntington surely expressed the view of most Pepin County residents when he tried to portray the lynching as a just and orderly proceeding, which was somehow not really lawbreaking at all, simply a local duty that was quietly and effectively performed:

> Mob law should always be frowned on by all respectable citizens, but this was *not* a mob. Less than 25 men seemed to have a hand in the matter. . . . The affair was conducted quietly—no loud talk or yelling, except the cry, "Hang the son of a b——h!"—which was evidently a signal agreed upon by the vigilance committee— and the [subsequent] signal of "Haul away!" . . .
>
> A regular legal execution could not have been conducted more quietly and orderly; and as soon as the murderer was suspended from the tree, the crowd commenced to disperse. Less than fifty of the large assemblage in the courtroom had the time to get out of the building before the tragedy was over. . . .
>
> All seemed to feel that a painful duty had been performed, and expressed fervent wishes that a like necessity should never occur again.

Huntington's comments revealed that he knew who at least some of the perpetrators were. He had been there, and he had talked with those who had done their so-called painful duty. His characterization of the lynching as an orderly, unemotional, almost-legal "necessity" also disclosed a self-righteous, punitive mind-set that refused to acknowledge either the humanity of the victim or the complex motivations of the mob. By portraying the murder as a "duty," an unavoidable cleansing process that would help ensure the future for "respectable citizens," Huntington was unintentionally revealing a horrible truth: The lynching was a psychological purgation, a communal slaying of the monster of aggression that lurked within the townspeople.

Of course, the lynching was not a "necessity" at all, but an act of disgusting public lawlessness, and other newspapers immediately saw it that way. A front-page article in the *Stillwater Daily Sun,* which was accompanied by two crude but dramatic drawings of the lynching, flatly condemned the vigilante action and called it what it was—a disgraceful murder by a mob:

LYNCH LAW IN WISCONSIN.
THE MURDER OF MAXWELL.

A Cowardly and Brutal Taking Off.

Menomonie, Wis., Nov. 21—Edward Maxwell was murdered by a howling mob at Durand, on Saturday. . . . In looking over the events since his arrest, there is much to force the conclusion that his death at the hands of the mob was anticipated both by officers and citizens. . . .

The crime of his taking off had in it many revolting features. Even the Ku Klux of the most benighted regions of the South covered their barbarism with some secrecy. But here, in the sovereign state of Wisconsin, after the telegraph and newspapers had for days predicted violence, a prisoner, practically undefended, with no protest . . . is taken by servants of the law into the midst of his bitterest enemies, and left to meet a death which disgraces the state, without the movement of a finger on his behalf. He was hanged in broad daylight, in the presence of an assembled community, under the eyes of officers and the court itself.

Fortunately, there need be no trouble in identifying the men who have thus boldly defied the law. If all the perpetrators are not known, enough witnesses are known to make it certainly possible that all the crowd can be brought to justice.

If difficulty is experienced in making arrests, the governor can easily obtain excellent assistance by giving immunity to

---

Lon Maxwell, and placing papers for the men wanted in his
hands. Better that one murderer should go untried than one
hundred.

No commentator more forcefully condemned public complicity in the
shameful act at Durand. If Ed was guilty of murder, so were the men who
killed him, and their combined assault on the justice system was more dam-
aging—because it had public support. Against them, even Lon might act
as a force for just punishment. Despite their smug moralism, the lynchers
and their supporters were regressing to bloody revenge, to "barbarism."

Other regional newspapers also quickly condemned the lynching. The
nearby *Pierce County Herald,* for example, argued that "there was no shadow
of an excuse for resorting to murder, to punish murder—burying one crime
under another," for Ed would have been convicted in court. Moreover, the
lawless mob action was anticipated by everyone and "should have been
prevented." In short, the authorities deserve censure for what happened,
whether or not they were in collusion with the mob.

In a commentary titled "THE DURAND MURDER," the nearby *Eau Claire
News* not only condemned the lynching but ridiculed Huntington's depiction of it as well: "The [*Pepin County*] *Courier,* in commenting on the
tragedy, claims that it was conducted 'quietly and orderly,' and that the
lynchers were not a 'mob,' only respectable citizens who had a 'painful
duty' to perform," but "dragging a helpless and manacled criminal down
the courthouse steps with a rope around his neck, and stringing him up to
a tree and launching him into eternity without the sanction of law might
be considered quiet and orderly business in the Cannibal Islands, but not
in Wisconsin. . . ."

More widely circulated newspapers also chimed in. In Madison the *Wisconsin State Journal* published a thoughtful commentary, recognizing that
"desperadoism is becoming too popular, and society would rest content if
such murderous ruffians as Ed Williams, the James [boys], the Youngers—
and imitators among the train robbers of the West—were put to death
[by mobs]," but "we must not override law and order, however great the
grievance." That editor excoriated "the wild and criminal lawlessness of
the mob" and concluded that "murders will always abound if the spirit
that 'murder justifies murder' is fostered."

The *Chicago Times* also deplored the Durand lynching—and the recent
ones in Michigan and Illinois as well—and suggested that the upper Mis-

sissippi Valley was becoming akin to "the uncivilized Southwest." In a very probing commentary, it also pointed out that the public slaying of Ed Maxwell was worse than the murder that provoked it:

> To kill a man except under the sanction of the law of the land, or of the natural law of self-protection, is murder, and it is just as much murder when it is committed by a hundred persons as it is when committed by one. And it is none the less murder when the person killed is a murderer. To lynch a man indicates the same contempt for law that the original murder indicates, and it does more: The original murder is the act of but one man, and is not sanctioned by others; a killing participated in by a hundred men and approved of by a thousand undermines respect for the law and regard for civil order, without which civilization is impossible. . . .
>
> Lawlessness is not to be remedied by lawlessness. As a cure for murder, mob violence may be said to be worse than the disease.

Similarly concerned about the continuation of western-style mob violence in the Mississippi Valley, the *New York Times* printed a scathing condemnation of the incident at Durand, asserting in an editorial, "No story of lynching reported from the wild south-western states can exceed in brutality . . . the hanging of [that] desperado by a Wisconsin mob," especially since the victim would have been "justly dealt with by the courts." The editor concluded that "acts like these are quite as dangerous to society as the perpetuation of crimes . . . for which Maxwell has been punished." In fact, lynch law simply undermined the rule of law itself. That was the great danger for America.

The murder of Ed Maxwell produced so much nationwide commentary—many dozens or scores of editorials—that by early December W. H. Huntington felt obliged to present some of it in the *Pepin County Courier.* Taken as a whole, that commentary revealed just how deeply the twin concerns of lawbreaking and lynching were bothering the American people in 1881—as the trial of the president's assassin was also continuing.

Some city newspapers—owned by upper-class businessmen who were alarmed by the rise in crime—clearly approved of the lynching. The *Chicago Inter-Ocean,* for example, praised "the open-handed, resolute, and determined calmness in the lynching," and asserted that "if lynching was ever justified, it seems so in this case." Likewise, the *Atlanta Constitution,* published in a state where lynching was common, concluded that "the lynching of Ed Maxwell was neatly and expeditiously accomplished"—and praised the mob for "anticipating the law."

Sharing that view, the *Milwaukee Sunday Telegraph* provided a long commentary that discussed the social dynamics of the case and commended the general practice of lynching. In a final word, it also reminded the public that Lon was still on the loose: "But the people of Durand and those who had a hand in the lynching must not forget that their victim's brother still lives, that no crime is too great for him now, and that he will devote the balance of his life to punishing those who had a hand in killing his brother. . . ." Again, Lon was portrayed as a well-motivated avenger who was bound to retaliate.

That newspaper and several others also called for the restoration of the death penalty in Wisconsin as a means of curbing the rise in crime and stopping the practice of lynching, but none of them mentioned the all-too-obvious data contradicting that notion: In the Mississippi Valley states that had a death penalty, such as Illinois and Missouri, both violent crime and lynching were more common than in Wisconsin. Executions did not prevent other men from breaking the law.

If the Milwaukee newspaper's closing comment was a reminder that Lon should be dealt with in the same way as Ed, the local public in western Wisconsin didn't need it. There was widespread feeling that Lon, too, should be lynched at the first opportunity. An anonymous letter in the *Pepin County Courier* claimed to speak for many local residents: "Our people almost to a unit say that the Spirit of Justice . . . triumphed in the execution of Ed Maxwell," and the time will come when "Lon's wicked, worthless, and forfeited carcass [will] dangle in mid-air at the lower end of a rope."

As that comment suggests, there was a certain satisfaction in expressing moral anger—because the more "wicked" and "worthless" you proclaimed some perpetrator to be, the more good and worthy you were, by implication. After all, you knew who deserved to be killed: that revealed your moral sense. And you could also avoid any obligation to consider the perpetrator's experience, psychological problems, or point of view, not to mention the details of the crime.

Naturally, editor W. H. Huntington made an elaborate defense of the lynching. Unfortunately, it was full of distortions and lies. He asserted, for example, that "Ed expressed no sorrow for his crimes, [and] repeatedly affirmed that his profession was that of a murderer. . . ." In fact, Ed had expressed his regrets to Mrs. Coleman while asserting that he and Lon had no intent to kill but had simply reacted to the sudden armed confrontation. And while he did say that his outlaw life, as a bandit, was a kind of profession, Ed explicitly stated that he and his brother were not murderers, just outlaws ready to use their guns if need be.

Huntington also claimed that the Coleman brothers were not just hunting the Maxwells for horse stealing "for the reward offered by Henderson County, Ill.," but "were endeavoring to arrest them on a warrant for assault with intent to kill one of our citizens, at whom they had fired several shots with their Winchesters"—a claim which might justify hunting them with guns in the streets of Durand. But no such assault with their Winchesters ever occurred, nor was any warrant ever issued. Moreover, Sheriff Anderson's "wanted for horse stealing" postcard, in Milton's pocket when he died, made the Coleman motive, which was legitimate enough, perfectly clear.

Huntington's most disturbing distortion of the situation was a blatant appeal to fear, expressed in his conclusion: "Ed Maxwell was hung, not in a spirit of revenge . . . but as a future protection to this and other communities," for he was "too dangerous a citizen to live, and any man or men who wipe such a dangerous desperado from the face of the earth should be commended instead of condemned."

That was, in fact, a chilling assertion of the American myth that would soon be enshrined in countless western stories and films—that violent lawbreaking is intractable evil, unable to be alleviated by the justice system, and so, for the protection of society, counterviolence is a necessity. And those willing to face the dangerous adversary and spill blood should be commended or admired. They are bold, manly heroes.

That American myth, so common in western films, always denies the complex realities of human motivation and selfish social purpose, and always portrays the justice system as ineffective and in need of substitutionary violence rather than improvement. It arose on the frontier, where law enforcement was sometimes ineffective, but it was an especially bogus rationale for lynching in Ed's case, for he was already helpless, unarmed and in chains, a threat to no one, and was surely headed for life in prison.

Huntington's effort to justify the mob violence by asserting that Ed was a uniquely dangerous desperado was elsewhere contradicted by his own words, as he misused his newspaper to threaten others with lynching. On November 25 he wrote,

> We hear of some threats having been made, by parties supposed to be in sympathy with the Maxwell brothers, of personal violence to men supposed to have taken part in the lynching of

Ed Williams—of burning their dwellings, etc. . . . This community understands its business, and proposes to be a peaceable, law-abiding community "if they have to fight for it." Any attempt at retaliation will be properly punished, "and don't you forget it." There is more rope here and plenty of responsible men who are not afraid to use it when the occasion demands.

This illogical declaration—that Durand was a "law-abiding community" because some citizens were always willing to set aside the law and commit violence—is as clear an expression of the American myth of necessary violence as one can find in the later nineteenth century. In another brief editorial, Huntington referred to mob violence as "heroic treatment," which many lawbreakers deserved but did not receive.

No wonder an isolated, still-frontierish county seat, dominated by a single newspaper, disgraced itself with an act of public lawlessness.

In another area involved with the Maxwell saga, the river bluff country of western Illinois, the *Alton Telegraph* also condemned the "lawless action" at Durand, and it expressed perhaps the major reason for the persistence of lynching—at least in the Mississippi Valley: "The people have lost confidence in the courts, knowing that with tricky lawyers, legal quibbles, time-serving judges, and ignorant juries, the chances are in favor of the acquittal of the most notorious criminals." That was probably true in general, but it was not a deciding factor in Ed's lynching, for people knew that he would be convicted. Rather, people in and around Pepin County had an overwhelming desire to even the score—to give the sheriff-killer what he deserved, in the public mind—rather than only what the law allowed, a long prison sentence, which might have included the possibility of eventual parole.

Ed had also become a scapegoat—a symbol of all the noted desperadoes who persisted in defying the law and evading the authorities. In a sense, he died for the crimes of his unassailable heroes, Jesse and Frank James.

And as the controversy over the lynching raged in the press, Ed was not without his defenders. Perhaps his most stunning support came from a group of "electors of the town of Spring Brook," near Menomonie, who published a signed letter in the *Dunn County News*—defending the rights of Ed and Lon, and criticizing the Coleman brothers. Among other things, they reminded the public that Milton Coleman was operating outside of his Dunn County jurisdiction: "Under what law and by what authority did

Milton Coleman assail, and with deadly weapons fire upon, the Williams brothers while they were quietly traveling on a highway in Pepin County?" Moreover, they asserted the same citizen's right to self-defense that Ed had been planning to plead in court, and they challenged the public to "explain to us the reason why the Williams brothers had no right to defend their lives." A thought-provoking document, signed by thirty men, the letter raised issues that were difficult to ignore.

Likewise, an editorial in the *St. Paul Daily Dispatch* not only condemned the mob that had lynched Ed and asserted his rights but reminded the public that he had exhibited certain admirable qualities:

> It is in order to discuss the quality of Wisconsin justice. . . . The prisoner [Ed Maxwell] had been caught 300 miles from the scene of his crime, having successfully evaded pursuit by a skill and hardihood that always command a degree of admiration. . . . He had displayed a coolness in the presence of hundreds of men eager to take his life, and had told the story of his crime and escape with such candor that he had won another point of advantage with the public. He had stated a good ground of defense, which should have had a lawful hearing in court. It seems that he and his brother did not even know for several weeks who their victims were. The Williamses were surprised by the Colemans, who were trying to arrest them for horse-stealing, and as Ed Maxwell claimed, they were fired upon before they used their [guns]. . . .
>
> [Maxwell] deserved punishment for certain crimes, and the evidence in the Coleman case might have required his punishment for the crime of murder. But when he died he was an innocent man legally. The men who took his life to avenge the death of the Colemans are as much murderers as the dead Maxwell. The moral effect of the lynching is deplorable in every respect. . . .

That editor, who commented that Ed's "bravery . . . in the face of death" had a certain appeal for at least some members of the public, was sensitive to the factors that would soon transform the Maxwells into dime novel heroes.

Because the Charles Guiteau trial had started in Washington on November 14, people across the country related that case—in which their desire for vengeance was being delayed and perhaps thwarted by the insanity plea—with the Ed Maxwell case, where no frustrating legalities prevented his execution by popular action. And the two cases were further related by the third unsuccessful attempt to murder Guiteau, while he was being taken from the courthouse back to the jail, which occurred on the very day that Ed was lynched while being taken from the courthouse at Durand.

In Nebraska, the *Hastings Gazette-Journal* viewed both incidents as evidence of public distrust of the courts. The "murder of Ed Maxwell, the notorious outlaw," and "at about the same hour, in the capital of the country, the third attempt [on] . . . the assassin, Guiteau," show the general feeling that "the courts are too tardy, too intricate, too technical, and too easily bribed."

The juxtaposition of the Guiteau and Maxwell cases in the public mind also prompted supporters of lynching to recommend "the Durand solution," and many of their comments were humorous. This is the way the *Stillwater Messenger* reported the attempt to kill Guiteau, in a front-page article: "If Guiteau should escape conviction, he should be sent to the jail at Durand, Wis., and fed on the insanity medicine which effectually cured Ed Maxwell of his mania for murder and robbery. One dose is warranted to cure." Likewise, the *St. Paul Pioneer Press* quipped, "Guiteau says he will be [acquitted, and be] a lecturer within a year. Let us trust that if his prophecy is verified, he will make his first appearance at the courthouse in Durand."

Editor Huntington of the *Pepin County Courier* also did not miss the opportunity to relate the two cases, and he employed the widespread hatred of Guiteau to support his contention that the lynching was justified: "Guiteau may be a greater crank than Ed Maxwell, but he is not half so good a shot, nor half so dangerous to society." To those who condemned the lynching, he retorted, "Stop your sniveling over Maxwell. . . ."

While most Americans continued to follow the Guiteau case—he was convicted in early January and hanged on June 30, 1882—the Durand lynching soon faded from the newspapers. But in Wisconsin, it remained a controversial topic for a long time.

In February 1882 a bill to legalize the lynching was actually introduced in the state legislature. It was never seriously discussed, however, and some considered it a satirical ploy aimed at those who had tried to justify the mob's lawlessness.

Perhaps the most even-handed comment on the lynching came from David Maxwell, who was interviewed soon after the mob violence at Durand. For Susan and him, "the crimes of the two boys [were hard to bear], and now the hanging by a mob of one of them [was] a terrible blow," as one newspaper put it. Of course, the public had forgotten that, in a sense, David and Susan were also victims of the lynching, for emotionally, parents always share the fate of their children. Normally avoiding any commentary for the press on his two notorious sons, David made an exception and, speaking to a reporter for the *Hastings Gazette-Journal,* summed up his feelings about what had happened: "Lon and Ed were bad boys. I haven't a bit of a wish to defend them. . . . They deserved punishment for their crimes, though I always shall believe they shot the Coleman boys in self-defense. But the same law they broke should have punished them—not a lot of cowards who feared to meet the lads when they were free."

It was a forceful statement, asserting the ethic of self-defense that Ed and Lon felt should apply, and affirming the justice system that had been violated by the lynchers. Indeed, the mob, unlike the Maxwell brothers, had no claim whatever to immediate self-defense, and their act of murder was clearly premeditated.

Although the anguished father admitted that Ed and Lon were "bad boys," in this brief response to the violence at Durand they seem somehow superior to the mob of "cowards," the unidentified men "who feared to meet the lads when they were free." He assumed that the lynchers must have been lacking in manliness—the very quality that Ed spent his short life trying to exhibit. Did David's focus on that issue contribute to Ed's neurotic obsession, his fear that he would not be regarded as manly? Perhaps, but in any case, David's comment was also true: However framed as an act of manly self-assertion, lynching was always an act of cowardice.

Despite the vast commentary on the lynching, no one raised the deepest, most troubling question of all: To what extent are violent lawbreakers responsible for their actions? If their lives are the unfolding of what they are, what they did not choose to be, then how much blame can we attach to them? And what kind of punishment is just? Ed Maxwell did not create or want the psychological problems, social conditions, and public attitudes that had produced him. And the same was true of Lon. They were fated to be themselves—impoverished, shamed, alienated, insecure, frustrated, and self-absorbed young men who resented authority, admired defiance, yearned for respect, and loved guns. Those factors and penitentiary dehumanization shaped their experience, including their sudden response to armed strangers in the street who could have shot them down. If the causal history of a violent act extends back well past the immediate provocation, to powerful, unchosen forces in the perpetrator's life, what response by society is appropriate?

Of course, the popularity of mob violence against lawbreakers in nineteenth-century America revealed societal unconcern with those complexities.

Through that cold, snowy December of 1881, the public in Pepin County remained agitated over the lynching. Some regretted the condemnation that had come to Durand; others were still defensive of the mob action. And many were full of anxiety, wondering whether any law enforcement effort would ever confront the lynchers, or whether Lon would return to avenge his brother.

Meanwhile, a local fortune-teller who viewed the lynching as "an act against God and law" predicted bad things to come for Durand—the village that had turned to violence. As the Christmas season came along, people were on edge.

And then something awful did happen: On Christmas Day a fire broke out in the downtown area and roared its way from one structure to the next, sending up huge volumes of smoke visible for more than ten miles. People from nearby areas rushed to watch the terrifying spectacle. By the time it was over, the entire Durand business district—thirty-four buildings—had gone up in flames.

The story was front-page news in the surrounding area, and perhaps the most vivid account appeared in the *St. Paul Pioneer Press:*

DEVASTATION OF DURAND.

The Entire Business Portion of That Village
Swept by Fire and Now a Heap of Ruins.
Not a Store or Shop Left Standing. . . .

Durand, Dec. 27—Last Sunday . . . the village of Durand, famous as the scene of the lynching of Ed Maxwell, was visited by a terrible conflagration which swept away the entire business portion of the place. Situated twenty-two miles from railroad or telegraph, it was not until Monday night that the news reached the outside world. . . .

A visit to the scene of the conflagration found a truly desolate prospect. Where a few weeks ago the representative of the *Pioneer Press* saw a bustling little inland town, its main street lively with blue and red-shirted lumbermen . . . there is now nothing but a long avenue of black ruins, the charred timbers lying heaped upon each other as the fury of the fiery deluge left them.

The fire began in the Ecklor House, the two-story hostelry that stood facing the visitor as he landed from the ferry across the Chippewa. The proprietor, W. H. Huntington, who combines hotel keeping with his editorship of the Durand *Courier,* stepped across the street about 1 o'clock to buy some oysters for his Sunday dinner at the hotel. As he threw down a coin to pay . . . the cry of "Fire," by a woman's voice, sounded in his ears. When he reached the street, the flames were piercing from the roof. The wind blew a gale from the south, and before the alarm had spread a dozen rods the Ecklor House and [its] barn were blazing, and Burton's meat market adjoining on the north was afire. . . .

The scene was frightful. Sheets of flame were torn from the seething mass and swept off high into the air. Shingles and clapboards were carried whirling away up the street, to fall on other buildings.

Suddenly, the cry was raised, "Topping's store's afire!" The fire had leaped a block's length and across the street, and began backing up against the wind. It was then clear enough that the whole business part of the village must go. . . .

As the fire got under headway, the crowd gradually retreated from the heat, which had now become intense. Groups of women assembled, and when the whole street was outlined with sheets of flame, one excited female shouted, "It's a judgment from God!" Indeed, the exclamation was on the lips of many of the spectators. . . .

It is an open secret that the men who planned Maxwell's lynching were limited to fifteen or twenty leading citizens of Durand, some of whom have lost their all by the fire. This fact recalled to the minds of the people of Durand and vicinity the threatening letter in the *Pioneer Press* signed by the "Voice of Justice". . . .

The rumor spread that Durand had been burned by the avengers of Maxwell, and by 5 o'clock, when the fury of the fire had spent itself, hundreds of farmers had flocked into town, attracted by the light of the fire and the exciting stories of violence which passed from lip to lip.

Upwards of fifty teams drove down to the west bank of the

Chippewa, and from there crowded wagonloads of people viewed the grand sight of the burning village. The conflagration virtually marched up one side and down the other, leaving not a single building standing. . . .

Articles on the Christmas Day fire were also carried in such major newspapers as the *New York Times* and the *San Francisco Chronicle.* The *Times* also made a connection between "threats of revenge upon the town and its people" for the lynching of Ed Maxwell and the mammoth fire, which was apparently intended "to burn the whole town." That article also may have been written by Edward Johnstone, but some other newspapers, without his input, made the same point.

Local officials soon looked into the origin of the blaze. They reported that the fire was accidental, having originated in a defective chimney at the Ecklor House, and they also discounted the idea that the author of the "Voice of Justice" letter, or any other critic of the unprosecuted lynch mob, had set the fire. But their motives were immediately suspect. To some of the vast public that had been judging the town's recent behavior, it seemed that local leaders, who surely knew the lynchers or had acted with them, simply did not want to affirm that the people of Durand had done anything to provoke such devastating retaliation.

Many were skeptical of the report—including the editor of the *Milwaukee Sentinel,* who remarked, "It is nevertheless hard to separate the calamity . . . from the recent threats by friends of [Ed] Williams. . . ." The fact that W. H. Huntington, the editor who had encouraged and defended the lynching, owned the hotel where the fire started, and that "nearly every participant in the hanging of Ed Maxwell [was] rendered penniless," seemed to prove that it was a well-planned act of vengeance.

Many Pepin County residents also reflected on the frightened woman's outcry, "It's a judgment from God!" In fact, a correspondent for the *Stillwater Daily Sun* who had talked to people a few days after the devastation reported just how widespread that view had become: "There are hundreds of good people who regard [the fire] as a direct punishment from Heaven, upon leading men among the murderers of Ed Maxwell. Even in Durand, and among sufferers from the fire, there are those who are inclined to regard the matter this way." In the minds of many, a vengeful community that had perpetrated, and excused, a heinous act of violence had gotten exactly what it deserved.

As that suggests, the huge fire made it even harder for people to ignore the fate of Ed Maxwell—and the cover-up that shielded his killers. Controversy over the lynching was so intense outside of Durand that a circuit court judge eventually summoned a grand jury, in April 1882, to look into the notorious event.

But that effort failed too. None of the many witnesses called to testify seemed to know anything. On April 19 the grand jury reported "no evidence before us to find an indictment"—and declared that no one "would be likely to give us any evidence that would throw more light on the matter." The folks in Durand clearly wanted the lynching forgotten.

But it never was. As a result of the nationally reported mob action, Durand earned a lasting reputation as "the town that lynched Ed Maxwell," as if the community had a propensity for that kind of violence. One development surely contributed to that: The locally despised account of the lynching, written by Johnstone, which depicted Ed as the heroically defiant victim of a mindless mob, was soon reprinted in the 1881 *History of Northern Wisconsin,* thus becoming a kind of "official" account—much to the dismay of Huntington and others in Durand. When that history book appeared, in fact, another nearby editor quipped, "It would be perilous for that individual [Johnstone] to visit the village of hemp and summary justice."

Durand's inability to shake off its reputation as "The Hanging Town" eventually gave rise to folklore that took care of the issue by asserting that local residents were, in fact, blameless. A 1963 newspaper article reported that tradition, without recognizing that it was folklore: "Although Durand was criticized by papers throughout the U.S., actual residents had little to do with the hanging. Reportedly, a small group of river rats arrived in town the preceding day, and had been overheard talking of the possibility of lynching Ed. Obviously the [local] people had been aware of the plan, but did not take part in it. . . ." Another version of this said that the lynch mob was composed of "lumbermen" who had come into Durand "to make trouble." Of course, if these folkloric accounts were true, the inquest jury and judge would not have failed to do their duty, and editor Huntington would not have tried so hard to defend the lynch mob.

In any case, for many years after Ed's death, "the Durand lynching tree" near the courthouse was a kind of unofficial Pepin County historic site, recalling the murder of Maxwell the outlaw. Every local schoolchild for generations knew what that tree had been used for, and many an elementary school class was taken there on a historical excursion.

Finally, in the summer of 1959, the ancient oak was cut down to make way for construction of a courthouse annex. But before the saws got to it, someone hung, by the neck, a human skeleton from the limb where Ed had been lynched. Photographed for the local newspaper, it was a stark reminder of that cold November day in 1881 when the townspeople had turned to violence.

17

The Mysterious Fate of Lon Maxwell

Unlike western novels and films, which are expressions of American myth, stories of real-life outlaws often have unsatisfactory endings. That the most famous outlaw of them all, Jesse James, should simply be shot in the back while dusting a picture in his parlor was immediately unpopular with many people, so the notion arose that another person, a substitute for Jesse, had died that day. Likewise, that legendary gunfighter Billy the Kid, who had escaped death so often, had been murdered in the dark by his old friend Pat Garrett also seemed unsatisfying, and suspicious as well, so rumors flew that his death had been faked and he was still hiding out. American robbers Butch Cassidy and the Sundance Kid continued their crime spree in Bolivia, where troops supposedly killed them, but folklore eventually asserted that Cassidy, the former leader of the Wild Bunch, had escaped to America and had lived in secret for many years, in California or Utah or some other state. In all three cases some members of the public were unwilling to accept the reported deaths of colorful desperadoes.

And the opposite happened as well: Some outlaws simply vanished, and endings for them had to be developed—for the public mind always wants to resolve the tension of loose ends by attaching them to something. California stage robber Black Bart, for example, vanished in 1888, but San

Francisco newspapers continued to print stories that either associated him with mysterious robberies or simply claimed that he had settled, under an alias, in some American city. In the Mississippi Valley, long after robber and killer Joe Brice had disappeared into the West, stories about how he had supposedly died circulated in his home state.

The Lon Maxwell case was similar. Nobody knows for sure what became of him, although many people over the years claimed that they did. The shocking reality of Ed's death—so public, so definite, and so controversial—drew attention to the fact that Lon's fate was a mystery.

He was last seen for sure near Aurora, Nebraska, east of Grand Island, shortly after Ed's capture, but a week later, the *Grand Island Times* reported that various posses had failed to find him, and nobody knew where he was: "Several [search] parties who have been out after Alonzo Maxwell think they were close upon him at times, but in every case, he managed to elude them. Some are of the opinion that he left the country at once after the arrest of his brother, while others think that he is still in this vicinity."

That period of intense searching for Lon, late in 1881, naturally caused enormous stress for his aging parents, especially after Ed was captured and lynched. In December of that year, they were visited and interviewed by a reporter for the *St. Paul Pioneer Press,* who was probably Edward Johnstone. David and Susan's brief comments reflected their parental concern for Lon's safety—and their intense anxiety because of the day-to-day uncertainty about his fate:

THE MAXWELLS

The old couple are highly respected by all their neighbors, and they suffer the most poignant agony over the fate of their wayward son. . . .

In reply to the question of whether he proposed to go to Durand to get Ed's body, he said: "No. I did think of doing that, but if I can find an upright, fearless lawyer, who is willing to undertake the bitter prosecution of Ed's murderers, I would give him the money the trip would cost—and more, too. . . .

Of Lon, the old gentleman said: "I fear he will be caught. I almost hope he will be, for this suspense is terrible to his mother and me. I don't believe he would make a very hard fight to escape if he could only be sure he would have a fair

---

trial and be punished according to law. I want you to use all the power of the *Pioneer Press,* if he is caught, to protect him from lynching. For God's sake, do all you can through your paper to give the boy, wicked as he is, the show [that should be] given to every man, bad or good."

Of Lon, the mother said: "Oh, sir, it is awful for me to think of my boy, bad as he has been, out in the cold, with every man feeling like a bloodhound toward him, and ready to take his life. I would be glad to know he was in prison, if I only could be sure he would not be hanged without a moment's notice."

Lon surely wanted to see his parents, but he must have realized that the authorities in Adams County would be looking for him. Whether he ever saw them again is unknown, but it is likely that Lon, who had written to his father and mother even while in the penitentiary, eventually sent them a message or two with no return address, indicating that he was still alive.

Of course, the uncertainty about where Lon might be prompted a host of reports that he had been seen somewhere. One that made the newspapers in late November 1881 referred to "a young fellow who came into Doniphan, near Grand Island, one evening, and did some drinking with the locals" but was secretive about his background and his business. Nevertheless, he "had a very vicious look" and "talked a good deal about the Williams boys." Then he beat his way out of town on a freight train. Of course, Lon would never have come into a community, nor would he have called attention to himself, but for many weeks, whenever the Nebraska public was confronted with a stranger, they thought of Lon.

Some of the "Lon stories" that circulated in upcoming months were focused on his apparent capture at some location. In late May 1882, for example, the police in the Chicago suburb of Hyde Park arrested a young man with "a light mustache and goatee" who resembled "in almost every way the published description of Lon Williams" and who had supposedly just arrived from Colorado. Reports indicated that he usually carried "a couple of revolvers." Although he gave his name as David S. Lee, the man was held for several days on suspicion of being Lon (whose real first name was David). Articles on the case indicated that a $2,500 reward was being offered at that time for Lon's capture, so the Hyde Park officers who made the arrest were anxious for Wisconsin authorities to confirm that their prisoner was the infamous desperado.

Unfortunately, like the William Kuhl case in Milwaukee, this was a matter of mistaken identity—no doubt demonstrated when Lee failed to have a missing toe on his right foot.

Several months later, major newspapers carried a report that "the notorious desperado and outlaw Lon Williams . . . had been captured by the authorities of Dodge City, Kas." That famous cattle town, which in recent years had been home to lawmen like Wyatt Earp and Bat Masterson, as well as gunfighters like Doc Holliday and Luke Short, was a likely place for the public to identify some gun-toting stranger as Lon Maxwell. In this case, the arrested man claimed that his name was "Jack Bass," but he loosely resembled Lon, so the authorities thought that was just another alias.

While this story was in the news, a dispatch from western Wisconsin asserted that "Williams will probably be lynched if he is brought to this vicinity." Fortunately for Bass, he also soon convinced the authorities of his identity.

Perhaps the encounter in Doniphan, Nebraska, with the young tramp who rode the rails inspired one of the many accounts of Lon's death. A 1903 newspaper story on the once-infamous Maxwell brothers asserted, "Lon's death was not so sensational [as Ed's], but well did he pay for his misdeeds: He died in a boxcar in a western city, alone, unattended, with a black past to view and a blacker future to contemplate." The vague nature of this account brands it immediately as folklore—an effort by the public mind to bring closure to the Maxwell saga by asserting that Lon, too, got the miserable end that he supposedly deserved.

That same psychological impulse lies behind a more colorful 1889 account of Lon's death, which appeared in the *Colchester Independent,* published not far from where the Maxwells had settled in McDonough County:

LAST OF THE MAXWELLS.

It has been published in the daily papers that Alonzo Williams, a horse thief, border desperado, and general all-around bad man, was recently captured by Montana cowboys while having in his possession some stolen horses, and was hanged with the customary informality.

The report says that there is no doubt of the identity of the man, and if it be the notorious Lon Williams, alias Maxwell, an accomplished villain has gone to his final reward. . . .

If caught in Montana, Colorado, Arizona, and other places out West, a horse thief or cattle rustler was frequently hanged without being identified, and that prompted folkloric connections between wanted men, such as Lon, and the lynched thief who was engaged in the same illegal occupation. This account does not mention the basis for identifying the hanged horse thief as Lon. Moreover, the same article is full of other Maxwell folklore.

One sure indication that the hanged horse thief story lacked substance was the continuing appearance of other death-of-Lon accounts. The following is another Montana-based item of Lon Maxwell folklore:

> The last definite record of Lon Williams . . . was when Williams was captured in a wheat field near Miles City, Montana, in 1884. Lon was being taken to the Montana State Prison at Deer Lodge when he jumped out of a window of the stagecoach at Livingston, in the dusk of evening, and made his escape by swimming across the Yellowstone River. An intensive search brought no results. Years later, the skeleton of a man with handcuffs was found in a wild mountain valley near Livingston, and it was assumed that Lon had died of starvation.

Actually, this exciting account is ultimately based on a story that arose in 1883. An unsolved bank robbery and murder had been committed in Waupaca, Wisconsin, in December 1882, and months later people were saying that it was "the work of the noted outlaw Lon Williams," according to an article in the *Chicago Tribune*. Supposedly, afterward Lon had traveled to Montana, where he lived and robbed under the alias "James Edwards." Captured in Custer County, he was convicted and sentenced to the state penitentiary. But "while the train was passing through a mountainous region, by some means Edwards managed to slip his irons and, awaiting his opportunity, jumped through a [railroad] car window," and all traces of him were lost. By 1889 the public mind had changed that story from a railroad to a stagecoach escape, dropped the connection to Edwards, and concluded it with the discovery of a mysterious dead body.

There was never any proof that the outlaw named Edwards was really Lon, nor was Edwards, apparently, the Waupaca bank robber and killer. Another man was eventually arrested and indicted for that crime.

The handcuffed skeleton was a memorable detail, however, and it was later worked into another folkloric death-of-Lon story. Early in 1898, almost seventeen years after the Maxwells had been talked about all over America, a Chicago newspaper printed the following dispatch from a Durand correspondent:

A MYSTERY IS SOLVED.

Skeleton of Lon Maxwell,
the Noted Desperado, Is Found.

Durand, Wis., Jan. 21—Lon Williams, known as one of the most notorious and daring of the Jesse James gang . . . escaped lynching here only to die of starvation in the "bad lands," or alkali plains, of Montana. Mob justice was, however, meted out to his brother Ed. . . .

All trace of Lon had been lost, although a big reward was offered for his capture, until word was received today by ex-Sheriff Knight that prospectors passing through the "bad lands" had found the skeleton of a man lying in a lonely gulch, with the wristbones attached by a pair of rusty handcuffs. The skeleton had evidently lain there for years. Upon being polished up, the words "Pepin County" were deciphered upon the handcuffs, and this fact finally led to the identification of the skeleton as the desperado who had long terrorized the citizens of Illinois, Wisconsin, and other northwestern states. . . .

It is thought that Lon managed to hide himself in a freight car and made his way westward. Leaving the train, it is evident that he hid in the "bad lands." Being unable to remove the handcuffs, he sought out the gulch where his skeleton was found, and there apparently starved to death.

Twenty years ago, the exploits of those daring [Maxwells] were on every tongue. . . .

While this account seems specific—because the handcuffs said "Pepin County"—the public mind that had connected the mysterious desperado with the handcuffed-skeleton story had simply forgotten, by 1898, that Lon was not wearing handcuffs when he escaped at Grand Island, nor was he ever in the custody of Pepin County authorities. Moreover, that supposedly authoritative article is full of other Maxwell folklore: that after his release from prison Lon "joined the James boys and became one of the boldest in the gang," that the Maxwells held up the bank at Fieldon and killed the cashier, that Lon escaped from captivity in Nebraska by plunging headfirst through the window of a speeding train, and so on. Of course, no cashier was killed at Fieldon, nor does any evidence connect the Maxwell brothers with that bank robbery. Lon never escaped in Nebraska—because he was never captured there. And neither of the Maxwells was ever associated with the James gang.

That story about Lon's death was immediately challenged in the pages of the *Colchester Independent*. In fact, a resident of that area who had known the Maxwells provided his own, more exciting account:

MISTAKEN SKELETON.

Another Story of How Lon Maxwell
Met His Death.

. . . Robert James, of Tennessee Township, was a schoolmate with the Maxwell boys and grew to young manhood with them. He was, prior to the first robbery by Ed Maxwell at Blandinsville, his intimate and confidential friend, and Mr. James claims to know something of the Maxwells after [the outlaws] were sent to the state penitentiary and Mr. and Mrs. Maxwell and their daughter had moved from this county to Nebraska.

He was talking to an *Independent* reporter and told an entirely different story as to the fate of Lon Maxwell, and of the capture at Grand Island. The information that Mr. James has, was learned through a correspondence between the parents of the Maxwells and some old friends in this county, some considerable time after the lynching of Ed Maxwell at Durand. . . .

Ed was taken to Durand and lynched, but Lon was not taken in the capture at Grand Island. After that time he was at his parents' home and secured some clothing and money. . . .

From Nebraska he went farther west to elude the officers and evade arrest, large rewards being offered for his capture. He joined a band of outlaws in the northwest territories, and was shot, with several others of the band, while attempting a cattle raid on a ranch in Montana. His pursuers were deputy marshals and organized ranchmen, and his fate [death] came in the flight of the pursuit. . . .

While this account seems plausible, it is still not very specific, providing no year of death or place in Montana where the killing by a posse supposedly occurred. Lon may have "joined a band of outlaws in the northwest territories," but it is well to remember that he had never carried out a single theft or act of resistance to the authorities without Ed, and Ed was gone. It is also apparent that Lon traveled east, away from the Maxwell homestead, in the days following Ed's arrest. And Mr. James evidently did not know that David and Susan Maxwell had five other children, not just a daughter, when they moved to Nebraska, which suggests that he may not have been as close to Ed as he indicated. In any case, this account, too, seems like the kind of appropriate-death story that the public mind wanted to conclude the Maxwell saga with—a successful pursuit-and-killing of the missing outlaw who had become legendary by repeatedly eluding pursuers, both with his brother and alone.

Interestingly, this hearsay account by Maxwell schoolmate Robert James was accompanied by his assertion that "he saw Lon Maxwell in the streets of Colchester two or three years after Ed was captured and hanged," but the notorious outlaw, who "positively recognized" James, disappeared from town before the latter could confront him. Again, it seems very unlikely that Lon would have returned to one of the few communities where he might have been recognized, nor would he have any reason to go there. Mr. James perhaps enjoyed the local notoriety that came to him as one who "claims to know something of the Maxwells," and it is also unlikely that David and Susan Maxwell ever wrote to unnamed "old friends" in Mc-Donough County, to inform them that Lon had been killed while continuing to act as an outlaw.

Another indication that all of these death-of-Lon stories were untrue, and were simply efforts by the public to create a satisfactory conclusion to the troubling Maxwell saga, is the fact that one lawman who had pursued the outlaws discounted them and continued to search for Lon into the twentieth century. After ending his career as Henderson County sheriff in 1886, James O. Anderson served several terms as a representative in the Illinois General Assembly and was sergeant at arms in the Illinois Senate. In 1899 he began a ten-year stint as a special agent assigned to investigate internal revenue law violations in Chicago. During all those years he continued to take an interest in the Lon Maxwell case, doggedly pursuing leads on the missing desperado because he was haunted by a sense of uncompleted duty. In the first decade of the new century he became convinced that Lon had recently tried to hold up a bank in Washburn, had been caught, convicted under an alias, and sent to the penitentiary at Joliet. His 1905 letter to Warden E. J. Murphy survives, and in it he explains his purpose:

> Pursuant to our conversation of yesterday, I have reason to be-
> lieve that you have, or have had, a criminal, sent up from Woodford
> County some two or three years ago, for burglary—attempting to
> rob what is known as the Ireland Bank at Washburn, Ills. I do not
> know what name he used when convicted this time, but if he is
> the man I think he is, his name is Lon Maxwell. . . .
>
> I was sheriff of Henderson County from 1876 to 1886, and in
> 1881 the Maxwells killed three men who were trying to arrest them
> under my orders. Ed Maxwell was captured and lynched, while
> Lon has never been apprehended. . . .

Anderson's reference to "three men" shows that he believed that Ed and
Lon had killed Sheriff Lammy as well as the Coleman brothers. In any
case, he was clearly still bothered by the notion that his warrant for the
Maxwells for horse stealing had led to the sheriff killings that had shocked
the upper Mississippi Valley in 1881.

Anderson was probably responding to local folklore from Woodford
County, which had apparently connected the convicted robber with the
long-vanished desperado from an earlier generation. Like the folks in Mc-
Donough County and in western Wisconsin, they too had the Maxwells
on their minds for many years.

Well into the twentieth century, reports were still circulating that claimed
Lon had been living under an assumed name somewhere in the far West,
and had killed someone else, or had been killed, or had finally killed himself. For example, the 1915 suicide of a mysterious Montana rancher, "a
crack revolver shot" who had once killed a man but had managed to avoid
conviction "on a plea of self-defense," prompted some residents there to
assert that he was actually Lon Maxwell living under an alias. That, too,
was probably a groundless rumor, but it revealed the still-lingering legend
of the sheriff-killing desperado who had vanished.

However, Lon may have returned to, or had some contact with, one of
the places where he had once lived. A few years after his disappearance,
a slate headstone, adorned with a weeping willow to symbolize grief, was
erected over Fannie's grave in the remote Waubeek Prairie Cemetery, one
mile west of the Chippewa River and a few miles northwest of Durand.
Although Fannie had become Mrs. "Williams" when she had married Lon,
and was surely shocked to discover his real name and his outlaw past
shortly before she died, her headstone tries to set things straight—and
it offers a testament in stone to his affection:

FANNIE B.

dau. of
B. & W. E. Hussey
and beloved wife of
Alonzo Maxwell
DIED
June 13, 1881,
AGED
17 yrs., 2 ms., 20 ds.

Down at the ground line is something else, something unusual—a personal message, a letter in stone to the lovely wife and daughter who had died so young. "Dear Fannie," it begins, and then becomes too weathered by time to decipher.

An uncommonly literate outlaw, Lon was a man who wrote letters— to his parents, his brother, his in-laws, even Sheriff Hays and Reverend Downer—and to him the gravesite was a sacred spot where he had come with Ed more than once in those dark days after her death to feel close to Fannie, express his grief, and perhaps apologize for lying to her, leaving the region, and reverting to his outlaw ways. Like gunfighter Will Munny in Clint Eastwood's western film masterpiece, *Unforgiven,* he may have been unable to forgive himself.

After the escape near Grand Island, Lon may well have been in contact with Bridget Thompson—at least by letter. After all, they shared an essential bond, an abiding love for Fannie. Of course, the predicted burning of Durand convinced some people that he had returned to Pepin County if only to avenge the lynching, and rumors that he had been seen in the Chippewa Valley continued to circulate for many years. In fact, an 1884 *Chicago Tribune* article, published at about the time Fannie's headstone went up, asserted that "the Lon Williams Gang of desperadoes" had been operating near Eau Claire.

And what about the Maxwell family in Nebraska? If Lon had contact with David and Susan before they, or he, died, it was also probably through the mail. Complete separation from his family was one of the penalties he paid for being a notorious desperado, regardless of when or how he finally met his death.

After years of increasing disability and weakness, apparently due to heart disease, David died in Adams County on December 9, 1887, and was buried in the Osco Cemetery. He was only fifty-five, but the rigors of tenant farming and, in his later years, homesteading, as well as health problems stemming from illness during the war, had taken their toll. He was already an old man. A photograph from late in his life reveals that he looked like he was at least seventy. The inscription on David's headstone proclaims his release from "a world of care."

At the time he died, thirty-year-old Alice was married to William Thorne, a surveyor and stock raiser in nearby Webster County, and they had two children. Flora was almost twenty-six; George was twenty-one; John was eighteen, and Gabe was just thirteen years old. Flora was a schoolteacher, as Alice had been before her marriage. Among Nebraska pioneers, the Maxwell family had finally achieved respectability.

However, David and Susan always lived in a sod house and remained fairly poor—chiefly because "for [his] last years [David] had to be taken care of a good deal of the time," and he could not work, as Susan pointed out in a letter shortly after he died. Consequently, his estate was modest. But he had "proved" his claim and thus owned 160 acres in Section 8 of Logan Township. He also had a "timber claim" to an adjacent 160 acres, which required that he plant many trees, but that responsibility was "not yet completed." Susan eventually received the patent deed to that land as well.

She died about three years after David, on January 12, 1891, at the age of fifty-seven. Her health was probably also impacted by their long pioneering struggle, but no one knows for sure. Susan was buried beside David in the Osco Cemetery—which is now so remote that no road passes near it. At her death, Gabe was just sixteen, so his unmarried brother John became his guardian.

Interestingly, brother George Maxwell, who had been just fifteen years old in 1881, possessed the same superb eye-hand coordination that had once made Ed and Lon renowned gunfighters. Fascinated with firearms, he eventually earned an international reputation as a marksman, performing with a rifle and a revolver in every state and several foreign countries before his death in 1936. Even more astounding, in midlife George lost his left arm in a hunting accident, but he continued to display his shooting skill, and not just with a revolver—operating the kind of weapon associated with his notorious brothers, a Winchester repeating rifle, with only one arm but with incredible speed and accuracy that two-armed competitors could not match. An annual Nebraska contest for marksmen was named in his honor.

Gabe died in 1915, apparently of tuberculosis; Alice died in 1925; and Flora in 1932. The last of the Maxwell siblings to pass away was John, who died in 1943. As a young man, he had been a cowboy, herding cattle for his brother-in-law, William Thorne, along the Blue River. Later, he lived in the village of Holstein, not far from where his parents had homesteaded in the 1870s. He married in 1891 and had three daughters. The oldest, Blanche, also married but died young, in 1920, leaving two small daughters of her own. Yetive Jacobson and her sister, Lorraine Riese, now elderly, were raised by their grandfather—who was just twelve years old when his brothers were wanted throughout the upper Mississippi Valley.

The granddaughters were never told much about their great-uncles, the Maxwell outlaws, for when they were young John and his remaining brother and sister refused to talk about relatives who were, of course, an embarrassment to the family. But both Yetive and Lorraine have asserted that when their grandfather was still an unmarried man, already living in Holstein, Lon turned up one day. Ill and impoverished, he was taken in by his younger brother and lived with him, quietly and secretly, for some months until he died. Neither woman could say exactly when that was, however, or where Lon was finally laid to rest.

Of course, that could be false too—a story that arose within a family, as stories sometimes do, to provide a satisfactory conclusion to a disturbing episode. If so, the tale of Lon's return is, at this writing, one of the last pieces of folklore about the Maxwell brothers that is still alive in anyone's mind.

There is another version of the "Lon's return" story, once known to residents of the area, which depicts the arrival of his body "from some place far off" so that relatives at the village of Bladen, where Alice (Maxwell) Thorne lived, could bury it "under cover of darkness, in some now-unknown location." That vague account has all the earmarks of folklore, and its point is apparent: A kind of closure to the outlaw saga finally came for the Maxwell family when they received and buried Lon's body. Whether that ever really happened will probably never be known, but some people surely hoped that it had.

Before his death, Lon probably spent years as an impoverished, regret-ful, anxiety-ridden fugitive living under an alias. Of course, he may have taken his guns and worked as an outlaw in Wisconsin or in the far West. Or he may have found a remote location where, now that Ed was gone, he could make the life change that he had once wanted. Or he may have done all of those things. We simply don't know.

Where there is no certainty, people are free to speculate, and getting a story right is not just a matter of compiling the available facts anyway. Wanting a certain kind of truth—a validation of their simplistic vision of good and evil, of victims and victimizers—Americans had exerted a shaping influence on the Maxwell saga from the beginning. And even in this document-studded account, the story of the once-famous outlaw brothers has been carefully composed and interpreted—in a sense, reimagined, so that we might comprehend the two lawbreakers differently, and more deeply, than people once did.

As every biographer realizes, accounts of anyone's character and experience are always approximate, never objectively true. More than most biographical works, this one shows why: We must anchor our historical truth in a heap of surviving, and often conflicting, reports, upon which folklore, fading memories, cultural myths, personal views, and sheer fictionalizing have had an inescapable impact.

But one thing is certain: The Maxwell brothers were even more complex than we can now determine. They were not just desperadoes, but men.

Epilogue

The Story Life
of the Maxwell Brothers

After Ed's death and Lon's disappearance, they continued to be famous outlaws, at least for a time, because of the stories that were told about them. While those accounts were generally inaccurate because they were folkloric or fictionalized, they provide insight into the significance of the Maxwell brothers for American culture, and they illustrate the rise of the outlaw hero in the later nineteenth century. More deeply, the story life of the ill-fated brothers helps us to understand why Americans were, and still are, fascinated by such violent lawbreakers.

Until sometime in the twentieth century, the general public lived not by facts or news reports, but by stories—narratives that appealed to them and warranted retelling. People seldom checked the accuracy of what they heard, or read, and in fact, they usually had no means to do so. Folklore, unrecognized as such, was common in every locality, often arising and spreading like wildfire as the public mind strove to "get the story" about some compelling person or event. Unrecorded details were consciously or unconsciously supplied, the story's emotional impact was heightened, connections were made to familiar places and people, and acceptable meaning was slowly derived from it all. By that means, tales became more dramatic and significant—but always, unfortunately, less accurate.

The preceding chapters on the Maxwells illustrate time and again how the public mind worked—and how often the newspapers reflected circulating inaccuracies. But many folkloric items about the outlaw brothers were not mentioned in this account of their lives, simply because those rumors and stories would have made the narrative even more complicated than it already is. However, such items indicate the impact of the Maxwell brothers on the public mind—and reveal the storytelling context of the dime novels that were inspired by their career.

Every county that had some relationship to the Maxwell saga developed folkloric rumors and stories about the outlaws, usually to intensify their lawbreaking and connect them with a specific locale. For example, an 1889 newspaper item from Colchester, in McDonough County, summed up their career in this way:

> They [the Maxwells] rapidly advanced in crime, and for the next dozen years their depredations were numerous in Illinois, Missouri, Kansas, and adjoining states. They were identified with a gang of horse thieves who for some years flourished in the Illinois River bottom near Beardstown. One of the "stations" of this gang, it was afterwards found, was at a house two miles west of Macomb on the Colchester road. . . .
>
> The brothers then went to Wisconsin . . . and from 1876 to 1882 terrorized the western portion of that state; and their arrest rewards, aggregating several thousand dollars, are still unpaid. They were the most desperate criminals that ever made their homes in that state. . . .

The article also asserts that "many of the crimes charged against the James brothers were actually perpetrated by the Maxwells," and it provides a dramatic retelling of the gunfight at Durand, in which the desperadoes fire their Winchesters from the hip, killing the Coleman brothers before either "could press the trigger of his cocked and leveled gun." The message is clear: The Maxwells were renowned bandits and peerless gunfighters whose activities had once embraced the Macomb-Colchester area.

In Wisconsin, popular storytelling heightened the already dramatic account of Ed's death by claiming that "on the drive down from Menomonie, [the captured desperado] predicted that he would never leave Durand alive," and by also asserting that, as Ed was being led from the courthouse, "he raised his manacled hands to utter defiance, and offered to take on two men at a time." His lynching was the story of the century in Pepin County, told and retold until it symbolized outlaw daring and defiance.

For similar reasons, many of the folks in Calhoun County refused to believe that it was not the infamous Maxwell brothers who had gunned down Sheriff Lammy in late September of that same year, despite Ed's flat denial of the act. They could not surrender the notion that their world had been touched by fascinating desperadoes whose enormous evil underscored the heroic goodness of their lawman who had been so willing to risk his life to protect the local public. The "Battle of Fox Creek," pitting Lammy against the Maxwells, remains a part of Calhoun County folklore.

Oral storytelling about the outlaws was no doubt much more common than we realize, and some of it was consciously concocted—by men like the yarn-spinning Buffalo Charlie, who had achieved notoriety during the Wisconsin manhunt. Tales from a similar storyteller were actually published in the *Chicago Herald* during that incredible summer of 1881. Titled "A Confederate's Story," the compilation of yarns was related to a reporter by an unnamed man who claimed that he had once shared exploits with the desperadoes:

> "I knew them both intimately. The fact is, I used to train [i.e., hang around] with them once—but that was several years ago. The family came from Virginia and settled in Illinois, just about the time the war broke out. Splendid fellows, those boys were. Hard? No, not exactly hard, but wild, untamed, and ready for any deviltry or any danger. . . .
>
> You ought to see those fellows on horseback. Ride! They'd ride anything that went on four legs. I believe either one of them'd jump at a chance to saddle and bridle a lion and gallop across the country on his back. And shoot! Well, there's no use talking about shooting when they are around. I'm a pretty good shot myself, but I ain't no marker to them. . . .
>
> At that time I was just as wild and reckless as they were. . . . I met Lon Maxwell in a saloon one night. There was a row, and the whole crowd was against him. I didn't like to see a dozen men against one, so I stepped up beside him and took his part. Afterwards I met his brother Ed, and we became fast friends. . . ."

The storyteller—a clear match for the garrulous yarn-spinner Simon Wheeler in Mark Twain's "The Celebrated Jumping Frog of Calaveras County"—went on to provide an exciting account of his only horse-stealing adventure with the Maxwells some years earlier in Kentucky, and their escape from a posse amid a hail of bullets.

The tendency to make the outlaw saga even more dramatic was common in Maxwell storytelling, whether that was accomplished through folkloric elaboration or the conscious development of new scenes that had no basis in fact. A retrospective account of the beginning of their outlawry, published in the *St. Paul Pioneer Press* in 1881, reflects both kinds of embellishment:

> Mr. Dines, the [Blandinsville] clothier, went out to the farm, to see if he recognized the thief. . . . The rascal evidently knew Dines, and as he passed him, Ed in a careless way unbuttoned his coat, displaying two revolvers and a bowie knife. Taking no notice of him, Mr. Dines passed into the house, and while he was there, the brazen-faced rascal stole his horse and rode rapidly away.
>
> Chase was made for him, and the officers sent to arrest him joined in the hunt, but the cheeky scoundrel doubled back on his track and returned to the farmer's house, where he slept until early morning, there being none but women at home. [Another version says that he slept with the farmer's wife.] He left the horse and made off after searching to see if there was anything worth stealing. . . .
>
> A few months afterward, he and his younger brother Lon . . . robbed ten farmers' houses near the adjoining town of LaHarpe. They would go from one farm to another, brandishing their revolvers and demanding everything of value. . . .
>
> The town marshal and a squad tracked them to the next town, and found them in a saloon. The marshal placed his hand on Ed's shoulder and remarked, "You are my prisoner." In a twinkling of an eye Ed covered him with a pistol and exclaimed, "Not by a d——d sight!" Lon and his comrade attended to the rest of the party [i.e., got the drop on the marshal's posse], and the ruffians retired backwards in good order, covering the officers with their pops [i.e., handguns]. . . .
>
> It is known that these desperate criminals have committed many crimes, but those recited give sufficient evidence of their terrible character and boldness. . . .

The closing comment explains what the fabricated details and dramatic saloon scene were intended to demonstrate, to a readership fascinated by the desperado mystique.

The *Pioneer Press* article was surely written by Edward Johnstone, who was so anxious to dramatize the Maxwell story that he used any exciting material that turned up, no matter how questionable it was. Another of his retrospective articles on the Maxwell brothers even dramatizes the use of "30 bloodhounds" and several frontier scouts during the great manhunt—features that had been exposed months earlier as fictions created by Buffalo Charlie. But that exciting account was part of a front-page story by Johnstone in the *New York Times,* and it almost certainly inspired the first dime novel about the Maxwells.

The cheap, paper-covered booklets called "dime novels" began appearing in 1860 and immediately found an immense market. Published by New York firms like Beadle and Adams, Street and Smith, Robert DeWitt, and Frank Tousey, they originally focused on frontiersmen and American Indians, as well as heroes of American wars, and later featured other exciting figures, especially detectives and adventurous boys.

A related publication was "the story paper," which appeared weekly or semimonthly carrying two or three exciting narratives—essentially serialized dime novels—in each issue, sometimes accompanied by poems, jokes, and other short fillers. Those serialized stories also featured sensationalized woodcuts of heroes in peril—escaping from Indians, fighting wild animals, confronting bandits, and the like. Similar illustrations also appeared on the covers of separately published dime novels, luring readers with the promise of high adventure.

Well over 100,000 pulp fiction titles, all characterized by stirring action and heightened description, appeared in one format or the other during the later nineteenth century and early twentieth. Their authors were hacks who turned out their formulaic stories as rapidly as possible, often under a pen name, for a mass audience of mostly men and boys who craved thrilling tales that took them away from their commonplace lives and dramatized ultimate matters—life-and-death struggles.

It is significant that most of those exciting narratives were set in the West, from the Mississippi Valley to the Pacific Coast, and as that suggests, they often reflected the mythic clash of civilizing forces (frontiersmen, homesteaders, and lawmen) and uncivilized antagonists (Indians, wild animals, and outlaws). Although simplistic in characterization, such forerunners of the modern western dramatized the self-assertive, heroic impulse in the making of America and sometimes reflected social class and justice issues.

By the late 1870s and early 1880s dime novels started to feature outlaw heroes as well—real ones like the James brothers and fictional ones like Deadwood Dick. The Maxwells had come to national notoriety at just the right time.

The first dime novel–type narrative about the Maxwell brothers started appearing in Frank Tousey's popular story paper called *The Boys of New York* on December 31, 1881. That was just six weeks after Ed had been lynched, showing how rapidly the author and publisher had moved to take advantage of the Maxwells' recent notoriety. Titled *The Williams Brothers; or, A Thousand-Mile Chase,* and divided into thirty chapters, it ran for twelve weekly installments, concluding on March 18, 1882, with Ed and Lon hiding out in Missouri and awaiting "storms of adventure in the near future, more wild and furious than any they had yet experienced."

The exciting serialized narrative was immensely popular, and it was soon followed by two continuations, *An Endless Chase: A True Story of the Williams Brothers,* and *Hunted Down; or, The Fate of Ed Williams.* The former ran from April 29 to July 22, in thirteen installments, and the latter followed immediately, running from July 29 to October 14, also in thirteen installments. Each also had thirty chapters. The three titles, consisting of ninety short chapters serialized in thirty-eight installments, were components of the same episodic saga, filled with violent confrontations and narrow escapes and climaxed by the lynching at Durand.

The author was "Robert Maynard," one of many pseudonyms, or "house names," used by writers for publisher Frank Tousey. Whoever he really was, "Maynard" became the chief creator of pulp fiction inspired by the Maxwell saga.

The trilogy that first appeared in *The Boys of New York* is the most significant fictionalized treatment of the famous desperadoes. As all three titles suggest, the "chase" after the outlaws unifies the series: Ed and Lon are fugitives, fleeing from those who don't know much about them but want to bring them in or kill them, and for that reason alone, they attract the reader's sympathy.

The author's preeminent addition to the story is his justification for their violence. At the opening of *The Williams Brothers,* they are "honest, upright, industrious young men," working for a "savage, penurious employer," lumber baron Mark Durham. Their real background as robbers and horse thieves is replaced by a mysterious crime in South Carolina, and a later one in Illinois, which eventually brought them to the forests of western Wisconsin—and caused them to replace the name "Maxwell" with the alias that is used throughout the novel. It is soon evident that they are not perpetrators so much as victims, for Durham has repeatedly swindled them out of their wages, and that has evidently been the pattern in their lives—victimization by mean-spirited capitalistic forces.

Epilogue

The author was clearly appealing to the rising sense of victimization among working-class Americans who had suffered through the recent depression and had developed animosity for owners and bosses—symbolized by Mark Durham, a man with economic power but no respect or concern for others. Ed and Lon were about to emerge as heroes in a drama that would examine the challenge of achieving justice in a rapidly changing nation where increasing social class inequality and economic unfairness devalued, and eventually alienated, hordes of poor, struggling workers like themselves.

In the story, the Maxwells' unfortunate social circumstance has been compounded by the public's unwillingness to see the complex reality of their situation, preferring instead to label them as evil and simply hunt them down. As Ed says in chapter 1, "The facts are, Lon, we seem born to be unfortunate. We have been wronged, and when we retaliate with a vengeance, the world turns against us. We are branded as outlaws and hunted as if we were wolves." His brother replies, "We seem likely to never get justice. . . ." As that suggests, the real antagonist in *The Williams Brothers* is the American public, which reduces criminal justice to a good-versus-evil melodrama that allows no comprehension of, or appreciation for, accused lawbreakers and, hence, often fosters more crime. That remarkable perception lends unusual significance to the trilogy. The Maxwells' quest for "justice" also gives them a certain stature and allows American readers to readily sympathize with them.

Before chapter 1 is over, the rich, corrupt, mean-tempered lumber baron arrives with six "cronies," disparages the two poor "vagabonds," refuses to pay them, and starts to beat Lon, which leads to gunfire. Durham is shot dead, along with two of his men. The others flee. As the brothers discuss their plight, Ed says, "I am not in favor of being lynched," thus establishing a tension that runs through all thirty-eight installments as they flee for their lives across several states. Before they rush out into the dark forest, Ed makes the author's social point: "[Durham] has driven us to desperation; he has made us outlaws. . . ." Because Durham symbolizes the uncaring, selfish, capitalistic system that so many of the poor felt oppressed by, the social context of American crime is effectively stated.

In the subsequent chapters of *The Williams Brothers,* the desperadoes shoot one of their pursuers, plunge over a Chippewa River waterfall in a canoe, kill the Coleman brothers in a gunfight (not in Durand, but at a backwoods cabin), elude the famous scouts Buffalo Charlie and Yellowstone Kelly, fight off eight Indians and a pack of vicious bloodhounds, get saved by a lovely woodsman's daughter (whom Lon is attracted to), suffer with gunshot wounds, survive hunger and thirst in "the big woods" while being chased by "at least a thousand men," evade and kill Chicago detective Bart Manning, escape from a family of demented backwoods killers, survive a gunfight with drunken and threatening bullies in a remote tavern, flee down the Mississippi River, kill an unnamed sheriff (based on Lammy) and wound two of his posse near Alton, shoot to death an aggressive policeman near St. Louis, reluctantly rob a stagecoach (pretending to be the James brothers), and, finally, seclude themselves in a Missouri village.

Their struggle to survive amid so much danger makes Ed and Lon heroic—a perception that the real Maxwell brothers identified with, as outlaws, and wanted to promote among the public. Indeed, while all of that dime novel adventure is going on, "the wonderful achievements and daring of the Williams brothers excited the interest of the entire nation" and "the great daily papers from New York, Chicago, Philadelphia, Boston, St. Louis, and, in fact, from all the cities of the United States, were devoting columns to their exploits." So, *The Williams Brothers; or, A Thousand-Mile Chase* refers to the massive 1881 publicity that made the real Ed and Lon nationally known, and prompted the fictionalized treatment of their saga. "Robert Maynard" knew that readers would identify with the fugitives if he simply made the tale *their story*—prompting emotional engagement with them rather than with the men they shoot.

This serialized, episodic story in which hunted and misunderstood men must survive by fleeing, avoiding capture (and lynching), and defending themselves against an array of violent people is an effective commentary on American culture in the Mississippi Valley during the later nineteenth century. A kind of picaresque novel of escape, like *Huckleberry Finn,* but with greater violence, *The Williams Brothers* was also a precursor of the popular TV series *The Fugitive,* which would engage American viewers almost a century later. Although the fictionalized Maxwell brothers are violent men, they also clearly live in an unfair, insensitive, and violent world, so an important point is repeatedly made: Violence is justified whenever a man is threatened or provoked. As Lon says in chapter 24, "It has always been with us, kill or be killed," and Ed responds, "I wish the public could only understand. . . ." Their struggle to be understood—or regarded as men of integrity in a violent, antagonistic world—lends a universal, and tragic, quality to the action-filled serial.

That Ed and Lon are not simply evil men is apparent not only from their reason for being outlaws but from their personal code, which prompts them to admire the courageous Coleman brothers in chapter 4 and to avoid killing the helpless Yellowstone Kelly in chapter 8. They shoot many others, but only in self-defense—to avoid being killed or being captured and lynched. Like so many gunfighter figures in later westerns, they adhere to a private set of values, a code of honor, that allows them to maintain self-respect and somehow rise above their circumstances. They are outlaw heroes.

An Endless Chase claims to be *A True Story of the Williams Brothers,* but it has even less relationship to the actual lives of Ed and Lon than the first story in the trilogy. Set entirely in northern Missouri, it begins with a gathering at Kirksville of three Chicago detectives who have come to pursue the Maxwell brothers because of "the immense rewards" for them. It is apparent that they are little more than bounty hunters, anxious to kill them for money. Later, three other detectives track the brothers as well. In a series of gunfights, Ed and Lon eventually kill all of them. The last is an intrepid Irishman named Terrence O'Rarry, who pursues them relentlessly until Ed finally shoots him in a thrilling, nighttime encounter. Most of the story, in fact, takes place in the dark as the desperadoes struggle to evade and eliminate their pursuers in the woods and at remote cabins.

The darkness is so pervasive that it becomes symbolic of the lurking presence of death in their lives. The two fugitives refer to death several times, always in connection with their destiny—as when Lon says that the only place safe "from all danger of pursuit," for men like them, is "in the grave." It is apparent, in fact, that the Maxwells are foredoomed to defeat. Their heroism in the face of bounty-hunting detectives can only delay the fate that stalks them. *An Endless Chase* thus reminds us of what the western is most deeply about—the testing of masculine character in potentially lethal circumstances. Confronting death.

Very flat, conventional characterizations and repetitious gunfights in the dark make *An Endless Chase* less captivating than the initial story. Also, the limited setting and emphasis on detective antagonists (rather than a mixture of violent Americans) give the story less cultural significance than *The Williams Brothers.*

Hunted Down; or, The Fate of Ed Williams begins with the two fugitives recalling their endless chase, "strewn for a thousand miles with bloodhounds, fire, lead, and steel," and with Ed's discovery that six more of "Pinkerton's Chicago detectives," together with a local posse, are pursuing them in the Missouri forest. As the story proceeds, the outlaws escape from an ambush in the woods, ride on the cowcatcher of a speeding freight train, kill a marksman hired by the detectives, hide from pursuers in a cornfield, exchange gunfire with posse members on horseback, shoot a threatening hunter, encounter belligerent local rustics at a dance (where Ed copes, in a comic scene, with a 200-pound girl named "Julia Solid"), survive a cyclone that is followed by a rainstorm and a flood, save a child who was blown into a treetop, rescue a young woman named Bessie and her aging mother, kill and wound more pursuers in another gunfight, swim across an icy stream, steal a boat to cross the Missouri River, hide in a farmhouse cellar and a barn, and shoot to death a farmer who fires on Lon and wounds him. In the midst of all this, Lon and Bessie fall in love, and a fabulous coincidence emerges: The outlaws discover that Bessie is the daughter of lumber baron Mark Durham, and that she and her mother had been forced to flee from his abuse many years earlier. Hence, the gunfight that had launched the "endless chase" of the Maxwells had, in fact, freed Bessie Durham and her mother from the dread of being discovered and killed. Although improbable, this coincidence emphasizes that in the trilogy Ed and Lon function as psychological projections of the reader's latent desire to destroy what is evil and rescue what is good—by assertive actions based on what the heart knows is right. They are not just survivors in a violent world, but heroes—like the central characters in later outlaw films such as *Jesse James, Billy the Kid, Badmen of Missouri* (about the Younger brothers), and *When the Daltons Rode.*

The final chapter—"the last dread scene in this truthful drama"—is focused entirely on November 19, 1881, as Ed appears at the Durand courthouse, pleads self-defense to the charge of murdering the Coleman brothers, and is hanged by a "wild and furious" mob—men who behave "like wild beasts clamoring and fighting to suck the blood of some animal." Society's culpability for the Maxwell tragedy is effectively realized here, as Ed becomes a kind of sacrificial scapegoat for violent drives that lie deep within the American public. In a sense, the mythic conflict of civilized and uncivilized forces, so typical of the western, has been reversed as the victimized, justice-seeking outlaw is brutally murdered by supposedly civilized townspeople.

Like the hero in a Greek tragedy, Ed in the trilogy is an essentially good person but is also flawed—by his willingness to use violence—and he refuses to compromise with the forces arrayed against him, suffers greatly as a result, and ultimately succumbs to defeat. But his destruction has a kind of salutary impact, for he reveals to all who identify with him that a human being—in this case, an American seeking justice—is capable of truly heroic self-assertion. This tragic pattern in the trilogy lifts it above the level of typical dime novel fiction, despite the sometimes shallow dialogue and contrived plotting.

Although Ed is called "the terror of the West," the narrative closes not with criticism of his lawbreaking but with condemnation of the lynching: "The mob went unpunished for the murder of Ed Williams, and all mankind, ashamed at the disgraceful death of one who, having been 'Hunted Down,' deserved a fair trial, have ceased to make any efforts to capture his brother, Lon, who is still at large in our great Western wilderness." The author is suggesting, of course, that Lon somehow deserved to go unsought and unpunished because the society that had hunted them relentlessly and had finally lynched Ed was itself guilty of great wrongdoing.

Throughout the trilogy there is ambiguity about the Maxwell brothers: They are presented as violent men who repeatedly kill those who pursue them, but they have essential integrity in a corrupt world, and they are models of determination, resourcefulness, and courage. As the author says in the first chapter of *An Endless Chase,* "While we cannot admire the cold-blooded deeds of the Williams brothers, their coolness and acts of daring have excited the interest of the world." Or at least, the interest of Americans, who were in a sense co-creators of the outlaw hero, who was emerging in pulp fiction to dramatize fearless individualism, to critique the limitations of the justice system, and to express American ambivalence about violent men.

The first separately published dime novel about the Maxwell brothers appeared in Frank Tousey's "Five-Cent Wide Awake Library" series on February 13, 1882, while the initial story about Ed and Lon was still being serialized. Titled *The Maxwell Brothers; or, The Chase of a Season,* it is an alternative, shorter version of the trilogy, and is the only pulp fiction about the outlaws to consistently employ Ed and Lon's real name rather than their alias. Some scenes and lines are identical to the trilogy, demonstrating that the same author had turned it out while writing the series for *The Boys of New York.* The author's name was given as "Kit Clyde," but that too was a house name used by various hacks writing for Frank Tousey.

Some scenes in *The Maxwell Brothers* are distinctive, if rather undeveloped. One depicts the fugitives' nighttime visit to Fannie's grave, where Lon breaks down, praises his young wife's innocence, and laments his own misery. Another shows Ed responding to a newspaper article titled "The Bloody Maxwells," which describes them, announces the sizable reward, and proclaims that they are coming. He remarks to Lon that, in a sense, the newspapers are "hounding us down." Whoever he was, "Kit Clyde" realized that the press had played a central role in the pursuit of the Maxwells.

Epilogue

In December 1882 Frank Tousey launched a new dime novel series, "The Five-Cent Weekly Library," which soon included three more titles about the Maxwell brothers, all written by "Robert Maynard": *The Williams Brothers as Fugitives* (June 22, 1883), *The Williams Brothers Afloat* (July 16, 1883), and *The Williams Brothers and the Detectives* (September 3, 1883). Just twelve chapters long, *The Williams Brothers as Fugitives* is a condensed version of the first third of *The Williams Brothers; or, A Thousand-Mile Chase*. It omits the pursuit by detective Bart Manning as well as all the scenes that occur during their escape down the Mississippi River and in Missouri. Nevertheless, it is an exciting account of pursuit in the Wisconsin forest. *The Williams Brothers Afloat* does not survive—at least, in a known collection. It is surely a revision of the middle third of that first story in the trilogy, which deals with Ed and Lon's adventures along the big river. *The Williams Brothers and the Detectives,* also just twelve chapters long, completely reworks the section on detective Bart Manning that appeared in the first story of the trilogy. In the 1883 dime novel, the daring Pinkerton agent is their chief pursuer, and the Maxwells do not kill him this time, but they do shoot dead his two associates. This work shows the huge drift toward robbers and detectives for the standard dime novel content that would mark the 1880s.

Two other serialized dime novels by "Robert Maynard" that reflect the Maxwell saga also appeared in *The Boys of New York* during 1883. The earliest was *Buffalo Charlie, the Young Hunter: A True Story of the West,* which started appearing on February 24. It was simply inspired by the yarn-spinning figure who had briefly conned the posse and the press during the great Wisconsin manhunt. The story depicts a buffalo-hunting youth in the far West, "beyond the borders of civilization," whose family is slaughtered by the Indians and who then becomes an Indian-fighting scout and frontier guide. In two later chapters he and his comrade Yellowstone Kelly attempt to catch the fugitive Williams brothers with the help of some friendly Indians, but after a gunfight the outlaws escape. As that suggests, the author probably found it difficult to mesh the far-western, Indian-fighting background of his hero with the famous outlaws of the Mississippi Valley.

By the fall of that year "Maynard" was experimenting with another concept. The growing popularity of detective heroes prompted him to create a more effective combination of plot forces, in a serialized dime novel that featured young sleuth Jerry Owens in pursuit of the elusive outlaws. *Pinkerton's Little Detective; or, The Dread of the Williams Brothers,* started appearing in *The Boys of New York* on November 3, 1883. It opens with the great detective chief Allan Pinkerton learning that the Williams brothers have killed his well-known agent Bart Manning—which connects the story to the recent trilogy about the outlaws. Pinkerton then decides to assign that case to an even better agent, Jerry Owens, a teenager known as "the Little Detective," who is renowned as a master of disguise.

As that suggests, Ed and Lon are not the protagonists of the story, but merely the antagonists, the thoroughly evil badmen that the young hero tries to bring in, dead or alive. The use of a boy hero reflects the increasing drift of pulp fiction toward young male readers, as does the popularity of *The Boys of New York* story paper in which it appeared.

The Maxwell brothers were eventually featured in three more detective stories that were serialized in *The Boys of New York: Jerry Owens and the Williams Brothers; or, Chased from Shore to Shore,* which started appearing on January 30, 1892; *Jerry Owens and the Beacon Light; or, The Signal Fires of the Williams Brothers, a Thrilling Story of Missouri,* which began appearing on June 11, 1892; and *Jerry Owens' Midnight Signal; or, The Williams Brothers Outwitted,* which started appearing on October 7, 1893.

Like the trilogy, *Jerry Owens and the William Brothers* reflects a sympathetic view of Ed and Lon, portraying them as outlaw heroes. As the story opens, they have been working as "axmen" at a mill in Michigan and are asking for their overdue pay, but they are insulted by the company's evil bookkeeper, Tom Hix, and then accused of being stage robbers by the rich, penurious owner, Colonel Elliott. A fight erupts and they flee. As in the trilogy, the Maxwells are clearly victims of society. "We would have lived like honest men if they had permitted us to," Lon says, but instead, "we have been wronged, driven by one misfortune after another to crime; and crime grows, so we never know when and where it will end." In short, they have become enmeshed by fate, and must flee, hide, rob, and defend themselves in order to survive. Alienation, and a life of theft and violence, have been forced upon them.

Early in the story, Lon—who is more prominent than Ed in the first half of the novel—explains to Colonel Elliott their unfortunate situation and their assertive response to it, and in the process, he crystallizes the ethic of the outlaw hero: "The Williams brothers have been branded as outlaws. Many crimes of which we are innocent are imputed to us, and if we should be captured we will hang. We are determined to die rather than be captured. We have never taken a life save in self-defense, and have never hesitated to kill, when necessary, to save ourselves." Later, another exchange between Lon and the selfish, insensitive Colonel Elliott reflects the issue of responsibility for violent crime that runs throughout the work:

> "What harm have we done you, Colonel Elliott? We did honest work, but you listened to Tom Hix, who slandered us," said Lon.
> "Honest work, indeed," said Colonel Elliott, white with rage. "You need not plead honesty in anything. Villains! You who rob, steal, and plunder at will!"
> "Necessity forces us to this."
> "Does it?"

The author's examination of this issue makes *Jerry Owens and the Williams Brothers* the most important narrative about Ed and Lon outside of the trilogy.

The serialized dime novel has a dual focus, both on the detective hero, Jerry Owens, who relentlessly and courageously pursues Ed and Lon, confronting them face to face several times, and on the outlaws themselves, who struggle to avoid capture and death. Like Deputy Marshal Samuel Gerard (Tommy Lee Jones) in *The Fugitive,* who pursues the brave and clever Richard Kimble (Harrison Ford) because that is his job and he is driven to succeed at it, Jerry Owens has an identity based on always succeeding as a detective and is relentless even when he admires his quarry—as he does in this case. He tells them, "I know you are brave men," and he even comments at one point, "It is all professional . . . and I hope you bear me no ill will." The outlaws, in turn, express admiration for him. Clearly, there is much similarity between the fugitives (especially Lon) and the detective, who possess the same essential decency and courage. As Ed tells Owens, "Men are never so bad but that you may find some good in them," and Lon adds, "Even outlaws. . . ."

The second half of *Jerry Owens and the Williams Brothers* emphasizes the episodic chase plot, as the fugitives flee to the West, managing one hairbreadth escape after another, but are unable to shake off or kill the resourceful detective, who tracks them through Missouri, Kansas, Colorado, Nevada, and California. They finally escape into Mexico, but not before Colonel Elliott locates them on a wagon train, pulls a gun on them, and is stabbed to death by Ed. As with the killing of Mark Durham in the trilogy, that is a justifiable act of violence, but it will simply be viewed by the public as another Maxwell murder.

Like the trilogy, *Jerry Owens and the Williams Brothers* dramatizes the difference between the public standard of right and wrong, enshrined in the law, and a more personal, and perhaps natural, standard developed by individuals who must repeatedly respond to violent confrontation. In a sense, the Maxwells' escape here is not just from a detective, but from an impersonal and inadequate system of justice that society is striving to impose on them. Many other stories about American outlaw heroes, in books and films, would later center on this issue, first dramatized in dime novel fiction about the Maxwell brothers.

Unfortunately, like *Pinkerton's Little Detective,* which appeared nine years earlier, *Jerry Owens and the Beacon Light; or, The Signal Fires of the Williams Brothers, a Thrilling Story of Missouri* simply depicts Ed and Lon as badmen, the detective hero's antagonists. In this case, they are trying to assemble and direct a gang of robbers by the use of beacon fires on a Missouri bluff. Also, the narrative revolves around someone other than Owens—an orphaned youth, Roy Mitchell, who is mistreated and driven out by his shortsighted relative, Squire Thornton, and temporarily joins the Williams gang. *Jerry Owens and the Beacon Light* is, then, a kind of cautionary tale about an essentially good young man who falls into bad company and finds that he has "compromised himself with crime." He is almost killed, both by the desperadoes, who soon regard him as a traitor, and by a lynch mob, headed by the unscrupulous Bob Cole, his rival for the love of fair-haired Carrie Thornton. But after various chases and gunfights, things turn out well in the end: The Maxwell gang is broken up, and Roy marries his lovely sweetheart.

Jerry Owens' Midnight Signal; or, The Williams Brothers Outwitted was the final dime novel related to the Maxwell brothers. Also set in Missouri, which had a national reputation for lawlessness, it pits the young detective against Ed, Lon, and other members of their infamous gang. The plot centers on the abduction of a rich farmer, George Lyons, who is held both to extort money and to coerce his lovely daughter Grace to marry the evil Joe Rush, a gang member. After an incredible number of gunfights, captures, and escapes—including the abduction, escape, and recapture of Grace herself—a climactic gun battle occurs at the outlaws' secret cavern, and the Williams brothers are aided by a new gang member, young Bill Dalton. Although defeated, the three of them survive—Ed and Lon to become "a terror to the West" and their comrade to eventually become "the chief of the Dalton gang." Those outlaws had, in fact, become famous train and bank robbers during the early 1890s, only to meet disaster at Coffeyville, Kansas, in 1892, one year before *Jerry Owens' Midnight Signal* started appearing. The only Dalton brother still on the loose in 1893 was Bill. "Robert Maynard" was, then, connecting his popular Maxwell brothers material with an outlaw who was more newsworthy in the 1890s.

In that decade Frank Tousey launched another dime novel series, "The New York Detective Library," in which he eventually published eight hundred titles. Eight of the "Williams Brothers" novels were reprinted for that series, including the popular trilogy (on February 8, May 17, and November 1, 1890), the first three of the Jerry Owens titles (on October 27, 1888; December 10, 1892; and March 17, 1894), and both *The Williams Brothers as Fugitives* and *The Williams Brothers and the Detectives* (published together on December 19, 1891). During the closing decade of the nineteenth century, those "Detective Library" titles provided a new, and probably larger, readership for fiction inspired by the Maxwell saga.

The fact that some dime novels about the Maxwells depict them as outlaw heroes, while others, including the last two, simply present them as badmen, shows the divided American view of western lawbreakers. Jesse James is perhaps the preeminent example of an outlaw whose robbery and violence were deplored but who was also admired by many for his courage and individualism. The notorious Nebraska horse thief and killer Doc Middleton was another. A convicted lawbreaker, he was eventually celebrated as an "absolutely fearless" man who "played a fair game" and "never took a life unless forced to do so."

From one viewpoint Ed and Lon are simply evildoers, antagonists to be struggled with, and triumphed over, by heroic figures like detective Jerry Owens. But from another perspective, they reflect aspects of the American male's mythic identity (courage, self-reliance, individualism, integrity), so their adventures reveal how heroically men can struggle against oppressive circumstances, especially violent pursuers. In one fictional guise, they symbolize American fears—for they are threats to the developing social order—and in the other, they symbolize American hopes—for they are powerless common men who refuse to be defeated and, in their quest to survive, reinvent themselves as heroes.

It is interesting to note that the fifteen or so dime novels on Billy the Kid depict him as a badman who robs and kills, for it was only in the 1920s that he finally emerged as an outlaw hero, worthy of public admiration—and depiction in numerous Hollywood films. But the transformation of the Maxwell brothers, in dime novel fiction, went in the opposite direction. They were outlaw heroes long before Billy finally made the grade, but they ended their story lives as badmen, in the final Jerry Owens novels, and were never revived as outlaw heroes for twentieth-century novels and films. One reason was surely the fact that they were never associated with the far West, which became the mythic Wild West, the obligatory setting for westerns. For great western mythmakers like director John Ford and writer Louis L'Amour, Illinois and Wisconsin were somehow unrelated to the world of outlaws and gunfights, sheriffs and posses—but the Maxwell saga demonstrates how untrue that was in the nineteenth century.

To the extent that dime novel outlaw heroes like Ed and Lon could also remain essentially good men who were somehow justified in using violence, they also reflected American myth—especially the cultural belief that unjust circumstances, and manly character, call for violent action. Surrendering to a sheriff or policeman and trusting your fate to a court of law is not an admired American response to perceived injustice, as countless western books and films would later demonstrate. Individualism demands self-assertion.

The real-life Maxwell brothers believed that too.

Shortly after the earliest pulp fiction about the Maxwells had appeared, another kind of book about them was also published. Entitled *Twice Outlawed,* it had a lengthy and sensationalized subtitle: *A Personal History of Ed and Lon Maxwell, alias the Williams Brothers, a Record of Highway Robbery, Horse Stealing, Romance, and Murder, to Which Is Added a Detailed and Graphic Account of the Arrest and Lynching of Edward Maxwell at Durand, Wisconsin, November 19, 1881.* The author was a certain "Adrian Percy," about whom nothing is known. The name was probably a pseudonym for someone who had followed, or had participated in, the evolving saga of the Maxwells.

It is tempting to conclude that Edward Johnstone of the *St. Paul Pioneer Press* was the author, especially since he had written more articles on the Maxwells than anyone else, for the *Pioneer Press* and other newspapers, and his "RED LETTER RECORD" article on their outlaw career obviously influenced the overall shape of the book. Moreover, at one point "Adrian Percy" refers to "The *Pioneer Press,* an excellent paper printed at St. Paul, [which] . . . had an expert correspondent in the field at an early day." That could be disguised self-praise, Johnstone's covert way of celebrating his work as an eyewitness reporter.

Whatever the case, *Twice Outlawed* is much indebted to Johnstone's coverage of the Maxwell story for the *Pioneer Press*—and to exclusive manhunt reports for the *Chicago Times,* which may also have been written by him. The 194-page book is undated, but it probably appeared in 1882.

Twice Outlawed is a true-crime narrative. That is, it intends to be a nonfictional account of the famous criminals, like Truman Capote's *In Cold Blood* and Norman Mailer's *The Executioner's Song*. Many contemporary true crime writers, including Capote and Mailer, have been accused of fictionalizing now and again as they struggled to engage the reader with their essentially factual narratives, so we should not be surprised to find that nineteenth-century writers sometimes did the same thing. In the case of *Twice Outlawed,* however, there is a great deal of fictionalizing—coupled with uncritical acceptance of Maxwell folklore—that makes for a very untrustworthy historical narrative. One might say, in fact, that unlike "Robert Maynard" and "Kit Clyde," the author stuck to the reported facts—however inaccurate they were—when he had them but did not hesitate to imagine whatever he thought would be appropriate to dramatize what might have happened.

The characterization of Ed is simply based on the notion that such an outlaw must have been shiftless and prone to crime when he was young: He "followed nothing in particular for a living," was "fond of dissipation," and caroused with wicked friends "that fast were dragging him onward and downward." Ed is, in fact, depicted as an "evil genius" whose "depraved mind" prompts him to lure his younger brother into a life of crime. In short there is no real psychological understanding of Ed—and very little of Lon. Hence, the author provides a good example of the uncomprehending American public that is the real antagonist in the dime novel trilogy—as he views Ed and Lon through the dark, mythic prism of the outlaw stereotype rather than depicting them as complex human beings.

As the account proceeds, some completely fictional scenes are grafted onto the developing story of Maxwell lawbreaking: The brothers drink and plot in a saloon, steal horses and sell them at a rural fair, sleep with whores at a dance hall, and so on. Sometimes the author quotes vague newspaper sources, as when an unnamed "St. Louis paper" records their arrest at a Minnesota whorehouse—which suggests that "Adrian Percy" was simply manufacturing some sources to lend a documentary quality to his narrative. Later, Lon's love affair with Fannie is fully dramatized, with sentimentalized commentary on their inner lives that no one could have reported.

Another great shortcoming of *Twice Outlawed* is the complete lack of cultural context. The true crime narrative has no meaning—other than the shallow, moralistic notion that drinking, whoring, and petty theft lead to violent crime—because the world of the Maxwells is never reconstructed. Nothing is understood about the nineteenth-century American culture that produced and pursued the desperadoes.

Epilogue

Since *Twice Outlawed* appeared in the early 1880s, no extensive nonfictional account of the Maxwells has been published. In 1971 a short article titled "The Day They Hanged Ed Williams," written by Earl V. Chapin, appeared in *Real West* magazine, and that was surely the most widely disseminated twentieth-century piece on the once-famous desperadoes. Despite the narrowly focused title, Chapin's article is a brief general review of their career. Based largely on *Twice Outlawed,* it is inaccurate as well. Various historical newspaper articles on the Maxwells have also appeared, but otherwise, the notorious outlaw brothers have been forgotten—which is to say that, unlike Jesse James and Billy the Kid, they no longer symbolize any troubling issues or mythic components of the American experience.

But they once did.

Acknowledgments

Because *Dime Novel Desperadoes* deals with the Maxwell outlaws and their pioneering family in several states and attempts to recover their rural and small-town cultural contexts in some detail, the assistance of a wide variety of local historians, archivists, librarians, and genealogists was essential. To the dozen people listed on the dedication page who responded to many requests for information, my special thanks.

I also extend my appreciation to the following people who provided information and research materials during the long period (1998–2007) when this book was in progress: Ruth Bauer Anderson, Minnesota Historical Society Library; John Barnason, Andersen Library, University of Minnesota; Jackie Behle, Grand Island (Nebraska) Public Library; Patti Blount, Durand Community Library; Marjorie R. Bordner, Fulton County Genealogical and Historical Society; Roger D. Bridges, the Rutherford B. Hayes Presidential Center Library; Margaret Bush, Tazewell County (Illinois) Genealogical and Historical Society; Karen Butler, Adams County (Nebraska) Genealogical Society; Russ Caplewski, Stuhr Museum of the Prairie Pioneer; Jim Cohlmeyer, Illinois State Archives; Nancy Dolan, Quincy (Illinois) Public Library; Karen Eckhardt, Holstein, Nebraska; Andrea Faling, Nebraska State Historical Society; Lois Frahm, Blue Hill, Nebraska; Roger Gambrel, Joliet Public Library; Betty Gibboney, Lewistown, Illinois; Meredith Gillies, Andersen Library, University of Minnesota; Dee Anna Grimsrud, Wisconsin Historical Society; Linda Hanabarger, Fayette County (Illinois) Genealogical and Historical Society; James L. Hansen, Wisconsin Historical Society; Dan Hanson, Dunn County (Wisconsin) Historical Society; Barron Holland, Stuttgart, Germany;

Katherine Hull, Upper Sandusky (Ohio) Community Library; Noel E. Hurford, Rosiclare, Illinois; Yetive Jacobson, Minden, Nebraska; Helen Janson, Taylor County (Iowa) Historical Society; Alyson Jones, Chalmer Davee Library, University of Wisconsin–River Falls; Jean Kay, Historical Society of Quincy and Adams Counties (Illinois); Karen Keehr, Stuhr Museum of the Prairie Pioneer; Sandy Kennedy, Bedford (Iowa) Public Library; Frank S. Kennett, Dunn County (Wisconsin) Historical Society; Ed Knight, Jerseyville, Illinois; Dan Kubick, Omaha Public Library; Avonelle Lamphere, Durand Community Library; Dave Lee, Barry, Illinois; Margaret Lewis, Tennessee, Illinois; Shirley Mahlin, Giltner, Nebraska; Wendy Martin, Havana, Illinois; Natalie McConnell, Blandinsville, Illinois; Mildred L. McCormick, Golconda, Illinois; Barbara Miksecek, Metropolitan Police Department Library, St. Louis; Loren Musgrave, Nevada, Ohio; Linda Oelheim, Illinois State Historical Library; Mary Osborne, Decatur, Georgia; Roy Ostenso, Dunn County (Wisconsin) Historical Society; Coryl Pace, Bedford (Iowa) Public Library; L. Emerson Retzer, Calhoun County (Illinois) Historical Society; Lorraine Riese, Holstein, Nebraska; John Russell, Menomonie, Wisconsin; Sandi Salen, Bedford, Iowa; Kay Shelton, Founders Memorial Library, Northern Illinois University; Vera Slabey, Pepin County (Wisconsin) Historical Society; David L. Smith, Cumberland County (Pennsylvania) Historical Society and Hamilton Library Association; Peggy Southerland, Stillwater (Minnesota) Public Library; Kevin Charles Stealy, Brainerd, Minnesota; Robert E. Sterling, Joliet (Illinois) Junior College; Geraldine Strey, Wisconsin Historical Society; Lynne Thomas, Founders Memorial Library, Northern Illinois University; John D. Waggoner, Macomb, Illinois; and Gene Q. Watson, former sheriff of Hall County, Nebraska.

To Bill Cook, Tom Joswick, Tracy Knight, Kathy Nichols, and Marla Vizdal, all of Western Illinois University, my sincere thanks for reading and commenting on drafts of the manuscript during 2005 and 2006. Their insights made this a better book. I am similarly indebted to Gerald Danzer, professor of history at the University of Illinois at Chicago, and Rodney O. Davis, emeritus professor of history at Knox College, who read and critiqued the manuscript for the University of Illinois Press.

Also, my thanks to the following staff members at Western Illinois University's Malpass Library: Sally McPherson, Archives and Special Collections; Kathy Dahl, Kate Joswick, and Krista Bowers Sharpe, Reference; Diane Billeter, Julie Hannen, and Linda Wade, Interlibrary Loan; Brian Andrews and Chet Derry, Computer Services; and Cecil Compton, IRAD intern.

My appreciation is also extended to Chad Sperry of the McDonough

County GIS Center at Western Illinois University, who prepared the maps employed in the book.

I am grateful for the wise counsel of Willis G. Regier, director of the University of Illinois Press, and the expertise of his staff, especially managing editor Rebecca Crist, copy editor Anne Rogers, and art director Copenhaver Cumpston.

Some financial support for research expenses was provided by the Haines Family Fund, established at Western Illinois University by Vilma Kinney. My sincere thanks to her as well.

Finally, I want to express appreciation to my wife, Garnette, who adapted herself to my busy work schedule, and my travel demands, during the nine years that it took to produce this book.

Notes

The following notes include hundreds of nineteenth-century sources, mostly newspaper articles. In using quotations from those sources, I have occasionally corrected spelling and altered punctuation for the sake of clarity, and I have standardized the spelling of geographical and personal names. Because some newspaper articles have extensive, multiline titles, I have generally cited just the first line or two of a title. Quotations from newspapers, if clearly dated in the text, are not cited. Photocopies of all the articles and public records employed in the book are available in the Hallwas Collection in the Archives and Special Collections unit of Malpass Library at Western Illinois University in Macomb, Illinois. That collection also has a lengthy bibliography of newspaper articles on the Maxwells.

Prologue

1   *"an open winter":* Hallwas, *Macomb,* 69.
     Macomb: On nineteenth-century Macomb, see Hallwas, *Macomb.* Also, Hallwas, *McDonough County Heritage,* includes a section on "Sources" for the community and county (187–89), including county histories published in 1878, 1885, 1907, and 1968.
     "mud-boats": Hallwas, *Macomb,* 69.
2   *"prosperity, progress":* "The Opera House," *Macomb Eagle,* Apr. 26, 1873.
     "McDonough County's most prominent citizen": History of McDonough County (1885), 1090. See also Hallwas, "Citizen Chandler," *McDonough County Heritage,* 89–91.
     "The Most Beautiful": "MACOMB ENTERPRISE," *Macomb Journal,* Apr. 17, 1873.

2 *"a drama":* "The John Whittley Dramatic Company," *Macomb Eagle,* Aug. 9, 1873. The play was based on an 1869 dime novel, *Buffalo Bill, the King of the Border Men.*

   "held his hearers": "SCHUYLER COLFAX," *Macomb Journal,* Feb. 17, 1876.

3 *"the greatest living":* Ad for Beecher's lecture, *Macomb Eagle,* Sept. 21, 1878.

   "to rise up from": Beecher, 102–3.

   "A DESPERADO": *Macomb Eagle,* Feb. 21, 1874.

4 *"a famous Cornwall boy":* "Jack the Giant Killer," *Macomb Journal,* Nov. 24, 1881.

   exploits with . . . robbers: LeSage, *Adventures of Gil Blas of Santillane,* vol. I, 16–36.

5 *a postwar crime wave:* Papke, *Framing the Criminal,* 8–9.

   an era of defiant lawbreakers: A thorough, if dated, outlaw bibliography is Adams, *Six-Guns and Saddle Leather* (1969). Brief, authoritative accounts of most of the outlaws mentioned here can be found in Horan, *Authentic Wild West;* Lamar, *Reader's Encyclopedia of the American West;* and Nash, *Virgin Land,* among others.

   "Western Bandit Volunteers": Before his execution, a gang member revealed the extent of this group's operation: "THE LAW VINDICATED," *Macomb Journal,* Mar. 20, 1873. On another gang, see "A Horse Thief's Autobiography," *Canton Register,* Feb. 13, 1874.

   less-noted outlaws: For an overview of Brice, see Hallwas, "Joe Brice: Fulton County Bad Man"; for Harrison Johnson, see "THE JOHNSON GANG," *Macomb Eagle,* June 28, 1866; for the Berry gang, see Conover and Brecher, *Lynch Law.*

6 *"I would be mobbed":* Letter to Governor Joseph W. McClurg, June 1870, in Horan, *Authentic Wild West,* 38–39.

   "more like a panther": "THE MAXWELL BOYS," *Macomb Journal,* Dec. 17, 1903.

7 *"reign of terror":* "The County's Worst Desperadoes," *Macomb Journal,* Mar. 17, 1924.

Chapter 1: The Maxwell Family Moves West

9 *The Maxwell family:* Information about the family background in Pennsylvania was derived from many sources, including Gary L. Jacobsen, "Descendants of William Maxwell" and other Maxwell family genealogical records; David Maxwell, "Descendants of William Maxwell" (genealogical typescript, 2005); John D. Maxwell, "Maxwell History" (handwritten, 1920, Cumberland County Historical Society); "Maxwell Report of Work in Cumberland and Franklin Counties" (typescript, from the Flowers Folder, Cumberland County Historical Society); Mary Osborne, "Descen-

dants of William Maxwell" (genealogical typescript); and correspondence with the author from Wilmer B. Maxwell, Jan. 30 2005; Stanley Miller, Researcher, Cumberland County Historical Society, March 26, May 26, July 23, 2004; Aug. 2, 30, 2005; David L. Smith, Librarian, Cumberland County Historical Society, Jan. 31, 2005; and Donna (Maxwell) Tivener (e-mailed records), May 24, 30, June 24, 2003. The Miller letters include photocopies of records from Cumberland County. Copies of all these are in the Hallwas Collection.

9 *Cumberland:* On early Pennsylvania and Cumberland County, see Dunaway, *History of Pennsylvania*; Lemon, *Best Poor Man's Country*; Majewski, *House Dividing*; and Wing, *History of Cumberland County*.

10 *the county's population grew:* Majewski, *House Dividing*, 39.

 William Maxwell served: Revolutionary War records, Fifth Series, Vol. 2.

 the Walnut Bottom Road: That road and the families who lived along it in 1858 are shown on the Southampton Township map, in the *Atlas Map of Cumberland County, Pennsylvania*, 18.

 he died in 1808: Township tax records show that he had 248 acres in the year of his death. See also the Will Book (1808), 284, Cumberland County Historical Society.

 the outlaws' grandfather: Jacobsen, "Descendants of William Maxwell," Hallwas Collection.

11 *their first child, James D.:* A handwritten page in the Maxwell family Bible provides the birth and death dates for all of their children; copy in the Hallwas Collection.

 George Lee: Schaumann, *Taverns of Cumberland County*, 182.

 1850 Southampton Township tax roll: Cumberland County Historical Society collection.

 An inventory of his possessions: Vendue record, William Maxwell (Oct. 10, 1852), M254, Box 18, Cumberland County Historical Society collection.

 population and . . . land prices: Majewski, *House Dividing*, 38–45.

12 *the outlaws' mother:* Jacobsen genealogical papers and letters to the author from Stanley Miller, Aug. 2, 30, 2005, both in the Hallwas Collection.

 she married David Maxwell: The family Bible incorrectly lists their marriage date as September 9. A handwritten account of the Maxwell family by a descendant, in the Jacobsen papers, Hallwas Collection, gives the correct date, as do church records.

13 *Sarah . . . married William Clark:* Jacobsen genealogical papers, Hallwas Collection.

 The 500-mile-long journey: For early routes used in Pennsylvania, see Cuff, *Atlas of Pennsylvania*, 96.

 Ohio: On early Ohio, see Havighurst, *Ohio*; Knepper, *Ohio and Its People*; and Roseboom, *History of Ohio*.

13   *Wyandot County:* See the *Atlas of Wyandot County, Ohio; History of Wyandot County, Ohio* (1884); Baughman, *Past and Present of Wyandot County;*
Howe, *Historical Collections of Ohio;* and Vogel, *Indians of Ohio.* Also
helpful is "Wyandot County: Past, Present, and Future," *Wyandot Pioneer,*
July 23, 1857.

14   *because of Indians:* Vogel, *Indians of Ohio,* 25–67.
David R. . . . bought eighty acres: His several land purchases in Crane
Township are noted in the land deed records, Recorder's Office, Wyandot
County Courthouse.
"one of the best known": "Death of D. R. Maxwell," *Wyandot County Re-
publican,* Sept. 27, 1894.

15   *later records find them:* The U.S. Census for 1870 finds them in Marshall
County, Indiana, but the birthplaces of their children show that they
had gone to Illinois at the end of the 1850s. The 1880 U.S. Census finds
them in Marshall County, Illinois.
the Maxwells' first child: A handwritten entry in the Maxwell family Bible
(copy in the Hallwas Collection) gives his name, "William Edmuston
Maxwell," and birth date.
railroads were spreading: See Knepper, *Ohio and Its People,* 159–62.
"GOING BY STEAM": Upper Sandusky *Democratic Pioneer,* Nov. 17, 1853.

16   *a . . . vision of the West:* On the West as myth, see Smith, *Virgin Land.*
"we are bound to rise": "Progress of Our Town," *Upper Sandusky Democratic Pioneer,* Apr. 6, 1854.
"street brawls": "ROWDYISM," *Wyandot Pioneer,* Feb. 19, 1857.

17   *two more children:* The birth dates for Alice and Lon, and later Maxwell
children, are from a handwritten page in the Maxwell family Bible, Hallwas Collection.
settlers were moving on: "Going West," *Wyandot Pioneer,* Apr. 13, 1854.
Illinois: See the histories by Howard, *Illinois,* and Davis, *Frontier Illinois.*
Hoffmann's bibliography, *Guide to the History of Illinois,* is superb.
a land of opportunity: An influential early account of the state was John
Mason Peck's *Gazetteer of Illinois,* which referred to Illinois as "the 'Ca-
naan' of America," a place "where enterprise and industry meet with a
sure reward" (328).
"Then move your family westward": "Elanoy," in Hallwas, *Illinois Literature,*
118.
"a man of very small means . . . land is cheap": "The Prairie State," 589, 591.
Sarah Maxwell: The 1860 federal census for Linn Township, in Woodford
County, reveals that William and Sarah Woodburn had their older children in Pennsylvania during the late 1830s, and their younger children
were born in Ohio from about 1841 to 1851.
older brother William: The history by Perrin and Hill, *Past and Present of
Woodford County,* 360, says he was at Washburn.

Chapter 2: The Maxwells in Troubled Fulton County

19   *Fulton County:* Helpful sources, listed in the bibliography, are the *Atlas Map of Fulton County, Illinois;* the *History of Fulton County, Illinois* (1879); the later histories edited by Bateman, Bordner, and Clark; and *Historic Fulton County.*

    Waterford: See the topographical characteristics, school and church locations, and names of the 1870 landowners in the *Atlas Map of Fulton County,* 116–17. That atlas also reveals the poverty of the township in a table of population and economic statistics, 5.

21   *Just as Pennsylvanians:* See Meyer, *Making the Heartland Quilt,* 204–7.

    In Waterford Township: U.S. Census, 1850 and 1860.

    By 1860 Lewistown: U.S. Census, 1860; also, Ethel Duval Henry et al., "Lewistown Township," in Clark, *History of Fulton County,* 194–203; and "Lewistown," in *Historic Fulton County,* 157–92.

    "We have not yet fully caught": "Fulton Seminary—Progress of the Enterprise," *Fulton Democrat,* June 18, 1859.

    Farm life in that era: See Schob, *Hired Hands and Plowboys,* as well as Schlereth, *Victorian America,* 35–43, and Sutherland, *Expansion of Everyday Life,* 132–46.

22   *"We got up at 4 A.M.":* As quoted in Carl Landrum, "Life on the Farm before the Civil War," *Quincy Herald-Whig,* June 21, 1992. Madison also depicts threshing wheat.

    By the age of seven: Garland, *Son of the Middle Border,* 31, mentions doing those kinds of chores at age seven.

    most boys hated it: Sutherland, *Expansion of Everyday Life,* 134, mentions this common attitude.

    "to reach the plow handles": Garland, *Son of the Middle Border,* 86, 88.

23   *Women's work was not much easier:* See Riegel, *America Moves West,* 85–88, 578–80.

    Maxwell family relationships: Luchetti, in her *Children of the West,* discusses typical frontier family life.

    "he was just": Garland, *Son of the Middle Border,* 20.

    another "undersized" boy: Utley, *Billy the Kid,* 11.

    Waterford School: "Waterford School, District No. 6," *Historic Fulton County,* 262; Seth Leads, "Waterford School, District 157, Waterford Township," in Bordner, *Fulton County Heritage,* 490–91.

24   *Fulton County men joined up:* See "Fulton County Volunteers," *History of Fulton County, Illinois,* 355–91.

    the Fulton Blues: "The 'Fulton Blues,'" *Fulton Democrat,* May 4, 1861, and "Our Boys," *Fulton Democrat,* May 18, 1861.

    Bordner . . . Clark: Their native state and years of arrival in Fulton County are given in the *Atlas Map of Fulton County,* 11; their land is shown on page 98. On the two Bordners, see *Historic Fulton County,* 187–88; Bordner, *Fulton County Heritage,* 43–44; and their obituaries in the *Fulton Democrat:* "Died [Jonathan]," Sept. 26, 1873; "The Death record [Moses]," Mar. 29, 1905. On Clark, see "Death of Venerable Charles Clark," *Fulton Democrat,* Dec. 1, 1887.

24   *"Christine" Church:* Interview with Marjorie Bordner, May 3, 2007; May 18, 2007, letter to the author from Bordner, and her *Fulton County Heritage,* 43.

25   *a "ruling elder":* "Death of the Venerable Charles Clark," *Fulton Democrat,* Dec. 1, 1887.

      "inclined to evil": "The Auburn Declaration," in Marsden, *Evangelical Mind,* 253, also 26. The Presbyterian mind-set was similar to most mainline Protestantism.

      "an individualistic mind-set": Huber, *American Idea of Success,* 109–10.

      Bordner School: For the location, see the *Atlas Map of Fulton County,* 98.

      He enlisted: Illinois Civil War Muster Rolls, Company H, 103rd Illinois Infantry, Illinois State Archives. See also *History of Fulton County, Illinois,* 380.

26   *103rd Illinois Infantry:* A "History of the One Hundred and Third Infantry" and a muster roll are provided in the *Report of the Adjutant General of the State of Illinois,* V, 635–40. See also "The Fulton County (103d) Regiment," *Fulton Democrat,* Sept. 5, 1862.

      "the crowd offered their salutes": "Departure of the 103rd Regiment," *Fulton Democrat,* Sept. 12, 1862.

      letter, "From the 103d Reg't": *Fulton Democrat,* Feb. 13, 1863.

      David was "excused from duty": Report from the Adjutant General's Office, War Department, Jan. 30, 1886, in Jacobsen genealogical papers, Hallwas Collection.

      "During the siege": Report of the Adjutant General of the State of Illinois, V, 636.

      "Int. [Intestinal] Fever": Report of the Adjutant General of the State of Illinois, V, 636.

      he "came home": Undated letter by Susan, to support her application for benefits as a soldier's widow, in the Jacobsen genealogical papers, Hallwas Collection.

27   *David was wounded:* On May 4, 1864, according to a handwritten account of the David and Susan Maxwell family, in the Jacobsen genealogical papers, Hallwas Collection. Wills, *Army Life of an Illinois Soldier,* 242, depicts the experience of soldiers in the 103rd Regiment at Resaca.

      He had . . . a $27 bounty: "The 103d Regiment," *Fulton Democrat,* Oct. 10, 1862.

      "hostility and contempt everywhere": Putney and Putney, *Adjusted Ameri-*

can, 61. Their entire chapter on "The Persecuted," 58–70, provides helpful insight into Ed Maxwell's kind of neurosis.

27 *"[a] man who has had inadequate":* As quoted in Huber, *American Idea
of Success,* 121.

28 *"Shame on Lewistown":* Fulton Democrat, Sept. 18, 1863.

"We learn that there": "Festival and Fair," *Fulton Democrat,* Dec. 24,
1863.

Relief Society: "The Relief," *Fulton Democrat,* Dec. 16, 1864.

"At the time he was discharged": Undated letter by Susan, op. cit.

29 *the 1860 presidential race:* "Official Vote of Fulton County—1860," *Fulton
Democrat,* Nov. 17, 1860.

"a hot-bed of rebellion": "Early Days in Central Illinois," *Macomb Journal,*
Dec. 29, 1881.

"zealous Republicans": "War in Our Midst," *Fulton Democrat,* Aug. 10,
1861.

"Brutal Outrage": Fulton Democrat, July 31, 1863.

"six or seven hundred armed citizens": Report by Fulton County Provost
Marshal William Phelps, Aug. 17, 1863, printed in the *History of Fulton
County, Illinois,* 353.

"REIGN OF TERROR": "REIGN OF TERROR IN FULTON COUNTY," *Fulton
Democrat,* Aug. 21, 1863. See also "Trouble in Fulton County," *Fulton
Democrat,* Aug. 18, 1863, and "The 'Fulton County War,'" *Fulton County
Ledger,* Aug. 25, 1863.

Copperheads: "Powwow at Lewistown," *Canton Weekly Register,* Oct. 5,
1863.

S. Corning Judd . . . the state commander: Howard, *Illinois,* 315.

30 *"our streets were the scene":* "Lewistown under a Reign of Terror," *Fulton
Democrat,* May 13, 1864. See also "Trouble in Lewistown," *Canton Weekly
Register,* May 16, 1864.

Assistant Provost Marshal: "An Assistant Provost Marshal Shot," *Fulton
Democrat,* Aug. 14, 1864.

"he was out notifying": "Mr. John A. Criss Shot," *Fulton Democrat,* Nov. 4,
1864. See also "Another Assistant Provost Marshal Shot in This County,"
Canton Weekly Register, Oct. 31, 1864.

Jackson Bolen killed . . . Mahary: History of Fulton County, Illinois, 311.

"the code of the West": See Hendricks, *Bad Man of the West,* 57–62; Rosen-
berg, *Code of the West,* 159–74; Utley, *High Noon in Lincoln,* 176–77; and
Brown, *No Duty to Retreat,* 39–49. On the code's Southern roots, see
Etcheson, *Emerging Midwest,* 27–31.

31 *"The people vs. Samuel Goodman":* "Circuit Court," *Fulton Democrat,* June
5, 1863.

a right to defend himself: On this outlook, see Brown, *No Duty to Retreat,*
3–37.

31   *"fifty-two murders"*: "Early Days in Central Illinois," *Macomb Journal,* Dec. 29, 1881.

increase in lawbreaking: In *Frontier Illinois,* Davis refers to "the profound tranquility and justice of frontier Illinois" (340), a period when "crime was low" (561). That view seems overly positive. In any case, during and after the war, lawbreaking was worse.

"The morals of Lewistown": "Lewistown Morals," *Fulton Democrat,* Jan. 30, 1863.

boys "from twelve to eighteen": "The Progress of Immorality," *Fulton Democrat,* Dec. 22, 1865.

32   *"No town"*: "Vandalism and Rowdyism," *Fulton Democrat,* Aug. 11, 1865.

such social disorder . . . continued: A poet who was raised in Lewistown after the war recalled that, on Saturdays, rowdies from the river bottoms came into town—men who drank, caroused, and "fought with knives and guns and knucks"; Masters, *Across Spoon River,* 411.

repeat offenders: On Ryan and Trent, see Murray and Wetmore, *Detective's Vade Mecum,* 70–71, 86–87; on Spidell, see "Escape of Prisoners from Our Jail," *Fulton Democrat,* Oct. 4, 1867.

horse theft was "rampant": J. W. Phillips, "Horse Thieves in Central Illinois," *Chicago Tribune,* July 19, 1865.

"horse stealing is being done": "Depredations," *Fulton Democrat,* June 16, 1865.

"There will be no security": "Horse Thieves," *Canton Weekly Register,* Feb. 19, 1866.

"Stealing horses": Untitled article, *Fulton County Ledger,* Aug. 30, 1867.

St. Clair and Jersey counties: On the St. Clair County lynchings, see "The Raid on Horse Thieves," *Chicago Tribune,*" May 8, 1866, and "From St. Louis," *Chicago Tribune,* May 16, 1866. On the Jersey County lynchings, see "MURDER IN JERSEY COUNTY," *Fulton Democrat,* May 11, 1866, and "The Recent Trouble in Jersey County, Illinois," *Fulton Democrat,* May 18, 1866.

33   *The People vs. John Metzer:* "Circuit Court," *Fulton Democrat,* Mar. 6, 1863.

Illinois law prescribed: Hurd, *Revised Statutes of the State of Illinois,* 378.

"He has killed me": History of Fulton County, Illinois, 312.

"a very quiet, inoffensive man": History of Fulton County, Illinois, 313.

"All [three] of these parties": History of Fulton County, Illinois, 313.

34   *"Murder and Lynching"*: Chicago Tribune, July 7, 1870.

dance at Lewistown: "BLOODY WORK!" *Fulton Democrat,* Dec. 29, 1866.

robber and horse thief named John Yarnell: History of Fulton County, Illinois, 312–13; "A Terrible Tragedy," *Fulton Democrat,* June 21, 1867.

David Waggoner: See "Death of David J. Waggoner," *Canton Weekly Reg-*

ister, Nov. 15, 1883, as well as *History of Fulton County, Illinois,* 815, and Bateman, 1154–55.

34   *During the Civil War:* "STORY OF A PAROLED PRISONER," *Fulton Democrat,* Nov. 7, 1862, and "Return of Maj. Waggoner," *Fulton Democrat,* Nov. 7, 1862.

Joe Brice: "CAPTURE OF THE NOTORIOUS MURDERER AND ROBBER JOE BRICE BY EX-SHERIFF WAGGONER," *Fulton Democrat,* June 2, 1865.

35   *"more than statewide":* "Our County Ticket," *Fulton Democrat,* Sept. 14, 1866.

"Song of the Emigrant": By A. J. Eidson, *Macomb Eagle,* May 29, 1868.

"He told the reporter": "How They Began," *Macomb Journal,* Nov. 24, 1881.

36   *Woodford County:* See Moore, *History of Woodford County;* Perrin and Hill, *Past and Present of Woodford County;* and the *Atlas of Woodford County.*

David's much-older cousin, Sarah: On the Woodburn family, see the 1860 U.S. census for Woodford County, and the Jacobsen genealogical papers, Hallwas Collection.

The Woodburn farm: For the location, see the *Atlas of Woodford County,* X.

Washburn: The *Atlas of Woodford County,* X, briefly describes the town.

William Maxwell: U.S. Census, Woodford County, 1870. See also the Jacobsen genealogical papers, Hallwas Collection.

"detected in petty thieving": "Hanged by a Mob," *Chicago Journal,* Nov. 21, 1881.

37   *"a kind father":* Rogers, *Prodigal Son,* 6–7. (Photocopy, Jacobsen papers, Hallwas Collection.)

"the law, which exercises authority": Duncan, *Romantic Outlaws,* 59.

Taylor County, Iowa: See *History of Taylor County, Iowa* (1881).

Brice . . . was afterwards convicted: "Escape of Jo. Brice," *Fulton Democrat,* Dec. 1, 1865; "THE TRIAL OF BRICE AND CRANS," *Fulton Democrat,* Jan. 5, 1866.

Chapter 3: The Maxwells in McDonough County

39   *McDonough County:* See Clarke, *History of McDonough County;* McLean, *Historical Encyclopedia of Illinois;* and the 1885 *History of McDonough County, Illinois.* Hallwas, *McDonough County Heritage,* includes a section on "Sources," 187–89. Rezab's recent book, *Place Names of McDonough County,* is also helpful for towns, schools, and so on.

41   *"Look out for the cars":* Hallwas, *Macomb,* 34.

"a foolish, vain, wicked": Hallwas, *Macomb,* 44.

Atlas Map of McDonough County: For a discussion of that volume as an expression of American myth, see Hallwas, *Macomb,* 60–61.

the Gospel of Success: Huber, *American Idea of Success,* 93–106.

41 *"through diligent effort":* Ashby, *William Jennings Bryan,* 2. This paragraph is indebted to Ashby, 2–5. For an 1870s item on this view, see "Success in Life," *Knox County Republican,* Dec. 12, 1877.

42 *"PROVERBS OF TRUTH":* Macomb Journal, Nov. 24, 1881. This is a scattered selection from the more than five dozen proverbs listed in that lengthy article.
    respectability . . . was always judged: Friedman, *Crime and Punishment in American History,* 203.
    many components . . . are determined: Pereboom, *Living without Free Will,* 187–97, and Wegner, *Illusion of Conscious Will.*

43 *Ebenezer Hicks:* On Hicks, see the U.S. census for Hire Township, McDonough County, 1850, 1860, 1870, and 1880; also *History of McDonough County, Illinois* (1885), 628–29, and "Death of Ebenezer N. Hicks," *Macomb Journal,* June 17, 1886.

44 *"When he purchased his place":* History of McDonough County, Illinois (1885), 628.
    a hard-nosed businessman: Interviews with Hicks family descendants Margaret Lewis, of Sec. 33, Hire Township (the former Ebenezer Hicks farmstead), April 21, 1983, and Natalie McConnell, of Blandinsville, May 31, 2003.

45 *the southern edge:* See the "Map of Tennessee Township" in the *Atlas Map of McDonough County, Illinois,* 64. This map, and the one for Hire Township, 46, show some of the many parcels of land owned by Ebenezer Hicks.
    "Maxwell (the father)": "How They Began," *Macomb Journal,* Nov. 24, 1881.
    "On Wednesday last": "The Eagle's Nest," *Macomb Eagle,* Nov. 28, 1868.
    one-third of the tenants moved: Schlereth, *Victorian America,* 41. Schlereth's entire discussion of tenant farmers, 39–43, is very good.

46 *hired hand named Moore:* "Moore Murder," *Macomb Journal,* Dec. 17, 1903.
    "The general character of the two men": "HORRIBLE AFFAIR: Bloody Work Done in Hire Township," *Macomb Journal,* Nov. 26, 1874.

47 *"works on a farm":* 1870 U.S. Census, McDonough County, 340.
    the Hicks School: It was in Hire Township, near the farm rented by the Maxwells. See the "Map of Hire Township," *Atlas Map of McDonough County, Illinois,* 46. For brief information about the school, see the *History of McDonough County, Illinois* (1885), 647. A later newspaper article, "The Maxwell Brothers," *Canton Register* (reprinted from the *Macomb Eagle*), Aug. 12, 1881, asserts that both Ed and Lon attended the Hicks School.
    James D. Maxwell . . . was born on the farm: His birth date is from the Jacobsen genealogical papers, Hallwas Collection.

47   *Charles Gilbert Maxwell . . . was born:* Jacobsen genealogical papers,
       Hallwas Collection.
       Colchester: See Hallwas, *Bootlegger,* 17–66.
       "They were quick and sharp": "How They Began," *Macomb Journal,* Nov.
       24, 1881.

48   *a nearby church:* On Friendship Church, in section 5 of Tennessee Town-
       ship, see the 1885 *History of McDonough County,* 563. The Maxwells ap-
       parently moved a mile or two east, to another tenant farm, and then
       attended the nearby Argyle Church.
       "Prof. George Fentem": "LAST OF THE MAXWELLS," *Colchester Indepen-*
       dent, Sept. 19, 1889.

49   *"the family attended church":* Hainline, "The County's Worst Despera-
       does," *Macomb Journal,* Mar. 16, 1924.
       "he could make pretty good flourishes": "How They Began," *Macomb Jour-*
       nal, Nov. 24, 1881.

50   *"Ed was a fine penman":* "The County's Worst Desperadoes," *Macomb*
       Journal, Mar. 16, 1924.
       Ed began to work: "QUICK WORK," *Macomb Journal,* Oct. 12, 1876.
       Sciota, a hamlet: History of McDonough County, Illinois (1885), 953–57,
       and "Sciota Correspondence," *Macomb Journal,* July 28, 1871.
       Blandinsville: See Clarke, *History of McDonough County,* 637–41; *History*
       of McDonough County, Illinois (1885), 879–900.
       John Isom and J. E. Carlisle: For the location of their farms, see the "Map
       of Hire Township" in the *Atlas Map of McDonough County, Illinois,* 46. For
       a biographical sketch of Isom, see the 1885 *History of McDonough County,*
       Illinois, 645–46.
       His employer . . . John Terrill: The exact location of the Terrill farm in
       Blandinsville Township is unknown. Neither the 1871 *Atlas Map of Mc-*
       Donough County, Illinois nor local land deed records show an owner by
       that name. He must have rented the land.

51   *hired hands . . . exhausting toil:* Schob, *Hired Hands and Plowboys,* 188–90,
       214–15; Sutherland, *Expansion of Everyday Life,* 134–35; 143–44.
       "laborer lives or starves": "Our Chatter Box," *Macomb Journal,* Mar. 12,
       1874.
       the population had almost tripled: Walker, *Statistics of the Population of*
       the United States, 116.
       a gang of horse thieves: "THE JOHNSON GANG," *Macomb Eagle,* June
       28, 1866. Reprinted from the *Oquawka Spectator,* this article is the only
       known source on the gang.

52   *William Randolph . . . was killed:* "Killing of William H. Randolph," *His-*
       tory of McDonough County, Illinois (1885), 345–48; Hallwas, "The Killing
       of William Randolph" and "The Randolph Murder Trials," *McDonough*
       County Heritage, 81–85.

52   *"There are bold, bad men there":* "Horrible Tragedy in Blandinsville Township," *Macomb Journal,* Jan. 27, 1871.
     "MORE LAWLESSNESS IN BLANDINSVILLE": Macomb Journal, Apr. 21, 1871.

53   *"had fear and loathing":* Crews, "Television's Junkyard Dog," in *Blood and Grits,* 145.
     the perennial poor: Sandage, *Born Losers,* 237.

54   *"a vale of tears":* Bruce, *1877,* 17. On the 1870s depression, see also Keiser, *Building for the Centuries,* 121–23.
     "Macomb has . . . thieves": "Thieves About," *Macomb Eagle,* Feb. 21, 1874.
     "Tramping Loafers": Macomb Journal, Aug. 12, 1875. See also Friedman, *Crime and Punishment in American History,* 101–4.
     the Grange: Woodward, "Northwestern Farmer," 142, refers to the farmer's self-image as a "victimized yeoman," championed by the Grange. On the local Grange chapters and the group's constitution, see "Patrons of Husbandry," *Macomb Journal,* Mar. 13, 1873.
     names like "Liberty" and "Equality": "McDonough County Granges, of the Patrons of Husbandry," *Macomb Eagle,* Aug. 9, 1873.

55   *"the money mongers":* "Wealth of McDonough," *Macomb Independent,* July 15, 1879.
     "On the night of the 10th": "A DESPERADO," *Macomb Eagle,* Feb. 21, 1874. For another, shorter account of the theft, pursuit, and arrest, see "A Bold Freebooter," *Macomb Journal,* Feb. 19, 1874.

56   *"Reminiscences of the Maxwell Boys":* Macomb Journal, Feb. 24, 1917.

57   *Charles Dines: History of McDonough County, Illinois* (1885), 296.
     "The wily thief": "How They Began," *Macomb Journal,* Nov. 24, 1881.

58   *"He is evidently a dangerous":* "A DESPERADO," *Macomb Eagle,* Feb. 21, 1874.
     "who is in and who is out": Friedman, *Crime and Punishment in American History,* 84.
     "a large Bowie knife": "Nabbed," *Oquawka Spectator,* Feb. 26, 1874.

Chapter 4: Law and Order, and Prison Life

60   *Ed pled guilty:* "Circuit Court," *Macomb Eagle,* Mar. 28, 1874.
     Damon G. Tunnicliff: Hallwas, *Macomb,* 95.
     "one year in the penitentiary": "Circuit Court," *Macomb Eagle,* Apr. 4, 1874. See also "Convict Register," Illinois State Penitentiary (April 2, 1874), Illinois State Archives.
     "Charley Dines and a host": "From Blandinsville," *Macomb Eagle,* Apr. 11, 1874.

61   *a thriving prairie town:* Hallwas, *Macomb,* 50–53, 56–57.
     There were no less than: "MACOMB," *Macomb Journal,* July 26, 1875.

61   *"Macomb is outstripping"*: "The Eagle's Nest," *Macomb Eagle,* Jan. 27, 1872.

      Macomb had 3,368 people: "MACOMB," *Macomb Journal,* July 26, 1875. That figure was based on a census taken by the local government. The population declined slightly, to 3,273, by 1880, probably because of the number of people who moved west (Hallwas, *Macomb,* 72).

62   *pioneers brutalized:* Hallwas, *Macomb,* 9.

      "a large gray timber wolf": "A Lively Chase," *Macomb Eagle,* Feb. 14, 1874. See also "Trapped," *Macomb Eagle,* Mar. 7, 1874, about a wolf killed at Wigwam Hollow.

      a permanent one: Hallwas, *Macomb,* 18.

      the third McDonough County courthouse: Hallwas, *Macomb,* 48.

      cornerstone ceremony: "CORNERSTONE LAYING," *Macomb Journal,* Aug. 20, 1869.

63   *"The county seems to be"*: "Thieves" *Macomb Eagle,* June 27, 1868.

      "Resident Thieves": *Macomb Journal,* Nov. 28, 1872.

      saloons were licensed: Hallwas, *Macomb,* 78.

      "during the past week": "Town and County," *Macomb Journal,* Aug. 20, 1869.

      Karr McClintock: Hallwas, *Macomb,* 74; for the two fights, see "Officer Assaulted," *Macomb Journal,* July 8, 1875, and "BILLY BALKED," *Macomb Journal,* Apr. 27, 1876, as well as a historical account, "A Great Fight," *Macomb Journal,* Dec. 17, 1903.

64   *Joseph Johnson . . . shot and killed:* "The Uncertainties of the Law," *Macomb Eagle,* Feb. 15, 1873; "Workings of the Law," *Macomb Journal,* July 31, 1873, and "The Johnson Trial," *Macomb Eagle,* Aug. 2, 1873.

      "juries are not always": "Murder," *Macomb Journal,* July 31, 1873.

      the penitentiary at Joliet: The only modern history of the prison is Robert E. Sterling's photographic volume, *Joliet Prisons,* but see also Richard Lawson's *The Joliet Prison Photographs 1890–1930.* Useful earlier sources are four books: Lathrop, *Crime and Punishment and Life in the Penitentiary;* Wetmore, *Behind the Bars: Life and Times in Joliet Prison,* and his much longer expansion of that work, *Behind the Bars at Joliet: A Peep at a Prison, Its History, and Its Mysteries*; and the anonymous *An Ex-Convict's Story: Life in Joliet Penitentiary, Joliet, Illinois.* See also the dissertations by Sanders, "History and Administration of the State Prisons of Illinois," and Shaw, "Economic Development of Joliet, Illinois," as well as the official reports on the Illinois State Penitentiary, starting in 1859, and the "Convict Register," both at the Illinois State Archives, Springfield. For a listing of six hundred notable criminals, most of whom spent time at Joliet, see Murray and Wetmore, *Detective's Vade Mecum.* The only available copies of this largely handwritten book are in the Library of

Congress and the Hallwas Collection. Also see Walter Brieschke, "Joliet Bibliography," in the Hallwas Collection.

65   *"Hell and Joliet"*: Mentioned in "The Chatter Box," *Macomb Journal,* Apr. 6, 1876.

"a backward spring": "A Backward Spring," *Joliet Signal,* Apr. 21, 1874.

it looked like a grim: This description is indebted to Wetmore, *Behind the Bars at Joliet,* 20–22.

66   *"The creaking of the big iron doors"*: Ex-Convict's Story, 26–30.

Prison records show: "Convict Register," April 2, 1874, Illinois State Penitentiary Collection, Illinois State Archives.

67   *"In the stillness of the night"*: Ex-Convict's Story, 34–35.

"so contracted, so repellant": Report of the Commissioners, 11.

68   the *"Auburn System"*: Friedman, *Crime and Punishment in American History,* 79.

"dropped dead . . . while marching . . .": "County Items," *Macomb Journal,* Feb. 19, 1874. See also "Circuit Court," *Macomb Eagle,* Feb. 15, 1873.

"engenders a secret hostility": "The Prison Keeper, No. 2," *Joliet Signal,* Oct. 3, 1876.

"silent, crabbed, and unapproachable": "The Prison Keeper," *Joliet Signal,* Sept. 26, 1876.

"M. Soley and Co.": "A Carthage Lawyer in the Joliet Penitentiary," *Carthage Gazette,* May 26, 1876.

69   *"such revolting, degrading self-effacement"*: Wetmore, *Behind the Bars at Joliet,* 51.

"the air in the cell houses": McClaughry, "Warden's Report," in *Report of the Commissioners of the Penitentiary,* 415.

"All conversation": Lathrop, *Crime and Punishment and Life in the Penitentiary,* 245.

70   *"The convict must always"*: Lathrop, *Crime and Punishment and Life in the Penitentiary,* 245.

"we had to annihilate": Wetmore, *Behind the Bars at Joliet,* 51.

"slow and daily tampering": As quoted in Friedman, *Crime and Punishment in American History,* 80.

Violation of the rules: See Lathrop, *Crime and Punishment and Life in the Penitentiary,* 250; *Ex-Convict's Story,* 41; and Wetmore, *Behind the Bars at Joliet,* 95, 119–23.

71   *"he had chained"*: "THE PENITENTIARY," *Macomb Eagle,* Sept. 12, 1874.

"charges of inhumanity": Report of the Joint Committee, 903.

a dozen or more prisoners went insane: McClaughry's "Warden's Report," 47, lists eighteen who were "sent to Insane Asylum" during a two-year period, but he also asserts that there are numerous others, "partially insane, or whose minds are affected," (48), who need but receive no treatment. McKelvey, in his *American Prisons,* 164, comments that prison repression sometimes led to "shattered intellects" as well as broken health.

71   *thirteen different wardens:* See "Wardens at Joliet Penitentiary," unpaginated typescript, Illinois State Archives, and "Joliet Wardens," a chronology compiled by Walter L. Brieschke, in the Hallwas Collection.

public concern: See the 1872 *Report of the Joint Committee* for an official inquiry into conditions at the prison.

Warden Elmer Washburn: "Major Wham," *Joliet Signal,* Sept. 8, 1876.

72   *"the escapes from Joliet Prison":* Wetmore, *Behind the Bars at Joliet,* 89.

"a Goddess of Liberty": Wetmore, *Behind the Bars at Joliet,* 171; see also Murray and Wetmore, *Detective's Vade Mecum,* 21.

"fresh fish": Wetmore, *Behind the Bars at Joliet,* 25.

"The young and inexperienced criminal": Report of the Joint Committee, 27.

convict jargon: See "The Rogues' Lexicon" in Wetmore, *Behind the Bars,* 53–56.

73   *"he had stolen over 100":* Murray and Wetmore, *Detective's Vade Mecum,* 29.

operated "all over the West": Murray and Wetmore, *Detective's Vade Mecum,* 32.

"He was first sentenced": Wetmore, *Behind the Bars at Joliet,* 185.

"Old Jim" Jones and "Old Bill" Miller: Murray and Wetmore, *Detective's Vade Mecum,* 36, 18. Miller is listed under the name "Oliver Davis."

Henry Williams: "Convict Register," Nov. 21, 1873, Illinois State Penitentiary Collection, Illinois State Archives.

74   *"the violent physical struggle":* "The Verdict," *Joliet Republican,* Jan. 3, 1874. For a record of the inquest, see "Testimony before Coroner's Jury," 861.

"literally drowned: "A Convict Killed," *Joliet Signal,* Dec. 16, 1873.

"There are but few [inmates]": Wetmore, *Behind the Bars,* 12.

"There's plenty on the outside": Wetmore, *Behind the Bars,* 11.

"I'm jugged [in prison]": Wetmore, *Behind the Bars at Joliet,* 155.

"Brace up, and stand your punishment": Wetmore, *Behind the Bars at Joliet,* 165.

75   *he was given:* Ex-Convict's Story, 65, describes the discharge routine.

It was March 2, 1875: The "Convict Register," April 2, 1874, Illinois State Penitentiary Collection, Illinois State Archives, indicates his discharge date.

Chapter 5: The Maxwell Brothers Become Outlaws

76   *"Eighteen hundred and":* "Building Improvements," *Macomb Journal,* Jan. 7, 1875.

"Times are hard": "Our Chatter Box," *Macomb Journal,* Dec. 31, 1876.

76 *Taylor County, Iowa:* When Ed and Lon were arrested in August, they claimed to be "residents of Taylor County, Iowa": "The Maxwells," *Macomb Eagle,* Aug. 28, 1875. David and Susan had probably moved there during the previous winter. On Taylor County, see the 1881 *History of Taylor County, Iowa* and Crosson, *History of Taylor County.*

77 *"to get away from their disgrace":* "The County's Worst Desperadoes," *Macomb Journal,* Mar. 17, 1924.
    "Hard times, low prices": "Brief Notes," *Macomb Eagle,* Feb. 8, 1879.
    Most of the settlers: U.S. Census, 1870, for Taylor County.
    "I wanted to be honest": "QUICK WORK," *Macomb Journal,* Oct. 12, 1876.

78 *"Indian warfare":* "What Our Boys Are Reading," *Scribner's Monthly* (March 1878): 681. The article is anonymous; the author's identity was determined by Bruce, *1877,* 14.
    scout Kit Carson: "An Indian Fighter," *Fulton Democrat,* Nov. 9, 1866.
    various tales: For example, "Peril of the Yard-Arm," *Fulton Democrat,* May 6, 1864.
    "with a revolver in each hand": "An Account of the Iowa Railway Robbery," *Macomb Journal,* July 31, 1873.
    "DARK AND BLOODY GROUND": *Macomb Eagle,* Feb. 15, 1873.
    The James-Younger band: See the books about Jesse James by Brant and Stiles, among many others.
    "the celebrated Missouri brigand": "Hot Springs Robbery: The Feats of Dick Turpin Eclipsed," *Macomb Eagle,* Feb. 21, 1874.

79 *a reader of dime novels:* In his 1907 history of McDonough County, Alexander McLean, who had been mayor of Macomb during the 1870s and had seen Ed and Lon in the local jail and had undoubtedly talked to many others about them, asserted that they "were great readers of the yellow-covered literature" (801)—or pulp fiction, which was commonly bound in yellow or saffron covers. He also may have recalled Ed's admission of that in the "QUICK WORK" interview, noted below.
    "fond of hunting": Willett, *Twin Trailers,* 27.
    "Boys' Literature": *Joliet Republican,* May 4, 1878.

80 *"yellow-covered literature":* "QUICK WORK," *Macomb Journal,* Oct. 12, 1876.

81 *"two men of suspicious":* "Pilot Grove," *Carthage Republican,* June 11, 1875.
    "Maxwell and Post": *Carthage Republican,* June 11, 1875.

83 *John A. Murrell was a legendary desperado:* See Wellman, *Spawn of Evil,* 155–239, 263–65. Several other books also deal with Murrell.

84 *"Out in Emmet, Sciota":* "Our Chatter Box.," *Macomb Journal,* Aug. 12, 1875.
    "Maxwell . . . and Post pounced down": "'The James Boys': The Arrest of Maxwell and Post," *Macomb Eagle,* Aug. 21, 1875.
    "that when he returned": *Macomb Eagle,* Aug. 21, 1875.

84　*"unwilling to bear":* Hobsbawm, 13. See his chapter on "The Social Bandit," 13–29.

　　"Of course, I'm interested in the money": Henry Starr, as quoted in Drago, *Outlaws on Horseback,* xxvii–xxviii. Noted outlaw historian Paul I. Wellman also commented that "the desire for adventure, for excitement, was a force possibly as motivating as the actual loot" for most bandits, in *Dynasty of Western Outlaws,* 14.

85　*"Excitement was running high":* "The County's Worst Desperadoes," *Macomb Journal,* Mar. 16, 1924.

　　"dead or alive": "BANDITTI," *Carthage Republican,* June 11, 1875.

　　"talk of lynching": "'The James Boys': The Arrest of Maxwell and Post," *Macomb Eagle,* Aug. 21, 1875.

86　*"nickel-plated revolvers":* "Maxwell Terrifiers," *Macomb Journal,* Sept. 30, 1875.

　　"Ed informed our reporter": "The Maxwells," *Macomb Journal,* Aug. 26, 1875.

　　Alonso McCally: Reprinted from the *Democrat* in "The Maxwells," *Macomb Journal,* Oct. 13, 1881. For another account of that episode, see "Table Grove," *Fulton Democrat,* July 22, 1875.

　　"When they got within": "EDWARD MAXWELL," *Pike County Democrat,* Nov. 24, 1881.

87　*"they would never be taken alive":* "The Maxwells," *Macomb Journal,* Oct. 13, 1881.

　　Soon one hundred men: "From Smithfield," *Fulton County Ledger,* July 23, 1875.

　　"They established a 'den'": "How They Began," *Macomb Journal,* Nov. 24, 1881.

　　"TWO DESPERADOES AT LARGE": *Fulton Democrat,* July 29, 1875. See also "The Maxwells," *Macomb Journal,* Oct. 13, 1881.

88　*a series of burglaries:* "Burglars on the Rampage," *Fulton Democrat,* July 29, 1875. See also, "Burglars," *Fulton Democrat,* Aug. 12, 1875.

89　*those robbers were indicted:* Actually, the indictment read, "William E. Maxwell, et al." See "Circuit Court," *Canton Register,* May 5, 1876.

　　Deputy Sheriff Charles C. Hays: For information on Hays and other Macomb lawmen, see the "Sheriffs and Marshals" file in the Hallwas Collection, as well as the 1885 *History of McDonough County, Illinois,* 322–26. Because Hays had been a soldier, see also the Illinois Civil War muster rolls at the Illinois State Archives.

　　"Arriving [at Beardstown]": Reprinted from the *Bushnell Record* in "The Maxwells," *Macomb Eagle,* Aug. 28, 1875.

91　*"On the way up town":* "The Maxwells," *Macomb Journal,* Aug. 26, 1875. The next several quotations on the capture and attempted escape are also from this article.

92 *"Personally, they do not at all":* Macomb Journal, Aug. 26, 1875.

perceived as "effeminate": A later *Journal* editor who had seen Lon in 1875 made that same assertion in "THE MAXWELL BOYS," *Macomb Journal,* Dec. 17, 1903.

Chapter 6: The Great Escape—and Recapture

93 *"our badly demoralized":* "'The James Boys': The Arrest of Maxwell and Post," *Macomb Eagle,* Aug. 21, 1875.

a two-story log building: Hallwas, *Macomb,* 14, includes a description and lithograph of that first jail.

two accused murderers: "ESCAPES FROM JAIL," *Macomb Journal,* Dec. 17, 1903.

a new brick jail: Hallwas, *Macomb,* 74.

94 *"during his entire term":* "The Retiring Sheriff," *Macomb Journal,* Dec. 16, 1870.

escapes were numerous: In the *Macomb Journal,* "Amusement at the Jail," Jan. 23, 1873, and "That Poor Jail," Jan. 6, 1876, discuss the jail's condition and the escapes.

there were several more: See, for example, "Jail Breaking," *Macomb Journal,* June 30, 1871, and "REVIEW OF JAIL RECORD," *Macomb Daily Journal,* Feb. 29, 1908.

the butt of local jokes: "ESCAPES FROM JAIL," *Macomb Journal,* Dec. 17, 1903.

"THE BEAUTIES OF BEING SHERIFF": Macomb Journal, Nov. 23, 1876.

95 *"the most desperate outlaws":* "ESCAPES FROM JAIL," *Macomb Journal,* Dec. 17, 1903.

"ESCAPED!": Macomb Journal, Sept. 2, 1875.

97 *"Ed Maxwell is about":* "The County's Worst Desperadoes," *Macomb Journal,* Mar. 15, 1924.

"quick, hard, and dangerous": L'Amour, *Hondo,* 1.

"There were . . . rumors": "The County's Worst Desperadoes," Mar. 15, 1924.

98 *rode with "the James and Younger gang":* A Durand, Wisconsin, newspaper item, "THE SEARCH! STILL UNSUCCESSFUL!" *Pepin County Courier,* July 22, 1881, is one of several articles that mention their association with the quintessential outlaw gang.

"got their inspiration from": "The County's Worst Desperadoes," Mar. 15, 1924.

Charley Roberts: 1870 U.S. Census for McDonough County; "Accident in a Coal Shaft," *Macomb Eagle,* Sept. 25, 1875, and "County Clippings," *Macomb Journal,* July 22, 1875.

on September 28, Lon was tried: "Convict Register," Illinois State Penitentiary, Oct. 8, 1875; "The Eagle's Nest," *Macomb Eagle,* Oct.9, 1875.

98 *that "he was arrested":* "City and County Items," *Macomb Journal,* Dec. 17, 1875.

"a man by the name": "GOT HIM! YES, GOT HIM!" *Macomb Journal,* Oct. 12, 1876. All the quotations on the Shortall-Venard correspondence are from this article.

99 *Stillwater:* See "Stillwater Lumber Business," *Stillwater Lumberman,* Apr. 23, 1875; "The Saw Mills," *Stillwater Lumberman,* July 16, 1880; Warner and Foote, *History of Washington County,* 512–56; Peterson and Thilgen, *Stillwater, Minnesota.* The Washington County Historical Society has an 1879 bird's-eye map of the town, which shows the mill locations and other features.

the state penitentiary: Warner and Foote, *History of Washington County,* 535–36; Peterson and Thilgen, *Stillwater, Minnesota,* 50–53.

The most famous inmates: For an overview of the Youngers' capture, trial, and arrival at the penitentiary, as well as a brief interview with Cole, see "Sentenced for Life," *Stillwater Messenger,* Nov. 24, 1876.

100 *The Northfield fiasco:* Brant, *Jesse James,* 173–83; Stiles, *Jesse James,* 332–35.

Younger brothers . . . photographs: "The Northfield Bank Robbery," *Stillwater Lumberman,* Oct. 3, 1876.

the Shortall brothers: "Death of John Shortall," *Stillwater Daily Gazette,* Mar. 23, 1888; "Matthew Shortall Dead," *Stillwater Gazette,* Sept. 15, 1903, and an untitled article, *Stillwater Messenger,* May 12, 1888, as well as Brent Peterson, "Matthew Shortall," *St. Croix Valley Press,* Nov. 13, 1997.

"one of the best police officers": "Matthew Shortall Dead," *Stillwater Gazette,* Sept. 15, 1903.

"AN UGLY CUSTOMER": *Stillwater Gazette,* Aug. 30, 1876.

101 *The mill . . . in South Stillwater:* See "New Saw Mill in South Stillwater" and the untitled article on businesses at that locality, *Stillwater Messenger,* July 23, 1881.

102 *"Not long after [the confrontation . . .]":* Untitled article, *Stillwater Messenger,* Oct. 6, 1876. Another account correctly indicates that the arrest took place in "a barn at Cottage Grove"; see "Taken In," *Stillwater Gazette,* Oct. 4, 1876.

the Stotesbury girl: According to the 1875 Minnesota Territorial Census, Bertha, Sarah, and Lucilla Stotesbury were living at home. Sarah was already married but may have been separated and seeking a divorce. The 1880 U.S. Census lists her as divorced.

Denmark Township: "Stroller's Strayings," *Stillwater Lumberman,* July 9, 1875, describes the rural township where Ed was living. See also Warner and Foote, *History of Washington County,* 353–64.

"honestly in love with a girl": "QUICK WORK," *Macomb Journal,* Oct. 12, 1876.

102 *"expressed . . . intended reformation":* "THE MAXWELL BOYS," *Macomb Journal,* Dec. 17, 1903.

"[h]e gave his name as": "Taken In," *Stillwater Gazette,* Oct. 4, 1876.

103 *"had shot and stabbed a sheriff":* "ANOTHER DESPERADO IN LIMBO," *Stillwater Lumberman,* Oct. 6, 1876.

"Maxwell . . . at the time": "Maxwell," *Macomb Eagle,* Oct. 14, 1876.

"was always flush with money": "ANOTHER DESPERADO IN LIMBO," *Stillwater Lumberman,* Oct. 6, 1876.

"I went to Minnesota": "QUICK WORK," *Macomb Journal,* Oct. 12, 1876.

"All last winter": "QUICK WORK," *Macomb Journal,* Oct. 12, 1876.

104 *On the night of his arrest:* "Maxwell," *Macomb Eagle,* Oct. 14, 1876.

"spent a merry time": "QUICK WORK," *Macomb Journal,* Oct. 12, 1876.

"Maxwell was visited": "Maxwell," *Macomb Eagle,* Oct. 14, 1876.

"confided all his misdeeds": "How They Began," *Macomb Journal,* Nov. 24, 1881.

"While in the jail": "ANOTHER DESPERADO IN LIMBO," *Stillwater Lumberman,* Oct. 6, 1876.

105 *"QUICK WORK": Macomb Journal,* Oct. 12, 1876.

106 *"that [he] had attained":* Wheeler, *Deadwood Dick,* 281. *Deadwood Dick* appeared in 1877.

"was not only willing": "QUICK WORK," *Macomb Journal,* Oct. 12, 1876, includes the interview, from which all of Ed's comments are quoted.

Chapter 7: Prison Time and Justice Issues

109 *Robert W. McClaughry: Biographical Encyclopedia of Illinois in the Nineteenth Century,* 65–66; *The National Cyclopedia of American Biography,* XXVI, 155–56; *American National Biography,* XIV, 859–61; and the following obituaries: "Major R. W. McClaughry," *Carthage Republican,* Nov. 10, 1920; "Major Robert Wilson McClaughry," *Carthage Gazette,* Nov. 20, 1920; "R. W. M'Claughry, Noted as Prison Expert, Is Dead," *Chicago Tribune,* Nov. 10, 1920. Also, see the chronology on McClaughry compiled by Walter L. Brieschke, Hallwas Collection, and the references to him in McKelvey's *American Prisons.*

"lost in a snowstorm": "Major R. W. McClaughry," *Carthage Republican,* Nov. 10, 1920.

110 *prison cleanliness:* McClaughry, "Warden's Report," in *Report of the Commissioners of the Penitentiary,* 417.

"a new penology": "Major R. W. McClaughry," *Carthage Republican,* Nov. 10, 1920. See also "CONVICTS HAVE SOULS," *Chicago Daily News,* May 10, 1913.

"he also abolished": Wetmore, *Behind the Bars at Joliet,* 123.

"brutal and capricious punishments": *American National Biography,* XIV, 860.

110 *one black prisoner:* "GAG AND STRAP," *Joliet Republican,* May 18, 1878.
     An investigation: See the 450-page Joliet Penitentiary Testimony Records,
     Box 1, Special Collections Research Center, University of Chicago Li-
     brary. The handwritten 1878 compilation records many accusations of
     brutality.
     "Major McClaughry": Wetmore, "Pennsylvania Industrial Reformatory,"
     332.
111 *Ed Maxwell subscribed:* "The Eagle's Nest," *Macomb Eagle,* Oct. 14,
     1876.
     "Our ever popular": "From the Prison," *Joliet Signal,* Oct. 3, 1876.
     a handsome, bearded man: Photograph, *National Cyclopedia of American
     Biography,* vol. 26, p. 155. See also "CONVICTS HAVE SOULS," *Chicago
     Daily News,* May 10, 1913. His physical features are also described in the
     Civil War Muster Records, Illinois State Archives.
     Illinois State Penitentiary had 1,520 males: "Joliet Prison Population"
     typescript, unpaginated, Illinois State Penitentiary Collection, Illinois
     State Archives.
     six prisoners escaped: "FROM THE PRISON," *Joliet Signal,* Oct. 24, 1872.
     a "general outbreak": "Felons Frustrated," *Joliet Signal,* July 17, 1877.
112 *Lon had been processed:* "Convict Register," Oct. 8, 1875, Illinois State
     Penitentiary Collection, Illinois State Archives.
     the Maxwells were typical: "Convict Register," 1870–75, Illinois State Peni-
     tentiary Collection, Illinois State Archives.
     boys as young as ten: Lathrop, *Crime and Punishment and Life in the
     Penitentiary,* 238.
     With good behavior: Lathrop, *Crime and Punishment and Life in the Peni-
     tentiary,* 252–53; Wetmore, *Behind the Bars at Joliet,* 186.
     "Criminal justice": Friedman, *Crime and Punishment in American History,*
     84.
     inequities in the prison sentences: "Convict Register," 1870–75, Illinois
     State Penitentiary Collection, Illinois State Archives.
     Frank Rande: "Convict Register," February 23, 1878, and mittimus file,
     Illinois State Penitentiary Collection, Illinois State Archives. On Rande's
     career, see the early books by Stephen R. Smith (1878) and John W.
     Kimsey (1897).
113 *"the most daring":* "A DESPERATE CHARACTER," *Macomb Eagle,* Nov. 24,
     1877.
     "Frank Rande, the Great Bandit": Kimsey, *True Account of the Capture of
     Frank Rande,* 103.
     "The American Brigand" . . . *"The Brilliant":* As quoted in Wetmore, *Behind
     the Bars at Joliet,* 109.
     "said to have killed": Kimsey, *True Account of the Capture of Frank Rande,*
     103.

113 *Rande attacked:* Kimsey, *True Account of the Capture of Frank Rande,* 150–56.

114 *inmates . . . received pardons:* For the examples referred to, see the *History of Fulton County, Illinois* (1879), 310–14.

179 men and three women: McClaughry, "Warden's Report," in *Report of the Commissioners of the Penitentiary,* 415.

outlaw John Tuggle: "THE INDUSTRY BURGLARS," *Macomb Eagle,* Sept. 30, 1876; "The Other Tuggle," *Macomb Journal,* Sept. 28, 1876; "BLASTED AND BUSTED!" *Macomb Journal,* Aug. 18, 1881; "GROWING WORSE!" *Colchester Independent,* Jan. 26, 1881, and "Tuggle the Outlaw," *Macomb Journal,* Dec. 17, 1903.

"He walked around": "Tuggle the Outlaw," *Macomb Journal,* Dec. 17, 1903.

115 *"leaving him in the hands":* Letter by James M. Blazer to Governor S. M. Cullom, July 22, 1880, Tuggle clemency file, Illinois State Penitentiary Collection, Illinois State Archives.

"kind hearted, fair haired": "From Industry," *Macomb Eagle,* June 22, 1878.

Charles Tuggle died: "Convict Register," Oct. 9, 1876, Illinois State Penitentiary Collection, Illinois State Archives. See Oct. 4, 1881, for John Tuggle's death entry.

In Tazewell County: Conover and Brecher, *Lynch Law,* 803–4.

116 *"a vigilance committee":* "LYNCH LAW IN ILLINOIS," reprinted in the *Macomb Journal,* Nov. 6, 1875.

"This is the fault": "Reign of Lawlessness," reprinted in the *Macomb Journal,* Nov. 6, 1875.

"[t]he facilities for obtaining pardons": Report of the Joint Committee, 26. "OUR ED": *Macomb Journal,* Mar. 22, 1877.

119 *"I. S. P":* "Reminiscences of the Maxwell Boys," *Macomb Journal,* Feb. 24, 1917.

121 *a new jail in 1876:* Hallwas, *Macomb,* 74.

122 *four men did escape:* "ESCAPES FROM JAIL," *Macomb Journal,* Dec. 17, 1903.

"the escape of prisoners": "Three Prisoners," *Macomb Independent,* Oct. 29, 1878.

"a laughing stock": As quoted from the *Eagle* in "UTTERANCES OF A FOOL," *Macomb Journal,* Mar. 6, 1879.

killed a . . . youth: "AN UNLUCKY SHOT," *Macomb Independent,* Sept. 10, 1878.

"he was so chagrined": "The Lost Page," *Macomb Journal,* Mar. 18, 1924. Hays moved to Woonsocket, S.D., where he died in 1918, according to burial records at the State Archives in Pierre.

no less than seven prisoners escaped: "ESCAPES FROM JAIL," *Macomb Journal,* Dec. 17, 1903.

123 *"It has grown into a proverb":* Untitled article, *Macomb Journal,* Feb. 17, 1881.

"The frequent . . . murders": "The Augusta Murder," *Macomb Eagle,* Oct. 11, 1879.

"Horse thieves are doing": "Brief Notes," *Macomb Eagle,* Aug. 4, 1877.

"horse thieves, house thieves": Clarke, *History of McDonough County,* 368. The local AHTA chapters were part of a national movement; see Brown, *Strain of Violence,* 125–26.

"to hang the culprit": "Horse-Thief Detective Association and Vigilance Committee," *Joliet Signal,* July 14, 1874.

Chapter 8: Lon's Struggle to Go Straight

124 *another of Warden McClaughry's reforms:* McClaughry, "Warden's Report," in *Report of the Commissioners of the Penitentiary,* 49.

Nebraska was a new state: For a contemporaneous account, see the 1882 *History of the State of Nebraska.* Olson and Naugle, in their *History of Nebraska,* provide a fine modern history.

125 *Adams County:* See Mattes, *Great Platte River Road,* especially 192–250; Creigh, *Adams County;* and "Annual Review," *Hastings Journal,* Jan. 1, 1880.

David Maxwell entered a claim: Register of Deeds for Adams County, at Hastings. His 160-acre claim was in the southwest quarter of Section 8, Logan Township, for which he received the patent on January 20, 1880. The adjacent southeast quarter eventually became the Maxwells' "timber claim," which required the planting of trees on some of those acres, and that claim was not proved until May 13, 1890, after David had died.

Osco: Bang, *Heroes without Medals* 70–71.

constructed a sod house: On sod houses, see Creigh, *Adams County,* 10–11.

126 *a lack of fuel:* Bang, 264–66.

"THE MAXWELLS": Reprinted in the *Bushnell Record,* Dec. 16, 1881.

"Died": *Juniata Herald,* Apr. 2, 1879.

127 *diphtheria epidemic:* Creigh, *Adams County,* 16.

Alice . . . Flora: Jacobsen genealogical papers, Hallwas Collection.

"During the season of 1878": "The Maxwells," *Bushnell Record,* Dec. 16, 1881.

Wheat was the dominant crop: "Annual Review," *Hastings Journal,* Jan. 1, 1880.

128 *Hastings: Hastings Journal,* Jan. 1, 1880. Also, "Hastings," *Hastings Journal,* Dec. 7, 1876; Creigh, *Adams County,* 14–17.

Juniata: "Annual Review," *Hastings Journal,* Jan. 1, 1880.

a band of thieves: "Hastings," *Hastings Journal,* Dec. 7, 1876.

Doc Middleton and his gang: Hutton provides the only extensive account of Middleton. He was captured in July 1879, but his gang continued to operate.

128   *a "Vigilante Committee":* Creigh, *Adams County,* 16.

    "A desperado": Untitled item, *Grand Island Times,* April 14, 1881.

    vigilantes . . . had been operating: Brown, *Strain of Violence,* 101.

    the fatal shooting of a homesteader: Creigh, *Adams County,* 499–500.

129   *"got the fine Winchester rifle":* "Ed Maxwell: His Reception at St. Paul," *Stillwater Daily Sun,* Nov. 18, 1881.

    a fabulous timber region: Merritt, *Creativity, Conflict, and Controversy,* 253–69.

    massive log rafts: Schob, *Hired Hands and Plowboys,* 164–65, briefly depicts rafting and cites many sources.

    "The lumber manufacture": Untitled article, *Pepin County News,* Dec. 24, 1880.

    some 250 million board feet: Merritt, *Creativity, Conflict, and Controversy,* 263.

    "the Mississippi Logging": "Local Brevities," *Dunn County News,* Jan. 17, 1880.

130   *crews struggled to move:* See "The Flood," *Pepin County Courier,* June 18, 1880.

    Pepin County had 4,659 people: "The Population of Wisconsin," *Dunn County News,* Sept. 4, 1880, gives figures for Pepin County, and Dunn as well, in 1870, 1875, and 1880. For historical overviews, see *History of Northern Wisconsin,* II, 690–95; Forrester, *Historical and Biographical Album of the Chippewa Valley,* 278–92; Curtiss-Wedge, *History of Buffalo and Pepin Counties,* 958–67, and *Pepin County History.*

    Durand: See *History of Northern Wisconsin,* II, 698–703; Forrester, *Historical and Biographical Album of the Chippewa Valley,* 291, 295–307; Curtiss-Wedge, *History of Buffalo and Pepin Counties,* 985–1005; *Historical Sketchbook for the Durand Centennial, 1856–1956.*

132   *the Pepin County Courthouse:* Forrester, *Historical and Biographical Album of the Chippewa Valley,* 291. The courthouse still stands and is on the National Register.

    the hamlet of Hersey: *History of Northern Wisconsin,* II, 962; Petronovich, *History of Hersey,* 3–7.

    some twenty-five million pounds: "Hersey," *Hudson Star and Times,* Feb. 18, 1881.

    "The streets are regularly laid out": *History of Northern Wisconsin,* II, 962.

    "E. S. Austin is the proprietor": *History of Northern Wisconsin,* II, 962.

    Austin was president: "Spring Lake," *River Falls Journal,* Feb. 13, 1896.

133   *"sawing shingles":* 1880 U.S. Census, Hersey, St. Croix County, Wisconsin.

    "Lon Williams had written": "Lon Williams," *Milwaukee Sentinel,* Oct. 25, 1881.

133 *"Lon Williams has been known":* "RED LETTER RECORD," *St. Paul Pioneer Press,* July 25, 1881.

he "occasionally drank rather freely": Percy, *Twice Outlawed,* 57, 75.

134 *"Lon Williams, when he came":* "The Durand Murderers," *Hudson Star and Times,* Aug. 29, 1881.

Fannie Hussey: 1880 U.S. Census, Hersey, St. Croix County, Wis.; "Died," *Pepin County Courier,* June 17, 1881; and letters to the author from Catherine A. Dodson and Stephanie J. Zeman, May 22 and Aug. 8, 2005, in the Hallwas Collection.

Waubeek Township: See Curtiss-Wedge and Jones, *History of Dunn County,* 224–25; Forrester, *Historical and Biographical Album of the Chippewa Valley,* 288; and Pinkowski, *Vanished Community.*

married in 1867: Pepin County "Registration of Marriages," vol. 1, p. 125½.

Arkansaw: Curtiss-Wedge, *History of Buffalo and Pepin Counties,* 1016–23; "Arkansaw, Pepin County," *Pepin County Courier,* Feb. 2, 1878.

135 *unreliable newspaper source:* "THE WILLIAMSES," *Chicago Times,* July 31, 1881.

"Lon Williams made the acquaintance": "RED LETTER RECORD," *St. Paul Pioneer Press,* July 25, 1881.

celebration in Hersey: "Hersey," *Hudson Star and Times,* July 7, 1880.

136 *"Five weddings occurred":* "Hersey," *Hudson Star and Times,* July 16, 1880.

One of those was: A *Dunn County News* article asserts that they were married on July 4, 1880: "A DOUBLE MURDER!" *Dunn County News,* July 16, 1881.

"Parson Downer": "THE OUTLAWS," *Milwaukee Sentinel,* July 26, 1881.

"all accounts [by local residents]": "THE WILLIAMSES," *Chicago Times,* July 31, 1881.

They apparently lived with the Thompsons: "THE WILLIAMSES," *Chicago Times,* July 31, 1881.

137 *He may have worked:* "A DOUBLE MURDER!" *Dunn County News,* July 16, 1881.

working . . . for Wilson, Van Vliet: "Worried in the Woods," *St. Paul Pioneer Press,* July 16, 1881.

"When I got married": "Worried in the Woods," *St. Paul Pioneer Press,* July 16, 1881.

Lon was injured: "Hersey," *Hudson Star and Times,* Feb. 18, 1881.

physician E. O. Baker: History of Northern Wisconsin, I, 283.

Chapter 9: The Wisconsin Desperadoes

138 *Ed was set free on January 21:* "Convict Register," Oct. 9, 1876, Illinois State Penitentiary Collection, Illinois State Archives.

138   *a black mustache:* See the July 23 "Wanted" description, reprinted in Klatt, *They Died at Their Posts,* 15.

     "good looking": "The Durand Tragedy," *Wisconsin State Journal,* July 12, 1881.

139   *Lon had written to Ed:* "Maxwell in Omaha," *Omaha Herald,* Nov. 16, 1881, prints a brief message: "Don't go to Nebraska. It won't be healthy for either of us. Come up to Wisconsin and have good chums." If this is genuine, Lon apparently suspected that Ed might return to lawbreaking—and perhaps feared involvement with him in a state marked by vigilante violence. In any case, Lon hoped that they would be together.

     Ed "assisted Lon": "RED LETTER RECORD," *St. Paul Pioneer Press,* July 25, 1881.

     Ed began stealing horses: Louise Miller, "Durand Once Had Reputation as 'The Hanging Town,'" *St. Paul Pioneer Press,* Aug. 18, 1963.

     "I could fill a column": "THE WILLIAMSES," *Chicago Times,* July 31, 1881.

140   *The Colt Navy revolver:* See Boorman, *History of Colt Firearms,* 48–49, 69.

     the 1876 model: "PURSUIT OF WILLIAMS," *Milwaukee Sentinel,* Nov. 12, 1881, even gives the serial numbers on their Winchesters: 1492 and 4346. On the Winchester rifle, see Boorman, *History of Winchester Firearms,* 30–47.

     "from the hip": Percy, *Twice Outlawed,* 79.

     The earliest . . . robbery: Untitled article, *Stillwater Messenger,* Apr. 16, 1881.

141   *"parties in South Stillwater":* Untitled article, *Stillwater Daily Sun,* Nov. 3, 1881.

     Sheriff Joseph Kelly: Neill and Williams, *History of Washington County,* 242. See also "A Similar Shot," *Hudson Star and Times,* July 8, 1881.

     "[Kelly] had a hair-lifting encounter": "BROTHERS OF BLOOD," *St. Paul Pioneer Press,* July 12, 1881.

142   *"They were here":* "THE DURAND MURDERERS," *Hudson Star and Times,* Aug. 29, 1881.

     "The people of Hersey": "A Brace of Thugs," *Hudson Star and Times,* Apr. 29, 1881.

143   *A horrific diphtheria epidemic:* See the following "Hersey" columns in the *Hudson Star and Times:* Jan. 21, 1881; Feb. 18, 1881; Aug. 12, 1881; and Sept. 16, 1881.

     "[t]hey were heavily armed": *Pepin County Courier,* May 20, 1881.

     Undersheriff Miletus Knight: "Old Citizen Passes Away," *Pepin County Courier,* Mar. 27, 1908; *History of Northern Wisconsin,* II, 702.

144   *returned to horse stealing:* "HORSE THIEVES AROUND," *Oquawka Spectator,* June 2, 1881.

     Sheriff James O. Anderson: History of Henderson County (1882), 755–56;

Bateman, *Historical Encyclopedia of Illinois and History of Henderson County,* 755–56.

145　*"On May 30th the brothers":* "RED LETTER RECORD," *St. Paul Pioneer Press,* July 25, 1881. An article in the *Canton Register,* "The Maxwell Brothers," Aug. 12, 1881, reports that the Maxwells vandalized the Hicks School, in Hire Township, on the night before they stole the buggy from W. H. Neece. There was no witness to the vandalizing, so that may have been simply an act that was later associated with them. However, the Maxwells may have been resentful of wealthy landowner Ebenezer Hicks, who maintained the school.

146　*"I have been going":* "Tolerably Certain," *Macomb Journal,* June 23, 1881.

147　*"went to a farmhouse":* Reprinted in "Tolerably Certain," *Macomb Journal,* June 23, 1881.

　　one such episode: "Memoirs of Maxwell," *St. Paul Pioneer Press,* Nov. 21, 1881.

　　"When the robbers": "RED LETTER RECORD," *St. Paul Pioneer Press,* July 25, 1881.

　　"with a warrant": "THE WILLIAMSES," *Chicago Times,* July 31, 1881.

148　*"the notorious Williams":* "Hersey," *Hudson Star and Times,* May 27, 1881.

　　"Died.—In Waubeek": *Pepin County Courier,* June 17, 1881.

　　death record: "Registration of Deaths," Pepin County, 1878–1907, vol. 1, p. 14.

　　"he recounted brief portions": Percy, *Twice Outlawed,* 94.

149　*a regretful letter:* "The Wisconsin Hunt," *St. Paul Pioneer Press,* July 23, 1881.

　　"Lon was strangely affected": "THE WILLIAMSES," *Chicago Times,* July 31, 1881.

150　*"Sunday Night, June 26, 1881":* First printed in "RED LETTER RECORD," *St. Paul Pioneer Press,* July 25, 1881. As the initials "L. D." suggest, the young outlaw started using "Lon" as his first name and "David" as his middle name by 1881.

153　*"Speaking of the history":* "THE SEARCH! STILL UNSUCCESSFUL!" *Pepin County Courier,* July 22, 1881.

154　*"We spent all the night":* "The Maxwell Brothers," unidentified 1881 newspaper clipping, in the Hallwas Collection. Lon's suicidal impulse at Fannie's gravesite is also mentioned by August F. Ender, "A Short Narrative of the Notorious Williams Brothers," *Durand Courier-Wedge,* July 22, 1937.

　　"We never went near her grave": As quoted in Percy, *Twice Outlawed,* 190.

　　"from a farmer living": "The Outlaws," *Pike County Democrat,* Oct. 13, 1881. Reprinted from the *LaCrosse Daily News.*

155   *the Chicago Times reported:* "THE WILLIAMSES," *Chicago Times,* July 31,
      1881. On the real thief, see "CORNERED IN A COOLEY," *St. Paul Pioneer
      Press,* July 17, 1881.

Chapter 10: The Gunfight at Durand

156   *a spectacular new comet:* Durand was among the thousands of towns
      where it was noted; untitled article, *Pepin County Courier,* July 1, 1881.
      "felt abashed to find": "The Comet," *La Harper* (LaHarpe, Ill.), July 1,
      1881.
      President Garfield was shot: Peskin, in his biography of Garfield, 582–613,
      provides a historical account.
157   *"The Bloody Comet Year":* Quincy Daily Herald, Oct. 6, 1881.
      record-breaking heat: "A STRICKEN CITY," *Chicago Times,* July 11, 1881.
      On the evening . . . it was still hot: Forrester, *Historical and Biographical
      Album of the Chippewa Valley,* 303.
      "THE OUTLAWS": Milwaukee Sentinel, July 26, 1881.
158   *"Lon Williams told":* "The Wisconsin Hunt," *St. Paul Pioneer Press,* July
      23, 1881.
159   *"Our idea was to":* Untitled article, *Jersey County Democrat,* Nov. 24, 1881.
      "an old granny": "Memoirs of Maxwell," *St. Paul Pioneer Press,* Nov. 21,
      1881.
160   *the Coleman brothers:* "A DOUBLE MURDER!" *Dunn County News,* July 16,
      1881; "SAD TRAGEDY," *Pepin County Courier,* July 15, 1881; "The Mur-
      dered Colemans," *Bloomington Daily Bulletin,* July 13, 1881; Kevin Charles
      Stealy, "The Life and Times of Charles G. Coleman," typescript, Hallwas
      Collection.
      "Charlie was shot": Untitled article, *Pepin County Courier,* Mar. 23, 1878.
161   *"HORRIBLE MURDER!":* Pepin County Courier Extra, July 11, 1881, in the
      Wisconsin Governor Proclamation Papers Pertaining to the Apprehen-
      sion of Criminals, Series 103, Box 1, Folder 1869–1889, Wisconsin Histori-
      cal Society, Madison.
      "A DOUBLE MURDER!": Dunn County News, July 16, 1881.
163   *The two-story home of . . . James T. Dorchester:* A photograph of the house
      and a description of its location appear in August F. Ender, "A Short Nar-
      rative of the Notorious Williams Brothers," *Durand Courier-Wedge,* July
      22, 1937. Because of the gunfight, the house was a noted landmark until
      it was moved in 1936.
      "[He] gave me the other barrel": "Memoirs of Maxwell," *St. Paul Pioneer
      Press,* Nov. 21, 1881.
165   *"We killed the Coleman boys":* "The Record of Crime: The Maxwell Lynch-
      ing," *Wisconsin State Journal,* Nov. 21, 1881.
      "He [Milton] must have been dead": "SAD TRAGEDY," *Pepin County Courier,*
      July 15, 1881.

166   *"hit his right arm":* "SAD TRAGEDY," *Pepin County Courier,* July 15, 1881.
You had no obligation to submit: See Brown, *No Duty to Retreat,* 3–37.

167   *"roughing it among hunters":* Untitled article, *Pepin County Times and Courier,* Nov. 21, 1879. Reprinted from the *Menomonie Times.*
Wild Bill Hickok: A useful reference work on the lawmen and outlaws mentioned here, and others of that era, is Lamar's *Reader's Encyclopedia of the American West.*
"Go prepared": "RED LETTER RECORD," *St. Paul Pioneer Press,* July 25, 1881.

168   *Anderson . . . then traveled:* "The Sheriffs Killed by the Maxwells," *Oquawka Spectator,* July 14, 1881.
W. H. Huntington: History of Northern Wisconsin, II, 694–95, 701; Forrester, *Historical and Biographical Album of the Chippewa Valley,* 753–54; *Pepin County History: Pepin County, Wisconsin,* 9.
"the mob again": Untitled article, *Pepin County Courier,* Dec. 20, 1878.

169   *"BROTHERS OF BLOOD": Macomb Journal,* July 21, 1881.
"the James and Younger band": "Officers Murdered," *Wisconsin State Journal,* July 11, 1881. The *Chicago Inter-Ocean* and other newspapers soon repeated that assertion. For a brief discussion of the possible connection between the Maxwells and the James gang, see "A Question of Identity," *Chicago Times,* July 31, 1881. But there was none.
"over the bodies of": "SAD TRAGEDY," *Pepin County Courier,* July 15, 1881, gives the inquest report.
"murder was the theme": "The Coleman Tragedy," *Chicago Times,* July 12, 1881.
"to give evidence": July 10, 1881, summons to appear at the inquest for Charles and Milton Coleman, Durand Public Library.
"the largest ever held": "SAD TRAGEDY," *Pepin County Courier,* July 15, 1881.

170   *"the funeral cortege from Durand":* As quoted in Percy, 118–19.
crepe arm bands: untitled item, *Pepin County Courier,* July 22, 1881.
"Charles Coleman, of this village": "HORRIBLE MURDER!" *Pepin County Courier Extra,* July 11, 1881.
"he was unable to engage": "To the Public," *Pepin County Courier,* Aug. 12, 1881.
a memorial fund: Untitled article, *Pepin County Courier,* Aug. 12, 1881.

171   *he was also engaged:* "SAD TRAGEDY," *Pepin County Courier,* July 15, 1881; "A DOUBLE MURDER!" *Dunn County News,* July 16, 1881.
"a model of Christian manhood": "To the Public," *Pepin County Courier,* Aug. 12, 1881.
"a man of exemplary character": "A DOUBLE MURDER!" *Dunn County News,* July 16, 1881.

171   *"Sweet Be Their Rest":* By Mrs. Mary Ingram, *Pepin County Courier,* Aug. 5, 1881.
      "A posse started": "Horrible Murder," *Barron County News,* July 15, 1881.
      "If [the Maxwells] are caught": "The Durand Tragedy," *Wisconsin State Journal,* July 12, 1881.
      "The excited men": "Worried in the Woods," *St. Paul Pioneer Press,* July 16, 1881.

172   *distanced people from the reality:* See Jacobs, *Choosing Character,* 93.
      they apparently hid in the woods: History of Northern Wisconsin, II, 700.
      Deputy Sheriff E. L. Doolittle brought: "A DOUBLE MURDER!" *Dunn County News,* July 16, 1881.
      "THE BLOOD AVENGERS": Chicago Times, July 15, 1881.

Chapter 11: The Great Manhunt

173   *Jesse and Frank remained at large:* Brant, *Jesse James,* 201–20.
      Billy the Kid: The best of the many biographies are by Robert M. Utley, *Billy the Kid: A Short and Violent Life,* and Michael Wallis, *Billy the Kid: The Endless Ride.* The latter, especially, records an array of experiences and psychological issues that have parallels in the life of Ed Maxwell.

174   *the biggest manhunt for outlaws:* The hunt for the members of the James gang, following the failed Northfield bank robbery, involved "at least 500" men (Brant, *Jesse James,* 186), operating in various groups at several locations, and the search was essentially concluded in two weeks. See, for example, the *St. Paul Pioneer Press* news coverage of that September 7 robbery and pursuit. In the manhunt for the Maxwells, Deputy Sheriff Doolittle's posse alone included at least four hundred men, and other posses searched in nearby counties. The Wisconsin state militia was also involved, and the manhunt continued well into the fall, with many often sizable posses in Illinois and Missouri, even though they were misled by rumor and mistaken identity, and still others in Nebraska, hunting for Lon.
      "bold bluffs, crowned with chaplets": Percy, *Twice Outlawed,* 125.
      "I cannot imagine": "THE WISCONSIN HUNT," *St. Paul Pioneer Press,* July 23, 1881.
      "One man carried both": "The Coleman Tragedy," *Chicago Times,* July 12, 1881.
      "distributing them into small squads": As reprinted in Percy, *Twice Outlawed,* 132–33.

175   *"grasp . . . the widest possible scope":* As reprinted in Percy, *Twice Outlawed,* 132.
      E. L. Doolittle: "Obituary: Doolittle," *Dunn County News,* Oct. 2, 1903; *History of Northern Wisconsin,* I, 284; Curtiss-Wedge, *History of Dunn County, Wisconsin,* 33.

175   *Dunn County then had about ten thousand:* U.S. Census, 1870, 1880.

      "the reputation": "THE WISCONSIN HUNT," *St. Paul Pioneer Press,* July 23, 1881.

      Sheriff Sever Seversen: History of Northern Wisconsin, I, 287; Curtiss-Wedge, *History of Dunn County, Wisconsin,* 33.

      "Hersey, Knapp": "Criminal Crookedness," *Wisconsin State Journal,* July 16, 1881.

      "There are rumors": "THE MURDERED SHERIFFS," *Chicago Tribune,* July 13, 1881.

176   *"CORNERED IN A COOLEY":* St. Paul Pioneer Press,* July 17, 1881.

      "Three Hundred Men Afraid": Illinois State Journal,* July 19, 1881.

      the reward money: A notice by Undersheriff Miletus Knight listed the various rewards: "$1,700 REWARD," *Pepin County Courier,* July 29, 1881. See also Governor William E. Smith's proclamation of the state's $500 reward in the Proclamation Papers Relating to the Apprehension of Criminals, Series 103, Box 1, Folder 1869–1883, Wisconsin State Historical Society.

177   *"old soldiers":* "Crimes and Criminals," *Milwaukee Sentinel,* July 15, 1881.

      "From these points": "PURSUIT OF THE WILLIAMS DESPERADOES," *Dunn County News,* July 23, 1881.

      Ed later reported: "Ed Williams," *Dunn County News,* Nov. 19, 1881.

      During their flight: "Ed Williams," *Dunn County News,* Nov. 19, 1881.

178   *"one of the armed scouts":* "'COME AND TAKE US,'" *Eau Claire Free Press,* July 21, 1881.

      "E. C. and Henry Coleman": "Criminal Crookedness," *Wisconsin State Journal,* July 16, 1881. The correspondent's report is dated July 15.

      their mother apparently begged them: "Corraled in the Woods," *St. Paul Pioneer Press,* July 15, 1881; "THE SEARCH! STILL UNSUCCESSFUL!" *Pepin County Courier,* July 22, 1881.

      "from fear of what they might do": "THE WISCONSIN HUNT," *St. Paul Pioneer Press,* July 23, 1881.

      the main posse swelled: The 1881 *History of Northern Wisconsin* (II, 700), says that "fully four hundred persons" were involved; "Ed Maxwell's Case," *Pepin County Courier,* Dec. 2, 1881, says there were 500.

179   *"While the main force":* "No Game Bagged," *Hudson Star and Times,* July 22, 1881.

      "an old and experienced detective": "The Criminal Record: The Williamses Still Out," *Wisconsin State Journal,* July 18, 1881.

      "one [side view] representing him": "The Criminal Record: The Williamses Still Out," *Wisconsin State Journal,* July 18, 1881.

      images . . . were copied: Untitled article, *Dunn County News,* July 23, 1881.

179   *"photographs of the Notorious":* Untitled article, *Pepin County Courier,* Aug. 12, 1881.

180   *"there are four men":* "Hunting the Coleman Assassins," *Chicago Times,* July 16, 1881.

181   *Both the St. Paul Pioneer Press:* The correspondent for both of those papers could have been Edward Johnstone. See the discussion below in the note to page 184.

       "THE WISCONSIN HUNT": St. Paul Pioneer Press, July 23, 1881. See also Percy, *Twice Outlawed,* 136–42.

182   *as Ed later stated:* "INTERESTING INTERVIEW WITH ED MAXWELL," *Chicago Tribune,* Nov. 18, 1881.

       Charles Scott: "Criminal Crookedness," *Wisconsin State Journal,* July 16, 1881.

       sympathizers . . . in the woods: "The Day's Crime: The William Brothers," *Wisconsin State Journal,* July 30, 1881.

       "assistants in the woods": Untitled article, *Pepin County Courier,* Aug. 5, 1881. Reprinted from the *St. Paul Pioneer Press.*

       rumors centered on the Wolf brothers: Pepin County Courier, Aug. 5, 1881.

       a July 30 letter: "The Durand Murderers," *Hudson Star and Times,* Aug. 29, 1881.

       "All sorts of rumors": "The Murderers," *Eau Claire News,* July 16, 1881.

183   *"Thomas Ricket":* "The Criminal Calendar: The Williams Brothers," *Wisconsin State Journal,* July 22, 1881.

       the outlaws had been tracked: "Dunn County Murderers," *Wisconsin State Journal,* July 23, 1881.

       Ed Maxwell had been spotted: "THE SEARCH! STILL UNSUCCESSFUL!" *Pepin County Courier,* July 22, 1881.

       the Ludington Guard: "The Williams Brothers Still at Large," *Dunn County News,* July 30, 1881; Percy, *Twice Outlawed,* 144–47; Klatt, *They Died at Their Posts,* 13–14.

       Captain T. J. (Thomas Jefferson) George: Percy, *Twice Outlawed,* 146; *History of Northern Wisconsin,* I, 284; Curtiss-Wedge and Jones, *History of Dunn County,* 33, 354–55.

       "Old Buckskin": Sept. 24, 2006, letter to the author from Frank Kennett, curator, Rassbach Museum, Dunn County Historical Society, in the Hall-was Collection.

       "served with gallantry": Percy, *Twice Outlawed,* 161.

184   *"THE PITILESS PURSUIT":* Chicago Times, July 28, 1881.

       Chicago Times . . . special correspondent: The exclusive reports of the *Chicago Times* correspondent (from July 27 to August 4, 1881) were "rewritten in great measure and altered by liberal additions" for *Twice Outlawed*

(147), so Percy's book is the most complete source for that reporter's dispatches, some of which never appeared in the newspaper. This use of revised material, of course, makes it likely that the *Times* correspondent and "Adrian Percy" were the same person. It is also likely that the *Times* correspondent was Edward Johnstone, who had simply decided to issue some exclusive dispatches to that widely circulated Chicago newspaper. Johnstone did send items to the *Times* that were variations of what he sent to the *Pioneer Press*. See, for example, "A LAWLESS LIFE," *Chicago Times,* Nov. 21, 1881, which mentions his name, so it is clear that he had a relationship with that newspaper as a "special correspondent."

184   *"You fellers will never ketch":* Percy, *Twice Outlawed,* 150–68.

"Maple Springs Camp": Percy, *Twice Outlawed,* 167–68.

185   *"Buffalo Charlie was no fool":* Percy, *Twice Outlawed,* 180–81.

an Associated Press dispatch: Percy, *Twice Outlawed,* 168.

"Camp Cady, Pierce County": Percy, *Twice Outlawed,* 170–1; see also 169–70, 174–75.

186   *"Bogus Charlie":* "BOGUS CHARLEY [*sic*]," *St. Paul Pioneer Press,* Aug. 1, 1881.

"Buffalo Charlie was": untitled article, *Pepin County Courier,* Aug. 12, 1881. Reprinted from the *Wabasha Herald.*

"The fact of the matter is": "The Record of Crime," *Wisconsin State Journal,* Aug. 2, 1881.

187   *"ex-Sheriff Doolittle":* "The Williams (Maxwell) Brothers Still at Large," *Macomb Journal,* Aug. 4, 1881. Reprinted from the *Chicago Inter-Ocean.*

On July 31, the Ludington Guard: "BOGUS CHARLEY [*sic*]," *St. Paul Pioneer Press,* Aug. 1, 1881. Apparently, the participation of the guard soon ended because wealthy families of some of the young guard members feared for the safety of their sons and circulated a petition that was sent to the governor. See "'Out of Mother's Eye,'" *Chicago Times,* Aug. 5, 1881.

"Terribly Torrid Weather": Pepin County Courier, July 22, 1881.

"TIRED OUT AND TRICKED": Chicago Times, Aug. 1, 1881.

"thousands of letters": "The Maxwell Brothers," *Grand Island Times,* Nov. 17, 1881.

more rumors: See, for example, "IN AN UPROAR," *Milwaukee Sentinel,* and "The Day's Crime," *Wisconsin State Journal,* both appearing on July 30, 1881.

"Frank Werner's saloon": "Where They Will Go," *St. Paul Pioneer Press,* July 14, 1881.

Another report claimed . . . and yet another: "Suspicious Parties in Wabasha County," *St. Paul Pioneer Press,* July 14, 1881, and "Crimes and Casualties: The Williamses at Sauk Rapids," *St. Paul Pioneer Press,* Aug. 5, 1881.

187   *A "perfectly reliable man":* "The Outlaws," *Milwaukee Sentinel,* Aug. 6, 1881.

188   *"a tramp who had stolen":* untitled article, *Pepin County Courier,* Aug. 12, 1881.

     "without any doubt": "The Williams Brothers," *St. Paul Pioneer Press,* Aug. 8, 1881.

     "undoubtedly the two men": Untitled article, *St. Paul Pioneer Press,* Aug. 12, 1881.

     "It is believed": "The Maxwell Brothers," *Canton Register,* Aug. 12, 1881.

     "At LaCrosse": "Return of Sheriff Anderson," *Macomb Journal,* Aug. 11, 1881. Reprinted from the *Oquawka Spectator.*

189   *raising money: Macomb Journal,* Aug. 11, 1881. Reprinted from the *Oquawka Spectator.* Also, untitled article, *Pepin County Courier,* Aug. 12, 1881.

Chapter 12: Another Gunfight—and the Renewed Manhunt

190   *Memorial services were held:* See, for example, the dozens that were briefly noted in "The Nation's Tribute," *Chicago Times,* Sept. 27, 1881.

     Charles Guiteau: Peskin, *Garfield,* 582–96, provides an excellent discussion of the assassin.

191   *"a prisoner . . . condemned":* "Dark Deeds," *Milwaukee Sentinel,* Sept. 28, 1881.

     below Pike County is Calhoun: See Carpenter, *Calhoun Is My Kingdom.*

     "made a capital place": Stanton, *They Called It Treason,* 154. Reprinted from the 1891 *Chicago Inter-Ocean.*

     "came over from Missouri": Memoir of C. C. Squiers, as quoted in Stanton, *They Called It Treason,* 55.

192   *"A Copperhead cheered":* Stanton, *They Called It Treason,* 153–54. Reprinted from the *Alton Telegraph.*

     By 1880 the county had: U.S. Census, Calhoun County, 1880.

     the Maxwell brothers had been seen: "THROW UP YOUR HANDS!" *Missouri Republican,* Sept. 27, 1881.

     Sheriff John Lammy: See the biographical sketch of his brother, "Chittic C. Lammy," *Portrait and Biographical Album of Pike and Calhoun Counties, Illinois,* 675, and these modern overviews: Chittick Lammy, "The Legend of John Lammy," *Calhoun News,* May 6, 1982; May 13, 1982; and "John Lammy, Sheriff of Calhoun County, 1839–1881," unpublished typescript, Hall County Collection, Stuhr Museum, Grand Island.

     Lammy looked very Irish: His photograph is in the Lammy File, Calhoun County Museum, Hardin, Illinois.

193   *"the most popular":* "Killed by the Williams Desperadoes," *Chicago Times,* Sept. 27, 1881.

193 *Sheriff E. W. Blades: History of Pike County,* 672.

"A SAD CALAMITY": Pike County Democrat, Sept. 29, 1881.

194 *"We divided our forces":* "THROW UP YOUR HANDS!" *Missouri Republican,* Sept. 27, 1881.

195 *"At this moment [Lon] Maxwell":* Letter to the editor, *Calhoun Herald,* Oct. 20, 1881; reprinted as "How John Lammy Was Killed," *Hardin Republican,* Jan. 5, 1905.

196 *Churchman . . . and McNabb:* U.S. Census, Calhoun County, 1880.

Churchman's account: There were other inconsistencies as well. For example, Churchman was in a posse focused on locating the Maxwell brothers, but he claimed that he approached the man with the gun at Fox Creek "not having any idea that he was one of the Maxwells." He surely made that remark to counter criticism that he and McNabb had acted hastily and foolishly in confronting men who were noted gunfighters. See, for example, "The Maxwell Desperadoes" in Springfield's *State Journal Register,* Sept. 28, 1881, which states that "the deputies seem to have rushed precipitately upon the fight." Churchman's report was apparently shaped to exculpate himself and shift the blame for the tragic event to others in the posse— despite the fact that he not only started the fight but also emptied his gun and failed to hit either of the outlaws, as Blades had pointed out.

"for three weeks": "THEY ARE COMING!" *Missouri Republican,* Sept. 28, 1881.

"have been located": "The Williams Outlaws," *Chicago Times,* Sept. 28, 1881.

"making their way down": "Pursuit of the Williams Brothers," *Milwaukee Sentinel,* Sept. 28, 1881.

197 *"THE MAXWELL BROTHERS": Alton Telegraph,* Sept. 29, 1881.

198 *A tall, slim, balding man:* Photograph and data at the Metropolitan Police Department Library, St. Louis.

"The chief says": "The Williams Brothers," *Milwaukee Sentinel,* Sept. 29, 1881.

"from the many reports": "The Cruise of the *Truant," Alton Telegraph,* Oct. 6, 1881.

"Sheriff Blades, of Pike County": "The Williams Brothers," *Milwaukee Sentinel,* Sept. 29, 1881.

"greatly alarmed": "The Williams Outlaws," *Chicago Times,* Sept. 28, 1881.

offered an additional reward: Residents of Bee Creek pledged $100; untitled article, *Pike County Democrat,* Oct. 6, 1881.

"CAUGHT": Milwaukee Sentinel, Sept. 30, 1881.

199 *Reports soon came in:* See the following articles from the *Missouri Republican*: "The Hue and Cry," Sept. 28, 1881; "They Didn't Catch Them,"

Sept. 30, 1881; "The Man Hunt," Oct. 4, 1881; "He Caught a Glimpse of Them," Oct. 15, 1881; and "We've Got Them," Oct. 18, 1881. In the *St. Paul Pioneer Press,* see "The Maxwells," Oct. 6, 1881.

199   *"a dozen" other places:* Untitled article, *Pike County Democrat,* Oct. 18, 1881.

"REVOLVER RULE": Milwaukee Sentinel, Oct. 3, 1881.

"500 men": "The Williams Brothers Again," *St. Paul Pioneer Press,* Sept. 28, 1881.

"each [of the outlaws]": "The Williams Brothers," *Chicago Tribune,* Sept. 27, 1881, and "FLYING FUGITIVES," *Milwaukee Sentinel,* Sept. 27, 1881.

"Lon, who killed Lammy": "The Maxwell Desperadoes," *Chicago Times,* Oct. 4, 1881.

200   *"Reports are":* "Killed by the Williams Desperadoes," *Chicago Times,* Sept. 27, 1881.

"from Clarksville": "The Williams Brothers," *Milwaukee Sentinel,* Oct. 4, 1881.

"three different posses": "The Williams Brothers," *Milwaukee Sentinel,* Oct. 4, 1881.

"roaming around": "The Williams Brothers," *Chicago Tribune,* Oct. 4, 1881.

"to search the woods": "Munchausen M'Grew, and His Thrilling Experience with the Maxwell Brothers," *Missouri Republican,* Oct. 23, 1881.

"A Mysterious Stranger": Alton Telegraph, Oct. 6, 1881.

201   *they were . . . gunmen:* Two helpful discussions of the gunman as a type of violent person are by Hollon and Rosa. Although neither mentions the Maxwells, the psychological profiles that they draw of such outlaw killers relate to what we know of Ed. See, for example, Hollon, *Frontier Violence,* 110, and Rosa, *Gunfighter,* 44.

"THE MAXWELL DESPERADOES": Oquawka Spectator, Sept. 29, 1881.

"the Mercer boys": Untitled article, *St. Paul Pioneer Press,* Nov. 19, 1881. See also, on the same page, "Murdered a Marshal."

"$500, for the capture": "The Williams Brothers," *Chicago Tribune,* Oct. 4, 1881.

"the telegraph lines": "Bowed by the Blast," *Chicago Times,* Sept. 26, 1881.

"the alarming rise": "Wisconsin Floods," *Milwaukee Sentinel,* Oct. 4, 1881.

202   *"the greatest flood ever known":* "Raging Floods," *Alton Telegraph,* Nov. 3, 1881.

"the destruction on both sides": "Raging Floods," *Alton Telegraph,* Nov. 3, 1881.

in Milwaukee, St. Louis, and other places: "The Williams Problem," *St. Paul Pioneer Press,* Nov. 4, 1881.

202   *"the largest concourse of citizens":* Untitled article, *Calhoun Herald,* Oct. 13, 1881, as reprinted in Chittick Lammy, "The Legend of John Lammy," *Calhoun News,* May 13, 1982.

     "an honored, brave": "In Memoriam," *Pike County Democrat,* Oct. 20, 1881.

     "The people of this county": Chittick Lammy, "The Legend of John Lammy," *Calhoun News,* May 6, 1982.

     Other stories: "The Legend of John Lammy," *Calhoun News,* May 6, 1982.

203   *$1,000 for an imposing monument:* "The Legend of John Lammy," *Calhoun News,* May 6, 1982.

     "the citizens of Calhoun County": "Another Murder by the Williams Brothers," *Jersey County Democrat,* Sept. 29, 1881.

     "Now all the bad management": Churchman, "How John Lammy Was Killed," *Calhoun Republican,* Jan. 5, 1905, as reprinted on page 9 in "John Lammy, Sheriff of Calhoun County, 1839–1881," unpublished typescript, Hall County Collection, Stuhr Museum, Grand Island. The Churchman article originally appeared in the *Calhoun Herald* in 1881, but that issue does not survive.

     the posse, who were too far away: As an article in Springfield's *Illinois State Register* pointed out, "At the time of the killing, Sheriff Blades and his posse were a mile and a half away. . . ."; "The Maxwell Desperadoes," Sept. 28, 1881, as quoted on page 5 in "John Lammy, Sheriff of Calhoun County 1839–1881," unpublished typescript, Hall County Collection, Stuhr Museum, Grand Island.

204   *legendary gunfighters:* On the characteristics of the gunfighter, see O'Neal, *Pimlico Encyclopedia of Western Gunfighters,* 3–9. Variously good or bad, they were simply men with a reputation for gunfights. Very few became nationally notorious. Focused on "Western" gunmen, O'Neal omits the Maxwells.

     "THE JAMES BOYS . . . ECLIPSED": "THROW UP YOUR HANDS!" *Missouri Republican,* Sept. 27, 1881.

     "The Williams' escape": Untitled article, *Dunn County News,* Oct. 8, 1881.

     "No criminals": "The Williams Boys," *National Police Gazette,* Dec. 3, 1881.

     had "committed a number of murders": "LON WILLIAMS," *Milwaukee Sentinel,* Oct. 25, 1881.

Chapter 13: Ed's Capture and Lon's Escape

205   *the gunfight at the O.K. Corral:* For a contemporaneous midwestern news report, see "Fight with Cowboys," *Missouri Republican,* Oct. 28, 1881. A fine historical account of America's most famous gunfight is Marks, *Die in the West.*

205   *"I do not want to fight":* Marks, *Die in the West,* 222.

      "a . . . Citizens' Safety Committee": Hollon, *Frontier Violence,* 201.

206   *Lon had been jailed:* "LON WILLIAMS," *Milwaukee Sentinel,* Oct. 25, 1881.

      "DREAD SUSPENSE": Milwaukee Sentinel,* Oct. 26, 1881.

207   *"William Kuhl" was simply another alias:* "THE ALLEDGED [*sic*] LON WIL-LIAMS," *Chicago Times,* Oct. 28, 1881.

      he "can not be mistaken": "Milwaukee's Mystery," *Chicago Times,* Nov. 1, 1881.

      National Police Gazette . . . article: "His Foot as Evidence," Nov. 19, 1881.

208   *"Coleman drew a large Navy":* "Identified as Lon Williams, the Outlaw," *Washington Post,* Nov. 1, 1881.

      "thoroughly identified": "Lon Williams," *Pepin County Courier,* Nov. 4, 1881.

      placed in the Dunn County Jail: "Lon Williams," *Pepin County Courier,* Nov. 4, 1881.

      "the man in custody": "The Williams Problem," *St. Paul Pioneer Press,* Nov. 4, 1881.

209   *"Dr. Baker avers":* "WAYS OF THE WICKED," *Milwaukee Sentinel,* Nov. 5, 1881.

      The district attorneys: "WAYS OF THE WICKED," *Milwaukee Sentinel,* Nov. 5, 1881.

      He sued for $25,000: "LAST OF THE MAXWELLS," *Colchester Independent,* Sept. 19, 1889. See also untitled article, *Pepin County Courier,* Nov. 18, 1881.

      a bulletin from St. Louis: "COLLARED AT ST. LOUIS," *Milwaukee Sentinel,* Nov. 3, 1881.

      the chief authority: Untitled article, *Pepin County Courier,* Nov. 18, 1881.

      "Edward Maxwell": "Ed Williams Caught," *Milwaukee Sentinel,* Nov. 9, 1881.

212   *A later report added:* "WHILE THEY SLEPT," *Macomb Journal,* Nov. 17, 1881.

      in the New York Times: See the items under "CRIMINALS AND THEIR DEEDS," Nov. 11, 1881, and "A LONG CRIMINAL RECORD," Nov. 12, 1881.

      "RUNNING DOWN WESTERN OUTLAWS": Philadelphia Evening Telegraph,* Nov. 11, 1881.

      "'DOWNING' A DEMON": Chicago Times,* Nov. 10, 1881.

      "THE SHERIFF KILLERS": Hastings Gazette-Journal,* Nov. 17, 1881.

      Sheriff Kilian: The file on Kilian at the Stuhr Museum of the Prairie Pioneer in Grand Island includes his obituary from the *San Bernardino Daily Sun* and other items. Among them is Gene Watson, "Hall County Sheriff Captures Outlaw Killer," *Grand Island Daily Independent,* July 3, 2000. See also the 1870 and 1880 U.S. Census for Grand Island.

212   *Grand Island:* See "NEBRASKA," *Grand Island Times,* Aug. 4, 1881, and "The Boom," *Grand Island Times,* Dec. 25, 1879. The history of Hall County by Buechler and Baker includes 1875 and 1879 photographs of the town on pages 96 and 108, and Bailey's history of Grand Island includes an 1874 bird's-eye map on page 13. The most recent history of the county, *Trails into Time* by Budde and Woitaszewski, includes an 1881 photograph on page 8.

     "He is a German": "Ed Williams' Captor," *Wisconsin State Journal,* Nov. 22, 1881.

     Kilian soon received: "Williams' Captor," *Omaha Daily Bee,* Nov. 25, 1881.

214   *"William Edward Maxwell":* The "Prison Calendar" of the Hall County Jail, Stuhr Museum, Grand Island.

     he tried to pick the lock: "WHILE THEY SLEPT," *Macomb Journal,* Nov. 17, 1881.

     "interviewed the prisoner": "WHILE THEY SLEPT," *Macomb Journal,* Nov. 17, 1881.

     "Undersheriff Knight": Untitled article, *Pepin County Courier,* Nov. 18, 1881.

     "The picture, though poor": "Told by a Picture," *Milwaukee Sentinel,* Nov. 16, 1881.

     "All of importance": "WHILE THEY SLEPT," *Macomb Journal,* Nov. 17, 1881.

215   *"this section":* "INTERESTING INTERVIEW," *Macomb Journal,* Nov. 17, 1881.

216   *"as fearless a desperado":* Untitled article, *Pike County Democrat,* Nov. 24, 1881.

     "[W]e both wanted": "Memoirs of Maxwell," *St. Paul Pioneer Press,* Nov. 21, 1881.

     he led a posse: "PURSUIT OF WILLIAMS," *Milwaukee Sentinel,* Nov. 12, 1881.

217   *"The party that has been":* Reprinted as part of "WHILE THEY SLEPT," *Macomb Journal,* Nov. 17, 1881.

     "sent a boy into a store": "Ed Williams," *Pepin County Courier,* Nov. 18, 1881.

     "lost the trail": "Nebraska News: Aurora," (Lincoln) *Daily Nebraska State Journal,* Nov. 15, 1881.

     "Several posses": "The Maxwell Brothers," *Grand Island Times,* Nov. 17, 1881.

218   *"a region of sand hills":* "Ed Williams Jailed at Omaha," *Chicago Tribune,* Nov. 16, 1881.

     "had a very vicious look": "Was He Alonzo Maxwell?" *Grand Island Times,* Nov. 24, 1881.

218 *an article . . . illustration:* "The Williams Boys," *National Police Gazette,* Dec. 3, 1881.

Chapter 14: The Desperado and the Public

219 *a complex relationship with the public:* Illuminating studies of the relationship between Jesse and Billy, as outlaws, and the nineteenth-century public are Settle's *Jesse James Was His Name* and Tatum's *Inventing Billy the Kid,* as well as Steckmesser's *Western Hero in History and Legend* on Billy (57–104). Also helpful on Jesse James, Sam Bass, and Billy the Kid is Meyer's "The Outlaw Hero." A more general study of this same relationship with the public is Prassel's *Great American Outlaw.*
"MAXWELL, THE MURDERER": Omaha Daily Bee, Nov. 16, 1881.

220 *"As he was going up":* "MAXWELL, THE MURDERER," *Omaha Daily Bee,* Nov. 16, 1881.
"Just as the party": "Ed Williams," *Pepin County Courier,* Nov. 18, 1881.
"Henry Coleman succeeded": "ED MAXWELL LYNCHED," *Grand Island Times,* Nov. 24, 1881.

221 *"The parents of the Maxwell boys":* "Juniata Jottings," *Hastings Gazette-Journal,* Nov. 17, 1881.
"ED MAXWELL": Stillwater Daily Sun, Nov. 18, 1881.

222 *"A NOTORIOUS WESTERN RUFFIAN":* New York Times, Nov. 18, 1881.
"MAXWELL IN MANACLES": St. Paul Pioneer Press, Nov. 18, 1881.

225 *"He further stated":* "A Card from Coleman," *Eau Claire Free Press,* Dec. 8, 1881.

226 *What Ed meant:* On the notion that people often strive to become what they were meant, by psychological drives, to be, see May, *Freedom and Destiny,* 92–96.
"had no shoe or stocking on one foot": "Another Murder by the Williams Brothers," *Jersey County Democrat,* Sept. 29, 1881.

227 *"Ed's arm was badly riddled":* "The Experiences of the Williams Desperadoes—How They Were Hunted Down," *Wisconsin State Journal,* Nov. 18, 1881.
"around Fieldon": "Bold Robbery," *Jersey County Democrat,* Oct. 20, 1881.
"the conviction [arose]": "The Fieldon Bank Robbery," *Chicago Times,* Oct. 22, 1881. See also "CRIMINALS UNCAUGHT," *Missouri Republican,* Oct. 2, 1881; "The Daily Calendar: The Fieldon Bank Robbers," *Chicago Times,* Oct. 21, 1881; and an untitled article, *Jersey County Democrat,* Nov. 24, 1881.
"a little lame": "From Fieldon," *Jersey County Democrat,* Nov. 3, 1881.

228 *good with their guns:* A later article said that searchers found tin cans pierced with holes, showing that the Fieldon bank robbers also practiced marksmanship with their guns; "The Fieldon Bank Robbery," *Jersey County Democrat,* Oct. 27, 1881.

228 *Edward Johnstone:* "Edward Johnstone Dies in East at 85," *St. Paul Pioneer Press,* Mar. 30, 1935; "E. L. [*sic*] Johnstone, 85, an Ex-Editor, Dies," *New York Times,* Mar. 30, 1935.

 "crowds thronged": "A RED-HANDED RASCAL," *Chicago Times,* Nov. 18, 1881.

229 *"seemed to be a disposition":* "Comments of the Press," *Pepin County Courier,* Dec. 2, 1881. This item is reprinted from the *Galesville Independent.*

 "TALKING ON THE CARS": This is part of "MAXWELL IN MANACLES," *St. Paul Pioneer Press,* Nov. 18, 1881.

230 *"[a] large but orderly crowd":* "The Capture of Ed Williams," *Wisconsin State Journal,* Nov. 18, 1881.

 "AT HOME: THE CAPTURED BANDIT": *Milwaukee Sentinel,* Nov. 18, 1881.

231 *"Small squads of citizens:* "AT HOME: THE CAPTURED BANDIT," *Milwaukee Sentinel,* Nov. 18, 1881.

 "Grave fears": "Exhibiting Williams," *Wisconsin State Journal,* Nov. 19, 1881.

 "People here talk freely": "MAXWELL IN MANACLES," *St. Paul Pioneer Press,* Nov. 18, 1881.

 "INTERESTING INTERVIEW": *Chicago Tribune,* Nov. 18, 1881.

 Ed's reiteration: On the importance of shame, and its avoidance, as a cause for violent behavior, see Gilligan, *Violence,* 103–36.

233 *"were suffering so terribly":* "TALKING ON THE CARS," *St. Paul Pioneer Press,* Nov. 18, 1881.

 "I don't lie, sir": "TALKING ON THE CARS," *St. Paul Pioneer Press,* Nov. 18, 1881.

 "After the shooting": "ED WILLIAMS," *Dunn County News,* Nov. 19, 1881.

234 *"During the hours":* "Memoirs of Maxwell," *St. Paul Pioneer Press,* Nov. 21, 1881.

235 *"Ed Maxwell appears":* Untitled article, *Milwaukee Sentinel,* Nov. 19, 1881.

237 *the supreme form of heroism:* Tompkins, *West of Everything,* 31.

 "Those who have led": "The Capture of Ed Williams," *Wisconsin State Journal,* Nov. 18, 1881.

 death would be: Paraphrasing Tompkins, *West of Everything,* 27, who discusses death and the hero.

Chapter 15: The Lynching at Durand

238 *"perish by mob violence":* "GUITEAU," *Milwaukee Sentinel,* Sept. 29, 1881.

 "The ball was started": Untitled article, *Pike County Democrat,* Sept. 29, 1881.

238 *the insanity plea:* For a discussion of this, see Friedman, *Crime and Punishment in American History,* 143–48.

He not only disclosed: For a good contemporaneous account of the insanity defense for Guiteau, see "Washington News," *Omaha Daily Bee,* Nov. 23, 1881.

239 *"a downright lunatic":* "Guiteau's Insanity," *Peoria Transcript,* July 7, 1881.

"When a man is sane": Untitled article, *Canton Register,* Nov. 25, 1881.

"a . . . bad man": "Conviction of Guiteau," *Pepin County Courier,* Feb. 3, 1882.

"a natural-born criminal": "Guiteau's Insanity," *Peoria Transcript,* July 7, 1881.

"a cowardly act": "Memoirs of Maxwell," *St. Paul Pioneer Press,* Nov. 21, 1881.

240 *The Chicago Tribune staff started:* "Dead and Gone," Jan. 1, 1883.

"The general growth": "Enforcement of Law," *Canton Register,* Nov. 4, 1881.

241 *"in our own city":* "Dead and Gone," *Chicago Tribune,* Jan. 1, 1883.

reliance on lynch law: For a historical overview, see Brown, *Strain of Violence.* See also the bibliography by Moses.

it reported 117: "Dead and Gone," *Chicago Tribune,* Jan. 1, 1883.

"'Lynched' . . . is a very common": "Philosophy of the Bloomington Lynching," *Chicago Tribune,* Oct. 4, 1881.

lynchings in almost every state: On the prevalence of lynching, see Cutler's *Lynch Law,* Gard's *Frontier Justice,* and "Necktie Parties" in Monaghan, *Book of the American West,* 298–307.

"TWO COWBOYS HANGED": *Chicago Tribune,* Nov. 10, 1881.

"cowboy" still had negative associations: Smith, *Virgin Land,* 109–11, and Courtwright, *Violent Land,* 87–89.

242 *An 1881 . . . newspaper article:* "The Moral of Lynch Law," *Pierce County Herald,* Dec. 7, 1881.

"a mob of forty": "CRIMINALITIES," *Milwaukee Sentinel,* Oct. 6, 1881.

Illinois also had lynchings: No comprehensive account of Illinois lynchings has been done. In the adjacent state of Iowa, there were at least seventy-seven victims of lethal lynching and twice that many cases of nonlethal brutality between 1834 and 1908, according to an early study; see Black, "Lynchings in Iowa." Illinois surely had a similar record.

"The custom in . . . communities": "Lynching," *Quincy Daily Herald,* Mar. 27, 1878.

a thief named David Hardy: "STRUNG UP," *Macomb Eagle,* Aug. 15, 1874.

In Carthage, Missouri: "An Outlaw Arrested," *Milwaukee Sentinel,* Aug. 6, 1881.

243   *"This [shooting of the jailer]":* "LYNCHED," *Chicago Tribune,* Oct. 2, 1881.

      "There is too much law quibbling": "The Bloomington Lynching for Murder," *Chicago Tribune,* Oct. 3, 1881.

      "If the State of Illinois": "The Lynching in Illinois," *Milwaukee Sentinel,* Oct. 4, 1881.

      a double lynching at Stevens Point: "The Scroll of Sin," *Chicago Tribune,* Oct. 29, 1875. See also "True or False, Lynchings in Wisconsin Made News," *Wisconsin Then and Now* 24 (June 1978): 4–5, 7, which includes a list of Wisconsin lynchings.

244   *"an occasional threatening remark":* "ED WILLIAMS LYNCHED," *Dunn County News,* Nov. 26, 1881.

      "a flimsy, insecure structure": "HIS LONG JOURNEY ENDED," *St. Paul Pioneer Press,* Nov. 20, 1881.

      "our jail would not hold": "ED WILLIAMS," *Pepin County Courier,* Nov. 18, 1881.

      the largest cell, containing: "HIS LONG JOURNEY ENDED," *St. Paul Pioneer Press,* Nov. 20, 1881.

      asked . . . if he would write his life story: "HIS LONG JOURNEY ENDED," *St. Paul Pioneer Press,* Nov. 20, 1881.

245   *"A DEAD MAN'S TALE":* *Chicago Tribune,* Nov. 21, 1881.

248   *"partly true and partly false":* "LYNCHED!" *Pepin County Courier,* Nov. 25, 1881.

      "We didn't get along": "Memoirs of Maxwell," *St. Paul Pioneer Press,* Nov. 21, 1881.

249   *"This morning between":* "SHORT SHRIFT," *Chicago Times,* Nov. 20, 1881.

      "You don't think I'm walking": "A DEAD MAN'S TALE," *Chicago Tribune,* Nov. 21, 1881.

250   *some five hundred people:* Louise Miller, "Durand Once Had Reputation as 'Hanging Town,'" *St. Paul Pioneer Press,* Aug. 18, 1963.

      "THE STORY OF AN EYE-WITNESS": *Macomb Journal,* Nov. 24, 1881.

251   *Wayne B. Dyer:* "Wayne Bidwell Dyer," *Pepin County Courier,* Sept. 1, 1899.

      "Hang him! Choke him!": "LYNCHED!" *Pepin County Courier,* Nov. 25, 1881.

253   *"STILL ANOTHER ACCOUNT":* *St. Paul Pioneer Press,* Nov. 26, 1881. Reprinted from the *Eau Claire Free Press.*

254   *the widow of Charles Coleman:* "Hanged by a Mob," *Chicago Journal,* Nov. 21, 1881.

Chapter 16: The Lynching Controversy and Durand's Fate

257   *"SNUFFED OUT AT LAST":* *Macomb Journal,* Nov. 24, 1881.

      "JUSTICE": *Chicago Tribune,* Nov. 20, 1881.

258   *"that he would suffer death":* "THE DURAND LYNCHING," *Milwaukee Sentinel,* Nov. 21, 1881.

258   *"Every witness of the hanging":* Untitled article, *Stillwater Daily Sun,* Nov. 26, 1881.

       "the body of Ed Maxwell": "Verdict of the Jury in the Ed Maxwell Lynching Case: He Fell from the Courthouse Steps and Broke His Neck," *Chicago Tribune,* Nov. 23, 1881.

259   *"an unmitigated, d—n liar":* "A Daisy of a Reporter," *Pepin County Courier,* Nov. 26, 1881.

       "to excite the citizens": "Pure Cussedness," *Pepin County Courier,* Nov. 26, 1881.

       "INQUEST UPON THE VIEW": Handwritten report, Ed Maxwell Inquest, "Williams/Maxwell" file, Pepin County Historical Society.

260   *"did all in our power":* "The Lynching of Maxwell—Card from Undersheriff Knight," *Wisconsin State Journal,* Nov. 25, 1881.

       "none of the mob were masked": "Sheriff Kilian Receiving His Reward," *Chicago Tribune,* Nov. 23, 1881.

       "I have not yet heard": "The Maxwell Tragedy—Explanation by the Sheriff," *Wisconsin State Journal,* Dec. 6, 1881.

261   *"murdered Ed Williams":* "The Foes of Society," *St. Paul Pioneer Press,* Nov. 24, 1881.

       "Lon Maxwell": "The Maxwell Lynching," *Chicago Times,* Nov. 24, 1881.

       "Murder, Murder": "Lynching" file, Pepin County Historical Society, Durand.

262   *"Mob law should always":* "LYNCHED!" *Pepin County Courier,* Nov. 26, 1881.

263   *"LYNCH LAW IN WISCONSIN":* *Stillwater Daily Sun,* Nov. 21, 1881.

264   *"there was no shadow":* "LYNCH LAW," *Pierce County Herald,* Nov. 30, 1881.

       "THE DURAND MURDER": *Eau Claire News,* Nov. 26, 1881.

       "desperadoism is becoming": "The Durand Lynching," *Wisconsin State Journal,* Nov. 21, 1881.

265   *"the uncivilized Southwest":* "SHORT SHRIFT," *Chicago Times,* Nov. 20, 1881.

       "No story of lynching": Untitled editorial, *New York Times,* Nov. 21, 1881.

       "the open-handed, resolute": "Comments of the Press," *Pepin County Courier,* Dec. 2, 1881. Reprinted from the *Chicago Inter-Ocean.*

       "the lynching of Ed Maxwell": "Comments of the Press," *Pepin County Courier,* Dec. 2, 1881. Reprinted from the *Atlanta Constitution.*

266   *"But the people of Durand":* "Comments of the Press," *Pepin County Courier,* Dec. 2, 1881. Reprinted from the *Milwaukee Sunday Telegraph.*

       That newspaper and several others: "The Moral of Lawlessness," *Pepin County Courier,* Nov. 21, 1881; "The Natural Result," *St. Paul Globe*; and an untitled editorial from the *Wabasha Herald* reprinted in the Dec. 2, 1881, issue of the *Courier.*

266 *"Our people almost to a unit":* Letter from Pepin (dated Dec. 6, 1881), *Pepin County Courier,* Dec. 9, 1881.

"Ed expressed no sorrow": "Ed Maxwell's Case," *Pepin County Courier,* Dec. 2, 1881.

267 *"We hear of some threats":* Untitled editorial, *Pepin County Courier,* Nov. 25, 1881.

268 *"heroic treatment":* Untitled article, *Pepin County Courier,* Nov. 25, 1881.

"The people have lost": "LYNCH LAW," *Alton Telegraph,* Nov. 24, 1881.

"electors of the town": "A Communication," *Dunn County News,* Dec. 3, 1881.

269 *"It is in order to discuss":* Untitled editorial, *St. Paul Dispatch,* Nov. 21, 1881.

270 *"murder of Ed Maxwell":* "LYNCH LAW," *Hastings Gazette-Journal,* Nov. 24, 1881.

"If Guiteau should escape": Untitled editorial, *Stillwater Messenger,* Nov. 26, 1881.

"Guiteau says he will be": St. Paul Pioneer Press editorial, quoted in the *Pepin County Courier,* Dec. 2, 1881. Other humorous commentaries linking the Guiteau case and Ed Maxwell's lynching appeared in the *Pepin County Courier* on Dec. 2 under "Comments of the Press" and on Dec. 16 in an untitled page-1 article.

"Guiteau may be a greater crank": untitled item, *Pepin County Courier,* Dec. 2, 1881.

a bill to legalize: Dunn County News report, *Pepin County Courier,* Dec. 2, 1881.

"crimes of the two boys": "THE MAXWELLS," *Eau Claire News,* Dec. 17, 1881.

271 *"Lon and Ed were bad boys":* "ED MAXWELL LYNCHED," *Hastings Gazette-Journal,* Nov. 24, 1881.

If their lives are the unfolding: Very helpful on this issue were Jacobs, *Choosing Character;* Moran, *Grammar of Responsibility;* Pereboom, *Living without Free Will;* and Wegner, *Illusion of Conscious Will.*

272 *"an act against God and law":* An 1881 comment in the *Pepin County Courier,* as quoted in the *Pepin County History,* 9.

"DEVASTATION OF DURAND": St. Paul Pioneer Press, Dec. 28, 1881.

274 *"threats of revenge":* "REPORTED BURNING OF DURAND," *New York Times,* Dec. 28, 1881.

"It is nevertheless hard": Untitled article, *Milwaukee Sentinel,* Dec. 28, 1881.

"nearly every participant": "Was It a Judgment?" *Canton Register,* Dec. 29, 1881.

"There are hundreds": "The Durand Fire," *Stillwater Daily Sun,* Dec. 28, 1881.

275   *"no evidence before us":* Report of [the] Grand Jury, April 19, 1882; Pepin County Circuit Court records, University of Wisconsin–Stout.

the 1881 History: II, 695–96. The book actually appeared in the winter of 1882.

much to the dismay: Untitled article, *Pepin County Courier,* Feb. 17, 1882.

"It would be perilous": "That History," *Pepin County Courier,* Mar. 3, 1882.

"The Hanging Town": Louise Miller, "Durand Once Had Reputation as 'Hanging Town,'" *St. Paul Pioneer Press,* Aug. 18, 1963.

"Although Durand was criticized": Louise Miller, "Durand Once Had Reputation as 'Hanging Town,'" *St. Paul Pioneer Press,* Aug. 18, 1963.

"lumbermen"... *"to make trouble":* Slabey, "Afterword," *Durand 1881,* n. p.

276   *someone hung*... *a human skeleton:* Untitled photographic item, *Durand Courier-Wedge,* Aug. 20, 1959.

Chapter 17: The Mysterious Fate of Lon Maxwell

277   *the notion arose:* Settle, *Jesse James Was His Name,* 168–71, provides a good brief discussion of this rumor and the various hoaxes that it spawned.

rumors flew: Several people have asserted that someone other than Billy died by the gun of Pat Garrett. Johnson's *Billy the Kid* provides a helpful critique of those assertions.

folklore eventually asserted: Nash, *Encyclopedia of Western Lawmen and Outlaws,* 70.

Black Bart... *vanished:* Drago, *Road Agents and Train Robbers,* 56–57. See also Drago's discussion of the disappearance of Nevada bandit Milton Sharp, 83–84.

278   *Joe Brice disappeared:* Hallwas, "Joe Brice: Fulton County Badman," 14.

"Several [search] parties": "The Maxwell Brothers," *Grand Island Times,* Nov. 17, 1881.

"THE MAXWELLS": *Eau Claire News,* Dec. 17, 1881. Reprinted from the *St. Paul Pioneer Press.*

279   *"a young fellow":* "Was He Alonzo Maxwell?" *Grand Island Times,* Nov. 24, 1881.

"a light mustache and goatee": "Lon Williams," *Chicago Tribune,* May 30, 1882. See also in that issue "Hyde Park," and in the May 31 issue, "Lon Williams."

280   *"the notorious desperado":* "Lon Williams," *Chicago Tribune,* Oct. 29, 1882.

"Williams will probably be lynched": "Lon Williams," *Chicago Tribune,* Oct. 29, 1882.

280   *"Lon's death was"*: "THE MAXWELL BOYS," *Macomb Journal,* Dec. 17, 1903.
      "LAST OF THE MAXWELLS": *Colchester Independent,* Sept. 19, 1889.

281   *"The last definite record"*: August F. Ender, "A Short Narrative of the Notorious Williams Brothers," *Durand Courier-Wedge,* July 22, 1937.
      "the work of the noted outlaw": "MEAD'S MURDERER," *Chicago Tribune,* Sept. 30, 1883. A later version of this asserted that the arrest and escape took place in 1910; Curtiss-Wedge and Jones, *History of Dunn County,* 42.

282   *"A MYSTERY IS SOLVED"*: *Colchester Independent,* Jan. 28, 1898.

283   *"MISTAKEN SKELETON"*: *Colchester Independent,* Feb. 4, 1898.

284   *After ending his career:* *History of Henderson County,* 756.

285   *"Persuant to our conversation"*: Letter to Hon. E. J. Murphy, Warden, Joliet State Penitentiary, Sept. 17, 1905, in the Penitentiary Mittimus File for Lon Maxwell, Illinois State Archives, Springfield.
      "a crack revolver shot": August F. Ender, "A Short Narrative of the Notorious Williams Brothers," *Durand Courier-Wedge,* July 22, 1937.

286   *"the Lon Williams Gang"*: "The Moon Family," *Chicago Tribune,* Feb. 5, 1884.
      David died . . . on December 9: Jacobsen genealogical papers, Hallwas Collection.

287   *he looked like he was:* A late photograph of David is in the Hallwas Collection.
      "for [his] last years": Undated letter by Susan Maxwell, in the Jacobsen genealogical papers, Hallwas Collection.
      his estate was modest: Inventory of the Estate of David Maxwell, Adams County Probate Records; copy in the Hallwas Collection.
      She died . . . on January 12: Jacobsen genealogical papers, Hallwas Collection. Data on the marriages and deaths of all of David and Susan's children are also in that file.
      he . . . earned an international reputation: "Councilman G. Maxwell Dies Today," *Hastings Daily Tribune,* Nov. 23, 1936; "Plans for Rites of Geo. Maxwell Not Completed," *Hastings Morning Spotlight,* Nov. 24, 1936.

288   *The last . . . was John:* Information on John and his family is from interviews with his granddaughters, Yetive Jacobsen and Lorraine Riese, June 16, 2005. See also "Funeral Services for John L. Maxwell Held," *Hastings Tribune,* Aug. 17, 1943.
      "from some place far off": Interview with Frances (Florence) Sidlo, on July 18, 2005, by Lois Frahm, who supplied a typescript. Filed in the Hallwas Collection. Another version of this story appears as "Items and Legends," *Bladen: The First 100 Years,* 79.

Epilogue

292   *"[the Maxwells] rapidly advanced":* "LAST OF THE MAXWELLS," *Colchester Independent,* Sept. 19, 1889.

"on the drive down from Menomonie": August F. Ender, "A Short Narrative of the Notorious Williams Brothers," *Durand Courier-Wedge,* July 22, 1937.

293   *folks in Calhoun County:* See, for example, the untitled article in the *Pike County Democrat,* Dec. 1, 1881, which expresses the view of many in Pike and Calhoun counties: "It was, in our mind, beyond all question the Maxwells who killed Lammy." Also, see George Carpenter, "Maxwell Bros. Kill Sheriff John Lammy," in *I Want to See a Lawyer,* 15, and Chittick Lammy, "The Legend of John Lammy," *Calhoun News,* May 6, 1982, and May 13, 1982, which reflects local twentieth-century tradition and celebrates Lammy as a hero slain by "the infamous Maxwell brothers." Also, an elderly man, Ed Knight, who had once rented the farm on which the killing of Sheriff Lammy occurred, told the author in an interview, September 7, 2006, about many aspects of the battle between "the Maxwell brothers and Sheriff Lammy's posse," which he had, in turn, heard from Calhoun County residents decades ago. His September 2006 letter to the author, in the Hallwas Collection, refers to other folklore about the Maxwells.

The "Battle of Fox Creek": Earl V. Chapin, "The Day They Hanged Ed Williams," *Real West,* Nov. 1971, 52. Also, interview with Ed Knight, September 7, 2006.

"'I knew them both'": "A Confederate's Story," reprinted from the *Chicago Herald* in "WISCONSIN OUTLAWS," *Macomb Journal,* Aug. 11, 1881.

294   *"Mr. Dines":* "RED LETTER RECORD," *St. Paul Pioneer Press,* July 25, 1881.

295   *"30 bloodhounds":* "ED WILLIAMS LYNCHED," *New York Times,* Nov. 20, 1881.

"dime novels": The best single source for information on dime novels is Cox, *The Dime Novel Companion.* His introduction, "Dime Novel Days," provides a helpful overview (xiii–xxv). See also Bold, *Selling the Wild West*; Jones, *Dime Novel Western*; and Le Blanc, "Brief History of Dime Novels," in Sullivan and Schurman, eds., *Pioneers, Passionate Ladies, and Private Eyes.* I use the term "dime novel" both for separately published titles that commonly sold for five or ten cents and for the often identical serialized fiction in story papers.

Frank Tousey: For information on Tousey, the publisher of all of the dime novels and serialized stories on the Maxwell brothers, see Cox, *Dime Novel Companion,* 265–66.

the mythic clash: On this myth in the literature of the American West, see Cawelti, *Six-Gun Mystique,* and Slotkin, *Regeneration through Violence.*

296 *The Boys of New York:* For information on this popular story paper, see Cox, *Dime Novel Companion,* 35.

"storms of adventure": The Williams Brothers, in *The Boys of New York,* Mar. 18, 1882, p. 7.

"Robert Maynard": On this "house name" used by publisher Frank Tousey, see Cox, *Dime Novel Companion,* 168–69. One prolific author who employed it was Francis W. Doughty; see Cox, *Dime Novel Companion,* 89–90. Also, the "Holiday Number" of *The Boys of New York,* Dec. 23, 1882, printed an image of Maynard, with other authors, on the cover, but that is probably a generalized sketch.

"honest, upright, industrious": The Williams Brothers, in *The Boys of New York,* Dec. 31, 1881, 2.

297 *"The facts are, Lon":* The Boys of New York, Dec. 31, 1881, 2.

"I am not in favor": The Boys of New York, Dec. 31, 1881, 2.

"[Durham] has driven us": The Boys of New York, Dec. 31, 1881, 2.

298 *"at least a thousand men":* The Boys of New York, Jan. 28, 1882, 5.

"the wonderful achievements": The Boys of New York, Dec. 31, 1881, 5.

"It has always been with us": The Boys of New York, Mar. 4, 1882, 3.

299 *a code of honor:* For commentary on the outlaw code, see Rosenberg, *Code of the West,* 159–74.

They are outlaw heroes: Meyer, in "The Outlaw: A Distinctive American Folktype," mentions a dozen qualities of the outlaw hero, based on his analysis of oral traditions about Jesse James and a few other figures. While helpful, his view of the outlaw hero is more narrowly defined than the one applied here, which reflects the content of dime novels—and, for that matter, later western books and films.

"the immense rewards": An Endless Chase, in *The Boys of New York,* Apr. 29, 1882, 2.

"from all danger of pursuit": An Endless Chase, in *The Boys of New York,* Apr. 29, 1882, 2.

"strewn for a thousand miles": Hunted Down, in *The Boys of New York,* July 29, 1882, 2.

300 *"the last dread scene":* The Boys of New York, Oct. 14, 1882, 7. The other quotations follow on the same page.

Like the hero in a Greek tragedy: For an excellent discussion of the outlaw hero as a tragic figure, see Tatum, *Inventing Billy the Kid,* 193–97.

301 *"The mob went unpunished":* Hunted Down, in *The Boys of New York,* Oct. 14, 1882, 7.

"While we cannot admire": An Endless Chase, in *The Boys of New York,* June 17, 1882, 7.

"Kit Clyde": On this house name used by publisher Frank Tousey, see Cox, *Dime Novel Companion,* 59–60.

"The Bloody Maxwells": Clyde, *Maxwell Brothers,* 12.

302   *"beyond the borders of civilization":* Maynard, *Buffalo Charlie, the Young Hunter,* in *The Boys of New York,* Feb. 24, 1883, 2.

    Yellowstone Kelly: This colorful name was also concocted by the yarn-spinning Buffalo Charlie during the great Wisconsin manhunt. Robert Maynard not only developed such a character for this novel, but also later wrote a novel focused on him. *Yellowstone Kelly: A Story of Adventures in the Great West* started appearing in *The Boys of New York* on July 26, 1884. However, that novel about a "famous hunter and scout" does not mention the Maxwell (or Williams) brothers.

303   *"We would have lived":* Maynard, *Jerry Owens and the Williams Brothers,* as reprinted in *The New York Detective Library,* Dec. 10, 1892, 4.

    "The Williams brothers": Maynard, *Jerry Owens and the Williams Brothers,* as reprinted in *The New York Detective Library,* Dec. 10, 1892, 1.

304   *"What harm have we done you":* Maynard, *Jerry Owens and the Williams Brothers,* as reprinted in *The New York Detective Library,* Dec. 10, 1892, 8.

    "I know you are brave men": Maynard, *Jerry Owens and the Williams Brothers,* as reprinted in *The New York Detective Library,* Dec. 10, 1892, 5.

    "It is all professional": Maynard, *Jerry Owens and the Williams Brothers,* as reprinted in *The New York Detective Library,* Dec. 10, 1892, 15.

    "Men are never so bad": Maynard, *Jerry Owens and the Williams Brothers,* as reprinted in *The New York Detective Library,* Dec. 10, 1892, 16.

305   *"compromised himself with crime":* Jerry Owens and the Beacon Light, in *The Boys of New York,* July 2, 1892, 6.

    a national reputation for lawlessness: Settle, *Jesse James Was His Name,* 63–64. See also in the 1881 *Chicago Times,* "The Outlaws' Paradise," July 26, and "A Lawless Land," Sept. 18.

    "a terror to the West": Jerry Owens' Midnight Signal, in *The Boys of New York,* Dec. 2, 1893, 3.

306   *The Williams Brothers as Fugitives:* For "The New York Detective Library" series, the title was changed to *The Williams Brothers as Fugitives and the Detectives,* although the dime novel has no detectives in it.

    an "absolutely fearless" man: Obituary of Middleton, as quoted in Hutton, *Doc Middleton,* 214–22. He also briefly depicts the Middleton legend on page 48.

307   *"The Pioneer Press, an excellent paper":* Percy, *Twice Outlawed,* 136.

    which may also have been written by him: See the notes to page 184.

308   *"followed nothing in particular":* Twice Outlawed, 11.

    "evil genius": Twice Outlawed, 16.

    "depraved mind" prompts him: Twice Outlawed, 12.

    "St. Louis paper": Twice Outlawed, 151.

309   *"The Day They Hanged Ed Williams":* Real West, Nov. 1971, 33–34, 50–53.

    Various historical newspaper articles: Quincy Hainline, "The County's

Worst Desperadoes," *Macomb Journal,* Mar. 15, 1924 and Mar. 17, 1924; August F. Ender, "A Short Narrative of the Notorious Williams Brothers," *Durand Courier-Wedge,* July 22, 1937; "Great Tragedy Here in 1881," *Durand Courier-Wedge,* July 9, 1942; Louise Miller, "Durand Once Had Reputation as 'Hanging Town,'" *St. Paul Pioneer Press,* Aug. 18, 1963; Buz Swerkstrom, "Durand Mob Made History with Lynching 100 Years Ago," *Eau Claire Leader-Telegram,* Nov. 13, 1981; "Lynching Case 100 Years Ago Gave Notoriety," *Durand Courier-Wedge,* Nov. 19, 1981; John E. Hallwas, "The Last Outlaws," "The Gunfight," and "Lynching the Maxwell Brothers," *Macomb Journal,* Apr. 4, 11, 18, 1982, respectively, reprinted in Hallwas, *Western Illinois Heritage,* 137–43; Chuck Rupnow, "Dying in the Line of Duty," *Eau Claire Leader-Telegram,* July 7, 1991; and Phil Luciano, "Last of the Outlaws," *Peoria Journal Star,* Aug. 30, 1998.

Bibliography

This historical account employs hundreds of newspaper articles, most of which are referred to only once and some of which are untitled, so those items are not listed in the bibliography. Of course, they are cited in the notes to the book chapters.

Collections at Archives, Libraries, and Historical Organizations

Adams County Historical Society Collection, Hastings, Nebraska

Area Research Center Collection, Chalmer Davee Library, University of Wisconsin–River Falls

Calhoun County Collection, Archives and Special Collections, Malpass Library, Western Illinois University, Macomb

Calhoun County Museum Collection, Hardin, Illinois

Cumberland County Historical Society and Hamilton Library Association Collection, Carlisle, Pennsylvania

Dunn County Collection, Archives, Library Learning Center, University of Wisconsin–Stout, Menomonie

Dunn County Collection, Russell Rassbach Historical Museum, Menomonie, Wisconsin

Fulton County Collection, Archives and Special Collections, Malpass Library, Western Illinois University, Macomb

Fulton County Collection, Parlin-Ingersoll Library, Canton, Illinois

Hall County Collection, Stuhr Museum of the Prairie Pioneer, Grand Island, Nebraska

Hallwas Collection, Archives and Special Collections, Malpass Library, Western Illinois University, Macomb

Illinois Civil War Muster Rolls, Illinois State Archives, Springfield

Illinois Newspaper Collection, Abraham Lincoln Presidential Library, Springfield

Illinois State Penitentiary Records, Illinois State Archives, Springfield

Iowa Newspaper Collection, Iowa State Historical Society, Des Moines

Joliet Penitentiary Testimony Records, Special Collections Research Center, University of Chicago Library

McDonough County Collection, Archives and Special Collections, Malpass Library, Western Illinois University, Macomb

Minnesota Newspaper Collection, Minnesota Historical Society, St. Paul

Pepin County Collection, Durand Public Library, Wisconsin

Pepin County Historical Society Collection, Old Courthouse, Durand, Wisconsin

Revolutionary War Records, Cumberland County Archives, Pennsylvania

St. Louis Police Library Collection, Metropolitan Police Department, St. Louis

Taylor County Collection, Bedford Public Library, Iowa

Washington County Historical Society Collection, Stillwater, Minnesota

Wisconsin Governor Proclamation Papers, Relating to the Apprehension of Criminals, Wisconsin Historical Society, Madison

Wisconsin Newspaper Collection, Wisconsin Historical Society, Madison

Wyandot County Collection, Upper Sandusky Public Library, Ohio

Newspapers

Alton Telegraph (1881)
Barron County News (1881)
Bushnell Record (1881)
Bloomington Daily Bulletin (1881)
Canton Register (1852–81)
Carthage Gazette (1875–76; 1881; 1920)
Carthage Republican (1875–76; 1881; 1920)
Chicago Times (1881–82)
Chicago Tribune (1866; 1875; 1881–84; 1920)
Colchester Independent (1881; 1889; 1892–93, 1898)
Daily Nebraska State Journal (1881)
Dunn County News (1880–1881)
Durand Courier-Wedge (1931; 1936; 1981)
Eau Claire Free Press (1881)
Eau Claire Leader-Telegram (1881)
Eau Claire News (1881)
Fulton County Ledger (1855–69; 1875; 1881)
Fulton Democrat (1855–69; 1875; 1881)
Grand Island Times (1880–81)

Hardin Republican (1905)
Hastings (Gazette-) Journal (1878–81)
Hudson Star and Times (1880–81)
Illinois State Register (1881)
Jersey County Democrat (1881)
Joliet Republican (1866; 1873–81; 1893)
Joliet Signal (1866; 1872–81; 1884)
Juniata Herald (1879–81)
M'Donough Independent (1854)
Macomb Eagle (1864–80)
Macomb Independent (1878–79)
Macomb Journal (1855–81; 1903)
Milwaukee Sentinel (1881)
Missouri Republican (1881)
National Police Gazette (1881–82)
New York Times (1881)
Omaha Daily Bee (1881)
Omaha Daily Herald (1881)
Oquawka Spectator (1874–75; 1881)
Pepin County Courier (1878–82)
Philadelphia Evening Telegraph (1881)
Pierce County Herald (1881)
Pike County Democrat (1881)
Quincy Daily Herald (1881)
Stillwater Daily Sun (1881)
Stillwater Lumberman (1875–76; 1881)
St. Paul Pioneer Press (1881; 1935)
Upper Sandusky (Democratic) Pioneer (1847–48; 1853–54)
Washington Post (1881)
Wisconsin State Journal (1881)
Wyandot County Republican (1894)
Wyandot Pioneer (1857)

Books, Theses, and Journal/Magazine Articles

Adams, Ramon F. *Six-Guns and Saddle Leather: A Bibliography of Books and Pamphlets on Western Outlaws and Gunmen.* 1954; rev. ed. Norman: University of Oklahoma Press, 1969.

American National Biography, ed. John Garraty and Mark C. Carnes. New York: Oxford University Press, 1999.

An Ex-Convict's Story: Life in Joliet Penitentiary, Joliet, Illinois. Chicago: L. T. Dunkley, 1892.

Ashby, LeRoy. *William Jennings Bryan: Champion of Democracy.* Boston: Twayne, 1987.

Atlas Map of Cumberland County, Pennsylvania. Philadelphia: H. F. Bridges, 1858, as "Adapted and expanded . . . by the Cumberland County Historical Society and the Hamilton Library Association" (1987).

Atlas Map of Fulton County, Illinois. Davenport, Iowa: Andreas, Lyter, 1871.

Atlas Map of McDonough County, Illinois. Davenport, Iowa: Andreas, Lyter, 1871.

Atlas of Woodford County and the State of Illinois. Chicago: Warner and Beers, 1873.

Atlas of Wyandot County, Ohio. Philadelphia: Harrison and Hare, 1879.

Bailey, Jack E. *Grand Island—Hall County Centennial, July 1–6, 1957.* Grand Island, Neb., 1957.

Bang, Roy C. *Heroes without Medals: A Pioneering History of Kearney County, Nebraska.* Minden, NE: Warp Publishing, 1952.

Bateman, Newton, et al., eds. *Historical Encyclopedia of Illinois and History of Fulton County.* Chicago: Munsell, 1908.

———. *Historical Encyclopedia of Illinois and History of Henderson County.* Chicago: Munsell, 1911.

Baughman, A. J. *Past and Present of Wyandot County, Ohio.* Chicago: S. J. Clarke, 1913.

Beecher, Henry Ward. "The Reign of the Common People," *Lectures and Orations of Henry Ward Beecher,* ed. Newell Dwight Hillis. 1913; rpt. New York: AMS Press, 1970. Pp. 94–127.

Biographical Encyclopedia of Illinois in the Nineteenth Century. Philadelphia: Galaxy, 1875.

Black, Paul Walton. "Lynchings in Iowa." *Iowa Journal of History and Politics* 10 (April 1912): 151–254.

Bladen: The First 100 Years. (Compiled by the Bladen Opera House Centennial Book Committee.) Marceline, MO: Walworth, 1986.

Bold, Christine. *Selling the Wild West: Popular Western Fiction, 1860 to 1960.* Bloomington: Indiana University Press, 1987.

Boorman, Dean K. *The History of Colt Firearms.* London: Salamander, 2000.

———. *The History of Winchester Firearms.* London: Salamander, 2001.

Bordner, Marjorie, ed. *Fulton County Heritage.* Dallas: Curtis Media, 1988.

Brant, Marley. *Jesse James: The Man and the Myth.* New York: Berkley Books, 1998.

Brown, Richard Maxwell. *No Duty to Retreat: Violence and Values in American History and Society.* 1991; rpt. Norman: University of Oklahoma Press, 1994.

———. *Strain of Violence: Historical Studies of American Violence and Vigilantism.* New York: Oxford University Press, 1975.

Bruce, Robert V. *1877: Year of Violence.* 1959; rpt. Chicago: Ivan R. Dee, 1989.

Budde, Gene, and Kathy Woitaszewski. *Trails into Time—Images of Hall County.* Marceline, Miss.: D-Books, 1997.

Buechler, A. F., and R. J. Baker, eds. *The History of Hall County, Nebraska.* Lincoln, Neb.: Western Publishing, 1920.

Carpenter, George W. *Calhoun Is My Kingdom: The Sesquicentennial History of Calhoun County, Illinois.* Hardin, Ill.: Board of County Commissioners, 1967.

————. *I Want to See a Lawyer: Murder in Calhoun, 1821–1981, and the Story of Our Calhoun Court Systems in the Past 160 Years.* Hardin, Ill.: George W. Carpenter, 1981.

Cawelti, John G. *The Six-Gun Mystique.* Bowling Green, Ohio: Popular Press, 1984.

Chapin, Earl V. "The Day They Hanged Ed Williams," *Real West,* Nov. 1971, pp. 33–34, 50–53.

Clark, Helen Hollandsworth, ed. *A History of Fulton County, Illinois, in Spoon River Country, 1818–1868.* Lewistown: Fulton County Board of Supervisors, 1969.

Clarke, S. J. *History of McDonough County, Illinois.* Springfield, Ill.: D. W. Lusk, 1878.

Clyde, Kit. *The Maxwell Brothers; or, The Chase of a Season.* New York: Frank Tousey, Feb. 13, 1882.

Conover, Jim, and James E. Brecher. *Lynch Law.* Pekin, Ill.: Lynch Law Productions, 1998.

Courtwright, David T. *Violent Land: Single Men and Social Disorder from the Frontier to the Inner City.* Cambridge, Mass.: Harvard University Press, 1996.

Cox, J. Randolph. *The Dime Novel Companion: A Source Book.* Westport, Conn.: Greenwood Press, 2000.

Creigh, Dorothy Weyer. *Adams County: The Story 1872–1972.* Hastings, Neb.: Adams County-Hastings Centennial Commission, 1972.

Crews, Harry. "Television's Junkyard Dog," in *Blood and Grits.* New York: Harper and Row, 1978. Pp. 134–51.

Crosson, Frank E. *History of Taylor County, Iowa, from the Earliest Historic Times to 1910; Biographical Sketches of Some Prominent Citizens.* Chicago: S. J. Clarke, 1910.

Cuff, David J., et al., eds. *The Atlas of Pennsylvania.* Philadelphia: Temple University Press, 1989.

Curtiss-Wedge, Franklyn. *History of Buffalo and Pepin Counties, Wisconsin.* Winona, Minn.: H. C. Cooper, Jr., 1919.

Curtiss-Wedge, Franklyn, and George O. Jones. *History of Dunn County, Wisconsin.* Minneapolis-Winona, Minn.: H. C. Cooper, Jr., 1925.

Cutler, James Elbert. *Lynch-Law: An Investigation into the History of Lynching in the United States.* London: Longmans, Green, 1905.

Davis, James E. *Frontier Illinois.* Bloomington: Indiana University Press, 1998.

Drago, Harry Sinclair. *Outlaws on Horseback.* 1964; rpt. Lincoln: University of Nebraska Press, 1998.

————. *Road Agents and Train Robbers: Half a Century of Western Banditry.* New York: Dodd, Mead, 1973.

Dunaway, Wayland F. *A History of Pennsylvania.* Englewood Cliffs, N.J.: Prentice Hall, 1948.

Duncan, Martha Grace. *Romantic Outlaws, Beloved Prisons: The Unconscious Meanings of Crime and Punishment.* New York: New York University Press, 1996.

Etcheson, Nicole. *The Emerging Midwest: Upland Southerners and the Political Culture of the Old Northwest, 1787–1861.* Bloomington: Indiana University Press, 1996.

Forrester, George, ed. *Historical and Biographical Album of the Chippewa Valley, Wisconsin.* Chicago: A. Warner, 1891–92.

Friedman, Lawrence M. *Crime and Punishment in American History.* New York: Basic Books, 1993.

Gard, Wayne. *Frontier Justice.* Norman: University of Oklahoma Press, 1949.

Garland, Hamlin. *A Son of the Middle Border.* New York: Grosset and Dunlap, 1917.

Gilligan, James. *Violence: Reflections on a National Epidemic.* 1992; rpt. New York: Vintage, 1997.

Hallwas, John E. *The Bootlegger: A Story of Small-Town America.* Urbana: University of Illinois Press, 1998.

————, ed. *Illinois Literature: The Nineteenth Century.* Macomb: Illinois Heritage Press, 1986.

————. "Joe Brice: Fulton County Badman," *Illinois Magazine,* July–Aug. 1988, pp. 13–14.

————. *McDonough County Heritage.* Macomb: Illinois Heritage Press, 1984.

————. *Macomb: A Pictorial History.* St. Louis: G. Bradley, 1990.

————. *Western Illinois Heritage.* Macomb: Illinois Heritage Press, 1983.

Havighurst, Walter. *Ohio: A Bicentennial History.* New York: Norton, 1976.

Hendricks, George D. *The Bad Man of the West.* 1942; rev. ed. San Antonio, Tex.: Naylor, 1970.

Historic Fulton County: Sites and Scenes—Past and Present. Lewistown, Ill.: Mid-County Press, 1973.

Historical Sketchbook for the Durand Centennial, 1856–1956. Durand, Wisc., 1956.

History of Fulton County, Illinois. Peoria, Ill.: Charles C. Chapman, 1879.

History of Henderson County. Chicago: H. H. Hill, 1882.

History of McDonough County, Illinois. Springfield, Ill.: Continental Historical, 1885.

History of Northern Wisconsin. 2 vols. 1881; rpt. Iron Mountain, Mich.: Ralph W. Secord, 1988.

History of Pike County, Illinois. Chicago: Charles C. Chapman, 1880.

History of the State of Nebraska. 2 vols. Chicago: Western Historical, 1882.

History of Taylor County, Iowa. Des Moines, Iowa: State Historical, 1881.

History of Taylor County, Iowa. Bedford, Iowa: Taylor County Historical Society, 1981.

The History of Wyandot County, Ohio. Chicago: Leggett, Conaway, 1884.

Hobsbawm, E. J. *Primitive Rebels: Studies of Archaic Forms of Social Movement in the 19th and 20th Centuries.* 1959; 2nd ed. New York: Frederick A. Praeger, 1963.

Hoffmann, John, ed. *A Guide to the History of Illinois.* New York: Greenwood Press, 1991.

Hollon, W. Eugene. *Frontier Violence: Another Look.* New York: Oxford University Press, 1974.

Horan, James D. *The Authentic Wild West: The Outlaws.* New York: Crown, 1977.

Howard, Robert P. *Illinois: A History of the Prairie State.* Grand Rapids, Mich.: William B. Eerdmans, 1972.

Howe, Henry. "Wyandot," *Historical Collections of Ohio in Two Volumes.* 1888; rpt. Norwalk, Ohio: State of Ohio, 1896, II, 885–911.

Huber, Richard M. *The American Idea of Success.* New York: McGraw-Hill, 1971.

Hurd, Harvey B. *The Revised Statutes of the State of Illinois, A.D. 1874.* Springfield: Illinois Journal, 1874.

Hutton, Harold. *Doc Middleton: Life and Legends of the Notorious Plains Outlaw.* Chicago: Swallow Press, 1974.

Jacobs, Jonathan. *Choosing Character: Responsibility for Virtue and Vice.* Ithaca, N.Y.: Cornell University Press, 2001.

Johnson, Jim. *Billy the Kid. His Real Name Was . . .* Denver: Outskirts Press, 2006.

Jones, Daryl. *The Dime Novel Western.* Bowling Green, Ohio: Popular Press, 1978.

Keiser, John H. *Building for the Centuries: Illinois 1865 to 1898.* Urbana: University of Illinois Press, 1977.

Kimsey, John W. *A True Account of the Capture of Frank Rande, "The Noted Outlaw," by the Late Frank Hitchcock, Sheriff of Peoria County, Ill., for Twelve Years.* Peoria, Ill.: J. W. Franks, 1897.

Klatt, Christine Granger, ed. *They Died at Their Posts: A True Historical Account of Murder and Lynching on the Wisconsin Frontier 1881.* Menomonie, Wis.: Dunn County Historical Society, 1976.

Knepper, George W. *Ohio and Its People.* 1989; 2nd ed. Kent, Ohio: Kent State University Press, 1997.

Lamar, Howard. *The Reader's Encyclopedia of the American West.* New York: Harper and Row, 1977.

L'Amour, Louis. *Hondo.* 1953; rpt. New York: Bantam, 1983.

Lathrop, Rev. S. G. *Crime and Punishment and Life in the Penitentiary.* Joliet, Ill.: Rev. S. G. Lathrop, 1866.

Lawson, Richard. *The Joliet Prison Photographs 1890–1930.* Carbondale: Southern Illinois University Press, 1981.

Le Blanc, Edward T. "A Brief History of Dime Novels: Formats and Contents, 1860–1933," *Pioneers, Passionate Ladies, and Private Eyes: Dime Novels, Series Books, and Paperbacks,* ed. Larry E. Sullivan and Lydia Cushman Schurman. New York: Hawthorn Books, 1966. Pp. 13–21.

Lemon, James T. *The Best Poor Man's Country: A Geographical Study of Early Southeastern Pennsylvania.* Baltimore: Johns Hopkins, 1972.

LeSage, Alain René. *The Adventures of Gil Blas of Santillane.* London: J. M. Dent, 1910.

Luchetti, Cathy. *Children of the West.* New York: Norton, 2001.

McClaughry, Robert W. "Warden's Report," in *Report of the Commissioners of the Penitentiary for the Two years Ending September 30, 1876.* Springfield: State of Illinois, 1876. Pp. 415–18.

McKelvey, Blake. *American Prisons: A Study in American Social History Prior to 1915.* Montclair, NJ: Patterson Smith, 1968.

McLean, Alexander. *Historical Encyclopedia of Illinois and History of McDonough County.* Vol. 2. Chicago: Munsell, 1907.

Majewski, John. *A House Dividing: Economic Development in Pennsylvania and Virginia before the Civil War.* Cambridge: Cambridge University Press, 2000.

Marks, Paula Mitchell. *And Die in the West: The Story of the O. K. Corral Gunfight.* 1989; rpt. New York: Simon and Schuster, 1990.

Marsden, George M. *The Evangelical Mind and the New School Presbyterian Experience: A Case Study of Thought and Theology in Nineteenth-Century America.* New Haven, Conn.: Yale University Press, 1970.

Masters, Edgar Lee. *Across Spoon River: An Autobiography.* 1936; rpt. Urbana: University of Illinois Press, 1991.

Mattes, Merrill J. *The Great Platte River Road.* Lincoln, Neb.: State Historical Society, 1969.

May, Rollo. *Freedom and Destiny.* 1981; rpt. New York: Bantam Doubleday Dell, 1989.

Maynard, Robert. *Buffalo Charlie, the Young Hunter: A True Story of the West,* in *The Boys of New York,* Feb. 24, Mar. 3, 10, 17, 24, 31, Apr. 7, 14, 21, 28, May 5, 12, 19, 26, 1883.

———. *An Endless Chase: A True Story of the Williams Brothers,* in *The Boys of New York,* Apr. 29, May 6, 13, 20, 27, June 3, 10, 17, 24, July 1, 8, 15, 22, 1882.

———. *Hunted Down; or, The Fate of Ed Williams,* in *The Boys of New York,* July 29, Aug. 5, 12, 19, 26, Sept. 2, 9, 16, 23, 30, Oct. 7, 14, 1882.

————. *Jerry Owens and the Beacon Light; or. The Signal Fires of the Williams Brothers, A Thrilling Story of Missouri,* in *The Boys of New York,* June 11, 18, 25, July 2, 9, 16, 23, 30, Aug. 6, 13, 20, 27, Sept. 3, 1892.

————. *Jerry Owens' Midnight Signal; or, The Williams Brothers Outwitted,* in *The Boys of New York,* Oct. 7, 14, 21, 28, Nov. 4, 11, 18, 25, Dec. 2, 1893.

————. *Jerry Owens and the Williams Brothers; or, Chased from Shore to Shore,* in *The Boys of New York,* Jan. 30, Feb. 6, 13, 20, 27, Mar. 6, 13, 20, 27, Apr. 3, 10, 17, 1892.

————. *Pinkerton's Little Detective; or, The Dread of the Williams Brothers,* in *The Boys of New York,* Nov. 3, 10, 17, 24, Dec. 1, 8, 15, 22, 29, 1883; Jan. 5, 12, 19, 26, Feb. 2, 9, 16, 23, 30, 1884.

————. *The Williams Brothers Afloat.* New York: Frank Tousey, July 16, 1883.

————. *The Williams Brothers as Fugitives.* New York: Frank Tousey, June 22, 1883. Reprinted as *The Williams Brothers as Fugitives and the Detectives.* New York: Frank Tousey, Dec. 19, 1891.

————. *The Williams Brothers and the Detectives.* New York: Frank Tousey, Sept. 3, 1883.

————. *The Williams Brothers; or, a Thousand-Mile Chase,* in *The Boys of New York,* Dec. 31, 1881; Jan. 7, 14, 21, 28, Feb. 4, 11, 18, 25, Mar. 4, 11, 18, 1882.

Merritt, Raymond H. *Creativity, Conflict, and Controversy: A History of the St. Paul District U.S. Army Corps of Engineers.* Washington, D.C.: Government Printing Office, 1979.

Meyer, Douglas K. *Making the Heartland Quilt: A Geographical History of Settlement and Migration in Early-Nineteenth-Century Illinois.* Carbondale: Southern Illinois University Press, 2000.

Meyer, Richard E. "The Outlaw Hero: A Distinctive American Folktype," *Journal of the Folklore Institute* 17 (1980): 94–124.

Monaghan, Jay, ed. *The Book of the American West.* New York: Bonanza Books, 1963.

Moore, Roy L. *History of Woodford County.* Eureka, Ill.: Woodford County Republican, 1910.

Moran, Gabriel. *A Grammar of Responsibility.* New York: Crossroad, 1996.

Moses, Norton H. *Lynching and Vigilantism in the United States: An Annotated Bibliography.* Westport, Conn.: Greenwood Press, 1997.

Murder, Murder, Public Murder! [broadside]. Durand, n.d.

Murray, Frank, and Sidney W. Wetmore. *The Detective's Vade Mecum.* Joliet, Ill.: n.p., 1878.

Nash, Jay Robert. *Encyclopedia of Western Lawmen and Outlaws.* 1992; rpt. New York: Da Capo, 1994.

The National Cyclopedia of American Biography. 1892–94; rpt. New York: James T. White, 1957.

Neill, Edward D., and J. Fletcher Williams. *History of Washington County and the St. Croix Valley, including the Explorers and Pioneers of Minnesota.* Minneapolis: North Star, 1881.

Olson, James C., and Ronald C. Naugle. *History of Nebraska.* 1955; 3rd ed. Lincoln: University of Nebraska Press, 1997.

O'Neal, Bill. *The Pimlico Encyclopedia of Western Gunfighters.* 1979; rpt. London: Pimlico, 1998.

Papke, David Ray. *Framing the Criminal: Crime, Cultural Work, and the Loss of Critical Perspective, 1830–1900.* Hamden, Conn.: Archon Books, 1987.

Peck, John Mason. *A Gazetteer of Illinois.* Jacksonville, Ill.: R. Goudy, 1834; rev. ed. 1837.

Pepin County History: Pepin County, Wisconsin. Dallas, Tex.: Taylor Publishing, 1985.

Percy, Adrian. *Twice Outlawed: A Personal History of Ed and Lon Maxwell, Alias the Williams Brothers, a Record of Highway Robbery, Horse Stealing, Romance, and Murder, to Which Is Added a Detailed and Graphic Account of the Arrest and Lynching of Edward Maxwell at Durand, Wisconsin, November 19, 1881.* Chicago: W. B. Conkey, n. d.

Pereboom, Derek. *Living without Free Will.* Cambridge: Cambridge University Press, 2001.

Perrin, William Henry, and H. H. Hill. *The Past and Present of Woodford County, Illinois.* Chicago: William Le Baron, Jr., 1878.

Peskin, Allan. *Garfield: A Biography.* Kent, Ohio: Kent State University Press, 1978.

Peterson, Brent T., and Dean R. Thilgen. *Stillwater, Minnesota 1849–1993: A Photographic History.* Stillwater, Minn.: Valley History Press, 1992.

Petronovich, Helen Hathaway. *A History of Hersey.* Glenwood City, Wis.: Glenwood City Tribune, 1980.

Pinkowski, Vern. *A Vanished Community: The Waubeek Sawmill Settlement.* n.p., 2004.

Portrait and Biographical Album of Pike and Calhoun Counties, Illinois. 1891; rpt. Evansville, Ind.: Unigraphic, 1975.

"The Prairie State," *Atlantic Monthly* 7 (May 1861): 579–95.

Prassel, Frank Richard. *The Great American Outlaw: A Legacy of Fact and Fiction* Norman: University of Oklahoma Press, 1993.

Proctor, George P. *The First Hundred Years: A History of the First Presbyterian Church of Lewistown, Illinois.* Lewistown, Ill.: First Presbyterian Church, 1936.

Putney, Snell, and Gail J. Putney. *The Adjusted American: Normal Neuroses in the Individual and Society.* 1964; rpt. New York: Harper and Row, 1972.

Report of the Adjutant General of the State of Illinois. Vol. 5. Springfield, Ill.: Phillips Brothers, 1901.

Report of the Commissioners of the Illinois State Penitentiary at Joliet for the Two Years Ending Sept. 30, 1900. Springfield: State of Illinois, 1901.

Bibliography

Report of the Joint Committee Appointed to Investigate into the Discipline, Management, and Financial Condition of the Illinois State Penitentiary. Springfield: Illinois General Assembly, 1872.

Rezab, Gordana. *Place Names of McDonough County, Illinois.* Macomb, Ill.: Gordana Rezab, 2006.

Riegel, Robert E. *America Moves West.* New York: Henry Holt, 1930; rev. ed. 1947.

Rogers, Rev. E. P. *The Prodigal Son; or the Sinner's Departure and the Sinner's Return.* New York: American Tract Society, 1862

Rosa, Joseph G. *The Gunfighter: Man or Myth?* Norman: University of Oklahoma Press, 1969.

Roseboom, Eugene H., and Francis P. Weisenburger. *A History of Ohio.* Columbus: Ohio State Archaeological and Historical Society, 1953.

Rosenberg, Bruce A. *The Code of the West.* Bloomington: Indiana University Press, 1982.

Sandage, Scott A. *Born Losers: A History of Failure in America.* Cambridge, Mass.: Harvard University Press, 2005.

Sanders, Wiley B. "The History and Administration of the State Prisons of Illinois." Ph.D. diss., University of Chicago, 1929.

Schaumann, Mary Lou. *Taverns of Cumberland County, Pennsylvania, 1750–1840.* Carlisle, Penn.: Cumberland County Historical Society, 1994.

Schlereth, Thomas. *Victorian America: Transformations in Everyday Life, 1876–1915.* New York: Harper Collins, 1991.

Schob, David E. *Hired Hands and Plowboys: Farm Labor in the Midwest, 1815–60.* Urbana: University of Illinois Press, 1975.

Settle, William A., Jr. *Jesse James Was His Name, or Fact and Fiction Concerning the Careers of the Notorious James Brothers of Missouri.* 1966; rpt. Lincoln: University of Nebraska Press, 1977.

Shaw, Fayette Baldwin. "The Economic Development of Joliet, Illinois 1830–1870." Ph.D. diss., Harvard University, 1933.

Slabey, Vera. "Afterword," *Durand 1881 . . . Verbatim Excerpts from the Pepin County Courier,* ed. Vera Slabey. Durand, Wis.: Pepin County Historical Society, 1987.

Slotkin, Richard. *Regeneration through Violence: The Mythology of the American Frontier, 1600–1860.* Middletown, Conn.: Wesleyan University Press, 1973.

Smith, Henry Nash. *Virgin Land: The American West as Symbol and Myth.* 1950; rpt. Cambridge, Mass.: Harvard University Press, 1976.

Smith, Stephen R. *A Journalist's Account of the Outlaw Rande, His Remarkable Career and Pending Trial, with a Sketch of His Early Life, Written by the Bandit in His Cell.* Burlington, Iowa: Hawkeye, 1878.

Stanton, Carl L. *They Called It Treason: An Account of Renegades, Copperheads, Guerillas, Bushwhackers, and Outlaw Gangs That Terrorized Illinois during the Civil War.* Bunker Hill, Ill.: Carl L. Stanton, 2002.

Steckmesser, Kent Ladd. *The Western Hero in History and Legend*. Norman: University of Oklahoma Press, 1965.

Sterling, Robert E. *Joliet Prisons: Images in Time*. St. Louis: G. Bradley, 2003.

Stiles, T. J. *Jesse James: Last Rebel of the Civil War*. New York: Alfred Knopf, 2002.

Sutherland, Daniel E. *The Expansion of Everyday Life 1860–1876*. New York: Harper and Row, 1989.

Tatum, Stephen. *Inventing Billy the Kid: Visions of the Outlaw in America, 1881–1891*. 1982; rpt. Tucson: University of Arizona Press, 1997.

"Testimony before Coroner's Jury to Inquire into the Cause of the Death of the Convict Henry Williams," in *Reports Made to the General Assembly of Illinois at Its Twenty-Eighth Session, convened January 8, 1873*. Springfield, Ill.: State Journal Printing, 1874. Vol. IV, 861–84.

Tompkins, Jane. *West of Everything: The Inner Life of Westerns*. New York: Oxford University Press, 1992.

"True or False, Lynchings in Wisconsin Made News," *Wisconsin Then and Now* 24 (June 1978): 4–5, 7.

Utley, Robert M. *Billy the Kid: A Short and Violent Life*. 1989; rpt. Lincoln: University of Nebraska Press, 1991.

———. *High Noon in Lincoln: Violence on the Western Frontier*. Albuquerque: University of New Mexico Press, 1987.

Vogel, John J. *Indians of Ohio and Wyandot County*. New York: Vantage, 1975.

Walker, Francis A. *The Statistics of the Population of the United States*. Washington, D.C.: Government Printing Office, 1872.

Wallis, Michael. *Billy the Kid: The Endless Ride*. New York: W. W. Norton, 2007.

Warner, George E., and Charles M. Foote. *History of Washington County and the St. Croix Valley*. Minneapolis: North Star, 1881.

Wegner, Daniel M. *The Illusion of Conscious Will*. Cambridge, Mass.: MIT Press, 2002.

Wellman, Paul I. *A Dynasty of Western Outlaws*. 1961; rpt. New York: Pyramid Books, 1964.

———. *Spawn of Evil*. New York: Modern Literary Editions, 1964.

Wetmore, Sidney W. *Behind the Bars: Life and Times in Joliet Prison*. Chicago: Ottaway, 1883.

———. *Behind the Bars at Joliet: A Peep at a Prison, Its History, and Its Mysteries*. Chicago: J. O. Gorman, 1892.

———. "The Pennsylvania Industrial Reformatory," *Frank Leslie's Illustrated Newspaper*, Dec. 12, 1891, 332.

"What Our Boys Are Reading," *Scribner's Monthly* (March 1878): 681–85.

Wheeler, Edward L. *Deadwood Dick, the Prince of the Road; or, The Black Rider of the Black Hills*, in *Reading the West: An Anthology of Dime Novels*, ed. Bill Brown. Boston: Bedford, 1997. Pp. 273–358.

Bibliography

Willett, Edward. *The Twin Trailers; or the Gamecock of El Paso: A Tale of the Texan Frontier.* New York: Beadle and Adams, 1872.

Wills, Charles W. *Army Life of an Illinois Soldier.* Washington, D.C.: Globe, 1906.

Wing. Conway, ed. *History of Cumberland County, Pennsylvania.* Philadelphia: James D. Scott, 1879.

Woodward, Margaret L. "The Northwestern Farmer, 1868–1876: A Tale of Paradox," *Agricultural History* 37 (July 1963): 134–42.

Index

JOHN E. HALLWAS

is Distinguished Professor of English, emeritus, at Western Illinois University. He is the author or editor of more than twenty books, including *The Bootlegger: A Story of Small-Town America, Cultures in Conflict: A Documentary History of the Mormon War in Illinois* (with Roger Launius), and *Western Illinois Heritage*.

The University of Illinois Press
is a founding member of the
Association of American University Presses.

Composed in 9.5/13 ITC Cheltenham
with Old Towne No. 536 display
by Jim Proefrock
at the University of Illinois Press
Designed by Dennis Roberts
Manufactured by Thomson-Shore, Inc.

University of Illinois Press
1325 South Oak Street
Champaign, IL 61820-6903
www.press.uillinois.edu